Quality

The third edition of this top-selling text continues to provide a complete knowledge platform for all those wishing to study the development of the theory and practice of quality management. Building upon previous editions' unique critical perspective on quality, this edition is enhanced by the inclusion of the latest contemporary developments in quality thinking, including Integrated Management Systems, Lean Manufacturing and SMART thinking, as well as updated, real-world examples in applying quality methods. In addition, existing understanding of the environmental impact of the quality movement will be extended into a broader understanding of environmental, financial, regulatory, and behavioural sustainability. The book also addresses the issues of Corporate Governance and Corporate Social Responsibility, which are now informing the decision making and behaviour of managers.

Key features include:

- Complete introduction to quality in the context of management thinking
- In-depth reviews of the contributions of 'quality gurus'
- Contemporary developments in theory and practice
- International case studies drawn from both public and private sectors
- Equal emphasis on both manufacturing and service sectors
- Practical 'case study' focused toolkits and applications

John Beckford is Visiting Professor in Information Science at Loughborough University, holds a Ph.D. in Organisational Cybernetics from the University of Hull, is a Fellow of the Cybernetics Society, a Member of the Institute of Management Services and a Fellow of the Royal Society for the Arts. He has published extensively and regularly delivers seminars, workshops and master classes.

He established Beckford Consulting in 1990 and works internationally with organisations in a variety of sectors including software, finance, steel, public and private healthcare, housing, public education, food, property, retail, manufacturing and transport. These organisations include SAP, Northern Rail, GNER, The Congregation of the Sisters of Nazareth, the BBC, InHealth Group, Arena Group, Fusion21, Alternative Futures Group, Hong Kong Quality Assurance Agency and Sunbase (Hong Kong).

100562261

Quality
A Critical Introduction

Third Edition

John L. W. Beckford, Ph.D.

Routledge
Taylor & Francis Group

NEW YORK AND LONDON

100562261

HD
62.
15.
B43
2009

First edition published 1998
Second edition published 2002
by Routledge
270 Madison Ave, New York, NY 10016

This edition published 2010
by Routledge
270 Madison Ave, New York, NY 10016

Simultaneously published in the UK
by Routledge
2 Park Square, Milton Park, Abingdon, Oxon OX14 4RN

Routledge is an imprint of the Taylor & Francis Group, an informa business

© 1998, 2002, 2010 John Beckford

Typeset in Garamond by
Swales & Willis Ltd., Exeter, Devon
Printed and bound in Great Britain by
TJ International Ltd, Padstow, Cornwall

All rights reserved. No part of this book may be reprinted or reproduced or utilized in any form or by any electronic, mechanical or other means, now known or hereafter invented, including photocopying and recording, or in any information storage or retrieval system, without permission in writing from the publishers.

Trademark Notice: Product or corporate names may be trademarks or registered trademarks, and are used only for identification and explanation without intent to infringe.

Library of Congress Cataloging-in-Publication Data
Beckford, John, 1958–
    Quality : a critical introduction / John Beckford. – 3rd ed.
        p. cm.
    Includes bibliographical references and index.
    1. Total quality management – Case studies.   2. Service industries –
Management – Case studies.   3. Manufacturing industries – Management –
Case studies.   I. Title.
    HD62.15.B433 2010
    658.5′62 – dc22   2009011321

ISBN10: 0–415–99634–1 (hbk)
ISBN10: 0–415–99635–X (pbk)
ISBN10: 0–203–88571–6 (ebk)

ISBN13: 978–0–415–99634–1 (hbk)
ISBN13: 978–0–415–99635–8 (pbk)
ISBN13: 978–0–203–88571–0 (ebk)

Brief Contents

Full Contents

List of Figures

List of Vignettes

Preface to the Third Edition

Introduction

The third edition of *Quality* continues to provide a complete knowledge platform for those wishing to study the development of the theory and practice of quality. In developing this edition, I have incorporated suggestions from users, readers and reviewers of the previous editions of this book, and have included contemporary developments in the world of quality thinking, such as Integrated Management Systems, Lean Manufacturing, and Systemic Quality Management. Recent practical experiences have also been brought to bear and, for completeness, this has led to the inclusion of thinking on corporate governance and corporate social responsibility, extension of the environmental impact dimension, and a broader understanding of financial, regulatory, and behavioural sustainability.

In preparing this edition of *Quality*, I have retained the structure and substantial content of the first three parts of the first and second editions, but have adopted a completely new approach to Part Four. Parts One, Two and Three follow the established pattern of the prior editions in embedding practical examples in an exploration of the development of the theory of quality, while Part Four now inverts the approach to embed the theory in the practice of quality. It achieves this by presenting Part Four as an extended case study, through which the theory and application of quality methods, tools and techniques are demonstrated.

As with the second edition, many minor revisions have been made for the sake of clarity, and substantial changes have been introduced to reflect developments in 'quality' knowledge and thinking since the last edition was written.

The aims of this book, its target readership, use and structure remain as explained in the preface to the first edition, and my intention is that the substantially revised approach to Part Four will enhance both the experience of reading the book and the utility of the ideas.

Acknowledgements

I am extremely grateful to all those who have helped in the development and production of this book. Many managers and students have debated quality and management ideas with me, and either deliberately or inadvertently have contributed to the ideas – especially Mike Gooddie, Ian Bevan, James Robbins, Simon Gimson, Tien Nguyen, Martin Hirtle and Doug Haynes; their theoretical and practical contributions have altered and shaped my views. Dr Peter Dudley, with whom I have enjoyed many robust discussions, worked with me in developing the idea of Systemic Quality Management – amongst many other things. Reviewers and readers of the first and second editions of the book have supported the work of preparing this edition, and have guided my thinking. While I have attempted to address the issues they have raised, I remain responsible for any errors, oversights or omissions. Many organizations have allowed the sharing of their quality experiences, specifically the following: The Congregation of the Sisters of Nazareth; GNER; Cathay Pacific; Derwentside District Council; Fletcher Challenge Steel, China; The Hong Kong Police Force (formerly the Royal Hong Kong Police Force); Kennet School, Thatcham, Berkshire; McDonalds, Hong Kong; and West Berkshire Music Centre. Thanks are due to Nancy Hale and the editorial team at Routledge, Taylor and Francis, for accepting the idea of the book and supporting its production. Special thanks are due to Sara, Paul and Matthew who continue to act as my critical friends – there are some things that only your wife or children can say!

Preface to the Second Edition

Introduction

In preparing this second edition of *Quality*, I have retained the structure and substantial content of the first edition. While many minor revisions have been made for the sake of clarity, substantial changes have been introduced to reflect the developments in my knowledge in the four years since the first edition was written, and especially to reflect recent changes in the quality arena such as the launch of ISO 9000: 2000, and increased use of the Business Excellence Model.

The aims of this book, its target readership, use and structure remain as explained in the preface to the first edition.

The Changes

Chapter 1, 'The Quality Imperative', has been extended to explore the notion of quality in greater depth, and relate quality directly to its justification which rests in increasing organizational effectiveness. The development and application of Skills-based Quality management, which takes advantage of the changes to ISO 9000, is discussed in Chapter 27, 'Sustainable Organization', and provides a wholly new Chapter 28.

Following the introduction of ISO 9000: 2000, Chapter 21, 'Quality Management Systems', has been completely revised to address the very substantial changes introduced to this standard. The links between these changes and the development of Skills-based Quality Management are explored. The chapter also examines ISO 14000 and The Business Excellence Model.

Chapter 22, 'Statistical Methods', was the subject of particular criticism from readers of the first edition. This has been rewritten to focus on problems surrounding the use of statistics while the gurus' methods are explored in the individual chapters of Part Two of the book.

I am grateful to readers and critics for the many complimentary comments and observations on the first edition, but where the comments were critical, I have attempted to improve the book to address them. If I have failed to do so, it is not the fault of my critics.

Preface to the First Edition

Introduction

The pursuit of organizational effectiveness and success – however that may be defined – through higher quality in products and services is a dominant theme for organizations throughout the world. However, many quality initiatives fail to achieve their objectives, or only partially succeed, contributing to improvement but not leading to the higher levels of organizational performance expected. This failure perhaps results from the narrow focus of many quality programmes and a consequent lack of breadth in the understanding of the true role and meaning of quality in organizational effectiveness. Contributing to this lack of success is the apparent desire of many organizations and managers to adopt a relatively simple pre-packaged programme, based upon a single approach to the achievement of quality.

Drawing on case studies from around the world in organizations such as McDonald's, Cathay Pacific, the Hong Kong Police and Fletcher Challenge Steel, China and many other private and public sector organizations, this book enables the reader to develop a unique and broad understanding of quality – one which will work for him or herself in a particular organization. The book shows the full breadth of approaches and tools available to support a quality initiative, and considers the importance of the socio-cultural context in selecting and using these approaches.

The Aim of This Book

There is a substantial body of literature already published in the field of quality – so why yet another book? The principal established texts in the field are those produced by the 'quality gurus' themselves. Each of these takes only the particular author's view of the subject, while books by other writers reflect a bias towards one aspect of the subject or one narrow view of it. None of these provides either the breadth of information or the critical stance adopted in this book. The 'discipline' of quality is now mature; the time is right to develop a non-partisan, complete approach to the subject.

Who Should Use This Book?

This book provides a complete and coherent knowledge platform for all those (whether students or managers) wishing to understand fully the theory and practice of quality. It does *not* offer the latest quality-focused 'miracle' cure for all organizational ills. Instead, the book brings together in a single text the plethora of ideas, approaches and methods espoused in the pursuit of quality in recent years. It draws on the published writings of many quality experts and incorporates the practical experience of the author and his associates in using these ideas throughout the world.

It features:

- a complete introduction to quality in the context of management thinking;
- in-depth reviews of the contributions of the 'quality gurus' and contemporary management authors to quality theory and practice;
- international case-studies drawing on the public and private sectors;
- particular emphasis on the neglected service sector as well as manufacturing industry.

Structure

The book is divided into four parts. Part One provides a foundation for the book by considering the arguments surrounding the pursuit of quality, the role of quality in the organization, barriers to its implementation, and the developments in management thinking which appear to underpin the quality movement.

Part Two provides a critical review of the works of those writers who have made a distinct and valuable contribution to the achievement of quality. These are Philip Crosby, W. Edwards Deming, Armand Feigenbaum, Kaoru Ishikawa, Joseph Juran, John Oakland, Shigeo Shingo and Genichi Taguchi.

Part Three moves beyond these traditionally based approaches to consider the value to be derived from contemporary management thinking. This part relates to the quality theme ideas ranging from the emergence of contingency theory to the more radical notions of critical systems thinking, re-engineering, and organizational learning.

Part Four shifts the focus away from quality theory to quality practice by introducing the methods, tools and techniques used for achieving quality. This section works from basic and common techniques, such as process analysis, through to current strategies for engaging all of the organization's stakeholders in the quality process, and concludes with guidance on implementing quality programmes.

How to Use This Book

This book, as with all textbooks, provides a simplified perspective of its topic and of the daily realities of pursuing quality in organizations. The information is presented in what seems to the author to be a logical, systematic order, teasing apart topics which are necessarily closely interrelated.

The clue to successful reading is to recognize the connections which exist between the various parts and topics (these connections are regularly made within the text). The chapters, then, while presented in one particular order, need not be read in that way. Equally, the chapters can be read in a fully sequential manner, although each is intended to be able to stand alone, offering a perspective on a particular topic. Hence, some chapters are short, some long.

Each part of the book commences with a user guide to the content, and makes suggestions about how to maximize learning from it. These introductions each summarize the major points made in the contained chapters.

Practical illustrations and short vignettes will be found in each chapter. These are intended to help consolidate learning, as well as being informative and entertaining. Many readers will find that remembering the story helps them to remember the key points of the associated chapter. These illustrations arise from the author's own knowledge and practice, or have been contributed by friends and colleagues drawing on their working experience in positions of responsibility for quality.

Each chapter concludes with a question. This may be used either as a formal assignment, or as a discussion topic for classroom or study group work. Attempting to answer these questions will help to reinforce and consolidate learning. If you cannot adequately answer the question, you should revisit the chapter to enhance your knowledge. Working through the book in this way will help you to develop your knowledge in a systematic and critical way.

The Author

John Beckford is Visiting Professor in the Department of Information Science at Loughborough University. He holds a Ph.D. in Organizational Cybernetics from the University of Hull, is a Fellow of the Cybernetics Society, a Member of the Institute of Management Services, and a Fellow of the Royal Society for the Arts. He has published numerous refereed journal and conference papers, and regularly delivers seminars and workshops to organizations internationally, in both the public and private sectors.

Starting his career at the Royal Bank of Scotland, John worked as an internal consultant on Organizational Effectiveness before leaving the bank to pursue his doctorate. He established Beckford Consulting in 1990 and has worked in the UK, USA, Middle East and Far East, Australia and New Zealand, with organizations in a variety of sectors, including software, finance, steel, public and private healthcare, public education, food, property, retail, manufacturing and transport. These organizations include SAP, Northern Rail, GNER, Fletcher Steel, Hoverspeed, The Congregation of the Sisters of Nazareth, the BBC, Diethelm Healthcare, In Health Group, Arena Group, Hong Kong Quality Assurance Agency, and Sunbase (Hong Kong).

John has researched, written and presented numerous management education courses for universities and commercial organizations. He regularly works with researchers and teams from Loughbrough University and Manchester Business School.

Quality:

n. the essential attribute of anything

Collins, *New English Dictionary*, 1968

Part One

Introducing Quality

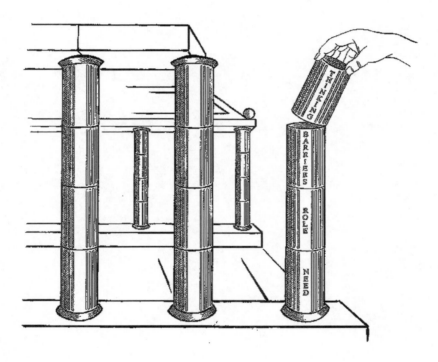

User Guide

Part One introduces the whole quality debate. Chapter 1, which has been substantially revised from the previous editions, examines the arguments for and against the pursuit of quality, considering both the needs and the opportunities. It examines the economic, social, environmental, and governance imperatives. For the first time, this includes how the requirements of corporate social responsibility and corporate governance relate to quality issues. Chapter 2 looks at the role of quality in the organization, considering the strategic and operational aspects of quality and the debate as to its fit to the organization. Chapter 3 focuses on barriers to the pursuit of quality, highlighting how the established cultures, systems, and processes of organizations inhibit quality initiatives. In Chapter 4, the 'classical' and 'human relations' schools of management thinking are introduced, and their apparent influence on the thinking of the quality gurus elaborated.

This part of the book provides the necessary foundation for a study of quality by examining the four key dimensions:

- the opportunity and need for quality;
- the role of quality;
- the barriers to its achievement;
- the thinking which underpins the dominant approaches to management.

1　The Quality Imperative

Integrate the three pillars of social well-being, economic prosperity and environmental protection
(Gisbert Glaser, International Geosphere–Biosphere Programme, cited
by James Lovelock, 2006)

Introduction

Quality has emerged and remained as a dominant theme in management thinking since the mid-twentieth century. While the initial ideas arose from American theorists and practitioners, early commercial applications were predominantly amongst Japanese companies. The need for enhanced quality was initially largely ignored or rejected in the West. Since the mid-1980s, when the success of Japanese companies began to impinge seriously on Western markets, commercial organizations throughout the world have embraced, at least in part, the theories and practices of quality, and many national governments are pursuing quality initiatives. For example, governments are under increasing pressure to achieve service levels equivalent to those of private organizations, and have sought to modernize and enhance public offerings through the application of quality methods, sometimes in conjunction with privatization or the creation of non-Governmental Executive Agencies. European governments engage in such initiatives as 'Best Practice' and 'Best Value' programmes and actively support the Business Excellence Model as a framework for service quality improvement.

This chapter is concerned with *why* quality has achieved this pre-eminence amongst the concerns of so many managers. It presents three arguments for the pursuit of quality – the economic, the social and the environmental – before considering the specific challenge for service organizations. Finally, the chapter considers the problems generated in organizations by the use of the word 'quality' itself. Each of these is pursued through the author's own perspective on management and achievement of quality.

1.1　The Economic Imperative

During the post-Second World War years, consumer demand grew to such an extent that the manufacturing focus in the Western world was on productivity: increases in volume of products and the efficiency of both the production equipment and the labour force. Effectively, growing markets were starved of products, and with increasing economic prosperity everything that could be produced could be sold. Unfulfilled demand meant that organizations were under no pressure to focus on the quality of product and perhaps perceived that they had already achieved the ultimate standards. Coupled to this, consumer expectations of product longevity and reliability were relatively low compared with those of today, as was the technology of both the products and the manufacturing processes.

As markets matured and growth consequently stabilized, organizations, faced with increasing costs of production – particularly the cost of labour, waste and, in the 1970s, the dramatic escalation in the cost of power – began to challenge their established ways of working. While some organizations further increased the pressure on workers for more productivity gains while pursuing cost reductions in raw materials and through research and development, others relied on the emerging technologies of automation, robotics and electronic data processing. Most adopted a mix of these approaches. Where technologically and financially feasible, other organizations followed the more trad-itional approach of exporting jobs to lower-cost manufacturing centres, especially in South East Asia, a practice that is still ongoing with the dramatic growth of manu-facturing in China and in the sub-Continent of India. Rather than reducing costs through improving their processes, these organizations relocated manufacturing plants to take advantage of lower-cost labour. Organizations have begun exporting service-based jobs through the creation of overseas contact centres and 'shared-service' centres, and increasingly jobs based on knowledge (such as software development) are following the same route, capitalizing on high levels of education in the Indian sub-continent.

This phenomenon of chasing cheap labour can be traced from the late nineteenth century, when manufacturing emerged in the US with its ready supply of cheap land and labour. At that time European organizations began to establish overseas operations. From the mid-1960s, Western organizations have developed operations in the so-called 'Tiger Economies' of Asia. The first of these to emerge, Singapore, Hong Kong and Taiwan, are now mature economies (GDP per capita is at, or approaching, Western levels) and they in turn have been losing jobs to their newly emergent and lower-cost neighbours such as Cambodia, Indonesia, Korea and Vietnam.

Change in the European economy over recent years has delivered a partial reversal of this trend. Many Asia-based companies have relocated some manufacturing operations to Europe as labour is, relatively, cheaper than before; the workforce has the skills required for high quality manufacturing operations; and the cost of transporting fin-ished goods is substantially reduced. Local manufacturing also helps to overcome import tariffs and other trade defence actions. Notable organizations following this trend include Sony, Nissan, Toyota and Honda from Japan, and Lucky Goldstar from Korea. One Asian airline relocated much of its paper processing and accounting work to Australia from Hong Kong, and a UK airline operates its customer call-centre from the Middle East. The number of emergent, relatively low-cost economies has also increased substantially in recent years, not just with the Far East countries but also with those of Eastern Europe. Each of these new producers and economies adds to the level of competition in the established markets.

It seems relatively clear that where technology and total costs enable such a move, employment is attracted to cheap labour. The economic consequences for the originat-ing economies are currently uncertain. However, it is easy to observe relative growth in the wealth of emerging economies and decline in those which are mature. While there may be profits for the 'home' economy to repatriate (after tax!), the jobs and much of the wealth remain in the host manufacturing economy, as this is where the workers spend their wages.

It would seem to be the case that work continues to follow low total production costs. If the observed cycle continues, it should be apparent that long-term decline of the mature economies is inevitable as emergent economies develop the skills and abilities necessary to absorb a greater proportion of both manufacturing and service sector jobs.

In parallel with this phenomenon, and notwithstanding the substantial apparent progress in products, services and information technology in recent years, it also appears to be the case that for many products, with the exception of certain emerging products and services such as computer games and leisure facilities, demand is in effect satisfied.

Consumers are operating in a replacement cycle for a large proportion of established products, for example, cars, domestic appliances, home entertainment equipment, even personal computers, albeit new features and functionality ensure a degree of obsolescence in some products. In this replacement phase of the product life cycle consumers are demanding greater reliability and longevity from their purchases, and these characteristics are significant in their decision making. It also appears that for many products, diversity and choice are expanding, with competitive products from emergent economies challenging those of the established players.

Vignette 1.1 Manufacturing Activity Drives the Service Sector

As the severe recession of 2008/9 is beginning to show, an economy without a sound manufacturing base is extremely vulnerable. As the UK has seen, a dramatic slowdown in financial services activity, which, by limiting the availability of credit, has a negative impact on every other aspect of the service economy, has a dramatically weakening effect on the whole economy – including manufacturing – because the products manufactured cannot be sold.

It can perhaps be argued that the wages of manufacturing workers drive prosperity in the domestic (as opposed to the international) service sector of an economy. Observation of any community which has lost its manufacturing base will tend to confirm this view. The UK, which has largely lost its mining, steel and shipping industries and much other manufacturing, continues to suffer high unemployment. In 2009, it has a depressed retail sector, falling house prices and relatively lower business volumes (and consequently incomes) for professional services such as legal and accountancy. Growth, which was apparent from the mid-1990s to mid-2008 and based on spectacular growth in financial services activity, has simply vanished with the limited availability of credit, apparent over-supply of products, and the effective conversion of what were once specialized high-cost items to commodities. It was believed that high-technology and service-based jobs would provide sustainable growth for the whole economy. This has not proven to be the case.

Since 1997 and the so-called 'Asian Economic Crisis' several of the emerging economies have been struggling to maintain employment and have seen sharp reversals in the previous patterns of economic growth. The impact of this crisis has been severe. Some countries, such as Indonesia, have seen massive collapse of their currency values, while major industrial combines have seen large falls in business volumes and looming bankruptcy. Hong Kong and Singapore saw substantial reductions in the numbers of both business visitors and tourists, with consequent impacts on the service sector: reduced hotel bookings, under utilized airport facilities, all knocking on to both service and manufacturing sector employment. This apparent reversal in the fortunes of these countries may not have been a crisis at all, but simply a reflection of the maturity of those economies. The long-established, supposedly post-industrial, economies, and those which are still emerging, need to recognize that manufacturing provides under-pinning strength and needs to be retained as a key element of sustainability.

So much for private industry, but what of the public sector? Does the same economic imperative apply? The pursuit of quality is equally important to this sector of every economy. From their behaviour and actions throughout the world, governments can be observed to be dissatisfied with the cost and effectiveness of many public services. For some years there has been a trend towards privatization, commercialization, or agency status of many public sector bodies. Such changes impose on them many of the same commercial constraints faced by private sector, profit-oriented institutions. It seems to be the case that the share of GDP absorbed by governments is unacceptable to many voters and potentially damaging to economies, given, for example, the tendency for organizations to relocate from high employment cost economies to lower-cost ones.

At the same time in those relatively wealthy established economies such as the UK, there has been a drift of public service consumers away from the public offerings towards private services, perhaps in conjunction with the emergence of executive agencies and the privatization of public services such as railways. An example of this is the creation of 'Foundation Trusts' in the NHS, which will generate organizations which, while still in public ownership, will be at arm's-length from government, finding and managing their own finances, albeit still dependent on the state for the bulk of their income. These changes occur where the public service is perceived to be failing to meet the needs of its consumers, where costs are very high and uncontrollable and where industrial relations challenges are likely to damage the standing of the party in government. If these public services do not address the problems which their users observe they must eventually fall into disrepair, either collapsing altogether through lack of public support or offering a second-rate service to the less-well-off members of the society which supports them, thereby increasing the unit cost of such provision. The pursuit of quality in their products and services offers these institutions the opportunity to provide comparable services to those available in the private sector. I argue that there is nothing inherently 'better' about a privately owned and offered service than a public one. It is merely that the economic imperative for survival has traditionally been greater in the private sector.

The economic imperative for quality is essentially quite simple: survival for the individual organization, industries and ultimately the total economy. The 'gurus' promise that achieving quality will reduce costs and improve productivity, and certainly many of the tools will lead towards these things. As consumers become more selective in their choices, quality has ceased to be an optional extra and become essential for any organization in a saturated marketplace and a weak economy – only the strongest will survive. From the perspective of the total economy of a nation, it is more cost-effective to cure quality problems than it is to export jobs or lose them to alternative or overseas suppliers.

1.2 The Social Imperative

In parallel with the developments in technology over the last fifty years or so, there has been a massive development in our understanding of humankind. Through the works of management writers and practitioners such as Barnard (executive functions), Mayo, Herzberg and McGregor (human psychology), Beer (organizational cybernetics), Ackoff and Checkland (soft systems), management theorists and scientists have become aware of many alternative ways of designing and managing jobs and organizations. However, clinging to the homespun philosophical and short-term arrogance of 'If it ain't broke, don't fix it', coupled with a level of complacency and/or fear of change – 'We've always done it like that' – managers and academics have collectively failed to embrace the many possibilities that these developments in thinking have made available to us. Many academics (though by no means all) at universities and colleges continue to teach classical methods, because either they are all they know or because they reject the 'new' ideas. Expansion of higher education opportunities has led to a situation where not all lecturers can be active researchers in the disciplines which they teach, and with increasing teaching loads it may be a struggle to keep up to date with emerging ideas. Those who are active researchers tend to be engaged in those relatively few institutions which are well established and well funded. Practically for managers it is often easier in the short term to keep things as they are, particularly when the focus is forced onto the short-term financial performance measures by higher management and external demands.

Managers in organizations predominantly pursue a short-term, small step-based improvement methodology, rooted in the established norms of their situation, rather than, admittedly somewhat more ambitiously, pursuing the true potential of their organization. Commonly, managers know only the 'budget' for their function, and are unaware of what *could* be achieved if constraining norms were overthrown and they truly realized the potential of the resources (human, mechanical and informational) they have at their disposal.

To bring about change in the established order of anything always involves the expenditure of energy: to overcome the initial resistance; to persist with the change programme through the 'painful' times; and to provide the changed infrastructure to support the new order. As Machiavelli suggested in *The Prince*:

> It must be considered that there is nothing more difficult to carry out, nor more doubtful of success, nor more dangerous to handle, than to initiate a new order of things. For the reformer has enemies in all those who profit by the old order, and only lukewarm defenders in all those who would profit by the new order, this lukewarmness arising partly from fear of their adversaries, who have the laws in their favour; and partly from the incredulity of mankind, who do not truly believe in anything new until they have had the actual experience of it.

Similarly, the impact of any change programme may, at least in the short term, reduce the ability of the organization to acquire fresh supplies of energy. This energy, for most organizations, is expressed in the form of money. Where the money is not made available, for example in the public sector or in low-margin industries (commodity manufacturing and distribution), or where the demand for high investment returns restricts the available cash, the change programmes will fail.

An equivalent energy is required from the most senior management in terms of their commitment to supporting the change. While most frequently expressed in financial terms, the failure of support very often rests in the very human desire of managers to work with what they understand, deliver what has worked in the past, and seek to preserve their power and position within the organization. It is a rare manager who will voluntarily relinquish his or her own power base for the good of the organization. Observing change programmes is a little like watching a corrupt game of musical chairs at the senior level: when the music stops everybody is sitting in a different place, but the total number of chairs has not changed! Consequently, the ways in which we run organizations and manage people are often extremely wasteful of the human capabilities and talent of the majority.

The emergence in recent years of the idea of 'corporate social responsibility' (CSR) is challenging managers in new ways. While the next section deals with environmental challenges, especially the idea of 'global warming', CSR is concerned with the wider impact of the organization on its stakeholders. Corporate social responsibility is defined in a wide variety of ways with no universal agreement. However, Crane, Matten and Spence (2008) have explained it as follows: 'The [six] core characteristics of CSR are the essential features that tend to be reproduced in some way in academic or practitioner definitions.'

The six core characteristics are shown in Figure 1.1.

Ohno, founder of the Toyota Manufacturing method (Ohno, 1978), takes as his theme the elimination of waste (*muda*) as the basis of effectiveness in organizations. This systematic approach, discussed at length in Chapter 11, recognizes that waste can encompass people, systems, production machines and society, and it is this societal

Voluntary	acceptance of responsibility for actions that goes beyond that prescribed by law;
Internalizing/Managing Externalities	recognising impacts beyond the organization and accepting them as belonging to it;
Stakeholders	recognizing responsibility beyond shareholders and customers to embrace the wider society;
Alignment	the understanding that there is no necessary conflict between CSR and profitability. Addressing the alignment of corporate and social interests;
Practices and Values	this is not simply about the adoption of 'good' practices as avoiding a negative, but about an internal belief system that recognizes CSR as a good thing in its own right;
Beyond Philanthropy	an assumption that CSR is a mainstream way of doing business, not an addition that keeps society happy

Figure 1.1 Characteristics of corporate social responsibility.

dimension that is dealt with here. From origination to consumption, and ultimately disposal or recycling, every action by an organization and its human actors imparts both positive and negative impacts to society. Corporate social responsibility argues that managers have a responsibility to minimize the negative impacts, and follows this into practical activities, whether they be enhanced company driver training to reduce accidents and improve economy, support for community activities such as sponsoring clubs, or involvement of local communities directly in the development of long-term plans. Each of these, and a myriad of other actions, are intended to soften the impact of the organization on its social environment and encourage it to 'behave' as a good 'corporate citizen'.

Both CSR and the Toyota method exploit the understanding that many of the people affected by inefficient, ineffective systems know that the system is ineffective and also, importantly, how to fix it. Such systems are not only wasteful but demoralizing and destructive to the talents of their members and users. It is staggering how often those responsible for a job can identify a short cut which enables the job to be completed on time and within specification, whereas the organization of the system itself would drive towards at least one, and often both, of these important parameters being missed.

One effect of the failure of organizations fully to exploit the talents they employ is that they lose them. Recent years have seen a huge rise in the number of new, small professional service organizations whose proprietors and directors, disenchanted with the limitations of life in large organizations, have the confidence and ability to build their own, independent concerns. The joke on the large organizations is that they then, very often, hire back at much greater expense the very set of talents and skills which they previously failed to exploit. The large organization loses in two ways: it has to compete actively to obtain the particular skills it needs at higher cost and the career model provided to young employees features the organization as victim rather than predator. The underlying message to talented young staff is that they will not be able to exploit their talents within the organization.

At the operational level, organizations have in many cases failed to respond to improvements in our understanding of human behaviour and in levels of education. They continue to manage their staff through a Taylorist mental model, imposing bureaucracy and regulation and insisting on mindless adherence to 'the procedure'. While there are many circumstances in which adherence to the procedure is essential for safety or consistency, there are similarly many circumstances where 'the procedure' inhibits rather than enhances quality. This particularly applies to the service sector and will be explored in Section 1.4, 'The challenge for service organizations'. However, even in manufacturing the regulatory and policing burden imposed by a heavily proceduralized organization could be substantially reduced by a higher initial investment in training and development, thus releasing the talents of those employed. Similarly, contemporary information systems have the inherent capability to release individuals from the drudgery of data capture and reporting, but are poorly designed and executed, most commonly replacing manual bureaucracy with an electronic equivalent, and thus allowing the same mistakes to be made faster and at greater cost. The benefit to be obtained from enhanced people development and effective Information Systems investment would dramatically outweigh the cost of providing it. A well-developed member of staff who understands *why* something should be done in a particular way will do so willingly, thus reducing the cost of supervision. Perhaps more importantly, he or she will be able to appreciate when the procedure has become inappropriate and, even if not free to change it, will at least be able to bring it to the attention to those who have that authority. 'I was only following orders' is not a guarantee of success in manufacturing any more than in any other walk of life. Relatively well-educated staff in a reasonably wealthy, high-employment economy have choices. If they are not treated appropriately they will exercise them! As was recently remarked, 'With every pair of hands you hire you get a free brain' – so why not use it?

If, as can be shown to be the case, individuals have the capacity to perform more complex tasks to higher standards or in greater volume than the system permits, then managers are wasting resources. This is in itself sufficient evidence of the need for change, quite apart from the potential benefit to the human spirit that change could offer. From the perspective of social cohesion, it must be the responsibility of every manager to maximize the opportunity for development for each of his or her fellow workers. This will surely lead to a more satisfied workforce, a commitment to the organization, and a society more at ease with itself.

The negative risk of minimizing apparent waste of human resources is that if quality is achieved and markets do not grow to absorb increased higher volume outputs, there may be a substantial increase in levels of unemployment. This will arise because organizations will find it unnecessary (and costly, since there are indirect additional costs involved in employing extra staff) to retain current numbers of employees. In the 1980s such pressures led to the fashion for downsizing in organizations, reducing staff numbers to the minimum level.

As has been seen in many conurbations in developed countries over the last twenty years, high levels of unemployment tend to create conditions of social isolation, a sense of hopelessness and unease, often leading to unrest and anti-social behaviour such as drug and alcohol abuse or increasing crime rates. Examples of such situations have been riots in Liverpool, Birmingham and other UK cities, the increase in drug abuse reported in crime statistics, increased levels of shoplifting, and the rise in illegitimate births, particularly amongst teenagers. It cannot be regarded as acceptable that by achieving quality we also achieve social destruction. Neither can it be regarded as sustainable to produce poor quality outputs in order to maintain employment in the short term – above all else, consumer markets will not allow this. A substantial debate is required to address this issue. After all, it may be argued that by succeeding in the pursuit of quality any particular country will act as an attractor of industries leading to economic success for that country. Inevitably this would have international consequences which are beyond the capacity of any individual or normal organization to address. Meanwhile the markets will not wait and action must be taken to preserve, maintain and develop all industries.

The second imperative for quality, then, stems from the responsibility of all managers to minimize waste of costly human resources and maximize satisfaction through work for their colleagues in order to support social cohesion within their own sphere of influence.

1.3 The Environmental Imperative

The third imperative for quality is environmental. Driven by the experiments and perspectives of writers such as Lovelock (1979, 1988, 1991) and the emergence of the environmental movement, it is now widely recognized that the world has only finite natural resources, particularly fossil fuels, and that the use of these appears damaging to the total ecology of the planet. Renewable energy sources, such as solar power, wind energy or wave energy, are not yet readily available, nor as cheap as may be possible in the future. While Lovelock in *Homage to Gaia* (2001) has presented an argument for the adoption of nuclear power as an available alternative to fossil fuels, this is unlikely to prove any more acceptable to the established power groups than his arguments against fossil fuels were in the 1970s.

In this early part of the twenty-first century, concern about damage to the environment has been elevated to a primary concern of governments of all nations. In particular, governments of the most mature economies are making substantial commitments, some legally binding, some not, to reduction in carbon dioxide emissions in particular, which are widely seen as a contributory factor in creating global warming. Although there is not universal agreement on the impact of such emissions, there is substantial agreement that they should be reduced.

International accords are being actively pursued to reduce fossil fuel emissions and the Kyoto Agreement, which demands substantial reductions in harmful emissions, also heralds the emergence of a market in which the right to produce emissions can be bought and sold. This provides an economic incentive for organizations to pursue the environmental imperative.

ISO 14000, the Environmental Management Standard, is becoming more widely accepted and adopted in the major economies and, like the early versions of ISO 9000, is becoming to be seen as the minimum acceptable standard with which companies should seek to conform.

While it might be argued that a narrow focus on environmental sustainability detracts from the broader arguments about the overall sustainability of organizations, projects such as SIGMA (Sustainability: Integrated Guidelines for Management) and the more recent international accords on environmental protection and emission reductions show that organizations can no longer afford to pay only lip service to this subject. For example, Europe has developed legislation designed to reduce both substantially and rapidly emissions from new motor cars (from inception to destruction), with lower acceptable levels of pollution being set for every manufacturer. Also, standards are increased and enforced for the recycling of the components of vehicles, and individual governments set tax incentives for consumers to drive less polluting vehicles. This has not yet been integrated with a revision to policy on pricing and incentives for the use of public transport, which is still subject to established rules on the provision of subsidies, but in the longer term this could be expected to happen.

Operating our organizations without a sharp focus on quality is wasteful of limited resources. Quality products, processes, systems and services minimize the use of all the factors of production (human, material, land and money), maximize the reliability and longevity of products, and thereby minimize lifetime damage to the environment. For example, a process which achieves Crosby's 'Zero Defects', Shingo's 'Poka-Yoke' or Ohno's *muda* standard involves no rework or rectification. Processes such as these then make minimum use of money, materials and labour in achieving output and consequently minimize damage to the environment compared with a process producing any number of defective outputs.

Clearly, with the exception of fictional characters such as Superman, it is too much to expect any one individual or organization to 'save the world'. Each individual or organization can, however, be expected to make a contribution to saving the world at an appropriate level, that is, their own level and the ones above and below. The levels could be thought of as the individual, the organization, the stakeholders, the local community, the national community, and the international community.

All individuals have a responsibility, along with their employers, to minimize the use of resources in the completion of their duties. This must be supported by organizations that create conditions which enable work to be carried out with minimum waste. This might simply mean ensuring that tools are properly functional (sharp, accurate), that sufficient time is permitted for the task to be carried out with appropriate care, and that the individual worker holds the necessary skill set to complete the given task competently.

Management have the additional responsibility of considering the total effectiveness of the organization in terms of its use of all resources and the environmental implications of their actions. This may mean undertaking additional investments to reduce environmental damage. This approach must, of course, be supported by the other stakeholders in the enterprise, in particular the shareholders. They must accept responsibility for the actions of the organization and be prepared to accept the returns generated by an organization which fully accepts its responsibilities, even if these are less in the short term than those offered by competing investments. This thinking links back to the notion of CSR outlined in Section 1.2.

A substantial conflict may arise for some companies when it comes to additional investment. In the chemicals industry, economic reality is that simply to keep pace with their competitors, organizations in this sector must reduce costs, year on year, by around 3 per cent. In an industry dominated by high-volume manufacturers of predominately low margin commodity products, this is a challenging target, especially for smaller companies. When coupled to increases in the regulatory load governing the behaviour of the organization, and the testing, storage and use of its products, the target becomes harder. To achieve sustainable improvements in quality (however that may be defined in the circumstances), to enhance the skill set of the employees and to ensure the long-term viability of the organization against this background of, in effect, falling margins is harder still. It may well be that the only truly sustainable business strategy (as far as the capital held by the organization is concerned) is to leave the industry! The ultimate challenge is not simply to improve quality and reduce costs to remain competitive, but to achieve a position which satisfies competing ethical demands: the imperatives to preserve jobs for society, to improve quality of product, to minimize damage to the environment, not to imperil the local (or wider) community, and to satisfy shareholder demands.

The community in which the organization exists must hold and impose expectations on the behaviour of the organization as regards environmental matters while at the same time accepting its own responsibilities. For example, if it wishes to continue purchasing the relevant product, the community must impose expectations regarding the dumping of waste, but must also provide an appropriate mechanism for such dumping to take place. Economically, certain resources can only be provided at the community level, for example, incinerators and recycling plants. The responsibility of the community is to ensure that these are available.

At a national level, the same considerations apply. The nation has a responsibility to itself, its constituents and the international community. This responsibility includes setting, maintaining and enforcing environmental standards and expectations, and creating conditions (perhaps through the use of taxes and duties) which reinforce those expectations.

At the international level, the responsibilities are much the same. Creation and enforcement of environmental standards must be undertaken by the international community. While other aspects of organizational life may be very different, for example wage rates, organizational culture and so on, the international community must demand common environmental standards from all those wishing to be part of that community.

At every level, there is a need and a responsibility to educate and inform on environmental matters, and to understand the needs from a total rather than a partial perspective. Thus the third imperative for quality is to address the rising desire for reductions in environmental damage, and so help to ensure the survival of all species. It is a responsibility which pertains at every level of the world community.

1.4 The Challenge for Service Organizations

The origins of the quality movement and the philosophies, tools and techniques reviewed in this book rest in the manufacturing sector. It was manufacturing that addressed the contemporary issue of quality and it might be argued that that has, at least at one level, 'solved' the specific problem of manufacturing quality. The organizational and economic world has, however, changed. Forty years ago, manufacturing was the dominant economic force in every advanced economy; the service sector was relatively small in comparison, employing small numbers of highly qualified professionals. In the 'post-industrial' or 'knowledge' economy, manufacturing is generally high-volume, highly automated, highly specialized and highly important, as already stated, but represents a relatively small proportion of total economic activity and employs a similarly small proportion of the workforce. The service sector is now the dominant employer and generator of economic growth. For example in Hong Kong, since the 1960s a strong manufacturing economy, around 70 per cent (depending on the basis of measurement) of economic activity is derived from the service sector. Similar proportions pertain in the Western economies.

The challenge for the service sector is to develop ways of addressing the 'quality problem' which are appropriate to the needs of a sector whose principal asset is people, and where the application of the skills and knowledge of those people it employs is the key differentiator between 'good' and 'bad' service. To date, the signs are not encouraging. Many organizations are simply adapting the manufacturing models of quality to the service sector to no great effect.

Manufacturing models of quality, as will be seen in Part Two, rely on an outmoded understanding of notions of quality, organization, people and consumers. They tend to be incremental in their impact and create bureaucracy, ultimately falling into disrepute and disuse. The focus of manufacturing-based quality systems has often been on doing that which is required to secure the necessary 'badge', not on delivering quality. Applied to the provision of services these models are mechanistic, alienating, lead to deskilling of the workforce, and devalue the notion of professionalism. They generate situations where the words used – 'Have a nice day' – are considered more important than the emotion conveyed. Words without meaning, without sincerity, without commitment will not suffice for quality in a service organization – particularly one where, however long the procedure chart, it never quite reaches the specific needs of the individual consumer (Beckford and Dudley, 1998; Dudley, 2000). Where the words are insincere, and the customers' problem or need does not fit the organization's procedures, the relationship has no future.

Whereas addressing quality in manufacturing rested on the resolution of tangible, visible, persistent issues, quality in services is totally different. Service quality is directly measurable only in relation to the tangible aspects of the transaction: did the teller cash the cheque and pass over the right amount of money? This is measurable, verifiable, and auditable. Did the teller handle this customer in the way that she or he wanted to be handled? Opinions might vary, the teller may well have used the 'right' words, but did he or she employ the 'right' manner? The teller may think so, the customer may not; neither can irrefutably prove their viewpoint.

Service quality is, then, intangible and instantaneous. It perishes with the completion of the transaction and cannot subsequently be verified or audited. It depends not on what actually happened but on how the parties to the transaction feel about what happened. The manufacturing models of quality cannot deal with the problem of service quality because they focus on the tangible not the intangible, and because the means by which they verify and audit quality are post-hoc. Service quality cannot be verified after the event; it must be assured beforehand.

The key to quality in service provision is not standardization and verification but skills, knowledge and education. To paraphrase Tony Blair, the key to quality in service provision is people, people, people! The challenge for service organizations is to embrace those notions of process control which can be usefully applied to the service environment and couple them to management of the skills of the staff to assure quality.

1.5 A Problem with 'Quality'

Inevitably there is more than one 'problem with quality'. The first problem, a precursor to the second, is the way in which organizations pursue quality programmes, very often adopting a neo-Taylorist or neo-managerialist philosophy (Taylor's work is briefly explored in Chapter 4) and driving quality through the traditional models espoused by the gurus (Part Two). The second problem is the understanding of precisely what is meant by quality and its role in generating effective organizations.

Section 1.2 explored the social imperative for quality. It is this imperative which must be recognized so that organizations can address the first problem of quality. Simply, the traditional, industrial model of quality focuses on control, conformance and standardization. This approach treats the human actors in the situation as expensive, unreliable, unthinking parts, and is, in many cases, actively distrustful of them. This leads to expensive, and often ineffective, inspection and audit routines, and on occasion to the generation of products and services which the organization wishes to make rather more than the consumer wishes to buy. In the manufacturing context, consumers simply purchase elsewhere; in the service context it leads to disuse of the service by the consumers or revolt. It has been observed, for example, that the methodology adopted by certain government agencies in the UK rests on this industrial model, and in more than one instance there has been vociferous protest from the affected professionals – the nearest they will get to revolution, although in some sections potential breakaway groups have emerged.

Those working within such organizations will, in general, not give their best work to these organizations because they do not want it. They simply require the workers to follow the laid-down procedures. They will act to produce those aspects of performance which the organizations measure (usually productivity and some narrow measure of quality such as reject rate) and do the job with the minimum of positive engagement. Given the opportunity they will seek work elsewhere. In adopting this model, such organizations will, over time, simply drive away those staff most capable of genuinely adding value to the functioning of these organizations.

The problem rests in a fundamental misunderstanding of the role and responsibility of managers, leading to a massive schism between the managers and the managed. The first core assumption underpinning the neo-Taylorist approach is that the managers know best. More often than not this is simply not the case (Townsend, 1970). The second core assumption is that when things go wrong, as they will in any organization from time to time, it is somebody's fault – and that somebody is not a manager (or at least not a manager at the level of the person identifying the fault). Thus we create organizations in which the managers instruct the workers in what to do and then blame them when it does not work. The key change required is the acceptance of real responsibility and accountability by those who give the instructions. A new generation of organizations is needed where genuine communication occurs between the managers and the managed and there is real collaboration between these participants to solve the problems of the organization.

The first problem is driven by the second problem, and that is the understanding of what quality really means in the context of creating an effective organization. Typically the focus of quality action has been very narrow, looking only at that part of the organization which makes a physical product or, in the service sector, directly interacts with the customer. The balance of the organization – very often the greater part of it – is uninvolved.

The narrow focus of quality programmes and initiatives followed the early development of the quality movement, which was focused on standardization and improving manufacturing performance. Such a focus can no longer be considered acceptable when what it often means is that the organization focuses on doing the wrong thing better rather than on doing the right thing! Quality improvement in a product no longer suited to its market, for whatever reason, will not solve the problems of the organization; it is futile. The organization will simply lose money at a slightly lower rate. Quality in this interpretation means doing the right thing right! By implication the organization must have a shared understanding of its present and future market or environment; it must have products positioned to meet the known and anticipated expectations of its customers or users; and it must have strategies in place to enable it to respond at an appropriate rate to the changes as they occur. For many managers this means that their egos must be subordinated to the organizational interest. Nobody can win unless the organization wins.

An effective organization is both capable of dealing with its current market or environment and of anticipating and responding to emergent changes in that market to ensure its own survival. Quality thought of in that way is not an operational, single function issue, but an organizational-wide systemic issue. In such an organization the impact, either direct or indirect, on every other part is explicitly recognized. Quality will then be embedded in every part and every level of the organization rather than isolated and handed over to the production or customer service director, who cannot possibly deliver it in isolation.

Summary

This chapter has identified and elaborated three imperatives for the contemporary pursuit of quality – economic, social and environmental – and has then moved on to examine the difficulties and challenges faced by the service sector. From these different perspectives, brief arguments have been developed which not only justify but also collectively demand that the idea of quality be pursued in every aspect of every organization.

KEY LEARNING POINTS

Five issues relating to quality: economic, social, environmental, service challenge, problem of quality

Economic:
mature markets; saturation coverage; work follows (relatively) cheap labour; manufacturing drives services income – economies must be balanced; the public sector must deliver better services at the same or lower cost to meet public expectations; ultimate demand is economic survival.

Social:
non-quality goods and services are wasteful of human capabilities and talent; working in a non-quality environment is ultimately demoralizing for the individual; the imperative is to minimize waste of talent and maximize satisfaction; corporate social responsibility is simply defined as the requirement (legal and social) for the organization to be a good citizen.

Environmental:
the world has finite material resources; we have a responsibility to minimize waste and environmental damage.

Service challenge:
services represent 70 per cent of post-industrial economies; industrial quality control models do not work in the service context; the key to quality in services is skilled people.

Problem of quality:
two problems: neo-Taylorist management approach and isolation of quality to the productive part of the organization; resolution through systemic approach to quality, based on doing the right things right in every part and level of the organization.

Question

Can an organization survive if it does not respond to the imperatives outlined in this chapter?

2 Quality: A Strategic Decision?

focus on quality, not quantity

(Jiang Zemin, President, Peoples Republic of China, 1996)

Introduction

The successful pursuit of a quality programme requires the dedication of substantial organizational resources, and it is vital to understand whether and how this generates value for the organization. It is evident from the citation above that China, the world's largest emerging economy consisting of 1.2 billion potential consumers, is treating quality not just as an organizational issue but as a national one. Evidence of its success can be seen in the massive and continuing economic growth of China since that exhortation, and its emergence as a significant manufacturer of a wide range of consumer goods, from electronics to cars. In 2008, China re-launched the MG brand in the UK, having re-established the final assembly of sports cars at the old Rover plant in Longbridge; the same year as it launched the brand with a range of cars in China itself. Such a position reinforces the message that all organizations and countries seeking to achieve economic success must take quality seriously.

In this chapter, the role and implications of quality in the organization will be explored through consideration of the conventionally recognized different levels of management decision-making (operations, administration and strategy). The idea of 'normative' decision-making (Beer, 1979), that is, decisions based on identity (values, beliefs, soul) will be introduced to enhance understanding. The implications for an organization of pursuing a strategy for quality will be assessed, starting with operational management.

2.1 Operations

Operational management is concerned with the day-to-day activities which ensure that the organization fulfils its present purposes and objectives. These may include short-run profitability and achievement of particular levels of output, yield or productivity. Operational decisions are generally more or less immediate in their impact on the organization, affecting what happens during a particular day, shift, or even part shift – for example, where there are product changes during the course of a shift. In the service sector, immediate operational decisions are often about the short-term allocation of staff resources to meet continuously varying customer volumes.

The objective of operational management is to deliver today's products and services into today's market but faster, cheaper and cleaner (more environmentally acceptable) than ever before. Operational management is not focused on the long term, but on creating an ever better version of 'now'.

The chapters in Part Four of this book will show how the traditional tools of quality are predominantly focused at this operational level. They are intended to assist the manager and staff in the production of quality goods and services on a daily basis, focusing on prevention of error and minimization of rework or rectification, aiming to minimize inspection and to achieve continuous improvement. These things are achieved through the use of measurement system outputs at the 'shop-floor' level to inform devices such as quality circles and work-improvement teams. These engage workers in reflection on the difficulties and problems experienced in creating a product or delivering a service, and through their joint efforts seek to reduce them.

In terms of the needs of the organization, an analogy can be suggested with Herzberg's (1959) ideas (Figure 2.1) on motivation theory. Herzberg suggested that working conditions affecting motivation fall into two broad bands: hygiene factors and motivating factors. Hygiene factors are those characteristics of the working environment which, if absent, will lead to dissatisfaction. Their presence will not motivate workers but will create conditions in which motivation becomes possible. Motivating factors are those characteristics of the work which will inspire those involved to greater efforts.

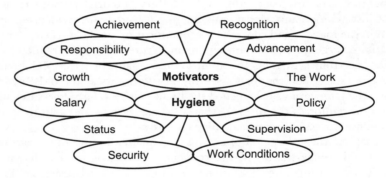

Figure 2.1 Herzberg's two-factor theory of motivation.

For the purposes of this analogy we can equate the hygiene factors to the need for operational quality. The absence of an operational quality focus will mean higher levels of error and failure. Its presence will not guarantee greater quality since so many aspects are driven by other parts of the organization, such as planning, design and marketing.

The role of operational management is to achieve the quality expectations of the organization, but this can only be done within the constraints imposed by higher-order decision making. Clearly, if product or service quality is not an inherent part of the thinking and decision-making at higher levels in the organization, it will be difficult, if not impossible, to achieve at the operational level.

2.2 Administration

Administrative management is concerned with the allocation, use and control of the current operational resources of an organization to achieve its present purposes and objectives. It is the control function for operational management. Administrative managers acting within the constraints imposed on them from higher management seek to maximize the use of resources in the pursuit of organizational goals.

At this level of the organization, reliance is placed more on data and information than on the physical artefacts themselves or the attributes of a service. Decisions are based on the recorded outcomes and achievements. Here organizations have missed something. While they have often automated production and service delivery quite extensively, there is, in many instances, a massive amount of work required to capture data about performance, collate that data, turn it into information for decisions and report it – promptly, accurately and usefully. Organizations could substantially benefit from reconsidering how *this* management loop on their production process could benefit from the more effective use of information technologies.

The administrative level allows the first serious constraint upon the achievement of quality to come into focus. The administrative manager, for example, a factory or production manager, may find her- or himself in a position of conflict between meeting the customer expectations in terms of volume of product delivered and meeting those customers' expectations regarding quality of product or service. At this point, the priorities imposed upon this manager (a reflection of the true values or identity of the organization) from above will determine the outcome of any conflict. The question is simply, 'Which does the organization regard as more important to deliver, volume or quality?' In addition to observation of the behaviour of the manager, clues to the answer can be discerned in an examination of the performance measurement system of the organization. If this emphasizes volume, then delivery of volume will prevail at the expense of quality and vice versa.

A quality management system (whether or not certified to ISO 9000: 1994, ISO 9000: 2000 or other standard systems) will, or should, form a significant part of the performance management system employed by the administrative manager. However, if quality is not perceived as a priority within the overall management system it will probably not be perceived as a priority at this level.

It is also important to realize at this stage that the pursuit of quality does not apply solely to the operational aspects of the organization but also to all of the support and administrative processes which enable it to function. For example, a personnel recruiting system should be thought of as a productive process delivering to the operational system (its customer) staff who meet the technical skill, attitudinal and behavioural criteria necessary to perform the tasks required. If it fails to do this then it is unreasonable to expect the operational processes to function to appropriate quality standards. The same thinking applies to training, reward systems, equipment and materials procurement, and so on.

The administrative manager, then, has a dual responsibility for the delivery of quality, neither of which is more important than the other; they are equally necessary. One is to create the operational conditions which make it possible for the product or service to meet customer expectations. The other is to ensure that his or her own systems and processes deliver outputs to the operational 'customers' which meet their needs and expectations.

2.3 Strategy

Strategic management is concerned with the scope of the organization's activities, its markets, products or services and market stance. It deals with the questions of how the organization should develop and adapt itself for the future. The strategic process necessarily leads to outcomes with a degree of uncertainty. Strategic decisions are, then, best thought of in terms of desirable results and probable outcomes rather than in the short-term absolutes which may be associated with operational or administrative decisions. Despite, or rather perhaps because of this, and as with administrative management, quality must be inherent in the strategic process itself to maximize the probability of success and reduce the chances of failed strategic decisions. The classic and often quoted example of such a failure is that of IBM, which determined that the future of computing rested in mainframe systems. This decision led to the organization falling behind competitors in the development of personal computers with associated failure, at least initially, to gain market share. The strategic process itself then must be subjected to the same rigorous approach to quality as the operational processes. However, it must be considered whether the decision to pursue a quality programme or become a quality organization is itself strategic.

Michael Porter, in the *Harvard Business Review* (1996), suggests that 'operational effectiveness and strategy are both essential to superior performance', but also makes the point that 'many companies have been frustrated by their inability to translate those gains [achieved from improved organizational effectiveness] into sustainable profitability'. He suggests that practices such as benchmarking and technology transfers between organizations create conditions where performance gains achieved by one organization are rapidly replicated in others, potentially leading to a sustained stalemate – no long-term winners and no long-term losers – with an increasing homogeneity of product and service characteristics. If strategic management is about creating and sustaining competitive advantage for an organization, this suggests that the pursuit of quality, particularly in a collaborative environment, may be the very opposite of strategic. If it acts to reduce competitive advantage rather than increase it, and to increase similarities between organizations, there is potential for all to pursue the same quality goal – which may not represent the true potential of the product or service.

However, that is not to say that the pursuit of quality has no strategic implications. Porter's work implies that every organization in a particular market will seek to emulate the behaviour of the one perceived as 'best'. This is inevitably not the case. Some organizations will not willingly collaborate. They may regard process knowledge (one key to organizational effectiveness) in the same proprietary manner as they regard a particular brand or item of intellectual property. For example, in the petro-chemical industry, the aphorism 'The product is the process' is used. In the USA it is not unknown for a process to be subject to patent. Equally, because of contextual differences, a working practice which delivers benefits for one organization in a particular cultural or social setting will not necessarily deliver the same benefits for another in a different cultural or social setting. Developing quality programmes internationally has highlighted the extent to which the success of any change or innovation and the business benefit it delivers is not simply a function of its apparent appropriateness to the process but, to a very great extent, the knowledge, skills, attitudes and behaviours of both the management and the workforce involved. An innovation which works in London or New York may not work well in Tokyo or Hong Kong, and vice versa. Even where cultures are more closely aligned, such as in South East Asia, what works in Singapore will not necessarily work in Hong Kong. Hofstede (1980) has examined this aspect in some depth. Thus the apparent loss of competitive advantage will not spread uniformly and universally across any industry, particularly where advantage can be gained through differentials in labour costs and/or the return on investment in technology.

Meanwhile, the leading organizations, that is, the ones against which others benchmark themselves, continually seek to further improve their products and processes to sustain their perceived advantage – always providing that they do not become complacent. It is possible to discern, then, that for any industry there will be leaders and followers with an inevitable time lag between the introduction of an improvement by the leader and its dissemination to others within the industry, either through benchmarking or creative imitation. This time lag will serve to sustain competition within the industry and hence support either price or cost advantage for the leading organizations. It is improbable that any innovation will bring benefits to an entire industry at the same instant except where it is externally driven, such as by governmental or regulatory authority involvement, or where the structure of the industry demands it. Innovation in the banking system, such as a new method of clearing payments between banks, would necessarily have to be adopted by a number of organizations at the same time to actually function. An improvement in operational effectiveness will, then, in most circumstances, generate a gain for the innovating organization until others emulate that improvement. A focus on constant innovation and improvement fits quite neatly into Porter's (1980) strategy of 'differentiation', the creation of a market perception of value advantage.

The strategic implications go much further than this, however. The comments on strategic management have, so far, been essentially inward-looking – to the organization and the industry. If we now look outwards at the environment, the effect of improved quality on customer behaviour can be examined. For perishable or consumption goods, there is little perceived impact. Improvement in the quality of a loaf of bread or a mushroom may affect customer choice but, if anything, is likely to lead to advantage for one player against others and a slight overall increase in volume, assuming a relatively mature market. It is when we examine consumer durables that the full impact becomes clear.

Any established consumer durable, especially one in the mature phase of its life cycle, will be subject to constraints of growth in volume. There is only a finite market for items such as cars, washing machines, microwaves or dishwashers. Buying activity in these circumstances is determined by the need to replace, or possibly upgrade, existing equipment. The products have entered the buyer's replacement cycle. In the consumer's mind, the quality of these items is perhaps determined by a number of factors. Inevitably these will include reliability and longevity as well as other factors, such as price, appearance, noise level in operation, and brand. If, as a manufacturer of consumer durables, we focus on improving reliability and longevity, the effect is to stretch the replacement cycle (the period of time between purchases), which has a direct impact on apparent market size. Thus improved quality will act to reduce the overall volume of sales of a particular item and, if the market is mature, the number of consumers who can be acquired from competitors determines the growth opportunity for any one supplier. In addition, the implications feedback into the organization to affect the volume of output necessary for the manufacturer to meet demand. This directly affects every strategic decision made by the organization, because those strategic decisions imply the commitment of substantial resources towards a desired outcome. Thinking which suggests that improving quality will increase sales which will increase manufacturing requirements, means that we have a requirement for additional capacity which may be fundamentally flawed. This is first because quality improvement will lead to greater volume output from existing facilities. Second, improvements in quality should substantially extend the replacement cycle, leading to a loss of total market volume. The motor industry exemplifies this potential.

Vignette 2.1 The Motor Industry

During the 1950s, 1960s and 1970s, the products of the motor industry (with a few honourable exceptions), whether American, British or European, were in general regarded as unreliable and expensive. These factors coupled to the then enormous labour cost difference across the East-West divide, and the quality improvement strategies being followed in Japan, enabled the very rapid growth of the Japanese motor industry and its substantial penetration into the established markets. Western cars were generally considered to have a relatively short life of five or six years, and after three years (or around 40,000 miles) to have become so unreliable and prone to breakdown that they needed to be replaced. The ancillary components, for example, clutches, steering systems, brake systems and electrical generators, were likely to need replacement at around this mileage.

Faced with the threat of extinction by the rapidly improving quality of imported vehicles, the industry eventually, and with much financial and personal pain, addressed its product quality. It is now usually expected that a car will generally be reliable for perhaps five or six years and that components, such as those specified above, have much longer life spans than previously. Mileage has also become a much less important factor in determining the reliability of a vehicle. Service history (that is, a good maintenance record) has become more important. The collaboration of manufacturers and their suppliers has so dramatically improved the quality of the outputs that, almost without exception, manufacturers are struggling to utilize the capacity of their assembly plants. Although the market for new cars is substantially larger than in the 1950s and 1960s, growth in capacity internationally means it has not grown to meet the potential numbers of vehicles now available. Consumers are able to rely on second user vehicles, and with improvements in the longevity of body work as well as other components, these maintain a greater proportion of their value. The cost of new vehicles and the rate of depreciation in retained value, particularly in the fleet purchaser-dominated UK market, has reached levels where the private consumer is often unwilling or unable to pay the manufacturer's price. What constitutes value for money for these consumers can adequately be met through the used car market.

These changes in buyer behaviour, driven by the quality improvements made by manufacturers, have in effect impacted adversely on strategic decisions to build new factories, launch new products, expand capacity, and so on.

It can be concluded, then, that the pursuit of quality must be considered as strategic. First, the process for formulating strategy must exhibit quality characteristics, that is, the process itself must be correctly designed and implemented. Second, the impact of the choice to pursue quality fits with the generic strategy of differentiation. Third, the pursuit of quality has an impact on strategic decisions, because it may generate changes in consumer behaviour. This in turn may obviate the need to establish additional facilities or new distribution channels.

2.4 Normative Decisions

The conventionally recognized levels of decision making in organizations have been considered. However, the changing nature of the world of organizations and the increasing concern with ethical issues such as morality, environmentalism, and so on, demands that we go further. Normative management decisions are concerned with these aspects, helping to define the nature and identity of the organization itself, that is, the values, expectations and beliefs espoused by its members. The norms so derived should ensure that the organization makes a good ethical fit with all of its stakeholders and with society in general – thus Corporate Social Responsibility.

Although all the component parts (people, factories, brands, products, services) of an organization may change, its identity may remain the same. That is, the essential attributes that define it as itself and nothing else can be sustained. These attributes, exhibited in the behaviours of its directors and employees, reflect its character. It might be honest, courageous, ethical or cowardly, abusive in its relations and lacking in integrity. Regardless of the specific products or services, such attributes come through in every engagement between the organization and its stakeholders. They define how it is treated in its market place and determine its success.

An organization which does not generate a good 'fit' of identity with its stakeholders will either lose customers, because it does not reflect their expectations, or fall into disrepute, as have branches of the civil service in many countries. Similarly, an organization which does generate such a fit is much more likely to be forgiven for an occasional lapse or transgression. While customer loyalty to organizations, and particularly brands, does exist – to the extent that some brands become synonymous with the product (such as the Hoover, Sellotape, Post-it Notes), and is encouraged through various loyalty schemes (such as Air Miles or Supermarket Bonus cards), such schemes will not retain customers who are genuinely unhappy with products or services. Political parties are particularly prone to failure of fit when they do not listen to an electorate that holds them in power. When the norms of a particular political grouping no longer reflect the wishes of their society they will be deposed, either through the democratic process or by revolution. Similar observations can be made of commercial organizations. When the characteristics of the products or services do not meet the expectations of consumers, or the behaviour of the organization is considered unacceptable, the customers will vote with their feet and buy elsewhere, and other stakeholders will follow. When sales and profit targets are not met, the shareholders in the organization, increasingly the large financial institutions, will depose the chief executive and appoint a new one in an attempt to correct the situation. Thus it is imperative for organizational survival (and for the self-preservation of those in power) that they listen to the demands of customers and formulate organizational norms which will meet them. For example, Marks & Spencer, which lost touch with its core market in the late 1990s, had by 2007/8 largely restored its previous position by paying close attention to what its customers wanted – and giving it to them. There is, however, speculation that in 2009 its core market is again being lost.

The pursuit of quality by so many organizations in recent years is precisely this kind of response. Consumers in mature markets are seeking the reassurance of reliable, high-quality goods and services (as defined by themselves), with the number and variety of choices available to them. Organizations which do not respond will fail.

The gurus of quality, as will be seen in Part Two, all stress the need for senior management commitment to the idea of quality in order to ensure its achievement.

Normative management is where this commitment arises. The feedback of consumer expectations to senior management closes the loop for the organization in determining behaviour. This loop explains why senior management must hold and believe in this commitment.

Normative decisions determine what questions and decisions are acceptable to the organization at the strategic level. They therefore pre-control (Espejo and Schwaninger, 1993) strategic decision making. Strategic decisions create potential new value for the organization: how profits will be made tomorrow. This, in turn, pre-controls the potential decisions at the administrative and operational levels – today's profits. At this point, and notwithstanding the potential for marketing activity to influence consumer behaviour, the organization largely loses control to the market. If the normative decisions are incorrect, the consumers will not buy.

In many organizations the normative decisions are expressed through devices such as mission statements or publicized 'visions' which attempt to express the values for which the organization stands. It is often considered that once this statement has been made the job is complete. However, if the values so expressed are not enacted in the behaviour of the senior management and in the performance measurement and reward systems of the organization, the junior management and operational staff will not respond to them. Rather, they will respond to the actual behaviour and expectations of the senior management measured by what they do and how they act, not by what they say. It is vital, as Professor Charles Handy so eloquently puts it, that the senior management 'walk the talk'.

Summary

This chapter has reviewed the role and positioning of quality in the context of the four levels of management decision making: operational, administrative, strategic, and normative. It has made clear that quality must be inherent throughout the organization in order for it to survive. While the principal traditional tools of quality focus on the operational and administrative aspects, this chapter has shown that it must extend well beyond this. If the senior management are not absolutely committed to quality in everything that they say and do, the organization will not 'care' about quality. If this caring is absent, it is impossible to build a quality organization.

KEY LEARNING POINTS

Four levels of management decision: operational; administrative; strategic; normative

Operational:
immediate impacts; day-to-day activity.

Administrative:
allocation of resources to achieve objectives.

Strategic:
activity scope; development directions.

Normative:
the nature of the organization; values, beliefs and expectations.

Quality must be inherent at every level.

Question

How closely aligned are the proclaimed 'norms' and values of your organization with the actual behaviour of the management?

3 Barriers to Quality

Passive resistance is the most potent weapon ever wielded by man

(Benjamin Tucker)

Introduction

This chapter aims to introduce readers to some barriers which prevent the achievement of quality. It will identify what those barriers are, how they arise and how they can be identified or recognized. The barriers have been grouped under four main headings:

- systems and procedures;
- culture;
- organization design;
- management perspectives.

These headings encompass a variety of other factors which are considered as symptoms rather than fundamental issues. The final part of the chapter will look at identifying the costs of quality, that is, the costs incurred by the organization in producing errors.

3.1 Systems and Procedures

Organizations of all sizes, especially those in the highly regulated business environments now existing, operate through a more or less bureaucratic process. That is to say, they are organized through a hierarchical system of offices or 'bureaux' (Weber, 1924) and maintain that organization through formal reports, documents and record-keeping, both internal and external. This is not in itself a bad thing; indeed, it is essential to the delivery of a standardized product, particularly in service organizations or in those operating through distributed delivery networks such as retail chains, fast-food operators or banks. Without a standardized approach the customer may easily be confused and the organization itself spiral out of control; standardization of everything is *the* key ingredient of commercial success for fast food chains.

However, problems can arise with such systems. First, systems and procedures can become fixed; that is, they become 'frozen' into the organization such that pressure for change and adaptation meets with high resistance. In this instance, when change is necessary to meet a new level of customer expectations it can be difficult to achieve. This is a barrier to the achievement of quality. It can be recognized when staff use expressions such as 'We've always done it like that'. This approach of using precedent as the basis of current decisions is common in many aspects of life, in particular in the practice of law which relies heavily on past cases and in civil administration. Readers may recall Lynn and Jay's *Yes Minister* (Lynn and Jay, 1982) when Sir Humphrey and the minister James Hacker were discussing the Honours system:

> I told him not to be silly. This infuriated him even more.
> 'There is *no reason*,' he said, stabbing the air with his finger, 'to change a system which has worked well in the past.'
> 'But it hasn't,' I said.

In the contemporary organizational climate, the reliance on precedent must be open to question if emergent threats are to be neutralized and advantage taken of opportunities, even if such precedents were at one time reliable. Organizations and individuals rapidly become comfortable with a learned pattern of response – the process – and lose sight of its effectiveness (or otherwise) in the pursuit of consistency and efficiency. 'Doing the wrong thing right' is often easier for an established organization than learning to do the right thing.

A particular problem arises from the use of procedures in service organizations. While procedures help to ensure standardization and repeatability, they can, as suggested in Chapter 1, miss the customer. Every service transaction is unique. While following a common pattern – each successive customer at the supermarket checkout goes through an identical process – the human interaction taking place is specific to the particular customer being dealt with – not the one before or the one after. If customers, as they often do, have problems or issues which do not fit the procedure then the transaction may 'fail', not in the process itself (though that is possible) but in the human interaction. The customer may walk away dissatisfied with the service.

It is often neither practical nor reasonable in a service transaction to attempt to create a procedure which covers every conceivable circumstance. It is the attempt to do so which leads to the bureaucratic management systems which so often fall into disuse and disrepute. Public and personal safety demand that before an aircraft departs, the cockpit crew work through extremely rigorous pre-flight checklists. These are designed to test and verify the functioning of every control and safety system to ensure that the aircraft is fit for the flight and that it will not endanger its crew, passengers or the public at large. This routine is essential and possible. The aircraft, a machine, has a defined and limited number of systems, each of which has two essential conditions: working or not-working. Failure or uncertainty in relation to any control or safety critical system means that the aircraft cannot depart.

Compare this with a visit to the dentist. While there is a set of procedural or process steps through which the dentist and patient must pass, neither the dentist nor the patient is a machine. The number of variables in the transaction is incalculable: the mental and physical condition of the dentist, the mental and physical condition of the patient, the moods of both, their past experiences of each other (and of other patients and other dentists), the extent to which the patient is currently suffering pain, the events they experienced on the way to the clinic. Each and every one of these factors will influence the transaction. Now, try to write the procedure chart for this! During the course of a quality project, a dentist was asked to do this. He had written seven pages before he got the patient's mouth open.

Variety, the number of possible states of the system, proliferates enormously in service transactions. Every possible question or requirement from a customer demands a specific response and a route for getting to that response. In a financial services organization it was calculated that for only six 'core' transactions with clients, variety had proliferated such that they had nearly 3,000 individual procedures, each an adaptation or derivation from another and each designed to meet the specific requirement of a customer or small group of customers. Even with this number of possibilities, there were numerous individual customers who fell through the gaps between the procedures. This has a number of drawbacks. Quite apart from continuing to fail in meeting customer expectations, the cost of maintaining, policing and auditing such a system far outweighs its benefit – to either business or customer. A better solution, especially given the highly qualified, professional staff employed, would have been to focus on the six core processes, develop and rely on the skills, knowledge and experience of the staff, and then allow them to exercise judgement in closing the gap between the high-order process outcome and the specific requirements of the individual customer. Human beings make excellent variety managers.

The second problem, the perception of what is important, is probably as great a barrier to quality, particularly in the context of a Crosby (1979) style quality programme. Such a programme relies heavily on an exhortative, evangelical approach. In most cases, managers and staff focus on achieving those aspects of performance which are explicitly measured. The systems and procedures of the organization, especially those involving performance measurement, tend to determine which characteristics of the organization receive most attention. For example, Beckford (1993) reports the case of a cake factory where the performance of the production department was monitored against two simple measures: volume throughput and labour utilization. The production managers sought to maximize these two characteristics in their daily work with considerable success. Complaints about quality, arising from either the internal quality control function or from the customers, were acknowledged but ignored in pursuit of productivity. A business issue arising from this case was that the production managers were, in effect, manufacturing for reject. The demand to increase throughput and labour utilization was not capped by the simple expression – 'to the extent of customer orders'. In order to keep the plant occupied the production managers were generating volumes significantly higher than customer demand. The excess production was sold off (at materials cost only) to a local secondary market trader. While outside the direct scope of Beckford's work, it was necessary for the subject organization to redesign its measurement system before any sustainable improvement could be achieved.

The barrier to quality revealed here is that of workforce perception, including all managers. Staff in an organization will seek to achieve the targets which are established through reported measurement, those things which the organization instructs them through its measurement system to regard as important. Discovering such a barrier in an organization is easy. It is simply necessary to look at the way in which performance is measured; this tells you what the organization regards as important. Even where quality performance is formally measured, and it often is not, its importance can be judged against the priority it is given when compared to productivity or other measures.

Overcoming these barriers will be dealt with in later chapters of this book. For now, it is sufficient to say that systems and procedures must be (re)designed to support the achievement of quality, with particular attention paid to the selection of performance criteria. If quality is a desired characteristic of the outputs of the organization, it will somehow, and to some degree, need to be measured and must take account of the expectations of customers, whether internal or external.

3.2 Culture

The development of a quality culture is a critical area of the achievement of quality, but what is culture? Clutterbuck and Crainer (1990: 195) describe it as:

> a set of behavioural and attitudinal norms, to which most or all members of an organization subscribe, either consciously or unconsciously, and which exert a strong influence on the way people resolve problems, make decisions and carry out their everyday tasks.

Schein, cited by Clutterbuck and Crainer (1990: 196), suggests that culture describes the 'artefacts, values and underlying assumptions' that govern behaviour within the organization. For the purposes of this book it is 'values' and 'beliefs' that are the key cultural drivers, although these may be expressed in a variety of ways. They often emerge from the measurement systems and procedures which are seen to communicate to staff and workers what senior management consider important about performance. Eventually, such aspects become culturally embedded – that is, they become a part of the value system of the organization.

Beliefs and values are also often expressed through the rituals, stories and myths of the organization. These are exchanged through both formal and informal processes, and may be seen as guiding new entrants towards particular forms of behaviour and attitudes. Those who do not conform may be seen as radicals and remain outside the 'cultural web' (Johnson and Scholes, 1993: 60) of the organization.

Entrenched norms of behaviour are some of the most difficult aspects of an organization to change. Where achievement of quality has previously not been considered important in comparison to achievement of some other target, it requires considerable determination and effort to change the established values. Again, a case history can perhaps explain the point. Many companies are currently abandoning the formal dress codes which grew up in the post-Second World War period, even enjoying 'dress-down Friday' when smart casual clothes are expected. Perhaps the most famous example of this is IBM which adopted a 'uniform' style of dress: grey suit, white shirt, boring tie. Adoption of this dress standard was seen as acceptance by the individual of his subordination to the organization – of his becoming a 'company' man. IBM, along with many other organizations, have formally abolished the requirement to wear standard office clothes, but how long will it be before the staff themselves accept the change? In the early twenty-first century, such informality has become normal – taking twenty years or so to pervade the workplace – but there is a slowly emerging trend back to the suit, although companies which consider themselves 'creative' or 'wacky' insist only that 'employees will wear clothes'. Contrarily, in some, but by no means all, Japanese companies, all employees, up to and including the chief executive, wear common corporate workwear. They argue that this approach helps to reduce or even eradicate differences between grades, enhances communication and that the sense of uniformity increases the common bond between employees. Relative to changing attitudes to quality, changing the dress code can be considered easy.

It has been shown that culture is often a very strong determinant of behaviour. In the next few pages some specific aspects of organizational culture will be considered.

'Politics' in the organizational context does not usually refer to overt competition between groups with differing ideologies, although this is possible. Normally, it refers to covert competition between various sub-groups in the organization for power; that is, for positions of influence and authority from which they can manage the organization to reflect their own preferences. These groupings may have their roots in a particular technical or functional ability, for example marketing, finance or production, or in common backgrounds such as groups who joined the organization at the same time and whose careers developed together, or who share the same school or university background, the same religion, the same home town or the same club tie. Working as a sub-cultural group within the organization's total culture, such groups often exercise immense, frequently tacit, influence. When such groupings are strong in an organization, they may place the interests of the group before those of the organization itself. This presents another barrier to quality. From the perspective of such sub-groups, achievement of quality must come to be seen as a meta-cultural requirement. The interests of the particular group must become aligned with, or subordinated to, the interest of the organization in pursuing quality.

Linking with some of the points already made about measurement systems and politics, do the employees of the organization care about the work and in particular about the quality of the product or service? If they do not, for whatever reason, then quality will probably not be achieved. Such attitudes are often driven by management through the priorities that they set and the results through which they manage the organization. For example, if those who are rewarded well by the organization are those who produce most, regardless of quality, then productivity (output) will be the focus of everyone's attention. If, on the other hand, quality is rewarded in preference to volume, then quality will be dominant.

Achievement of quality, particularly in the *kaizen* (continuous improvement) sense, depends upon an appropriate level of innovation. Creativity (the origination and implementation of new ideas or innovations) is often suppressed in organizations in pursuit of the status quo. This is revealed through the use of such expressions as 'Don't rock the boat', or 'Yes, you're right, but in the interests of your career/overtime/colleagues . . .'. A lack of creativity in the organization is not a sign that the people are not creative, because creativity is inherent in all of us. More frequently it is a sign that creativity is stifled by the organization, its processes and managers, and thus has become expressed outside the workplace.

Large or successful organizations often emit a 'hum' of satisfaction. They have an air of smugness, complacency and contentment with the way things are which can be almost tangible. This 'hum' comes through in their advertising, their websites, and often in the patronizing air of their customer service staff. Such a situation imposes an immense barrier to quality since there is no apparent compulsion or impetus for change. Frequently such satisfaction is present in organizations which have a short-term focus, perhaps a lack of foresight. They assume that if all is (or appears) right in this period, then everything will surely be all right in the next. Disasters and near disasters frequently overtake such organizations.

Vignette 3.1 The Banks and the Credit Crunch

For the fifteen years to 2008, the mature economies led substantial economic growth driven by a variety of factors. One of the most significant was the availability of credit, at least partly driven by the growth in derivative markets, that is, those where value has become dissociated from the value or earnings of underlying assets.

The profits generated by banks through this growth and the ever-increasing supply of credit led the leaders of those banks to either ignore the underlying risk, believing that somehow they had become 'super bankers', or perhaps they simply did not understand how their businesses were being managed.

Believing in their own myth, and drowning out expressions of concern by increasing the volume of the 'hum' of self-satisfaction, they engaged in ever more ambitious strategies, including, for example, the highly leveraged acquisition of big banks by little banks.

In 2007 and 2008, as the poor value and earnings of the underlying assets became clear and the risks transparent, the credit boom retracted and the hum of satisfaction became cries of terror.

This is maybe an extreme example; however, it is always the case that the 'bubble' bursts, and often the underlying realities are rotten. One of the tasks of the responsible manager is to challenge what the organization believes about itself.

Perhaps the best illustration of lack of foresight is given by Handy (1990a: 7–8):

> I like the story of the Peruvian Indians who, seeing the sails of their Spanish invaders on the horizon, put it down to a freak of the weather and went on about their business, having no concept of sailing ships in their limited experience. Assuming continuity, they screened out what did not fit and let disaster in. I like less the story that a frog if put in cold water will not bestir itself if that water is heated up slowly and gradually, and will in the end let itself be boiled alive, too comfortable with continuity to realize that continuous change at some point becomes discontinuous and demands a change in behaviour.

In the prevailing turbulent business environment, an assumption of continuity is highly dangerous. While pursuing quality with its implications of continuous improvement, standardization and regularity, it is equally vital to be alert to the potential for discontinuous change, especially since strategic advantage may rest in such discontinuities.

The last barrier to quality, which will be briefly explored under the general heading of culture, is that of accountability. Achievement of quality requires that errors be acknowledged, that sources of error be tracked down and rectified, and that both curative and preventative action be taken by those involved.

In many organizations this process is inhibited by a sub-culture which adopts a penal attitude. The realization of error is followed by a process of detection, prosecution – sometimes persecution – and punishment. This book is not the place for a debate on the societal value of such an approach, but it may be suggested that it is likely to be essentially negative in its effects. This may in turn lead to a situation where, as Deming (1982: 107) suggests, 'fear grips everyone'. In such a situation, errors may be suppressed or hidden. Where this is not possible, for example, in manufacturing organizations, there will be a tendency to avoid punishment by blaming others and by a refusal to accept responsibility.

This barrier can be overcome by recognizing that errors are normally opportunities for learning, and the basis for modifying a process, system, skill or behaviour to inhibit or prevent future occurrences. Naturally there must be a limiting case, when the error is consciously or deliberately provoked, when those responsible must be found and an appropriate response generated. However, in most organizations, and in many circumstances, the cause of error can be traced to some failure in the design or execution of a process, in the training of the employee, or in the equipment provided for the completion of the task. These aspects should be the first focus of attention, and in a quality organization will inhibit the use of disciplinary action. In many cases, though, they are the last. Managers often prefer to find someone to blame, perhaps because it is easier to do this than to accept responsibility for their own failure, and from this approach arises the blame culture. For example, one organization employed a group of administrative staff to operate a post office and administration system, servicing the needs of an off-site sales force. The salesmen rarely visited the office and relied heavily on the administrators to maintain diaries and timetable customer visits. An activity-based reward system meant that the sales force were absolutely reliant on the administrative system to ensure that they were paid the correct amount for the work done. Time lags in the system caused regular delays in payment. Work done was not paid for, and adventurous salesmen submitted claims for work which was incomplete, relying on the time lags to beat the system. Inevitably, problems arose in this operation. Members of the sales force began to fall behind with commitments, others received no pay at the end of certain months. After some delay, an administrator and two of the sales force left the organization; their temporary contracts were not renewed due to poor performance. Today, no member of the workforce will take any action without at least one management signature. This ensures that they have to take no responsibility. The system, the driver of the problems, is unchanged.

3.3 Organization Design

When discussing organization design, it is not simply the organization structure – the classic pyramidal hierarchy, or, more recently, the very flat organization chart – which is to be considered. It must also incorporate the interactions between units, the information and management systems, and their total interrelatedness. As Beer (1985: i) suggests, the organization chart may be seen as 'frozen out of history', revealing who to blame when things go wrong, but not showing how the organization actually works. A number of barriers to achievement of quality can be found in this area.

The first, and most frequent, error is what can be termed institutionalized conflict. This means that an organization has been designed in such a way that conflict between quality and some other characteristic, such as productivity, is inherent. This is commonly found where the quality control or assurance manager reports to the production manager. In such a case, the need to meet customer orders will often override the need to achieve quality standards. The quality manager is, in effect, redundant, since no value is added to the operation of the organization by his or her presence. Flood (1993: 210–21), reports how when production fell short of customer orders at 'Tarty Bakeries', the production manager would pass as acceptable output which had already been rejected by the quality inspectors.

This situation, replicated in many organizations, presents a major barrier to quality. A structure must be created in which the quality function is independent of the production function, and, as shall be seen, where quality is inherent in the product, the process and, importantly, in the culture. This leads to a situation where rather than rejects and errors being 'inspected out', quality can be 'baked in' to the product.

The second barrier to quality in this context is the design of the organization's information systems. This does not simply mean the computerized management or executive information system, but the whole of the data generation and capture, data processing and information reporting activity of the organization, both formal and informal. These activities must generate the right information, in the right format, at the right time, and deliver it to the right decision maker(s) if it is to be of any benefit. Vitally, the information itself must be presented in a way that informs the decisions that managers need to make. Most frequently, users of information spend much time analysing and discussing historical errors while paying little attention to the current situation and none to the future. While they may be criticized for this, it is as much a function of the design of the information system as a matter of managerial desire. Hindsight is always twenty-twenty, and a common requirement in organizations is for managers to explain what went wrong, to justify mistakes and failures. Such organizations are attempting to manage their past and not their future, perhaps because they find this easier to do. It is a little like driving a car by looking in the rear view mirror to see where you have been.

The informal system refers to communication through devices such as unions and other staff bodies, and the grapevine. Beer (1985: 58–9) encourages this informal communication between functions, which may be concerned with immediate operational matters such as the timing of the next batch of a product, or with longer term issues such as competition for capital. However, he specifically sees this communication as supplementary to, and not in place of, the formal systems. Beckford (1993: 300–23) shows how the union and the grapevine were perceived by both management and staff as the most reliable information sources in an organization. It is worth making the point at this stage that managers cannot stop communication within an organization. Data will find a means of transmission whatever barriers are placed in the way, but the organization will only be effective if the communication channels are properly designed.

Another aspect of this information system is performance measurement. Briefly recapping on Section 3.1, performance measurement tends to determine which aspects of the organization will be perceived as important. Those characteristics or outputs which are measured will be the focus of the workforce; those that are not measured may well be ignored. Thus the design of the measurement system, its prime content, and the way its outputs are responded to by managers, may be expected to drive the performance of the organization.

Similarly, many organizations operate with no formal measurement system at all; everything is done by 'gut feel' and rule of thumb. In such circumstances, quality simply cannot be known to have been achieved, since even if it has been defined it is not being measured. As the conversation goes in Alice in Wonderland (Carroll: 1866):

'Would you tell me, please, which way I ought to walk from here?' [said Alice]

'That depends a good deal on where you want to get to.' [said the Cheshire Cat]
'I don't much care where.' [said Alice]
'Then it doesn't matter which way you walk.' [said the Cheshire Cat]
'So long as I get *somewhere*.' [said Alice]

An appropriate form and degree of measurement is vital. That is enough to know what is happening, but not so much that the 'measured' feel burdened or oppressed by the system, since in such a case they may seek to pervert the results. Perhaps, as Beer (1985: 102) proposes in the context of autonomy, we should have as much measurement 'as guarantees cohesion'.

The next barrier to quality is one of role understanding and articulation within the organization, particularly amongst the staff involved in the control and development functions: general management, marketing, human resource management, accounting, strategic planning, and so on. There is a tendency amongst many such staff to delve down into the operations of the organization, perhaps taking direct control when errors occur or the unexpected happens. While doing so they will be neglecting their own roles within the organization. This 'fire-fighting' or 'crisis' style of management is perceived by many organizations to be heroic, with plaudits and awards handed to those who perform in this way. However, as the apocryphal saying goes, 'When you are up to your armpits in alligators, it's easy to forget that the original objective was to drain the swamp.'

Solving today's crisis is extremely important, but, as suggested by Senge (1990: 15), that is to deal with 'symptoms not underlying causes'. A low-level intervention by senior management will rarely address the root, or fundamental cause, of the problem, and *that* is their proper role, not to deal with operational matters. The operational managers must be allowed the freedom and given the support to solve their own problems. If senior management continually intervene in a junior manager's daily problem-solving activity, two things will occur. First, the junior manager will never learn to solve his or her own problems, thus reducing organizational effectiveness and increasing costs. Second, the senior manager's work will never get done, and consequently the organization will hurtle out of control into the nearest obstacle because nobody is watching where it is going.

The final barrier which will be explored in this section is that of irrelevant, or inappropriate, activities. This section is entitled 'Organization Design', but frequently the truth is that an organization has not been designed; it has grown and undergone metamorphoses almost of its own accord. Many features of an established organization, whether they be structural, such as department or units; organizational, that is, activities and procedures; or cultural and attitudinal, have not been intentionally and deliberately created. Often they just grow. They develop, perhaps to support some long-forgotten or superseded purpose of the organization, and are simply never stopped. Cases are common where procedures have become institutionalized and carried on for years. In one example a manager once requested a particular report which had to be produced by hand. That the manager had long since moved on (and retired) and no further request had ever been received for the report was not seen as a reason for stopping, 'After all, you never know!' Equally, that a computerized version of the same report was available had not been noticed, and 'Anyway, the technology is unreliable'.

A similar process occurs with what, in Business Process Re-engineering (BPR), are known as cowpaths. These are the routes through an organization which develop naturally without the purposeful intervention of the staff. A procedure in use may never have been the subject of deliberate design; it may have simply developed and its users become accustomed to it, complete with all its unique peculiarities and foibles. Such processes, often developed around the talents and skills of individuals, become the 'norm'. They are, however, often inefficient, sometimes ineffective, everybody complains about them, but they are seen as nobody's responsibility.

These cowpaths and inappropriate processes may well present barriers to the achievement of quality, since they are an 'unconscious' part of the organization and their quality-inhibiting properties may not be recognized.

3.4 Management Perspective

Management perspective does not simply refer to the attitude to quality, but to the whole management ethos of the organization as it impacts on quality, a subject which was touched upon in the previous chapter. The issue of corporate politics has already been raised in Section 3.1, so will not be covered again here.

In order for an appropriate attitude to be developed to quality, it must be recognized as an issue. This means that the poor quality of a product or service must be openly acknowledged. Frequently, companies adopt an ostrich-like attitude to quality; they find it easier to blame poor performance on a host of other reasons. For example, when a previously successful sales performance declines, a common reaction is to focus on market changes, the sales team, or activity on the part of competitors rather than on the product or service itself. Issues such as pricing and margins are often raised, perhaps leading to a focus on manufacturing performance in terms of productivity. Rarely is quality of product or service considered as a potentially primary issue at the outset.

It is essential that quality be treated as a potential part of the problem and considered as a possible cause of decline. Even where a company is performing well, a positive attitude to quality needs to be developed and maintained. A product which is considered 'good enough' probably is not in today's competitive markets. There is no room for such complacency. Over the last twenty years, the motor industry has fully understood this, with every successive generation of vehicles being 'better' in all respects than its predecessors. Where a manufacturer gets the wrong idea — as they will from time to time — the market punishes them by not buying the product.

A further barrier to achievement of quality is a focus on short-term results, that is, the result in a particular shift, day, week, quarter or even year. Often, salary or wage packages and performance bonuses are related directly to current period performance. Therefore currently acceptable performance parameters are used as a reason (or excuse) for not addressing the issue of quality. While not necessarily so, it is often the case that a focus on quality, or any other major change programme, will lead to a short-term decline in performance (particularly of productivity) while staff and management adjust to changes. This is known as the 'hockey stick' effect. This may be related to a complete change of emphasis, where achieving quality of output needs to override, perhaps for the first time, achieving quantity of output. The change required in management attitudes is fundamental: away from pure productivity to productivity with quality. After all, output which is rejected, either internally or by the customer, cannot really be considered as output at all: it is waste.

Thus a major barrier to achieving quality may be built in to the reward system of the organization. This can only be overcome by changing that system; it cannot be overcome through exhortations, evangelism, penal action or statistical measurement. Effective change may mean negotiating fresh terms with a variety of stakeholders in the enterprise, from the workforce and their bonus system to the shareholders or providers of equity and loan capital, whose short-term interests may be affected and will need to be addressed.

Management often focuses on 'output today at all costs'. No real concern with, or interest in, quality is evident. In order to boost performance, a focus is maintained exclusively on current output. In the event of an apparent or expected shortfall in output, the rate of production is increased in an attempt to compensate. Such increases are usually doomed to failure unless the system of production itself is addressed.

A food factory case study highlights the problem. The production lines had an established level of throughput for each of their various product lines, an optimal rate at which the equipment and operators could cope and a 'satisfactory compromise' was reached between productivity and quality. The established or recorded reject rate, with which the management were quite content, was 10 per cent.

In the event that production was likely to fall short of customer orders, the throughput rate across the product range would be increased from an average of twelve units per minute to an average of sixteen units per minute. It was assumed by the factory management that this would give a net increase of around 33 per cent in output over the running time compared to optimal-rate running. In practice, an increase of only about 10 per cent was achieved, the balance of additional throughput being rejected for failing to achieve the required quality standard. Naturally, the management's reaction was to speed up the process even further, seeking to gain the elusive extra output. Figure 3.1 shows the effect of slipping clutch syndrome diagrammatically.

While portrayed for the sake of simplicity as a step change, in practice, the quality gap widened on a progressive basis with every small increase in output. The greater the throughput, the greater the reject rate, every increase in running speed generating an ever-reducing increase in acceptable output. One other major factor in this case was that the necessary work rate of the individual members of staff had to increase in line with the speed of the production belt, something which would not generally be sustainable regardless of the quality issue. The major solution applied in this particular case was to reduce throughput and thereby reduce the quality gap, ensuring that operators had sufficient time with each unit to reach the appropriate quality standard. A series of other measures were also taken; simply changing production rates was not the entire solution to the subject company's quality problems.

Each of the barriers highlighted in this section reflects a common mindset on the part of management. That mindset is called reductionism, the belief that anything can be understood by continually breaking it down into parts, breaking the parts down into further parts, and so on. This is often called an analytical approach. The reductionist mindset seeks individual causes for individual effects, and reflects the mechanistic thinking which has dominated Western science.

Contemporary thinking suggests that a holistic approach to problem solving is more effective. That is one which deals with systems as wholes, which recognizes the interrelationships and interdependencies between parts of a system, which acknowledges that fixing one part of a system will not necessarily improve the whole and might even

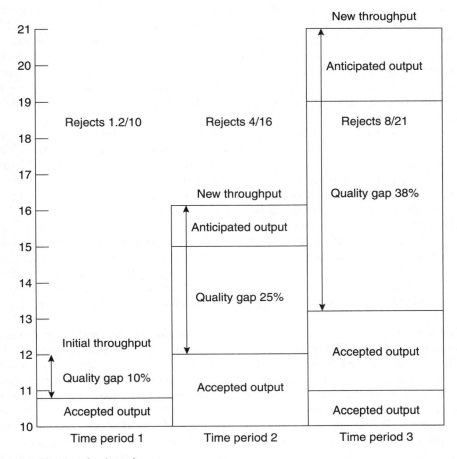

Figure 3.1 Slipping clutch syndrome.

make it worse. Such an approach broadens the attack on a problem by widening the scope of enquiry to study also those factors which influence it – its inputs – as well as considering the consequences of any changes – the effect on outputs. Simply replacing the tyres on a motor car, while potentially improving grip, will do little or nothing to improve the overall performance of the car.

3.5 Costs of Quality

The last issue to be briefly explored in this chapter is the costs of quality. This means the direct and invisible costs unnecessarily incurred by any organization which does not have an effective quality system in place – what Ohno calls *muda* or waste. Direct costs in this context means those costs arising as a result of the non-achievement of quality and visibly attributable to that fact. Invisible costs in this context means those costs arising in the organization as a result of not achieving quality but not visibly attributable to that fact, those where the relationship between non-quality and the cost may not have been discerned by the organization.

Any production system for a product or service which is not designed to achieve the quality standard 'first time, every time' will incur re-work and rectification costs. These are the costs of putting right errors, performing again a particular task or disassembling and reassembling (or scrapping) a product. Traditionally such costs have been treated by organizations as part of the overall cost of production, and a percentage is included in the price of every item sold for the ones that go wrong. Thus acceptance of error is institutionalized, carefully hidden but properly accounted for – surely this makes everybody happy?!

In the era of quality, with lean production systems and just-in-time delivery, these costs need to be uncovered and attention paid to their reduction and eradication. They must be challenged, not accepted. All processes receive inputs in the form of either materials or information from prior steps in the chain. That is to say that each process is the customer of either an internal or an external supplier. If the inputs received are defective, then costs may be incurred in a number of ways.

The first way, and potentially the most damaging, is that entire consignments have to be returned, holding up or stopping production and leading to unfilled orders and lost revenue. A commonly used answer to this is to increase holding stocks, ensuring that there is sufficient to cover a break in supply. Such an approach simply increases stocking costs, reducing the supply of working capital available to the organization and inhibiting its overall performance; it does nothing to solve the quality problem.

The second way is that costs are incurred in validating the quality of goods or information received before it is processed, inspecting out failures from suppliers and, in effect, absorbing part of the suppliers' operating cost. Costs can also be incurred by not inspecting goods received, leading to the use of defective parts or information at the next stage of production. This ensures that the final product will also fail, leading back to re-work and rectification.

A third way is that goods received are inspected and defective parts rectified before use. This again generates costs which should have been incurred by the supplier.

Inspection, as an auditing activity, can never be completely eradicated. Reports generated by inspection provide higher level management with information necessary for them to control and develop the operation. However, inspection is most commonly used as *the* quality mechanism, the one procedure which attempts to ensure that products and services are being provided at the agreed level. For such an approach to quality to work requires at least a statistically valid sampling approach, and 100 per cent confidence requires 100 per cent inspection, an impossible task in nearly all industries. Although frequently attempted, this is rarely successful and is always inordinately expensive. Also, it is often impractical. Beckford (1993: 308) refers to an inspection system with a notional target of 100 per cent; in practice 5 per cent was supposedly achieved. The target figure was not practical given throughput, and was in any case irrelevant, since the product to be inspected was sealed into a plastic bag, inside a cardboard box; the only inspection was of the box, not the product, provided by an independent external supplier!

The level of inspection can be significantly reduced where quality is inherent in both the product and the process. Effective auditing can be substituted. This has a direct impact on both the cost of the activity and its utility.

Invisible costs are much harder to identify and specify, but are nonetheless incurred when quality has not been addressed properly. They may include:

- dissatisfied customers who fulfil future needs with an alternative supplier;
- customer site service and maintenance costs, often operated as a separate business division. The costs of customer service are very often driven by the inadequacies and failures of the design and manufacturing process;
- in-process re-work costs (costs incurred by remaking unfinished products within a process). Beckford (1993:300–23) reports a case where the reported reject figure of 10 per cent ignored in-process rectification which amounted to a further 25 per cent of throughput;
- high staff turnover, leading to increased recruitment and training costs as a result of dissatisfied staff leaving;
- capital costs for equipment and warehousing to provide for rectification of defective parts and storage of additional materials;
- reduced availability of internal working capital, leading to unnecessary reliance on loan/overdraft capital (that is, increased gearing).

Such costs are rarely attributed directly to the quality issue. However, they are in an interdependent relationship with all the other factors of the business and so to a large extent they are related to, and driven by, quality.

Summary

This chapter has reviewed a number of the barriers to quality, looking particularly at the issues of systems and procedures, culture, organization design and management approach. The chapter concluded with a brief look at some of the costs of quality.

KEY LEARNING POINTS

Four principal barriers to quality: systems and procedures; culture; organization design; management perspectives

Systems and procedures:
supporting or inhibiting the pursuit of quality?

Culture:
attitudes, values and beliefs. Is the culture supportive of quality?

Organization design:
does the organization design support or inhibit quality achievement?

Management perspectives:
is quality recognized as a problem? Is the focus right for achieving quality? Is the mindset holistic or reductionist?

Two categories of quality cost: direct; invisible

Direct costs:
re-work, rectification, defective inputs, inspection.

Invisible Costs include:
lost customers, in-process errors, high staff turnover, unnecessary capital costs, reduced availability of working capital.

Question

Identify barriers to quality under each of the key headings in your own organization. For each barrier identified, consider what might be done to overcome it.

4 The Emergence of Management

These all look like 'Whats'. It's the 'Hows' that I have trouble with

(Winnie-the-Pooh on Problem-Solving, Roger E. Allen, 1995)

Introduction

The purpose of this chapter is to introduce the principal models that still appear to govern much management behaviour. The formal study of management has emerged as a discipline in its own right only over the last hundred years or so; indeed, it is still considered by many (particularly practising managers) as being at least as much 'black art' as science. Theoretical and practical development of the discipline have more or less paralleled the emergence of the major corporations – though it is evident that many are still managed according to a Taylorist–Weberian model that is scientistic and bureaucratic. Prior to the emergence of the joint stock company and the industrial revolution, permanent large-scale organizations (other than states which were then extremely volatile) were limited to the various churches and the standing armies and navies of the wealthier nations. The majority of the workforce were either agricultural labourers living at not much better than a subsistence standard of living, land-owning farmers, tradesmen and craftsmen or professionals such as doctors and lawyers.

Following the industrial revolution, agricultural workers were drawn from the country to the towns and cities to improve their standard of living, often becoming factory workers. The increasing size of factories (and the factory owners' increasing wealth and desire to pursue other interests) created the opportunity for the emergence of professional managers, those whose job it is to oversee and supervise the activities of workers on behalf of owners. The need to manage these large-scale organizations and the drive for additional profitability can be interpreted as having given impetus to the study of management. The development of early management theories is the topic of the next sections.

The principal early models in organization (or management) theory are the Classical, also known as the Traditional or Rational, and the Human Relations. The two approaches have their own particular strengths and weaknesses which will be explored. These theories are to some extent considered as the causes of many quality problems, and as being reflected in the dominant quality models, which will be considered in the next part of the book.

4.1 Classical Theory

The classical or 'machine' (Morgan, 1986: 20) model of organization reflects the scientific management approach developed by Frederick Taylor, the classical theory of Henri Fayol, and Max Weber's Bureaucracy Theory. Collectively, these still dominate mainstream management thinking. Each approach seems to regard the design of organizations as a technical exercise only, and depends upon the reduction (fragmentation or dissection) of an organization into its component parts for analysis and redesign for efficient operation.

The 'machine' approaches to organization arose in the late nineteenth and early twentieth centuries, and may be considered as logical extensions of the advances then being made in machine technology. Machines are, in general, designed to perform specified tasks at known input/output rates and within specified tolerances; these management approaches assume that organizations can be similarly designed.

Frederick Taylor's *The Principles of Scientific Management* (Taylor, 1911) is based on four key principles (see Figure 4.1) of scientific task design, scientific selection, management-worker cooperation and equal division of work.

Huczynski and Buchanan (1991: 282–3) see Taylor's objectives as being first to improve efficiency by increasing output and reducing 'underworking', what Taylor described as 'natural soldiering' and 'systematic soldiering'. Second, to achieve 'standardization of job performance, by dividing tasks up into small and closely specified sub tasks'. Finally, to instil discipline 'by establishing hierarchical authority and introducing a system whereby all management's policy decisions could be implemented'.

While Taylor recognized that the worker in a given situation had a 'mass of rule of thumb or traditional knowledge', which constituted his 'principal asset or possession', he had a poor view of the capabilities and intelligence of the worker. For example, he believed that:

> the science of handling pig iron is so great and amounts to so much that it is impossible for the man who is best suited to this type of work to understand the principles of this science, or even to work in accordance with these principles without the aid of a man better educated than he is.

Frederick Taylor:

'....develop a science for each element of a man's work, which replaces the old rule of thumb method.'

'....scientifically select and then train, teach and develop the workman, whereas in the past he chose his own work and trained himself as best he could.'

'.... heartily co-operate with the men so as to insure all of the work being done in accordance with the principles of the science which has been developed.'

ensure that '....There is an almost equal division of the work and the responsibility between the management and the workmen. The management take over all the work for which they are better fitted than the workmen, while in the past almost all of the work and the greater part of the responsibility were thrown upon the men.'

Figure 4.1 Frederick Taylor's principles of scientific management.

Taylor saw the organization as a machine, capable of being specified, designed and controlled by management to achieve a given purpose. The workmen were viewed as standardized machine parts, interchangeable with every other of like design, and to be used at the sole discretion of management. Gilbreth and Gantt, who both attempted to humanize scientific management, recognizing the need for rest (Gilbreth) and human needs and dignity (Gantt), later followed Taylor's approach. However, Taylor's key assumption that the worker was principally motivated by money was retained and this assumption still underpins management thinking in many organizations.

Henri Fayol (1916) used the 'machine' metaphor in writing that:

> The body corporate of a concern is often compared with a machine or plant or animal. The expressions, 'administrative machine', 'administrative gearing', suggest an organism obeying the drive of its head and having all of its effectively interrelated parts move in unison towards the same end, and that is excellent.

This perception of the excellence of the 'machine' view is evident in his proposals for organizing and managing. He proposed that 'to organize a business is to provide it with everything useful to its functioning: raw materials, tools, capital, personnel', and saw the organization as comprising six sets of activities: Technical, Commercial, Financial, Security, Accounting and Managerial. Fayol's proposed duties of managers reinforce this view; these are given in Figure 4.2.

The managerial duties reflect Fayol's fourteen principles of management, shown in Figure 4.3.

Some of these managerial duties and principles of management appear to conflict with the machine view and with each other. For example, take 'Define duties clearly' and 'Encourage a liking for initiative and responsibility', or 'specialization' and 'initiative', the first of which in each case would appear to preclude, or at least make more difficult, the second.

The admonition to managers to 'fight against excess of regulation, red tape and paper control' stands in sharp contrast to Fayol's view that the work should be 'clearly divided, judiciously planned and strictly carried out', aspects which carry with them an implication of machine-like precision and heavy reliance on record-keeping.

The overall impression remains that Fayol, like Taylor, viewed the organization as a machine. The management were responsible for forecasting, planning, organizing, commanding, co-ordinating and controlling, while the 'workers', distinguished by 'technical ability characteristic of the business', were component parts to be fitted into the machine at the most appropriate place with 'a place for everyone and everyone in his place'.

Max Weber's Bureaucracy Theory is developed from his views of three types of legitimate authority in organizations; rational, traditional and charismatic. Traditional authority rests on established acceptance of a natural order of society – the rulers and the ruled – perhaps reflecting the idea of monarchy. Charismatic authority rests on the personal devotion of individuals to a particular leader. Both these styles of management exist in organizations today. For example, traditional authority is found in many of the patriarchal family-owned businesses of Asia, while charismatic authority may be considered as the style of organizations such as easyJet, Virgin Atlantic and some religious organizations. Rational authority is the principal interest in this text as it has come to dominate many large organizations.

Henri Fayol:

To ensure that the plan is judiciously prepared and strictly carried out.

See that the human and material organization is consistent with the objectives, resources and requirements of the concern.

Set up a single, competent, energetic guiding authority.

Harmonize activities and co-ordinate efforts.

Formulate clear, distinct, precise decisions.

Arrange for efficient selection - each department must be headed by a competent, energetic man, each employee must be in that place where he can render greatest service.

Define duties clearly.

Encourage a liking for initiative and responsibility.

Have fair and suitable recompense for services rendered.

Make use of sanctions against faults and errors.

See to the maintenance of discipline.

Ensure that individual interests are subordinated to the general interest.

Pay special attention to unity of command.

Supervise both human and material order.

Have everything under control.

Fight against excess of regulation, red tape and paper control.

Figure 4.2 Henri Fayol's duties of managers.

Henri Fayol:

Division of work (specialization)
Authority
Discipline
Unity of Command
Unity of Direction
Subordination (the interest of the organization is more important than that of the individual)
Remuneration
Centralization (a question of continuously varying proportion)
Scalar chain
Order
Equity
Stability of tenure
Initiative
Esprit de corps

Figure 4.3 Henri Fayol's principles of management.

Max Weber:

Specialization: Each office (or 'bureau') has a defined area of expertise;
Hierarchy: Supervision and control of lower offices by higher ones;
Rules: Exhaustive, stable rules, learned by all;
Impersonality: Equality of treatment for all according to the rules;
Appointment: Selection according to competence not election;
Full-time: Occupation of office as the primary task of the individual;
Career: Promotion, tenure and seniority within the system;
Segregation: The official activity is distinct from the private individual.

Figure 4.4 Max Weber's principles of bureaucracy.

Rational authority was seen by Weber (cited in Pugh, 1990: 3–13) as representing legal authority, with 'obedience owed to the legally established impersonal order'. He considered that the 'purest type of exercise of legal authority is that which employs a bureaucratic administrative staff', and that bureaucracy was not simply desirable but indispensable to cope with the then complexities of organizations. He also considered that the increasing general technical knowledge had, as a consequence, a need for an increase in the particular technical knowledge of individuals, so that they could effectively administer an organization.

Weber saw a bureaucracy as being composed of a hierarchical organization of 'offices' (bureaux), each acting according to the rules and norms of the organization within a specified area of competence. Individuals within this structure were appointed on rational grounds to perform a specified function, without gaining rights to that appointment or having ownership of the organization. All decisions, rules and acts were to be recorded in writing in order, together with the 'continuous organization of official functions', to 'constitute the office'. Weber saw a clear choice in organizations between 'bureaucracy and dilettantism', and proposed that bureaucracy was an inevitable requirement to support large organizations.

The machine view is evident again in this case, Weber proposing that every function and every act of every office is capable of being specified to an exact degree. People were clearly viewed as functionaries within the bureaucracy, bringing no human element to the conduct of the affairs of the organization.

4.2 Critical Review

Several assumptions about the world and organizational life seem to underlie these three rational views of organization. These need to be stated before considering their strengths and weaknesses.

The first assumption is that an organization can be regarded as isolated from the influence of its environment. While this may have been an acceptable view in a fast-growing producer-led economy, it clearly cannot be considered appropriate in consumer-led, low-growth and highly competitive markets. Despite the observations of Galbraith (1974) concerning producer dominance, organizations must respond to the needs and demands of external stakeholders if they are to survive. In the mature, post-industrial economies, enabled by instant communications and ready access to global sources of information via the Internet, the informed consumer really does have the potential to determine the fate of organizations. A good example of this was the perception by UK consumers in the 1990s that motorcars cost too much relative to their value. Numerous consumers, taking advantage of the open European market and reliable communications, simply chose to purchase their cars in cheaper countries, thus saving 25 per cent or more of the UK purchase price. The manufacturers and dealers, encouraged by the European parliament, responded to this threat, and pan-European pricing is now much more closely aligned; indeed in 2009 many comparable cars are cheaper in the UK than in mainland Europe. An internally focused organization does not have the capability to respond in this way.

The second assumption is that an improvement in the performance of a part of the organization will necessarily improve the performance of the whole. There appears to be some merit in this idea at the purely mechanical level – the repair or replacement of a defective part will possibly generate some improvement. However, the approach ignores interdependence within the organization. This means that the whole will only perform at the level of the weakest or slowest part. Similarly, the idea of 'emergent properties'– the notion that the whole may be more than the sum of the parts – is ignored. The ideas of systemic thinking will be pursued explicitly in Part Three of this book; in the meantime it is sufficient to suggest that organizations often have characteristics or properties which belong only to their entirety and not to any of their individual parts. These characteristics cannot be addressed except by considering the capacity for interaction. It was suggested in Chapter 1 that quality is not an issue which can be isolated but must be pursued systemically, organization-wide. The classical model of organization cannot cope with this need.

The third assumption is that the organization must be studied only from the perspective of the goals of management. Later studies have shown that true organizational effectiveness depends on the co-operation of many parties involved with the organization. Commonly called 'stakeholders', these parties include owners, employees, customers, suppliers, and those outside the organization who are affected by its activities and behaviour. The contemporary concept of 'good corporate citizenship', expressed through the emergent literature on Corporate Social Responsibility, recognizes the need for organizations to take account of the wishes of the community in which they exist. This assumption is further challenged by the change in the ISO 9000 standard which now sees the customer as the focus of organizational performance and, as mentioned above, capable of sophisticated, informed behaviour.

The final assumption is that an organization can be designed and understood in 'machine' terms. It can be created to perform a given task, and, once designed, need not be adapted. Operating in a global economy, which is best characterized as turbulent and dynamic and subject to rapid changes in technology and customer expectations, any organization which cannot adapt reasonably readily cannot expect to survive.

Apart from the foregoing comments, each of these assumptions has been challenged through developments in thinking about organizations and in ideas about human well-being during the current century. Practical experience of using the model in organizations has also shown that the assumptions are flawed.

4.3 Reiteration

Flood and Jackson (1991: 8–9) provide a useful summary of the 'machine' view. They consider that it is useful in practice when the organization operates in a stable environment, performing a straightforward task such as repetitive production of a single product, and when the 'human parts' are prepared to follow 'machine-like' commands.

They suggest that its usefulness is limited, since it reduces the adaptability of organizations and that the 'mindless contribution' is difficult to maintain with 'mindful parts', leading to dehumanization or conflict.

The strengths of the model are that:

- it enables systematic, methodical analysis of specific tasks;
- it provides assistance in establishing order in organizations;
- it is a useful guide to creating organizations where demands on individuals need to be precise or exact, for example, in the nuclear industry or in multiple-outlet operations such as banks.

Its weaknesses are thought to be:

- its failure to recognize environmental interaction;
- the lack of acknowledgement of the interdependence of parts;
- no inherent capacity for adaptation;
- it is static not dynamic;
- people are 'dehumanized';
- goals are inherent in the design;
- the focus on control may encourage inefficiency;
- it cannot help with informal or virtual organizations such as network arrangements which are increasingly common;
- it is diagnostic but not prescriptive.

It can be seen, then, that while the machine view offers some assistance, its weaknesses are such that it must be considered an inadequate approach for managers today. The impact of this thinking on quality will be considered in Section 4.7.

4.4 Human Relations Theory

While benefits could, and may still, be obtained from the rational approaches, their lack of humanity is demonstrated by the difficulties which emerge during their application with the people involved. The Human Relations Model of organization emerged as a means of addressing these difficulties, and was the first significant challenge to the 'machine' view.

The 'organic' or 'organism' (Morgan, 1986: 39–76) analogy stems from the origins of modern systems thinking in the biological sciences and attempts to deal with attainment of survival of the system or organization rather than achievement of particular goals. While survival may be seen as a legitimate goal, it may not sufficiently represent the purpose of the organization. This organic view first found expression in organizations through what has become known as the Human Relations Model. This considers that attention must be paid to the human aspects of organization and gives primacy to the roles, needs and expectations of the human participants. Particular emphasis is given to issues of motivation, management style and participation as critical success factors.

The 'Hawthorne' studies of Roethlisberger and Dickson with Elton Mayo (Mayo, 1949) may be interpreted as an early systems approach to management (Flood and Carson, 1988). Although they were originally focused on the application of scientific management principles, the findings led away from this perspective. They later recognized the need to capture and understand the relatedness of all the parts involved. Later work in this field by Maslow and Herzberg did not adopt the systemic perspective. These later developments still adopt a reductionist and 'closed system' view of the organization, concentrating on improving the performance of parts rather than the whole, and emphasizing internal rather than external influences on the organization.

Mayo (1949) argued that:

> In modern large-scale industry the three persistent problems of management are:-
>
> - the application of science and technical skill to some material good or product;
> - the systematic ordering of operations;
> - the organization of teamwork – that is, of sustained co-operation.

Following Chester Barnard, Mayo saw that the first two of these would operate to make an industry effective, the third to make it efficient. He considered that the application of science and technical skill and the systematic ordering of operations were attended to, the first by continuous experiment, the second being already well developed in practice. He saw the third element as neglected but necessary if the organization as a whole was to be successful.

Mayo became involved in the 'Hawthorne' studies after they had examined the effects on workers of changes in the physical environment. Experiments had shown that social and psychological factors were present and the studies became focused on these human issues. Records were kept of every aspect of changes made and their impact, to establish a 'systemic' view. Further experiments were conducted and followed by formal interviews, which revealed that many of the particular organization's difficulties related to emotional rather than rational conditions. Further experiment showed that informal group pressures had more influence on output and performance than the economic pressures of the formal organization.

The 'Hawthorne' studies are credited with having discovered the importance of groups in organizations, the influence of the observer on the observed, and the need to ensure that the goals and objectives of staff are not in conflict with those of the organization. Notwithstanding subsequent criticisms of the research methodology and interpretation of the findings, the studies are generally seen as the foundations of the human relations approach.

Maslow (1970), while seeing that the 'individual is an integrated, organized whole', proposed a hierarchy of human needs. These needs were: physiological (food and health), safety (security), belongingness and love (the need to belong to a group), esteem (the need to be valued by oneself and others), and self-actualization (the need to be all that one can be). He suggested that the needs were all contained within each other such that 'if one need is satisfied then another emerges', although the satisfied need remains present. That means that each need is ever-present, even when not 'prepotent'.

Maslow's 'Hierarchy of Needs' is usually presented as in Figure 4.5.

Frederick Herzberg (Hertzberg, *et al.*, 1959), in his studies of motivation in the industrial and commercial context, built upon the foundation laid by Maslow. Through a series of observations and interviews with samples of people at work, he found that two sets of factors influenced the level of motivation. These were the 'hygiene' and 'motivating' factors discussed in Chapter 2. Briefly, 'hygiene' factors concerned the

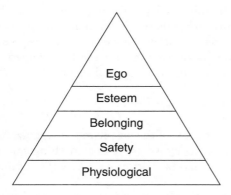

Figure 4.5 Maslow's hierarchy of needs.

maintenance of conditions that were conducive to satisfaction. If satisfactory conditions did not pertain the worker would be dissatisfied with his job position; conversely, achievement of a satisfactory standard would not positively motivate. Positive motivation would be derived from 'motivators', that is, factors which were seen as actively encouraging an increased contribution. They tend to be unique to each individual. These factors were illustrated diagrammatically in Chapter 2, Figure 2.1.

Summarizing, Herzberg concluded that in order for organizations to achieve improved levels of performance, they must address both types of factor. He considered that 'good hygiene will prevent many of the negative results of low morale', but that this on its own was not enough, suggesting, 'our emphasis should be on the strengthening of motivators'. This he saw as being achieved by restructuring jobs; providing workers with some degree of control over their achievement; meaningful job rotation; selection of staff to match the needs of the task; effective supervision through planning; organizing and support (a link with Taylor's work); and appropriate participation.

Finally, Herzberg recognized that 'there are large segments of our society to which these prescriptions cannot possibly apply'. He considered that these people could obtain a good life from 'fruitful hobbies and improved lives outside the job', and that 'the greatest fulfilment of man is to be found in activities related to his own needs as well as those of society'.

4.5 Critical Review

Again, several assumptions about the world and people seem to underpin the Human Relations approaches to organization, some of which represent a major shift in thinking from the machine view. From the organization design perspective, the influence of the environment is still largely neglected and there continues to be a focus on improving the performance of parts rather than the whole.

The first major shift, and perhaps the most significant, is the assumption that people may be motivated by rewards from work other than money. This assumption is of great significance in mature economies where ever-rising salaries and wages are not realistic prospects. If motivation is to be maintained in such circumstances, it is vital that managers recognize this assumption and discover which characteristics of the work and its environment are likely to stimulate staff.

The second assumption is concerned with the abilities of people. Whereas the machine view largely assumes limited ability and finite competence, the human relations view assumes much greater, albeit variable, competence and encourages a greater degree of autonomy and flexibility. It stresses delegation of decision making and enrichment of jobs, in direct contrast to the simplification associated with classical theory.

4.6 Reiteration

The Human Relations model gives primacy to the role of the people in the organization and suggests ways of increasing their satisfaction. However, it does nothing for the achievement of the objectives of the organization and says little about how the complex tasks of the organization could be structured.

Flood and Jackson (1991: 10) consider that the 'organic' view is of practical value when there is an open relationship with the environment, when survival or adaptation needs are predominant and when the environment is complex. They believe that the Human Relations view fails. First, because it does not recognize that organizations are socially constructed phenomena which, it can be argued, need to be understood from the perspective of the participants. Second, because the emphasis is on harmonious relations, whereas conflict and coercion are often present. Third, because change is often environmentally driven, rather than driven by the organization itself.

The principal strength of the 'organic' model is the emphasis that it places on the human element of organizations, recognizing that people are not 'machine' parts but individuals who have needs and desires. There are, though, a number of weaknesses in this approach that make it inadequate for the needs of contemporary managers. First, notwithstanding the warning from Herzberg that human needs could be and, for some people, need to be met outside the workplace, the assumption underlying many applications of the Human Relations approach is that these needs must be met at work. Second, the human relations model does not allow for the supremacy of organizational goals and objectives, needs driven by technology, or the operating environment, over human goals and needs. Such supremacy may be necessary to ensure the survival of the organization. Finally, the model does not assist with the specifics of designing and structuring organizations to cope with the complex tasks faced by contemporary managers, or with the interface of the organization with its environment.

This 'organic' view, while offering some significant advantages over the 'machine' view, still appears inadequate.

4.7 Relevance to Quality

The Classical and Human Relations theories of management have relevance to quality for a number of reasons. First, they remain the dominant approaches to management in many cultures and contexts. They retain this dominance because they do have considerable value and appear to offer simple, fast solutions to management problems while serving to support the currently powerful groups in organizations. Second, many management schools and training organizations do not teach the more contemporary and, arguably, radical ideas, rejecting them in favour of traditional approaches. It must be acknowledged that in a newly developing country where the workforce are perhaps unfamiliar with the concept of having a job, the highly disciplined and somewhat autocratic styles which fit with the traditional view of organization may offer advantages in the short term. In more sophisticated contexts, however, this is unlikely to be the case, and may indeed be directly damaging to the organization.

Furthermore, there is the loss of skill and status associated with the introduction of modern highly productive and factory-based methods of working. For example, when agricultural or craft workers left the land or traditional occupations to work in factories, their accumulated store of knowledge became redundant. The progressive deskilling of the workforce, particularly associated with increased specialization and mechanisation in factories, has served to reinforce this situation. Previously a worker would have exercised a large share of his or her skill, knowledge and abilities in the completion of a task. However, the factory-style operation requires far fewer of these qualities, and for this reason much of the pride of the worker in the job has been lost. This may reasonably be considered to be a primary driver of quality problems in organizations. Trist and Bamforth (1966, cited in Pugh, 1990: 393–416) make this point in relation to the sociological idea of 'responsible autonomy' in a three-man coal-getting team.

While the human relations approach, which emerged in response to the problems associated with the classical school, may appear to offer the solution to quality problems, this is not the case. The human relations view gives priority to the needs of individuals over the organization. In this case, the potential exists for the needs of the customers to be completely ignored in the pursuit of employee satisfaction. Thus it may be considered more important to go home on time, or take a tea break, than to meet a customer's expectations. Similarly, the organization may develop products and services which exercise the skills knowledge and aspirations of its workers rather than fulfilling a customer's needs.

Clearly, both of these schools of thought offer advantages to the organization. All too often these advantages are pursued internally (because they are internally focused) while the needs of the customer are neglected.

Part Two of the book considers the work of those we call the 'quality gurus'. The influence of the classical and human relations schools of management thinking on these writers will be apparent. While all stress the importance of the customer, perhaps in response to the internally focused approaches outlined above, they also place emphasis on tools and techniques which seem to sit most comfortably with the traditional approaches, and suffer from many of the same problems in the contemporary context.

Summary

This chapter has, through a critical review, shown the inadequacy of the dominant classical and human relations theories used by managers to deal with the complexity of contemporary organizations. In the final section, a comment was offered on the relevance of these theories to quality.

KEY LEARNING POINTS

The study of managing has emerged in parallel with the emergence of large organizations

Principal dominant models of organization:
Classical – 'machine' model; Human Relations – 'organic' model.

University of Ulster LIBRARY

Classical management theorists:
Frederick Taylor – Scientific Management; Henri Fayol – Administrative Management; Max Weber – Bureaucracy Theory.

Human Relations theorists:
Elton Mayo – Hawthorne Studies; Abraham Maslow – hierarchy of human needs; Frederick Herzberg – two-factor theory of motivation.

Each model is considered responsible for some aspects of contemporary quality problems.

Question

How relevant are the models of management outlined in this chapter to *your* organization?

Part Two

The Quality Gurus

User Guide

Part Two provides a comprehensive introduction to nine writers, whose individual ideas continue to dominate the quality movement. This edition for the first time includes the work of Taiichi Ohno, the prime force behind the 'Toyota' method, which has greatly informed the development of 'Lean Manufacturing' ideas, and is increasingly being adopted for service environments.

In every significant field of human endeavour, there is continual change and development. Many ideas and approaches to addressing specific issues are considered and tried, but very few withstand the rigours of testing to become established in the mainstream of theory and practice, and become conventional wisdom in the field. Those writers and practitioners whose ideas come to form this body of accepted knowledge, who lead and advise a movement, become known as 'gurus'. It is notable that although quality systems and approaches continue to develop, no new individuals appear to be emerging in this field. It might be thought, therefore, that the issue of quality has been resolved as knowledge in the field has matured, but as will be seen in this section the thinking is incomplete, and there is no single authoritative source.

This part of the book focuses on the theory and practice espoused by nine writers and practitioners of quality management. They are those whose philosophies, methods, and tools have survived and have become best practice; collectively, I call them 'the quality gurus'.

The aim of this part is to assist readers in the development of a critical appreciation of the contributions to the quality movement of Philip Crosby, W. Edwards Deming, Armand V. Feigenbaum, Kaoru Ishikawa, Joseph Juran, John Oakland, Taiichi Ohno, Shigeo Shingo and Genichi Taguchi. These writers are perceived as having made the most significant and enduring contributions to quality management, and include John Oakland, the dominant European contemporary practitioner of quality management. The work of each is explored through a five-point critical framework:

- philosophy
- assumptions
- methods
- successes and failures
- critical review.

Through this approach, the reader should develop a platform for understanding the strengths, weaknesses, and different perspectives of each writer. While each of those featured has much in common with the others, there are significant differences in their interpretations of the quality problem and their solutions. Although the work of some may be more widely applied than others, none of the views is either 'right' or 'wrong'; they are simply different, formed from the differing backgrounds, knowledge, and experiences of the various writers. Each is based on the particular guru's view of the world, and is valid from his theoretical and practical perspective. While we might be critical of these perspectives in our own contemporary contexts, it is important to respect the contexts in which the approaches were developed.

5 Philip B. Crosby

Quality is not only right, it is free. And it is not only free, it is the most profitable product we have
(Harold S. Geneen, cited by Crosby, 1979)

Introduction

Philip Crosby (1926–2001) graduated from Western Reserve University and had a professional career in quality management. Following military service, he went into quality control in manufacturing, where he worked his way from line inspector to quality director and corporate vice-president of ITT. Based on many years of practical experience, his first book became a best-seller and led him to establish the consulting organization Philip Crosby Associates Incorporated and the Quality College based in Florida. He is described by Bendell (1989) as 'particularly well marketed and charismatic', by the *Financial Times* (26 November 1986) as having 'the look of a sunbelt Senator rather than a man from the quality department', and by Bank (1992) as exhorting his message with 'almost religious fervour'. Clearly, he is a man who acted as he spoke or 'walked the talk'. His approach has been well received: over 60,000 managers have been trained at the Quality College and his quality books, particularly *Quality is Free* (1979) and *Quality without Tears* (1995), continue to sell well.

5.1 Philosophy

Crosby's philosophy is seen by many, for example Gilbert (1992), to be encapsulated in his five 'Absolutes of Quality Management' (Figure 5.1). Each of these absolutes will be examined in turn to consider its meaning.

Philip Crosby:

- Quality is defined as conformance to requirements, not as 'goodness' nor 'elegance';

- There is no such thing as a quality problem;

- It is always cheaper to do it right first time;

- The only performance measurement is the cost of quality;

- The only performance standard is zero defects.

Figure 5.1 Philip Crosby's five absolutes of quality management.

First is Crosby's definition of quality. It suggests that when he talks about a quality product or service he is referring to one which meets the requirements of the customer or user. This in turn means that those requirements must be predefined, and that 'measures must be taken continually to determine conformance' (Flood, 1993: 22). The requirements may, of course, include both quantitative and qualitative aspects, although as will be seen, Crosby's target emphasis is towards the quantitative, that is, 'Zero Defects'. The first fundamental beliefs, then, are that quality is an essentially measurable aspect of a product or service, and that quality is achieved when expectations or requirements are met.

Crosby's second absolute is that 'There is no such thing as a quality problem.' He is implying that poor management creates the quality problems; they do not create themselves or exist as matters separate from the management process. In other words, a product and its quality do not exist in a vacuum; they are a result of the management process and if that process has inherent quality then a quality product will emerge. The second belief, then, is that management must lead the workers towards a quality outcome.

His third absolute is that 'It is always cheaper to do it right first time.' Logothetis (1992) suggests that 'A company which relies on mass inspection of the final output to improve quality is doomed to stagnation.' It is possible to go further than this, and suggest that a company focused on inspection will be achieving more than it deserves if it stagnates. In the long run, it is more likely to fail altogether. Here, Crosby is making clear his belief that inspection is a cost, and that quality needs to be *designed into* a product, not that flaws should be *inspected out*. This is taken as a belief in the potential to achieve quality, that is, conformance to requirements, by developing a quality process and product from the outset, with no expectation of failure. Prevention of error is better than rectification.

The fourth absolute is that 'The only performance measurement is the cost of quality.' Crosby clearly believes that the cost of quality is always a measurable item, for example, in terms of re-work, warranty costs and rejects, and that this is the only basis on which to measure performance. It is, as suggested by Logothetis (1992: 85), the 'price of non conformance'. As a practical measurement of quality, this might generally be considered to be useful, although it cannot be seen as the only measure. Rather, it is a direct monetary measure of quality within the overall performance of the organization. Crosby's belief in a quantitative approach is evident.

Finally, 'The only performance standard is zero defects.' The idea here is that perfection is the standard to aim for, through sound initial process and product design, continuous improvement, and, underpinning that, 'Zero Defects' is an achievable and measurable objective. Here again, Crosby's fundamental belief in the quantitative approach to quality is made clear, with perfection, that is, zero defects, proposed as the target.

Summarizing Crosby's perspective on quality, there appear to be three essential strands:

- a belief in quantification;
- leadership by management;
- prevention rather than cure.

Quality is then suggested by Crosby to be an inherent characteristic of the product, not an added extra. He believes, for example, that 20 per cent of manufacturing cost relates to failure, while for service companies this is around 35 per cent. He considers that the workers must not be blamed for error; rather, that management should take the lead and that the workers will then follow. Crosby suggests that 85 per cent of quality problems are within the control of management.

5.2 Assumptions

The assumptions about the world that seem to underpin Crosby's approach will now be considered.

First, it can be clearly seen that Crosby focuses attention on the management process as the key driver of quality. That is to say that if the management process is not designed and operated to achieve quality, a quality product or service will not arise. If a causal chain view of the development of a product or service is adopted, it is easy to see value in this assumption. For example, if quality is defined as 'conformance to requirements', it is absolutely essential that requirements are defined and communicated amongst all stakeholders. If this first step is not taken, for example, the company manufactures what it can rather than what consumers demand, there will be an eternal quality problem, since customer requirements can never be met. This constraint, to define conformance requirements, must be met for every aspect of the product: design, function, colour, delivery, price, and so on.

The second assumption is that 'Zero Defects' is an achievable objective. The implication here is that any product can reliably be made, in relevant volumes, entirely free from defects. This raises the question of exactly what constitutes a defect. Working in this respect from Crosby's quality definition – conformance to requirements – any product which conforms to requirements is defect-free. This again highlights the importance of the product specification in determining what constitutes quality.

The third assumption is that it is possible to establish a company that 'does not start out expecting mistakes', where errors are not expected or inevitable. While this is an admirable ideal, it must be considered exceedingly difficult to achieve in practice. Culture, staff, levels of training and skill, and aptitude for the particular task, are all aspects that move over time. For example, in any large manufacturing facility, labour turnover at the shop floor level is likely to run at a level of 5–10 per cent, simply from natural causes such as ill-health and retirement. To achieve and maintain a consistency of expectation of zero defects in these circumstances may be seen as unreasonable, unless the management is sufficiently determined in its resolve to achieve quality. Operationally, and particularly where some qualitative or subjective judgement element applies to a product, managers are often faced with a dilemma between delivering volume and achieving conformance to requirements.

This problem was frequently met by management at 'Tarty Bakeries' (Flood, 1993: 209–21), makers of hand-decorated cakes, where the production manager could fulfil one or the other requirement exactly. More often he would make a subjective decision that cakes rejected at inspection actually conformed to requirements! This again leads back to the basic issue of 'requirements': What are they? How are they defined? Who decides them?

Crosby is not particularly illuminating on this issue which, as can be seen, has critical impact. In the context of a physically hard and readily definable product, specifying requirements is essentially straightforward. In the context of services or natural products such as foods, whether processed or not, and services, certain characteristics of the product are less tangible, or even intangible, except at the point of consumption. Consequently it is very difficult to specify requirements and even more difficult to know whether these have been met. The Chesswood Produce story illustrates this point. Since you cannot have your cake and eat it, it is difficult to know if it has matched the requirements unless these requirements are so loosely specified as to be almost meaningless.

Vignette 5.1 Chesswood Produce Ltd.

Chesswood Produce is a long-established and successful mushroom-growing business. Operating from two sites in the UK, it supplies mushrooms to the major supermarket chains and the wholesale market. Mushroom-growing is a twenty-four-hours a day, all-year-round business.

As with other production businesses, the keys to success in a highly competitive market are productivity, yield and quality. To ensure that quality standards are maintained, the staff at Chesswood adhere to rigorous controls in the entire process of growing, cropping and packing the mushrooms, that is over 400,000 lbs (180,000 kg) per week, around 200 tons!

The eight-week growing process starts with the preparation of compost, which is mixed and matured to a standard 'recipe', consisting of straw, different kinds of manure, water and various trace ingredients. Once pasteurized, the compost is run with spawn, placed in trays and cased with a protective layer of peat. The mushroom spawns are sourced from a single supplier and, once again, adhere to rigorous quality and performance standards. The cased trays are then moved to climate-controlled growing sheds, where they are monitored during the growth period. The monitoring system controls the air temperature, moisture content of the trays, and air movement, with the aim of maximizing yield and minimizing damage to the very delicate crop. To meet the demands of the supermarket customers, careful planning is required to enable sufficient quantities of mushrooms to be available on the correct day of each week; mushrooms have a very short shelf life.

Despite these efforts and the considerable skill and expertise of the mushroom growers, the crop matures at slightly different rates, so that the mushrooms do not all appear at the same time and are not all the same size. Each one doubles in size every twenty-four hours in the final stage of growth. Some are early and are ready to pick ahead of the others, while others are late.

This presents a problem. The mushrooms will not grow to meet accurately the exacting specifications laid down by the supermarkets. Each quality specification fills a binder covering around eight product categories, from buttons, through closed cups and open cups to flats (open field-type mushrooms). The specification covers the size, shape and colour of the mushrooms, as well as the packaging and labelling standards. While these latter standards can be specified and met exactly, when it comes to the mushrooms themselves, Chesswood and their customers are relying on the judgement of individuals. This natural product just cannot be 'made' to a standard specification.

Chesswood is continually under pressure from its customers to improve quality – whatever that may mean in the circumstances. Eight lorry-loads a day leave their site; very few mushrooms are returned as out of specification!

5.3 Methods

Crosby's principal method is his fourteen-step programme for quality improvement (see Figure 5.2). It is essentially very straightforward and relies on a combination of both quantitative and qualitative aspects.

The first two steps may be seen as addressing cultural aspects of the organization. The first is about management commitment. This means the management accepting responsibility for, or an obligation to, achieving quality. Such a commitment constrains management to consistently behave in a quality achievement-oriented manner. This may proscribe or inhibit many of the traditional ways in which they have managed, however effective or ineffective.

When linked to the second step – the formation of quality improvement teams – a further traditional boundary is broken. Organizations are still structured predominantly on functional lines. Crosby specifically requires multidisciplinary teams. This means that managers and other staff must break out of their comfort zones and inevitably relinquish some of the 'expert' and 'position' power (Handy, 1985: 124–6) that goes with the functional organization. A wholehearted embrace by management of these two steps alone may be considered a major achievement.

The third and fourth steps are quantitative and again directly linked; the fourth is simply not possible without the third. Measurement is a necessary precursor to evaluation.

These steps in turn provide a platform for the fifth step: raising quality awareness, a more qualitative issue. To make the quality training relevant for supervisors and managers, it needs to be set firmly in the context of the quality status of the firm as evidenced by the measurements. This step may also be seen to act as reaffirmation of the first two steps: gaining commitment and the multifunctional approach. Through measurement and evaluation, the interrelatedness of quality issues across internal boundaries can be highlighted.

Step six is take action. The other steps are worthless unless they lead to preventative and corrective action. At this point, staff really must 'walk the talk'. It has both qualitative and quantitative aspects. If the numbers generated through the measurement system are used simply as clubs to beat the heads of the staff, they are unlikely to prove very helpful. The numbers must be used to provide guidance and support to the action taken, and the actions taken must be in harmony with the words spoken.

Once step six has commenced, the organization can be seen to have established a sound platform for quality improvement: staff and management are committed and action is being taken. It could be argued at this stage that provided the momentum of improvement is maintained, quality will continuously improve. Crosby's process, however, sees this as insufficient; with the process firmly established he proposes an increased effort and impetus towards 'zero defects' (ZD). This is the thrust of step seven – zero defects planning – which strives to establish a ZD programme, an essentially quantitative target but achieved through both soft and hard approaches.

Philip Crosby:

Step 1) Establish management commitment – it is seen as vital that the whole management team participates in the programme, a half hearted effort will fail.

Step 2) Form quality improvement teams – the emphasis here is on multi-disciplinary team effort. An initiative from the quality department will not be successful. It is considered essential to build team working across arbitrary, and often artificial, organizational boundaries.

Step 3) Establish quality measurements – these must apply to every activity throughout the company. A way must be found to capture every aspect, design, manufacturing, delivery and so on. These measurements provide a platform for the next step.

Step 4) Evaluate the cost of quality – this evaluation must highlight, using the measures established in the previous step, where quality improvement will be profitable.

Step 5) Raise quality awareness – this is normally undertaken through the training of managers and supervisors, through communications such as videos and books, and by displays of posters etc.

Step 6) Take action to correct problems – this involves encouraging staff to identify and rectify defects, or pass them on to higher supervisory levels where they can be addressed.

Step 7) Zero defects planning – establish a committee, or working group to develop ways to initiate and implement a Zero Defects programme.

Step 8) Train supervisors & managers – this step is focused on achieving understanding by all managers and supervisors of the steps in the Quality Improvement Programme in order that they can explain it in turn.

Step 9) Hold a 'Zero Defects' day to establish the attitude and expectation within the Company. Crosby sees this as being achieved in a celebratory atmosphere accompanied by badges, buttons and balloons.

Step 10) Encourage the setting of goals for improvement. Goals are of course of no value unless they are related to appropriate time-scales for their achievement.

Step 11) Obstacle reporting – this is encouragement to employees to advise management of the factors which prevent them achieving error free work. This might cover defective or inadequate equipment, poor quality components, etc.

Step 12) Recognition for contributors – Crosby considers that those who contribute to the programme should be rewarded through a formal, although non-monetary, reward scheme. Readers may be aware of the 'Gold Banana' award given by Foxboro for scientific achievement (Peters & Waterman, 1982).

Step 13) Establish Quality Councils – these are essentially forums composed of quality professionals and team leaders allowing them to communicate and determine action plans for further quality improvement.

Step 14) Do it all over again – the message here is very simple: achievement of quality is an ongoing process. However far you have got, there is always further to go!

Figure 5.2 Philip Crosby's fourteen-step quality programme.

Step eight involves training of supervisors and managers so that they can pass on the programme to their subordinates. This tactic of 'train the trainer' is a powerful mechanism for culturally embedding the behaviour changes that are required – always provided that the more senior managers similarly embrace the changes.

Step nine, Zero Defects Day, may be seen as both a celebration of achievements to date and a new beginning to the quality improvement programme. This takes zero defects as a very precise, quantifiable, and achievable objective. Following the previous steps, it should be accepted as possible and necessary by the whole organization. Step ten is a natural consequence of step nine, and requires commitment to achieving goals for improvement tied to defined and relatively short-term timescales. Again, it is quantitative in nature, the results being directly measurable.

Step eleven – obstacle reporting – is a communication device which recognizes that failure to achieve quality in one area may be related to failure in another, or to local factors which inhibit quality achievement. This process enables those facing problems to report them and, importantly, it places obligations on management to address those issues. Time-frames for response and action are built into this step, which requires both a change in culture – the acceptance by management of criticism from the workers – and a change in the nature of managers' roles. It will be insufficient for managers to concentrate on their own direct areas of responsibility, particularly as regards problems which cross functional boundaries, They will have to work with managers of other areas to achieve the targets.

Step twelve requires acknowledgement of the contribution of staff to the process – a direct reward for the efforts made. Crosby is very specific that these rewards should be formal but non-monetary. This step is largely cultural in its impact. Recognizing and rewarding contributors to the programme is a device for reinforcing a particular kind of behaviour amongst the whole staff, thus further embedding a quality culture.

The establishment of quality councils at step thirteen is seen as 'institutionalizing' the quality programme – making it a part of the embedded culture. At this stage it becomes an integral part of the way in which the company is managed and controlled. Mainly qualitative in nature, it will affect many aspects of the way in which the staff of the company behave in the future.

The final step – 'Do It All Over Again' – should be seen as a reminder that quality improvement never stops. Any change programme will, over time, lose impetus and thrust, simply because the original, perhaps revolutionary, leaders will achieve the objectives which they set themselves. They may find it difficult to maintain the initial enthusiasm and drive. In order to sustain and develop the programme, it will be necessary to pump new energy into it by the appointment of fresh people and the establishment of new objectives.

Crosby's 'Quality Vaccine' (Logothetis, 1992: 82–83) is an essential part of his process. It is based on three principal ingredients:

- integrity;
- dedication to communication and customer satisfaction;
- company-wide policies and operations which support the quality thrust.

Logothetis proposes a triangle (Figure 5.3) of interaction between these three ingredients, which must be supported by Crosby's belief in how the vaccine is administered. This again has three strands:

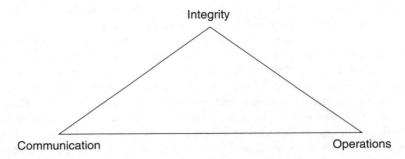

Figure 5.3 Philip Crosby's triangle of interactions.

- determination – awareness that management must lead;
- education – for management and staff;
- implementation – creating an organizational environment where achievement of quality is regarded as the norm, not the exception.

This chapter is not intended to provide an exhaustive account of methods, tools and techniques; those are introduced in the case study in Part Four, where aspects of Crosby's approach will be discussed in more detail. The 'How' rather than the 'What' will be dealt with in the appropriate chapters. This section has, however, provided an introduction to the principal strands of Crosby's method, which can be seen to be based largely in quantitative outcomes and to rely heavily on an evangelical attitude, amongst both the management and the staff.

5.4 Successes and Failures

Quality gurus, like doctors, are prone to advertising their successes and burying their failures. Companies act similarly: a successful quality programme will be advertised in order to attract customers; a failure will be swept under the carpet, with executives pretending that it never happened. It thus becomes impossible to find reported empirical evidence of failure.

Success, on the other hand, is shared. The guru proclaims the success of his or her method, while the company proclaims the success of its strategy, and acknowledges the contribution made by its interpretation of the particular guru's approach. Chrysler's Lee Iacocca, for example, cited by Bank (1992: 75), says: 'we established our own Chrysler Quality Institute in Michigan, modelled after his [Crosby's] operation – our company's put about twenty thousand of our people through it . . . and I admit they do return with QUALITY stamped on their foreheads.'

Here, it can be explicitly seen that Crosby's contribution has been acknowledged and that Chrysler have used his work as a model. What we cannot see is how closely the model follows the original.

With his consulting company, Quality College, and overseas operations firmly established, Crosby must be acknowledged as having been successful. It is also the case that sufficient client organizations must have found the approach useful to have sustained the development and growth of that organization over a lengthy period of time. It must be concluded that there is some real value to be found in his approach.

Flood (1993: 27–8) acknowledges this in identifying five strengths to Crosby's work. Summarizing, he sees these as:

- clarity;
- recognition of worker participation;
- rejection of a tangible quality problem; acceptance of the idea of solutions;
- Crosby's metaphors – 'vaccine' and 'maturity';
- Crosby's motivational style.

Flood also criticizes perceived weaknesses. He sees:

- a danger of misdirected effort from 'blaming' workers;
- an emphasis on marketing more than recognition of barriers;
- the management and goal orientation of the fourteen-step programme as failing to 'free workers from externally generated goals';
- the potential for 'zero defects' to be interpreted as zero risk;
- the ineffectiveness in coercive power structures.

Looking at the strengths, it could be argued that clarity and simplicity of approach are not necessarily beneficial in dealing with increasingly complex problems. The adequacy of any problem-solving tool must be measured in terms of its suitability for the problem being addressed. This must be considered when selecting an approach – the complexity of the process and tools used must at least match that of the problem.

The value of worker participation cannot be denied. First, the people who do the work may be the only people who can recognize the roots of a particular problem. Second, their involvement implies easier acceptance of ownership of the programme and the solutions.

The idea that all quality issues can be resolved is very useful in provoking ideal goal-seeking behaviour amongst the participants in the situation. Bank (1992: 23) compares this to the ice-skaters Torville and Dean aiming for perfect scores, even though they may not be attainable. He cites Thomas J. Watson, founder of IBM, as saying 'It's better to aim at perfection and miss than it is to aim at imperfection and hit it.' Acceptance that certain problems cannot be solved could be seen as reinforcing behaviour and attitudes which ensure that they never will be.

Creativity and leadership must be seen as essential strands in quality improvement. However, while some writers see great strength in Crosby's approach to this, there is also, perhaps, inherent danger. The 'charismatic' or 'evangelical' style adopted by Crosby has been criticized by Joseph Juran. Crosby, cited by Bank (1992: 76) says, 'Dr. Juran seems to think I am a charlatan and hasn't missed many opportunities to say that over the years.' The founding charge here seems really to be one of a lack of substantial underpinning to Crosby's approach, perhaps reflecting other comments about promotion 'through slogans and too often full of platitudes'.

There can be no doubt that many of the most sustained management theories and approaches over the years have been well marketed, yet when examined by others have been demonstrated to have either theoretical or methodological weaknesses. This is almost inevitably true. Theories validated within one paradigm can probably always be disputed from within another. Similarly, it is often said that there is no such thing as bad publicity, and to quote Oscar Wilde in *The Portrait of Dorian Gray*, 'There is only one thing in the world worse than being talked about, and that is not being talked about.'

That Crosby was an effective self-publicist cannot be denied. However, this does not necessarily detract from the value of what was being said. Perhaps the comments of another great self-publicist, Winston Churchill, Britain's Second World War Prime Minister, should be noted. Churchill is known to have annotated his speeches with what might be seen as stage directions. One of his most well known is the reported admonition in the margin of a speech: 'Weak point – SHOUT!'

Regarding the weaknesses, it is arguable whether the interpretation of Crosby as blaming the workers is reasonable. Bendell (1989), for example, states that Crosby 'does not believe that workers should take prime responsibility for poor quality; the reality, he says, is that you have to get management straight first'. Bendell further suggests that in Crosby's approach, 'management sets the tone on quality and workers follow . . . the initiative comes from the top'. Thus it could be argued that rather than creating a 'blame the workers' culture, the Crosby approach is a form of empowerment, led by the management. The difficulty rests in how the messages are translated by the managers in the middle, and that to a large extent depends upon how they receive them and how competent they are to re-transmit them.

The issue of platitudes and lack of substance has already been largely addressed, and goal orientation comes into focus. It is clear that Crosby only considers one goal for the organization and that is zero defects. Flood's criticism here is much better founded. The external setting of goals by the management is far from empowering or emancipating, and it neglects to address workers' perception of their own values and needs. It must be recognized, however, that the requirement for quality is being driven from the environment of the organization. If survival of the organization is to be achieved, quality products, which conform to requirements, are an essential feature.

Misinterpretation of zero defects as meaning the avoidance of risk is another reasonable point. There will always be an element of risk involved in a change of behaviour or process. To overcome the danger of risk-aversion, management must develop a cultural environment where risks can be calculated and minimized, and where learning from mistakes is encouraged, perhaps incorporating ideas of the Learning Organization (Senge, 1990; see Chapter 19 of this book).

Flood's strongest criticism is of the assumption that people will work in an open and conciliatory manner. He makes it clear that in a political or coercive context this will not apply. Many management writers agree that an element of politics and coercion is present in most organizations, whether or not this is explicit. There will always be a dominant group or sub-group, and it is suggested that a fully open and conciliatory atmosphere is an ideal rather than an easily achievable objective.

5.5 Critical Review

Overall, the foundation of Crosby's approach can be seen in two elements. First, his extensive professional background in quality will have provided the quantitative bias to his method and, second, his reportedly charismatic personality will have provided the qualitative aspects.

The general value of measurement in establishing standards and objectives for quality is readily recognizable, while the principals are transferable between organizations and people. The value of the qualitative issues is much harder to evaluate and transfer.

The majority of managers would not perhaps consider themselves to be 'charismatic' leaders; an epithet more readily used in respect of others than it is for oneself. A wholehearted commitment to quality achievement throughout the organization is undoubtedly required; what is questionable is whether the exhortative, inspirational slogans and platitudes will work in all circumstances and for all managers.

It has to be concluded that the process and quantitative aspects of Crosby's programme – a word which in itself implies a discrete activity rather than ongoing management behaviour – may be readily transferable. However, the management style adopted will have to reflect the needs, values and personalities of those involved in the programme.

Similar comments can be applied to other aspects of the approach. For example, while encouraging rewards, Crosby suggests that these should not be monetary. The reward, to be truly meaningful to the recipient, should reflect his or her needs and aspirations. For an individual whose focus is professional achievement, public recognition of his or her contribution may be all the reward that is required. For an individual on low wages, perhaps seeking to reduce personal indebtedness or, in an extreme case, to pay for life-preserving medical treatment, a monetary reward may be precisely what is required.

Reflection is also necessary on the suitability of the approach for different industries. With his manufacturing background, Crosby has developed an approach which reflects that it is essentially possible in the manufacturing environment to know when a defect-free product is achieved. This is far more difficult in the service sector, where definitions of the product are harder to generate and delivery is almost impossible to control.

Certain aspects of service are relatively straightforward to quantify. For example, how many times the telephone rings before it is answered, or precisely what words of greeting are used – although there have been cases reported where the telephone has been answered too promptly, thus frightening the customers! Other aspects are less susceptible to measurement and control, for example, tone of voice. The nature of many of these transactions is that the service is provided and consumed instantly. While they can, to some extent, be designed and planned, their production is uncontrollable. They also depend on factors which are perhaps outside the ability of the organization to influence effectively. These factors include the expectations of the customer, his or her mood, the sort of day the customer has already experienced, and the level of service he or she has previously received. These factors cannot be known until after service has commenced.

Crosby's approach, therefore, has to be marked with some cautions about its general applicability across a range of industries and cultures. What works very well for Philip Crosby at ITT, or for Lee Iacocca at Chrysler, may not work in a bank in Hong Kong, or on a North Sea oil production platform.

Summary

This chapter has presented the work of Philip Crosby through a five-point critical framework. It has described his philosophy and its underpinning assumptions, outlined his principal methods, examined the successes and failures of the approach, and summarized these in a brief critical review. Readers may refer to Crosby's own works, particularly *Quality is Free* (1979), to enhance and develop their own knowledge and understanding.

KEY LEARNING POINTS

Philip B. Crosby's definition of quality: conformance to requirements

Five absolutes of quality management:

- quality as conformance;
- no such thing as a quality problem;
- always cheaper first time;
- only measurement of performance is the cost of quality;
- zero defects.

Three key beliefs:
quantification; management leadership; prevention.

Principal methods:
fourteen-step quality programme; the 'quality vaccine'.

Question

Consider the management process in your organization. How does it support or inhibit quality goods or services?

6 W. Edwards Deming

A prophet is not without honour, save in his own country

(Matthew 13:57)

Introduction

W. Edwards Deming, who died in 1993, is considered by many to be the founding father of the modern quality movement. Perhaps the most widely known of the gurus both within and outside the quality field, Deming held a doctorate in physics from Yale and was a keen statistician, working in the US government for many years in the Department of Agriculture and the Bureau of Census. According to Bendell (1989: 4), Deming rose to prominence in Japan, where he was closely involved in the post-war development of quality, for which Bendell suggests he is considered largely responsible. Heller (1989) sees Deming as having a 'passionate belief in man's ability to improve on the poor and the mediocre, and even on the good', a belief which can be seen as evident in both his theory and his practice. Logothetis (1992: xii) sees Deming as advocating 'widespread use of statistical ideas, with management taking a strong initiative in building quality in'. Bank (1992: 62) cites Hutchins's belief that a major contribution made by Deming to the Japanese quality movement was in helping them to: 'cut through the academic theory, to present the ideas in a simple way which could be meaningful right down to production worker levels'.

Summarizing, Deming's approach can be seen as founded in the traditional scientific method (arising from his physics and statistics background). He was also a very capable communicator. Although as Bendell (1989: 5) suggests, it is 'difficult to delimit his [Deming's] concepts', owing to the constant refinement and improvement of his ideas, his successful and widely read book *Out of the Crisis* (1986) presents his approach to both management and quality in its most succinct, coherent form.

6.1 Philosophy

Deming's initial approach, largely rejected by US industry at the outset, was based on his background in statistical methods. His quantitative method provided a 'systematic, rigorous approach to quality' (Bendell, 1989: 4). Drawing on the work of the statistician Walter Shewhart, his tutor, Deming urged a management focus on causes of variability in manufacturing processes.

Deming's first belief can be seen here: that there are 'common' and 'special' causes of quality problems. 'Special' causes are seen as those relating to particular operators or machines and requiring attention to the individual cause. 'Common' causes are those which arise from the operation of the system itself, and are one of the responsibilities of management.

Deming believed in the use of statistical process control (SPC) charts as the key method for identifying special and common causes, and for assisting diagnosis of quality problems. His aim was to remove 'outliers', that is, quality problems relating to the special causes of failure. This was achieved through training, improved machinery and equipment, and so on. SPC enabled the production process to be brought 'under control'. Remaining quality problems were considered to be related to common causes, that is, problems inherent in the *design* of the production process, not its operation. Eradication of special causes enabled a shift in focus onto common causes to improve quality further.

Deming's second belief is apparent here: a quantitative approach to identifying and solving problems. It is suggested by Bendell (1989: 4) that this statistically based approach brings its own problems. He reports lack of technical standards and limitations of data and, perhaps more importantly, 'human difficulties in the form of employee resistance and management lack of understanding as to their roles in quality improvement', particularly in the US applications. Bendell considers that perhaps 'too much emphasis was being given towards the statistical aspects'. It can be suggested that Deming's approach strongly reflects the 'machine' view of organizations outlined in Chapter 4. It is also fair to make two further observations. First, the usual level of learning about statistics for most students does not proceed beyond the age of sixteen, with the grasp of the subject usually being tenuous. Consequently, it is difficult to understand fully what the results achieved really mean. Second, given contemporary information technology, the results which Deming's methods reveal could be presented more meaningfully. As with other experts in their respective fields, the value of Deming's work could be obscured by our ability to interpret it.

Notwithstanding these problems Deming became a national hero in Japan, and his methods were widely taken up. In 1951 the Deming Prize for contributions to quality and dependability was launched, and in 1960 he was awarded the Second Order of the Sacred Treasure, Japan's premier Imperial honour.

A third strand to Deming's work was the formulation of his systematic approach to problem-solving; an approach which is now commonplace and frequently reinterpreted in other methodologies, for example, the EPDCA cycle in Oakland's work, and is central to the application of the ISO 9001: 2000 standard. This has become known as the Deming, Shewhart or PDCA cycle – Plan, Do, Check, Action – illustrated in Figure 6.1.

The cycle is continuous. Once it has been systematically completed, it recommences without ceasing. This is in agreement with Crosby's admonition, already considered, to 'Do it all over again'. The approach is seen as re-emphasizing the responsibility of management to be actively involved in the organization's quality programme, while Logothetis (1992: 55) considers that it provides the basis for a 'self-sustaining quality programme'.

Two further beliefs can be derived here. First, there is a belief in a systematic, methodical approach, which contrasts sharply with the *ad hoc* and random behaviour found in many quality initiatives. The second belief is in the need for continuous quality improvement action. This contrasts sharply with the overtones in Crosby's approach, which suggest a discrete set of activities.

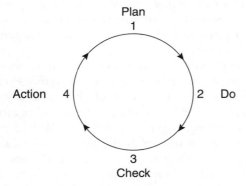

Figure 6.1 W. Edwards Deming's PDCA cycle.

Deming's later work focused on Western, particularly US, management. Here, Deming (1986: 97–148) elaborated seven fundamental beliefs (the Seven Deadly Sins, Figure 6.2) about bad management practices, which he considered must be eliminated before Western styles of management could be transformed to support the implementation of a successful quality initiative.

Sin 1, 'lack of constancy', is seen by Logothetis (1992: 46) as urging 'an absolute and constant commitment on the part of senior management to quality, productivity and innovation'. Inherent in this is a continuing drive towards better quality and reliability of product in order to drive down costs, protect investment and employment, create and enlarge markets, and hence generate more jobs. It is seen as providing a positive and achievement-oriented focus for the organization. Deming (1986: 98) criticizes management, particularly in US industry, for being 'run on the quarterly dividend'. It is certainly true that today ever more organizations throughout the world are managed according to the 'flavour of the month', with senior managers flitting from miracle solution to miracle solution, while more junior managers keep their heads down and wait for the passion to pass.

Sin 2, short-term profit focus, is seen to challenge and potentially defeat the 'constancy of purpose' previously urged. Deming (1986: 99) suggests that:

> Anyone can boost the dividend at the end of the quarter. Ship everything on hand, regardless of quality: mark it shipped, and show it all as accounts receivable. Defer till next quarter, so far as possible, orders for material and equipment. Cut down on research, education, training.

W. Edwards Deming:

Sin 1) Lack of constancy;
Sin 2) Short term profit focus;
Sin 3) Performance appraisals;
Sin 4) Job-hopping;
Sin 5) Use of visible figures only;
Sin 6) Excessive medical costs;
Sin 7) Excessive costs of liability.

Figure 6.2 W. Edwards Deming's seven deadly sins.

Here, Deming is making clear his belief in a management approach with a long-term orientation. He gives explicit recognition to the need to satisfy shareholder expectations, but points out that these expectations must go beyond the immediate return on capital to consider the long-term future of the organization.

Much criticism has been levied in recent years at what is now known as 'short-termism' in the City of London, on Wall Street, in Exchange Square, or Raffles Place. The underlying reasons and causes are not the subject of this book, but readers may wish to consider issues such as the increasing ownership of shares by financial institutions and the difficulties of making money by making products in a harsh business environment. Pension and investment companies are frequently the largest stockholders in public companies; it is worth thinking about their requirements and the reward packages of their employees, which are often tied to short-term performance measures. Similarly, investment bankers and traders in 'derivative' financial products are further dissociating the underlying value of products and companies from the valuation of the business itself.

Sin 3, performance appraisal, is considered by Deming (1986: 102) to 'nourish short-term performance' and 'leave people bitter, crushed, bruised, battered, desolate, despondent, dejected, feeling inferior', a somewhat damning indictment. Logothetis (1992: 47) sees appraisal as encouraging 'rivalry and isolation' and demolishing teamwork, again leading back to a focus on individual and short-term results, noting that 'people who attempt to change the system (for the better) have no chance of recognition'.

While acknowledging Deming's belief in the potential damage that a poor appraisal system can cause, this is rather more a function of a badly designed and badly operated system than a necessary outcome of performance review. As with the quality of a manufactured product, the quality and impact of an appraisal system will depend upon the quality of its design. Most of us need and enjoy recognition of our achievements, and can benefit from the guidance delivered through a constructive and effective appraisal system. This perhaps partly reflects the esteem element in Maslow's hierarchy of needs.

Sin 4 is job-hopping, that is, regular movement of management between jobs, either within or between organizations. Originally seen as a particular attribute of Western management, this has been increasingly common in Far Eastern locations such as Singapore and Hong Kong, although recent economic reversals in those and other economies have challenged the trend. Job-hopping is considered to lead to instability and further reinforce the short-term orientation of the organization. Logothetis (1992: 39) suggests that job-hopping destroys teamwork and commitment, and ensures that many decisions are taken in whole or partial ignorance of the circumstances surrounding them. The belief this time is in the need for commitment of management to the long-term future of the organization.

Sin 5 is 'the use of visible figures only'. Here, Deming criticizes the failure to recognize and evaluate the intangible aspects of the organization, for example, the additional sales generated through satisfied customers, the benefits to productivity and quality derived from people feeling part of a success story, and the negative impact of performance appraisal or barriers to achieving quality. Deming (1986: 123) considers that managers who believe that everything can be measured are deluding themselves, and suggests that they should know before they start that they will be able to quantify only 'a trivial part of the gain'. This should be seen as a belief in intangible, invisible benefits arising from good management practice. It does, however, conflict with his espousal of statistical methods, since the reliable measurement of intangibles is notoriously difficult. That said, the measurement of performance across the business processes, rather than simply in the vertical silos, is both achievable and beneficial. Lessons could perhaps be drawn from organizational psychology, which can help to measure some of the aspects that Deming considered intangible, and by re-examining the organizational and financial structure of the organization, which often obscures where the true profits and costs arise.

Sins 6 and 7, as revealed by Deming, are given little attention by other writers on his work. His points are simply made. The sixth sin, medical costs, both in direct lost labour costs and indirect in the sense of medical insurance premiums, are met largely by the employer. Thus, they are an additional cost to be recovered in the price of the product. Deming (1986: 98) refers to William Hoglund of the Pontiac Motor Division, who informed him that the direct cost of medical care to the company exceeded the amount spent on steel for every vehicle produced! This cost continues to be a major issue for organizations, as does the provision of other benefits such as pension provision.

Claims experience and actuarial expectation drive the cost of insurance, and it is arguable whether Deming is making a fair point here. Medical costs are currently covered in every developed nation. If they are not supported by private insurance schemes, such as those that prevail in the USA, France, Singapore and many other nations, they may be met by a national scheme such as the National Health Service in the UK. Either way, the company may be considered to bear the cost, through direct contribution, or by increased basic wages which enable the employees to meet the cost themselves. For example, in the UK, employees receive an appropriate level of income pay of between 7 per cent and 12 per cent of their wages in a National Insurance scheme, which is intended to cover costs of primary health care and provision of a state pension. In addition, employers pay a contribution of around 10 per cent of total salary costs into the same scheme on behalf of the employees. It is doubtful whether there is any real difference in the cost related to this between employers in the USA or the UK.

Sin 7, the final sin, is one that is now considered to be gaining further ground: liability costs. There is evidence throughout the industrial and post-industrial world of an increasingly litigious public, perhaps encouraged by lawyers working on a 'no win, no fee' basis. While many potential liability issues are insurable, many others are not. The costs of these must be borne by the organization. Whether management and manufacturers can reasonably be blamed for this issue is certainly arguable, and it is questionable whether it is within their power to control it effectively other than through improvements in product and process design. It is suspected that it relates to broader societal changes, such as an increasing trend towards individual, rather than collective, values, and the hunt, whenever things go wrong, for the often elusive 'someone to blame'.

Summarizing Deming's philosophy, we can identify a number of clear strands. There are evident beliefs in:

- quantitative, statistically valid, control systems;
- clear definition of those aspects under the direct control of staff, that is, the 'special causes' – and those which are the responsibility of management – 'the common causes'. Deming suggests that the latter are as high as 94 per cent;

- a systematic, methodical approach;
- continuous improvement;
- constancy and determination.

Taken together, these cover the first five of his 'Deadly Sins'. The other two are highly questionable.

Along with Crosby, Deming (1986: ix) considers that quality should be designed into both the product and the process. He believes that 'transformation of the style of American [sic] management' is necessary, requiring a 'whole new structure, from foundation upward'.

6.2 Assumptions

The assumptions about the world that Deming seems to make to underpin his approach will now be explored.

First, it can be seen that while initially focusing attention on existing processes to derive immediate improvement – the eradication of 'special causes' of failure – attention is rapidly refocused on the management process and attitudes. Deming seems to believe that these must be, in his own words, 'transformed', in order for sustained improvement to be achieved. The management is seen to be responsible and, significantly, to be capable of undertaking the proposed transformation. He does not, however, suggest, in organization design terms, how this should be achieved.

Second, is the assumption that statistical methods, properly used, will provide quantitative evidence to support changes. At the same time, Deming recognizes that some aspects of the management process and attitudes cannot easily be measured, and suggests that managements frequently fail to take seriously those aspects which they consider unmeasurable.

The third key assumption is that continuous improvement is both possible and desirable. Taking his definition of quality as 'meeting the needs of the customer, both present and future' (1986: 5), this has to be questioned. If the needs of the customer are fully understood and fully met, where is the benefit in further improvement?

A further aspect to this is perhaps more significant in the twenty-first century. The assumption is that continuous improvement, supported by a long-term orientation, will enable the organization to meet customers' future needs. If, however, the contemporary world is characterized as Handy (1990a) suggests by 'discontinuous change', a long-term view and continuous improvement may no longer be enough. Perhaps organizations have to be built which can anticipate and prepare for sudden, maybe catastrophic, change. The bankers example in Chapter 3 illustrates this point; continuous improvement and incremental change may not be sound recipes in a discontinuous world. The 'boom and bust' of the dotcom businesses is another example, as is the catastrophe which faced the world in 2008. While many of these businesses were undoubtedly built on weak foundations, many others should have been able to survive. The inevitable collapse of the weak, and the strong who through unconstrained risk-taking became weak, brought down many of the strong.

Deming's final assumption, as with Crosby, is related to the service sector. Simply, he sees that the prime role of the service sector, in the context of a national economy, rests in enabling manufacturing to do its job. For example, he suggests (1986: 188) that:

A better plan for freight carriers would be to improve service and thus to decrease costs. These cost savings, passed on to manufacturers and to other service industries, would help American industry to improve the market for American products, and would in time bring new business to carriers of freight.

While offering specific advice in the same text about quality improvement in the service sector, Deming, unlike Crosby, does explicitly recognize the difficulty of measuring certain aspects of it. He also seems to assume an initially altruistic effort, which contrasts sharply with his accusations of short-termism. To some extent he is possibly correct: cost-savings should be passed back down the chain, and in a systemically developed solution this could occur. Such a move, though, is probably more a function of truly competitive and open markets rather than an altruistic or collaborative gesture, and is a common thread in cost and performance improvement in, for example, highly integrated industries such as automotive and computer hardware manufacture.

The implications of his assumption about the role of services should also be considered. As suggested in Chapter 1 (manufacturing activity drives the service sector) it has been observed that few local communities thrive when their manufacturing base is lost. For example, the shipbuilding and coal-mining communities in the UK continue to suffer slow economic growth, social fragmentation, and significant unemployment. Notably, many service-sector jobs and organizations can now be clearly seen to have depended upon local manufacturers, through the direct purchase of services by the major organizations and the expenditure of wages by the employees. The wealth generated by the employer was in large part expended in the same community. As the manufacturing sector has declined, so too has the service sector in those communities.

Those sectors where services have thrived are in areas of specialist technical expertise, such as banking, insurance, finance and other knowledge-based industries. These industries have a less dependent relationship on the manufacturing sector than, say, retailing and real estate. Notwithstanding these particular aspects, there is perhaps a warning at a national and multinational level. If individual communities cannot be adequately sustained when manufacturing is lost to them, is there any future for nations if the manufacturing base as a whole is lost?

6.3 Methods

Deming has four principal methods:

- The PDCA cycle;
- statistical process control;
- the fourteen principles for transformation;
- the seven-point action plan.

The PDCA cycle has been introduced and will not be dealt with further here. Statistical process control will be properly explored in Part Four. The fourteen principles for transformation and seven-point action plan will provide the major content of this section.

Statistical process control is a quantitative approach, based on the measurement of process performance. Essentially, a process is considered to be under control, that is, stable, when inevitable random variations in output fall within determined upper and lower limits. That is seen by Deming as the process having achieved a position where the special causes of failure have been eradicated.

A control chart, a sample of which is provided in Figure 6.3., is used to record the value of a measurement associated with an event in a process. Statistical analysis of the values recorded will reveal the mean value and the normal distribution. Normal variation from this mean value for the particular process in its established state is conventionally taken as any value within +/− 3 standard deviations of the mean. Events which fall outside that normal variation are considered to be 'special', and should prove tractable to individual diagnosis and treatment. Events falling within the norms are considered to have 'common' causes, that is, they are a product of the organization of the system and require treatment at the system level. Here we can refer directly to Deming (1986: 315) and re-emphasize the role of management in the development of quality:

> I should estimate that in my experience most troubles and most possibilities for improvement add up to proportions something like this:
>
> 94% belong to the system (responsibility of management)
> 6% special.

It has to be acknowledged here that Deming's split of special and common causes, and consequently his allocation of responsibility for error, relates directly to the product of SPC. At +/− 3 standard deviations in a stable system, it is inevitable that 95 per cent of errors will belong to the system; 95 per cent being 2 standard deviations in a normal distribution. Three standard deviations (99.7 per cent approximately of results) are recognized through SPC as representing stability: the system is under control. The standard (+/− 3 sigma) was originally devised by Shewhart to minimize

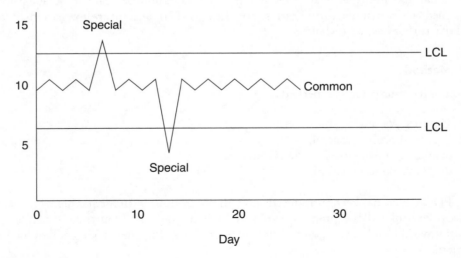

Figure 6.3 Sample control chart.

net economic loss from rectifying mistakes, the objective of Taguchi's 'quadratic loss function', which will be elaborated in Chapter 13.

We can now turn to the first main focus of this section: Deming's fourteen Principles for Transformation. These, like Crosby's fourteen steps, are essentially straightforward, and rely on a combination of statistical and human, or cultural, aspects. The principles will be reviewed in turn.

W. Edwards Deming:

Principle 1) Create constancy of purpose to improve product and service.

Principle 2) Adopt a new philosophy for the new economic age with management learning what their responsibilities are and by assuming leadership for change.

Principle 3) Cease dependence on mass inspection to achieve quality by building quality into the product.

Principle 4) End awarding business on price. Award business on total cost and move towards single suppliers.

Principle 5) Aim for continuous improvement of the system of production and service to improve productivity and quality and to decrease costs.

Principle 6) Institute training on the job.

Principle 7) Institute leadership with the aim of supervising people to help them to do a better job.

Principle 8) Drive out fear so that everyone can work effectively together for the organization.

Principle 9) Break down barriers between departments. Encourage research, design, sales and production to work together to foresee difficulties in production and use.

Principle 10) Eliminate slogans, exhortations and numerical targets for the workforce since they are divisory and anyway difficulties belong to the whole system.

Principle 11) Eliminate quotas or work standards and management by objectives or numerical goals: leadership should be substituted instead.

Principle 12) Remove barriers that rob people of their right to pride in their work.

Principle 13) Institute a vigorous education and self-improvement programme.

Principle 14) Put everyone in the company to work to accomplish the transformation.

Figure 6.4 W. Edwards Deming's fourteen principles for transformation.

The first three principles – creating constancy of purpose, adoption of a new philosophy, and ceasing dependence on mass inspection – may all be seen as focused on the cultural aspects of the organization. The first principle is aimed at creating a 'team' type of environment, where all are working together towards a common goal. It requires the management to commit to achieving ever-improving quality as a primary objective of the organization. The story of the regeneration of Kennet School illustrates this point.

Vignette 6.1 Kennet School: A Tale of Constancy and Determination

Kennet School presented a disappointing picture. The lack of coherence and consistency in support of the teachers constrained them from exploiting their talents and abilities. While some pupils performed exceptionally well, certain parents perceived the school as a glorified youth club; somewhere to send the children to keep them occupied while they were out at work. Limited leadership was in evidence; there was little communication between members of staff; parental complaints were ignored; and the buildings were neglected. The school was suffering a falling pupil roll, threatening the sixth form, comprising only ninety pupils, with closure. In measured performance terms, only 28 per cent of pupils obtained five or more passes at grades A to C in the General Certificate of Secondary Education (GCSE) examinations – a dismal record.

Now, despite the provision of extra buildings, the school is practically at capacity in pupil numbers, and the sixth form is thriving. Examination results show 63 per cent of pupils obtaining five or more GCSE passes at grades A to C. The standards attained by the school led to it being listed as outstanding in examination results and inspection. Kennet School is one of only sixty-three secondary schools in England and Wales, and the only school in West Berkshire, recognized in this way.

The achievement of this turnaround has been through constancy and determination, rather than the use of a miracle cure, or the adoption of any particular gurus' methodology. A new headmaster adopted a classical approach to management in the early days. He imposed discipline on both the children and the staff, letting 'nothing go by that [he] didn't like'. Development and imposition of rules and standards for staff and children was immediate. These covered issues such as movement, behaviour, uniform, and homework, and were supported by action on his part; the smooth functioning of the school now rests on these rules which received high visibility at the outset. A staff handbook is in use, which sets out the aims of the school, and is supported by clarity of responsibility with everyone now knowing who is responsible for what.

The priority of the school is academic excellence. Sporting success (a regular achievement) and pastoral issues are regarded as important in supporting the academic objectives – the means to achieve educational ends, rather than ends in themselves. The creation of an 'inner cabinet', chaired by the headmaster, emphasizes this priority. The cabinet consists of the heads of the eleven academic faculties within the school, together with one head of house. This unbalanced representation confirms in action the words of the headmaster: 'walking the talk'.

The headmaster recognized that some 'early wins' were required to ensure that his different way of running the school would be perceived as correct. Ten members of staff left in the first three years, some voluntarily, some less so. Two children were expelled. There was necessarily some conflict during those early days, and while there was much discussion with the people affected, the headmaster held, and still holds, an absolute veto on all matters – although he exercises extreme caution in using this. He recognizes the need to achieve a balance between making things happen and doing everything himself, a possible outcome of an autocratic approach.

With a system of rules in place and acceptance by the staff of the new way of working, much of the decision-making power has been passed to the heads of departments, notwithstanding the headmaster's veto. Their decisions, as well as those referred to the headmaster, rest on one simple question: What is the benefit in the classroom? If there is no benefit then the proposal will fail. The criterion for the introduction of new ideas or approaches is simply educational benefit.

   Creation of a three-year rolling development plan for the school is undertaken by the heads of departments and their staff, and subjected to a 'round robin' process of modification and refinement. Every member of staff receives a copy of the completed plan. The final column of the plan shows who is responsible for what aspects, thus making accountability open and public. The senior staff undertake a review and refocusing of the plan at termly intervals.

   The school, now managed in a much more decentralized manner, with trust given to staff and pupils wherever possible, still adheres to three global targets:

- continuous improvement in academic standards;
- staff development;
- improved behavioural standards and sustained improvement in the environment of the school.

In 2008, Kennet School was listed for the second time as providing 'outstanding care and education', and at a recent regulatory inspection as 'outstanding in overall effectiveness'.

   In the words of the headmaster, 'There is so much more to do.'

The second principle, that of embracing management learning and a leadership-based style of management, concerns acceptance by the management that the responsibility for developing and achieving the changes is theirs. It requires explicit recognition by management that the workers are not necessarily to blame for quality deficiencies. This may well require a dramatic change in both words and actions on the part of management, particularly if they have been accustomed, as so many have been, to pushing the blame down through the hierarchy.

   The third principle, ceasing dependence on mass inspection by building quality into the product, requires a further dramatic change in management approach, and has major implications for issues such as organization structure and information management. A simple abandonment of mass inspection, not supported by changes in other aspects, will potentially be disastrous. A successful example of such a change is the introduction in recent years of multidisciplinary product development teams in organizations such as John Deere Tractors. These teams include both design and production engineers, so that products are now designed with production requirements in mind rather than having to be re-engineered for production. This speeds up the development of new products, reduces manufacturing complexity, and leads to improved quality. Other major manufacturing companies are following the same route.

   The fourth principle, the ending of awarding business on price rather than on total cost, is recognition that the invoiced unit price of a sub-assembly, or part, is only a fraction of its total potential cost (or value) to the organization. For example, a part which has the lowest unit cost may carry with it a high level of rejects. This leads to either high inspection costs to identify poor quality parts, or to a poor quality of finished product, leading in turn to high inspection and rework costs, and potential for product failure in the hands of the customer.

   A number of aspects need to be considered in the identification of the total cost of a purchased item. These may include unit cost, quality (failure and reject rate), inspection costs, inventory costs (for example, the potential for implementing a 'just-in-time' or *kanban* system), and ease of use in the manufacturing environment – that is, the impact of the supplied item on labour and other costs. The other aspect that must be considered is the purchase of items which support the manufacturing process, such as machine tools, conveyor systems, and control systems. Particularly with these latter items, the ongoing running costs are often a far greater part of the total lifetime cost than the initial purchase price. Significant benefits can be obtained by bearing a higher initial cost in order to generate longer term savings. A prime example of this is with Mercedes motor cars. While the initial capital costs of buying a Mercedes are significantly greater than for competitors' equivalent models, the average Mercedes is reputed to depreciate at a far lower rate, under 40 per cent over the first three years life, compared to more than 60 per cent than its competitors. With greater component reliability and longevity, it also has lower running costs, although many other car manufacturers are now achieving comparable levels of performance. Toyota, through its Lexus brand, has achieved comparable product quality to Mercedes, but at lower cost and less premium pricing.

Deming also recommends a move towards single suppliers. As with so many things, this approach has both advantages and drawbacks. The principal advantages are that it provides the purchaser with significant leverage in negotiating improvements in product quality and price; it enables long-term relationships based on trust and mutual support; and it provides a more secure financial platform for the provider. Conversely, reliance on a single source of parts supply makes the purchaser vulnerable to any failure on the part of the supplier, either financially or in quality. Such exposure may give cause for concern to bankers and other financiers. A worthwhile approach here would be to consider the use of a single supplier based on Porter's (1980) model for competitive rivalry. Where supplier power is weak (there are many suppliers and the product is undifferentiated or non-critical), a single supplier strategy may bring significant benefits to the company, enabling it to take effective control of its supplier. Where supplier power is strong (there are few suppliers, the product is differentiated or critical), the organization may maximize its position by supporting more than one supplier.

The fifth principle, aim for continuous improvement, if considered appropriate to the customer's needs and industry circumstances, gives greater substance and focus to the first two principles by focusing attention on productivity, quality and decreasing costs. Objectives at this stage can be made more quantifiable, moving from the ideals of the first principles to a more practical achievement orientation.

The sixth principle, on-the-job training, emphasizes the need to improve competencies and skills in the practical context. While not excluding classroom-based training, this principle suggests that the objective of continuous improvement applies at least as much to people as it does to processes.

The seventh principle, leadership, is again qualitative and cultural, and is closely associated with the eighth principle, 'drive out fear'. These principles are connected with the management style of the organization. The objective here can usefully be seen as a requirement to move away from an adversarial style of management towards a collaborative style. Effective management in this way, supported by the SPC techniques, will focus attention on how to improve the individual (special causes), or the system (common causes), rather than on whom to blame. The approach will target curing the diseases rather than convicting the victims.

The ninth principle, breaking down barriers, can be seen to be linked to the fourth.

The suggestion here is, in effect, for the creation of multidisciplinary teams for product and service development that aim to enhance the development, production and delivery of new products or services. Deming does not discuss how this can be achieved, or how to specifically recognize the difficulties that can be associated with it. There are a number of cultural and professional issues which often emerge in the creation of multidisciplinary teams, and any reorganization into either a matrix form of management or project teams needs to be associated with commensurate changes in salary and bonus packages to enable congruence of individual and organizational goals. Contemporary developments in project management, such as business communications engineering (*The Five Dimensions of Project Planning*, Schmied and Brown, 2009), are intended to address precisely this problem, and have been applied very successfully in parts of the European automotive industry.

The tenth principle, 'eliminate slogans, exhortations and numerical quotas', is again more of a cultural than a quantitative statement. Here, Deming is suggesting that these features may act more to vex the staff than encourage them. His argument is simple: if, through the use of SPC, the 'special causes' of failure related to individual machines and workers have been removed, then all other causes of failure relate to the system itself. These are seen as the responsibility of management, so no amount of slogans, exhortations and quotas will have any positive effect. Instead, Deming (1986: 67) suggests they will 'generate frustration and resentment'. This principle clearly links to the second, which requires management to accept their responsibilities.

The eleventh principle, 'eliminate quotas, work standards and management by objectives or numerical goals and substitute leadership', seems to be something of a contradiction. Improvement targets must be an inherent part of measuring and monitoring achievement, and statistical process control provides one form of measurement of achievement. Deming's point here is that if the system is stable, as will be revealed by the control charts, its performance cannot be improved by the setting of targets, only by changes to the system. As with slogans and exhortations, Deming sees the setting of targets and quotas as potentially both meaningless and divisive, unless accompanied by a specific action plan to improve the process. This may well mean reappraising what the system is designed to achieve.

The removal of barriers that rob people of their right to pride in their work is the twelfth principle. Here, Deming distinguishes management and workers from each other. He sees that annual appraisal or merit review focuses the attention of management on the matters that will be covered in the appraisal or merit system. He implies that they will strive to achieve those things regardless of the impact on quality or productivity. They will do the right thing by the appraisal system, not by the customer.

Deming sees the workers as being constrained by uncertainty of employment; by lack of definition as to what constitutes acceptable workmanship; by poor quality materials, tools and machines; and by ineffective supervision and management. He suggests that if these aspects are corrected, quality products will follow. Deming (1986: 85) suggests, 'Give the work force a chance to work with pride, and the 3 per cent that apparently don't care will erode itself by peer pressure.' He seems to ignore the idea that the whole organization of many factories, based on the principles of classical management theory, is established, whether or not intentionally, to remove pride in achievement from the workers by fragmenting tasks.

The thirteenth principle is to institute a vigorous education and self-improvement programme. This is Deming's recognition that if the organization is continuously to improve, the people must also continuously improve. He suggests that future competitive advantage will be achieved through application of knowledge, a conclusion with which there can be little argument.

The fourteenth and final principle is to put everyone to work to achieve the transformation. This suggests that the whole programme can only be successful if a total approach is taken. This will require a strong, unified and cohesive culture within the organization, with commitment from top to bottom. Such a culture can only be achieved when the behaviour of management is consistent with their words, that is, when they 'walk the talk'.

Taken together, these principles can be summarized as proposing wholesale attitudinal change throughout the organization (a qualitative approach), supported where appropriate by reliance on validated statistical analysis (quantitative).

To enable the principles to be implemented, Deming proposed a seven-point action plan. This action plan is perhaps best interpreted as a series of statements about what to do, rather than the more important how to do it.

W. Edwards Deming:

Point 1) Management must agree on the meaning of the quality programme, its implications and the direction to take.

Point 2) Top management must accept and adopt the new philosophy.

Point 3) Top management must communicate the plan and the necessity for it to the people in the organization.

Point 4) Every activity must be recognised as a step in a process and the customers of that process identified. The customers are responsible for the next stage of the process.

Point 5) Each stage must adopt the "Deming" or "Shewhart" Cycle - Plan, Do, Check, Action - as the basis of quality improvement.

Point 6) Team working must be engendered and encouraged to improve inputs and outputs. Everyone must be enabled to contribute to this process.

Point 7) Construct an organization for quality with the support of knowledgeable statisticians.

Figure 6.5 The seven-point action plan.

The first three points clearly focus attention on the top management group, and are based on attitudes and communication. They suggest that this group must understand what they are trying to achieve, commit themselves to a successful outcome, and then communicate to subordinates throughout the organization why this is necessary. This has distinct overtones of Crosby's more directly evangelical approach, and reflects what may be thought of as the ethical aspect of the programme: the need for quality to be embraced in the values and beliefs of *all* members of the organization. It can surely be agreed that if the management are not wholly committed to the programme, and are unable, or unwilling, to communicate it effectively to the workforce – who must similarly accept it – it will not work.

The fourth point recognizes the process-based work flow of most organizations, and calls for the processes to be divided into stages. Each stage becomes a clear task, with the recipients of its outputs being treated as its customers. Thus at every stage there are customers whose needs must be identified and satisfied. This can be seen as an attempt to overcome the problem of workers in many processes, for example in the manufacture of sub-assemblies. These staff are often unaware of customers and do not recognize the sub-assembly as a product in its own right, but rather as a part of a larger product which perhaps they never see. It is suggested that this shift of emphasis enables workers to take a pride in their work that is otherwise absent.

The fifth point is simply to implement continuous improvement at every stage through the PDCA cycle. Achievement of implementation in this way implies acceptance, by both management and workers within each process, of responsibility for the process. This in turn implies that higher management must allow others within the organization authority to develop and implement the changes.

The sixth point, participation in teamwork to improve all inputs and outputs, can be seen to operate at several levels. First, a team culture must be developed within each process to improve it internally. Second, since changes in one area may have implications in another, a team culture must be engendered between process owners (the management) to enable effective communication between them. Third, to be truly effective, a means of sharing and developing improvements across processes must be developed; this links the whole programme back to top management.

The seventh point, construction of an organization for quality, is perhaps a further development of the third part of stage six, improvement across processes. The requirement is to build an organization which reflects and nurtures the achievement of quality. Deming suggests the use of knowledgeable statisticians to support this aspect, perhaps reflecting his own background. It is useful to go well beyond this, and propose the support of a multidisciplined team of management scientists and experts, such as cyberneticians, psychologists, statisticians, and accountants to work with the management team in pursuit of the programme. This emphasizes the collaborative nature of achieving quality. It is not suggested that management scientists develop and impose a programme of change; this would almost certainly be doomed to failure. Rather, it is suggested that management and workers should be responsible for the whole programme, having both control and ownership. The role of the management scientists is to use their expertise in a supportive, guiding manner, as experts within the team.

The introduction to Deming's approach is now complete. Statistical process control and methodologies for implementing quality will be addressed in the appropriate chapters. This section is concluded by reaffirming the view that while initially Deming's approach was rooted in quantitative methods, it later came to be supported by more qualitative techniques.

6.4 Successes and Failures

While overall Deming can be said to have been very successful in his achievements, in fact there have been both successes and failures. His movement into Japan, for example, was to some extent a result of the early rejection of his ideas by US managements. This perhaps reflects the maxim that 'a prophet is not without honour save in his own country'. It was only after his substantial successes with Japanese industry that Deming was able once again to turn his attention to the problems of industrial America.

Here, what Flood (1993: 14) calls Deming's fundamentally mechanistic approach ran into strong workforce resistance, from both the managers and the workers. Deming, taking account of these issues, together with matters of reliance on technology, standards of practice and cultural issues, substantially revised his methods. This is reflected in the shift in emphasis from quantitative to qualitative approaches, and in the codification of the 'Seven Deadly Sins'.

Adapting from Flood (1993), the principal strengths of Deming's approach are considered as:

- the systemic logic, particularly the idea of internal customer–supplier relationships;
- management before technology;
- emphasis on management leadership;
- the sound statistical approach;
- awareness of different socio-cultural contexts.

Significant weaknesses are also recognized:

- lack of a well-defined methodology;
- the work is not adequately grounded in human relations theory;
- as with Crosby, the approach will not help in an organization with a biased power structure.

Reviewing the strengths, the value of the systemic and logical approach cannot be denied; put simply, it is an organized and systematic, rather than chaotic, approach. The 'Plan, Do, Check, Action' cycle as a mechanism for organizational learning is recognized in other areas of management as a learning cycle. Handy (1985), for example, refers to a process of:

- questioning and conceptualization – fundamental parts of effective planning;
- experimentation – trying out ideas, the testing and evaluation of hypotheses;
- consolidation – the alteration of habits, the basis for future action.

Handy sees this as the basis of human learning, leading to continuous personal improvement. It is unsurprising that a similar process works for organizations which, after all, have people as their fundamental organizational units. This cycle will be seen echoed in Chapter 20 on organizational learning.

Deming's prioritization of management before technology represents a reversal of the attitudes of many managers. The British adage that 'a bad workman always blames his tools' recognizes that the tendency for most managers is to look for external rather than internal factors as being responsible for failure. If, as Deming suggests, 94 per cent of problems belong to the management, then acceptance of responsibility by them is a primary step in enabling change. Equally, even the worst tools can be made to perform better in the hands of a good workman, but a bad workman will not achieve good performance, however good the tools.

The recognition of the importance of leadership and motivation can be seen to reflect the development of human relations theory as a major strand of management thinking, although Deming does not draw heavily on the body of knowledge that became established in that area during his productive years.

Regarding the strong quantitative base, perhaps Flood does not go far enough. It is suggested that some form of measurement system, relying on both hard, physical measures, and on softer aspects using techniques from organizational psychology, is fundamental to achievement of quality. A simple attempt to 'do better', will always be followed by questions such as 'How much?' or 'When?' Vagueness on these issues would be expected to have a dispiriting effect on the participants, while a form of achievement target orientation would be motivational. Success is said to breed success, but first of all it must be known that success is being achieved.

The recognition by Deming of different cultural contexts is a vital strength. His failure to draw heavily on the literature of human relations theory for this aspect suggests that his embrace of it was driven by pragmatism rather than desire, perhaps a reluctant recognition that it was necessary to allow the other ideas to work. Nonetheless, the recognition of different cultures, and adaptation to them, are essential in achieving success. Hofstede (1980) produced the principal work in this area. In the context of quality, the recognition needs to go well beyond the country differences highlighted by Hofstede to recognize the particular culture of organizations themselves, and even sections, functions and departments within organizations. These frequently have unique, perhaps very strong, cultural contexts.

Flood's criticism of a lack of a clear Deming method can be seen as reasonably well justified. Like many gurus and experts, Deming suggests what to do, without indicating very precisely how to do it. While perhaps constraining on the one hand, this lack of precision can be seen as potentially dis-emprisoning and empowering. It encourages experimentation and debate within each individual context, to find an approach which will work, rather than using an approach which was developed in another time and context. Perhaps the most important issue is reliance on Deming's principles.

The second weakness having been covered within the strengths, we can examine the third. Deming is criticized for saying nothing about intervention in political and coercive situations, but then perhaps nothing needs to be said. The second principle, and the first three points of the action plan, all call on management to accept their responsibility for quality and productivity, and to embrace a new philosophy. These remarks are targeted directly at the most senior members of the management team, that is, those who hold power in a political or coercive context. If they do not accept responsibility at the outset, they are ignoring the principles, and, by default, not following the Deming method. If they seek to impose a quality approach on others, failure will certainly follow. Deming's whole approach rests on the attitude of management.

6.5 Critical Review

The foundation of Deming's approach can be seen in his statistical background and in his training in the science of physics. These essentially 'hard' sciences, based in scientific method, will have informed the development of his early approaches. It must be acknowledged that they continue to make a major contribution to work in the field of quality.

The principles and practice of SPC have been demonstrated over time to have considerable value to organizations in both the service and manufacturing sectors. They also have value for the workers who use them, providing rapid and personal performance feedback information, enabling them to recognize their own successes and failures, and to take corrective action where appropriate, always provided that the outputs are expressed in a language which they can understand.

Deming's work in relation to the softer issues is considered to be narrow and underdeveloped, failing to take account of much of the thinking in that area over the period of his career. It must, though, be acknowledged that Deming did not claim to be an expert in this area. Nevertheless, the value of his approach could have been further enhanced by a clearer focus on this aspect.

The Plan, Do, Check, Action cycle is a clear directive to both management and workers that achieving continuous improvement is the purpose of the quality activity. This contrasts directly with the overtones of a discrete programme suggested in Crosby's work.

Deming makes quite clear reference to the service sector in his work, but again places much emphasis on quantitative aspects of this area. For example, he refers to aspects such as how long a telephone is out of action before it is repaired. While this is of great importance, of equal importance is the tone of voice that a person uses in answering the telephone when it rings. This may be a stronger determinant of how the customer perceives the level of service quality than the number of times that it rings, or even the words that are said; readers will recall the comment on this issue in the previous chapter.

It is often the case that managers take measurements of the things which are easy to measure, rather than the things which, while difficult to measure, are of greater importance. In a world which relies ever more heavily on telecommunication devices, these aspects, which are more difficult to quantify, will have increasing importance. The reliability and clarity of modern digital telecommunication systems are such that these are no longer significant issues, and many businesses are run entirely through them, for example, telephone-based banking and insurance services. Of increasing importance, then, is tone of voice, since technical issues are less problematic and digital technology makes tone of voice transparent to the listener. The more recent development of video-phone technology and Internet telephony, which are not yet widespread, will have further impacts on this area of service.

It is accepted that Deming has probably made the most substantial contribution to quality management. However, enthusiasm must be tempered with the knowledge that if he had provided a clearer method, a more explicit and developed recognition of the human aspects, and a precise focus on what constitutes quality of service in the contemporary world, the value of his work would have been enhanced.

Summary

This chapter has presented the main strands of the work of W. Edwards Deming through the five-point critical framework. Readers wishing to develop their knowledge further should read the relevant chapters in Part Four of this book, and refer to Deming's own work, in particular, *Out of the Crisis* (1986).

KEY LEARNING POINTS

W. Edwards Deming's definition of quality: a function of continuous improvement, based on reduction in variation around the desired output

Seven Deadly Sins:

- lack of constancy;
- short-term profit focus;
- performance appraisal;

- job-hopping;
- use of visible figures only;
- excessive medical costs;
- excessive liability costs.

Five key beliefs:
quantification, recognition of failure causes, systematic approach, continuous improvement, constancy.

Principal methods:
fourteen principles for transformation, the seven-point plan.

Question

Deming suggests that 94 per cent of quality problems are a function of the design of the system (the common causes of error). What actions can be taken to resolve these?

7   Armand V. Feigenbaum

Quality is simply a way of managing a business organization
(N. Logothetis, *Managing for Total Quality*, 1992)

Introduction

Armand Feigenbaum originated the approach to quality known as Total Quality Control (TQC), which has a clear industrial focus. After completing a doctorate at MIT (Massachusetts Institute of Technology), Feigenbaum joined the General Electric Company where he was manager of worldwide manufacturing operations and quality control before becoming president of General Systems Company. His book, *Total Quality Control*, completed while he was still a doctoral student, and his other works, were discovered by the Japanese in the early 1950s. He was also involved with them through his business contacts with Hitachi and Toshiba.

Bendell (1989: 15) states that Feigenbaum presented a case for a 'systematic, or total approach to quality', and it is argued by Bank (1992: xv) that Feigenbaum was the first to do so. Logothetis (1992: 94) suggests that to Feigenbaum 'quality is simply a way of managing a business organization', while Gilbert (1992: 22) concurs with that and adds that Feigenbaum sees 'quality improvement as the single most important force leading to organisational success and growth'.

Feigenbaum's contribution has been widely recognized. He was founding chairman of the International Academy for Quality and is a past president of the American Society for Quality Control, which awarded him the Edwards Medal and Lancaster Award for his international contribution to quality and productivity (Bendell, 1989: 15).

7.1 Philosophy

Feigenbaum's philosophy is clearly founded in his early idea of the 'total' approach, reflecting a systemic attitude of mind. He saw it as fundamental to quality improvement that all functions in an organization should be involved in the quality process, and that quality should be built in to the product rather than failure being inspected out. He defines quality as: 'best for the customer use and selling price', and quality control as 'an effective method for co-ordinating the quality maintenance and quality improvement efforts of the various groups in an organization so as to enable production at the most economical levels which allow for full customer satisfaction'.

Reflecting on Feigenbaum's approach, there is no difficulty in accepting the systemic nature of his philosophy. While the work of both Deming and Juran can be interpreted in a systemic manner, Feigenbaum is explicit from the outset that this is vital. In the contemporary, complex world of organizations, there is every need to manage from a systemic perspective – recognizing and dealing with interactions across internal and external organizational boundaries, and at all levels within them, as well as with the suppliers, customers and other stakeholders in the enterprise.

The issue of building quality in can also be addressed here. This recognizes that organizations do not simply manufacture products; they also design and develop them. Feigenbaum appears to be suggesting that many quality problems can be eradicated from both the products and the manufacturing process by paying attention to the quality issue from the conception of the idea, right through to delivery of the first and subsequent items. Basic design techniques here might include colour coding wires, so that electronic products cannot be incorrectly wired, or varying bolt positions in otherwise apparently symmetrical pieces of metal so that they can only be mounted correctly.

Looking at Feigenbaum's definition of quality, two constraints are discovered which have not previously been detected: 'customer use' and 'selling price'. The first of these is perhaps no different from Deming's 'needs of the consumer', or Crosby's 'conformance to requirements', but it suggests a constraint rather than an ideal to aim for. It seems to imply that there are, perhaps, limits to useful quality. The issue of selling price clearly indicates that for any given price Feigenbaum perceives limitations to the expectations of quality. This can perhaps be interpreted as saying that a quality differential, in terms of perhaps longevity, performance or reliability between, say, a car costing US$10,000 and one costing US$100,000, is to be expected and is acceptable. This also implies developing an understanding of the real use to which a customer will put the product.

Feigenbaum's definition of quality control emphasizes the integral nature of the quality process, stressing 'co-ordination' of maintenance and improvement efforts across 'groups'. It is notable that he does not say 'functions' or 'departments'. This can be interpreted as a recognition of the human relations aspects of organizations.

To summarize Feigenbaum's philosophy, a commitment to a systemic, 'total' approach, and an emphasis on designing for quality and involving all departments, is evident. Supporting this is recognition of, and reliance on, the human aspects of the organization, with statistical methods being used as necessary. This contrasts quite sharply with the greater statistical emphasis in the work of Deming.

7.2 Assumptions

Feigenbaum's apparent assumptions about the world reveal a different understanding to that of the gurus already reviewed.

First is his explicit assumption of a world composed of systems. He works with the interrelationships that he perceives to exist between all aspects within the organization, and, importantly, in its environment or market. He recognizes the contribution made by suppliers and the constraints, particularly on performance expectations and price, imposed by customers.

The systemic view is clear again in his second assumption, that human relationships are a basic issue in quality achievement. This concurs with the developments in management thinking being made by the human relations school that were occurring at the time of his early work.

In these assumptions, he clearly focuses attention on the whole enterprise, from suppliers to users, through every function and to all the groups who are involved in it. The development in more recent times of global businesses serving global markets, of ever more complex and interdependent relationships between organizational, social and individual well-being, and the emergence of many more virtual organizations based on strategic partnerships, leads to the conclusion that this systemic view must be sustained.

An organization can today be more clearly seen to exist within an ecosystem, comprised of economic and social relationships, in which it will ultimately either thrive or become extinct. Although not explicitly referring to adaptation of the organization, Feigenbaum's commitment to 'full customer satisfaction', implies constant awareness of customer needs and expectations within the organization and the need for change to satisfy them.

Vignette 7.1 Great North Eastern Railway (GNER) – Applying Kobayashi's Twenty Keys

GNER decided to adopt Iwao Kobayashi's (1995) *20 Keys to Workplace Improvement* at Kings Cross station and Bounds Green train servicing depot. This was an interesting departure in an industry which remains very conservative and resistant to change.

The programme was launched with a 'Quick Wins' project, where a cross-functional team, supported by limited consultancy, were invited to consider how the Kings Cross and Bounds Green organizations could work better together. They quickly decided to work on 'right [on] time every time', that is, getting trains to depart on time with the correct catering stores and also ensuring that they were fully clean. Benchmarking their ideas, they adopted a pit-stop approach they called 'Project Schumacher'.

The team discovered that many of the problems associated with overnight servicing were caused by late despatch of trains from Kings Cross to Bounds Green. This happened because station staff had no understanding of the consequences of tardy processes at Kings Cross. The project was successful, partly because it was empowered to investigate and act on issues without having constantly to seek approval from more senior managers. This energized the team. It was notable how energized the team became and how hard they worked to deliver improvements to operating practices.

The improvements were noted both within GNER and by external stakeholders within the infrastructure body, who commented that it was like 'watching a Formula 1 racing team'!

At Bounds Green, the 'twenty keys' were introduced throughout the depot and resulted in increased productivity, a better working environment, and improved quality. Staff satisfaction improved, as did attendance. There was a significant improvement in cleanliness and output, and a massive reduction in waste of stores. The major servicing schedules for locomotives were reassessed, using process-mapping techniques which enabled improved productivity and better work flow.

In the travel centre at Kings Cross, staff were consulted about changes to working practices. A standard layout was adopted for the workstations, which led to improved service standards for customers and reduced queuing times. The introduction of a nightly cleaning regime for the ticket printers, carried out by the existing night staff, reduced faults by over 40 per cent.

Despite initial cynicism, most staff came to realize that the 'twenty keys' delivered improvements to their work and to the company.

Feigenbaum further assumes that continuous improvement is both desirable and achievable. Referring again to his definition of quality, we can see the potential for conflict and contradiction. For example, if customer expectations on performance and price are met, then quality, by his definition, has been achieved. However, unless the process of total quality control (TQC) ends, further improvement will arise. This, in turn, implies a need for the organization to interact with its customers, aiming to alter their expectations of quality, perhaps as suggested by Galbraith (1974). There is a danger, therefore, that, as with Crosby, Feigenbaum's approach can be interpreted as a finite, ends-oriented and discrete programme, whereas his intent appears to have been for continuous improvement.

7.3 Methods

While Flood (1993: 35) reduces Feigenbaum's philosophy to a four-step approach, these steps (Figure 7.1) should be viewed as a simplification of his overall method.

Armand V. Feigenbaum:

Step 1) Set quality standards;
Step 2) Appraise conformance to standards;
Step 3) Act when standards are not met;
Step 4) Plan to make improvements.

Figure 7.1 Armand V. Feigenbaum's four steps to quality.

These steps may certainly be seen to capture the fundamental essence of Feigenbaum's approach, which is intended to lead to a 'Total Quality System'. This is defined by Bendell (1989: 16) as:

The agreed companywide and plantwide operating work structure, documented in effective, integrated technical and managerial procedures, for guiding the co-ordinated actions of the people, the machines and the information of the company and plant in the best and most practical ways to assure customer quality satisfaction and economical costs of quality.

The Weberian, bureaucratic overtones and dangers inherent in this definition are quite clear. A heavy reliance on documentation and integration of procedures, and on co-ordinating the people, machines and information, certainly present an opportunity to those 'keener on talking about work than doing any' (Beckford, 1993). The recent ISO 9000: 2000 challenges this notion of documentation, with its shift from compliance with documented procedures to a focus on customer satisfaction and continuous improvement, and with particular attention paid to active management of skills – a change which Feigenbaum would surely have welcomed. It is fair to say that contemporary information technology supports a radically different approach to the availability of information than was possible when Feigenbaum formulated his approach.

To counter the danger, in the first sentence Feigenbaum used the word 'agreed'. This stresses that everyone must be committed to the design of the organization through effective communication. However while proposing that gradual development of the programme is preferred, little is said about how agreement is achieved which permits scope for either autocratic or democratic processes to be employed. While Feigenbaum proposes participation as a means of harnessing the contribution of people and encouraging a sense of belonging, it remains the case that the approach need not be used in this participative manner.

A further tool is the measurement of what Feigenbaum calls 'operating quality costs'. These are divided into four self-explanatory categories, and have been met before in Chapter 3:

- prevention costs, including quality planning;
- appraisal costs, including inspection costs;
- internal failure costs, including costs arising from scrap and rework;
- external failure costs, including warranty costs and complaints.

It can be seen how Feigenbaum's concept of total quality extends from product development right through to product use, that is, product quality in the hands of the consumer. Bendell (1989: 16) states that:

> reductions in operating quality costs result from setting up a total quality system for two reasons:
>
> 1. Lack of existing effective customer-orientated customer standards may mean current quality of products is not optimal given use.
> 2. Expenditure on prevention costs can lead to a several fold reduction in internal and external failure costs.

The proposal overall is that by measuring quality at every critical stage, the total costs of running the organization will be reduced. A similar concept is met in the food manufacturing industry, which uses a system called Hazard Analysis Critical Control Points (HACCP) to evaluate and ensure food product quality and safety at points of risk. This would include aspects such as temperature. If, for example, a product must be boiled then the HACCP system would test it to ensure that boiling point is actually reached. The emphasis on design again stresses the importance to Feigenbaum of designing quality into the product.

Overall, Feigenbaum's approach is best seen as part of the *kaizen* management practices, which are oriented towards management responsibility and involve effective team-working across the organization. These tools will be examined in more depth in the appropriate chapters.

7.4 Successes and Failures

Feigenbaum's approach has undoubtedly been successful, and has been adopted in whole, or in part, by a number of organizations. There is little doubt that his recognition of quality as a way of running an organization, rather than as a secondary activity, was a major breakthrough to thinking in this area. Yet even today, many organizations continue to consider quality as an added extra rather than a fundamental of organizational effectiveness. Recent experience with a number of organizations internationally has shown that many continue to focus on 'badge-hunting' through a quality management system, rather than on organizational survival through quality products or services. Finally, his systemic concept of 'total', that is, quality running throughout the organization, from its inputs to its outputs, has immense value.

Flood (1993: 36) again provides a summary of the principal strengths and weaknesses of Feigenbaum's approach, from which the following is adapted. He sees the main strengths as that:

- there is a total or whole approach to quality control;
- there is emphasis on the importance of management;
- socio-technical systems thinking is taken into account;
- participation is promoted.

Principal weaknesses identified are that:

- the work is systemic but not complementary;
- the breadth of management theory is recognized but not unified;
- the political or coercive context is not addressed.

It can be added to this critique that the industrial orientation of the approach provides little of real value for service-based organizations. Similarly, it could be said that, as with Deming, there is a lack of clarity of method; ample instruction in what to do is not supported by guidance on how to do it.

The necessity and contribution of the systemic view proposed has already been acknowledged. Similarly, the focus on the importance of management to the process is supported, although as Bendell (1989: 16) suggests, 'modern quality control is seen by Feigenbaum as stimulating and building up *operator responsibility* and interest in quality'.

While this is achieved through management commitment to the programme, the need for management to *sell* the ideas is stressed, suggesting a certain resistance by employees to accept the concepts of quality. While fully accepting the value of a participative approach, the question has to be raised again: how is such participation to be achieved? Even Flood's choice of the word 'harnessing' in respect of individual contributions is suggestive of a less than wholehearted commitment, having overtones of compulsion.

Looking at the weaknesses, Feigenbaum's work says nothing about the identification and selection of tools, whether management theories or systems approaches, which are most appropriate for a particular organizational or national context. For contemporary managers, this issue is of great importance. Many organizations are globally based, and to achieve agreement, which Feigenbaum requires amongst the top management, account must be taken of the varying cultures and expectations of the participants. An approach which works well in Hong Kong may fail completely in Tokyo, Los Angeles or London.

Finally, Flood's comment that nothing is said about political or coercive contexts is valid. Feigenbaum's assumption that people can and will work together for the improvement of the organization and its outputs is clear in his work. However, his recognition of the need to *sell* the total quality concept perhaps suggests that a degree of political or coercive pressure may, for him legitimately, be brought to bear to achieve the end result. That said, it is perhaps a little unfair to criticize someone for not offering a solution to a problem he did not set out to address.

7.5 Critical Review

There appear to be three basic ideas relating to Feigenbaum's work: his acceptance of the systems paradigm; his belief in appropriate measurement; and his recognition of participation as a means of developing and encouraging support for change and enabling creativity. Feigenbaum's strong academic background in issues of quality control, supported by his extensive practical managerial experience, undoubtedly provided a substantial platform for the further development and successful application of his ideas with considerable success.

The apparent lack of a well-developed, clear methodology telling managers how to proceed with his approach is a major drawback. It is suspected that personal and management styles are much greater factors in the success or failure of a TQC initiative than is normally recognized. Adoption by the most senior management of a collaborative, team-based working pattern is not easily achieved or maintained, especially in a world where, predominantly, rewards are calculated against personal, rather than team, achievement.

Functionally structured companies, for example, normally have power bases within each function. If these power bases are strong, they may resist the perceived loss of individual or function power that arises from any other orientation. Companies are often heard of which are 'production led', 'marketing led' or 'accounting led'. These are companies which are dominated by a particular power group within a professional specialization. They appear to perceive the world from a particular professional standpoint, and in doing so, perhaps undervalue the contribution of other professions. Adoption of a team-based approach where each profession is valued for its contribution to the whole, perhaps in the form of a project or matrix management system, is unlikely. Similar comments can be made about issues such as sexual orientation, gender and race; for example, consider the privileged position of the White Anglo-Saxon Protestants (WASPs) in the USA, Oxbridge graduates in the UK, and *Bumiputras* (indigenous Malaysians) in Malaysia. Professional and other biases must be overcome in the creation of organizations based on expertise; Feigenbaum says nothing of how to achieve this.

The quantitative aspects of Feigenbaum's approach are welcome. Reliance on statistics 'where appropriate' is a useful guide, encouraging managers to use discretion in their choice of measurements. This contrasts sharply with the strong emphasis on measurement proposed by Deming. Feigenbaum is quite selective about what it is useful to measure and when. Like Deming, he proposes, through the four-way division of operating quality costs, a form of customer chain analysis which can be seen to be helpful, not simply in identifying the costs of quality but, very importantly, where they arise.

It is accepted that Feigenbaum has made a substantial contribution to work in the field of quality, and certain contemporary developments in quality management carry powerful influences from his work. However, enthusiasm for his approach must be tempered by recognizing some weaknesses with respect to methodology and cultural context, and it is important to understand that his work does not go beyond the industrial sector.

Summary

This chapter has introduced the principal strands of the work of Armand Feigenbaum, presenting and reviewing his philosophy, assumptions, methods and successes and failures. Readers may wish to refer to Feigenbaum's own work *Total Quality Control* (1986) to enhance and further develop their understanding.

KEY LEARNING POINTS

Armand V. Feigenbaum's definition of quality: a way of running a business organization

Key beliefs:
systems thinking, relevant measurement, participation.

Principal methods:
the four steps to quality, operating quality costs.

Question

The chapter suggests difficulties might arise from Feigenbaum's definition of a 'Total Quality System' with its 'Weberian, bureaucratic overtones'. Critically review Feigenbaum's work in the context of this suggestion.

8 Kaoru Ishikawa

'At last,' he said, '*el pueblo*'

(Salvador Allende, President of Chile, in Beer, 1981: 258)

Introduction

Kaoru Ishikawa, who died in 1989, started his career as a chemist, held a doctorate in engineering, and was Emeritus Professor at Tokyo University. Bank (1992: 74) cites him as the 'Father of Quality Circles', and as a founder of the Japanese quality movement. He became involved in quality issues in 1949 through the Union of Japanese Scientists, and Engineers (JUSE), and subsequently became a worldwide lecturer and consultant on quality. Gilbert (1992: 23) suggests that Ishikawa was the first guru to 'recognize that quality improvement is too important to be left in the hands of specialists'. Ishikawa's writings explaining his approach include the *Guide to Quality Control* (1986) and *What is Total Quality Control? The Japanese Way* (1985), which have both been translated into English. Ishikawa was widely honoured for his work, receiving the Deming, Nihon Keizai Press, and Industrial Standardization prizes, and the Grant Award from the American Society for Quality Control.

8.1 Philosophy

Gilbert (1992: 23) and Logothetis (1992: 95) see the philosophical roots of Ishikawa's work in the concept of 'Company-Wide Quality'. Ishikawa himself, cited by Bendell (1989: 18) said: 'The results of these company-wide Quality Control activities are remarkable, not only in ensuring the quality of industrial products but also in their great contribution to the company's overall business.'

Bendell (1989) proposes that Ishikawa defines quality as meaning 'not only the quality of the product, but also of after sales service, quality of management, the company itself and the human being'.

Flood (1993: 33) interprets Ishikawa's approach as involving 'vertical and horizontal co-operation'. Thus, the approach takes account of communication and co-operation between different levels of managers, supervisors and workers, and from suppliers to customers. Ishikawa's first belief is that everyone involved in, or affected by, the company and its operations should be involved in the quality programme. This is similar to the 'total' approach advocated by Feigenbaum, which has been reviewed in Chapter 7.

The extent of involvement proposed is also significant. Ishikawa asks that the programme be not just company-wide (and beyond), but that it involve *active* participation

– as opposed to passive tolerance. His approach to participation emphasizes greater worker involvement and motivation, which Bendell (1989: 19) sees as being created through:

* an atmosphere where employees are continuously looking to resolve problems;
* greater commercial awareness;
* a change of shop floor attitude in aiming for ever increasing goals.

These strands stress three words, all of them qualitative rather than quantitative: atmosphere, awareness, and attitude. They are cultural requirements which have direct implications for the behaviour of management.

An 'atmosphere where employees are continuously looking to resolve problems' implies acceptance by management that:

* workers have the ability to recognize both problems and solutions;
* management will either: accept the need for change and implement proposals, or explain why a proposed change is not possible or desirable in a way which maintains the employees' enthusiasm.

A 'greater commercial awareness' imposes two responsibilities on management. The first is to facilitate training and education for the workforce in this area. The second is to provide accurate, meaningful and timely data to the workforce regarding the company's performance, as well as that of its competitors. In this regard, although commercial awareness is stressed, these matters should be considered equally important in a public sector or not-for-profit organization, which, rather than focusing on profit, should be focused on delivering the maximum level of service within a constrained resource; that is, value for money.

The third strand, 'a change of shop floor attitude' towards a focus on ever-increasing goals – the culture of continuous improvement – again implies management responsibility. Management must align their behaviours and words to enable such a culture. Any inconsistency between words and actions will be destructive. Deming's concern about 'exhortations' is important here, as well as Crosby's promotion through slogans and platitudes.

Clearly, Ishikawa believed that effective participation, like effective communication, is a two-way street and, as suggested by Hagima Karatsu, Managing Director of Matsushita Communication (cited by Bendell, 1989: 19), 'creative co-operation' between people is an absolute requirement for a quality organization.

A third element to Ishikawa's work is the emphasis on direct, simple communication. Bendell (1989: 17) states that Ishikawa saw 'open group communication' as critical, particularly in the use of his tools for problem-solving. A fundamental part of communication for Ishikawa seems to have been an emphasis on simplicity in his methods. For example, the book *Guide to Quality Control* was deliberately written as a 'non-sophisticated' text (Bendell, 1989: 17), and Bank (1992: 75) suggests that Ishikawa worked in a 'straightforward manner'. Logothetis (1992: 95) stresses that Ishikawa concentrated on 'simple statistical techniques for data collection and presentation'. The requirement for simplicity covers both the qualitative and quantitative issues.

The emphasis on simplicity and using the language of the shop floor is considered to have an empowering effect. The workers, having been trained in the appropriate methods, are not obliged to use obscure or arcane terminology. Management are unable to hide behind complex approaches and sophisticated language, which often seem to betray a lack of real understanding. Since training is given to all levels of employee, a common quality language is spoken by all, which in turn aids and enhances communication.

Three principal strands can be identified in Ishikawa's philosophy. First, in company with Feigenbaum, is the systemic or holistic approach advocated by 'Company Wide Quality', an all-embracing view. Second, is participation: active and creative co-operation between those affected. The third element is the emphasis on communication through two strands of thinking: simplicity of analysis and method, and commonality of language.

8.2 Assumptions

Ishikawa's apparent assumptions about the world will now be explored.

It can be seen that Ishikawa's first assumption is concerned with interrelatedness, a 'total', or systems, view. He explicitly recognizes that every aspect of the organization, and the relevant parts of the environment, must be considered. As with Feigenbaum, it is difficult to argue with his approach, although whether Ishikawa's techniques and methods may be thought of as systemic will be considered in the next section, since some of these seem to rely heavily on a reductionist perspective.

Ishikawa's second assumption is that a fully participative approach can be adopted. This implies a belief that every individual within the organization can, and will, commit him- or herself to addressing the quality issue. This suggests that a quality 'religion' or creed must become established, and that the achievement of higher quality becomes a superordinate goal, overriding all others as a requirement for organizational success. The primacy of this goal, while perhaps accommodating the requirements of the management or even the owners or shareholders, seems to assume that the primary goals of the workforce will be congruent with those of the organization. However, little is said about how such a state can be achieved, and, for example, Bendell (1989: 19) says that '[quality] circle members receive no direct financial reward for their improvements'. Commitment to quality, then, very like religious belief, is considered to be its own reward. This can be contrasted with Crosby's dictum to reward those who contribute to the quality programme.

A third, implied, assumption is that the quality activity takes place in an organizational environment which is free from political or power relations between participants. While this may be an admirable ideal, it must be perceived as being unrealistic. Both Eastern and Western organizations are subject to internal issues of power and potential coercion. These may be dominant or subordinate issues in the management of the organization, but they nonetheless exist. Ishikawa is silent on this aspect and how it may be addressed, perhaps reflecting the strength of his own position, or a lack of awareness of the problems faced by others, less educated, or in less privileged positions. Alternatively, it may simply reflect the strongly collective nature of the Japanese value system.

The fourth assumption, effective communication, is to some extent associated with the second. Participation relies on effective communication for its success. While the development of a common 'language' for discussing quality issues throughout the company is considered to be a substantial benefit in this regard, it is still possible that communication will be inhibited by cultural or political issues which prevent viewpoints from being expressed. For example, respect for age or status, or fear of loss of face, may prevent an open exchange of views. In such a case, no real communication takes place and the 'loser' in the transaction, who may have a valid viewpoint, is not heard.

Finally, we can turn to the assumption that 'simplicity' in technique and method is useful. While acknowledging that the sophistication of tools must match that of the people who work with them, Ishikawa's work to some extent may be seen as undervaluing or underestimating the people in the organization, in assuming that they can only cope with simple concepts and methods.

If the complexity of life of an individual is considered, in either the West or the East, it must be recognized that the majority of people deal extremely well with a highly complex existence. For example, coping with accommodation requirements, raising children and managing families (surely the ultimate management challenges), organizing pensions and health matters, dealing with state bureaucracies, even driving a car, require complex problem-solving, communication, and organizational skills. These skills are rarely expressly articulated and acknowledged, but nonetheless they exist and are used for the most part very well. To assume, as Ishikawa appears to, that everything must be simplified, is perhaps arrogant. To forget that starting from simple skills that we all acquire as children we can develop, through education and experience, the ability to handle greater complexity, is to underestimate the potential of the workforce, and perhaps sow the seeds of future discontent.

Another assumption apparently being made is that problems of quality will be tractable when examined, using simple methods and approaches. Products and services are considered by many to be becoming more complex, as are the environments in which organizations exist and the organizations themselves. There are increasing numbers of interrelationships between factors; at the same time, there are perhaps more factors to be considered. The complexity of any situation may be suggested to be increasing through these two prime driving forces. Experience suggests that simple problem-solving approaches are unlikely to be adequate in these circumstances. Other, more sophisticated but not necessarily less accessible, tools must be used. Despite their increasing availability and prominence, especially in Western nations during Ishikawa's time, he does not appear to have taken account of them. Some, as will be seen later in this book, reflect values in relation to the workforce which accord well with those of Ishikawa and would have, perhaps, enhanced his approach.

8.3 Methods

Ishikawa's overarching method is 'Company-Wide Quality Control'. This he sees as being supported by the 'quality circles' technique, and the 'seven tools of quality control'. These will be dealt with in turn.

Company-Wide Quality Control has already largely been addressed as the founding philosophy of Ishikawa's approach, and deals with organizational aspects. It is seen as embracing all departments and functions, and uses the tools which will be described in the following pages. Bendell (1989) suggests that fifteen effects arise from this approach (Figure 8.1).

While acknowledging that these are benefits, it cannot be agreed that they are necessarily consequent upon the Company-Wide Quality Control approach being adopted. Perhaps, as Logothetis (1992: 96) suggests, 'kaizen consciousness [implied

Kaoru Ishikawa:

Effect 1) Product quality is improved and becomes uniform. Defects are reduced;

Effect 2) Reliability of goods is improved;

Effect 3) Cost is reduced;

Effect 4) Quantity of production is increased, and it becomes possible to make rational production schedules;

Effect 5) Wasteful work and rework are reduced;

Effect 6) Technique is established and improved;

Effect 7) Expenses for inspection and testing are reduced;

Effect 8) Contracts between vendor and vendee are rationalized.

Effect 9) The sales market is enlarged;

Effect 10) Better relationships are established between departments;

Effect 11) False data and reports are reduced;

Effect 12) Discussions are carried out more freely and democratically;

Effect 13) Meetings are operated more smoothly;

Effect 14) Repairs and installations of equipment and facilities are done more rationally;

Effect 15) Human relations are improved.

Figure 8.1 Kaoru Ishikawa's fifteen effects of company-wide quality control.

within Ishikawa's work] can only be established when management changes the corporate culture', an area which is not discussed by Ishikawa.

Quality circles are Ishikawa's principle method for achieving participation. They comprise between four and twelve workers from the same area of activity, and are led by a workman or supervisor. Their function is to 'identify local problems and recommend solutions' (Gilbert: 92). Bendell (1989: 18) identifies three aims:

- to contribute to the improvement and development of the enterprise;
- to respect human relations and build a happy workshop offering job satisfaction;
- to deploy human capabilities fully and draw out infinite potential.

Gilbert (1992: 92) suggests that there are a number of cornerstones to successful quality circles (Figure 8.2). The first four of these factors apply to every successful quality programme – management at all levels must be committed, and workers must be trained and be willing participants. The 'shared work background' has some limitations, as it may fail to address cross-functional or interdepartmental needs. Solution-orientation is a means of ensuring that quality circles do not simply descend into complaint sessions, where the focus is on what the management, or adjacent processes, can do or cannot do. Considerable benefit can be gained in using Ishikawa's approach, if the notion of the

J. Gilbert:

- Top management support;

- Operational management support and involvement;

- Voluntary participation of the members;

- Effective training of the leader and members;

- Shared work background;

- Solution-oriented approach;

- Recognition of the Quality Circle's efforts;

- Have an agenda, minutes and rotating chairmanship;

- Keep to the time allowed for the meeting;

- Members should inform bosses of meeting times;

- Make sure that Quality Circles are not hierarchical.

- If seniority plays any sort of part you'll find the MD's [CEO] secretary thinks she's too good to attend the regular secretaries Quality Forum.

Figure 8.2 Cornerstones to successful quality circles.

willing participant, and how to encourage willingness, has been addressed. In adversarial cultures, or where loyalty between the organization and its employees is limited, as is often found in Western organizations, such participation is often very unwillingly provided.

Recognition of efforts is a difficult area. If there is only effort and no achievement, should this be recognized? To maintain efforts and encourage further attempts, it is probably valuable to recognize the work done. However, the difference between effort and substantial achievement should also be acknowledged.

Minutes and an agenda provide, in essence, control devices for the circle. They enable the circle to consider what has or has not been achieved since the last meeting; to keep track of implementation of solutions; and to maintain a focus within the circle on innovation rather than reiterating old points. The agenda provides the opportunity both to control the discussion once a meeting has started and, if issued in advance, to give thinking time to the participants before the meeting to consider the issues to be raised. Keeping to time is a matter of good discipline, which will be supported by the previous two items.

Informing bosses of meeting times is both courteous and good communication practice. He or she may wish to attend, or to provide some input to the meeting, either in the form of ideas or implementation progress, or to support the effort in other ways.

Ensuring a non-hierarchical approach will very much depend on the culture and political issues within the organization. If an ethos of equality in problem-solving has genuinely been achieved, there will be little difficulty with this aspect. However, experience of working within quality circles and other team-type environments suggests that hierarchy, of some sort, will very often emerge.

Vignette 8.1 Quality Circles Inaction

In the late 1970s, a retail distributor with several hundred outlets decided to launch a service quality initiative to improve its performance in an increasingly competitive and over-supplied market. The organization, apparently committed to this initiative at its head office, selected quality circles as the driving mechanism to be used at the outlet level.

The senior management of the organization at head office attended training sessions to learn the rules for quality circles, and this training was then extended to the outlet managers themselves. After some time had elapsed, all the training events had been completed and the programme was ready to be launched. Staff were informed by a letter to each outlet from the head office that the organization was to adopt quality circles as a device for improving service quality. The letter further informed them that the local manager would be arranging these events. Other than the outlet managers, no one at the local level was provided with any training whatsoever.

The local managers then called the staff together – at the end of the working day – and informed them that the first meeting of the quality circle would take place at 5 p.m. the following Wednesday. Overtime would not be paid, and all staff were expected to volunteer to join the circle. At the first meeting the rules would be explained, and roles allocated within the circle.

The first meetings took place, at which the managers naturally took the role of chair and explained the purpose of the circles. The meetings were then thrown open to suggestions from the staff to improve service quality. Discussion in one outlet focused on the number of ashtrays in the customer-facing areas: were there enough, not enough, too many? Another focused, perhaps quite usefully, on the issue of opening hours – until the manager ruled the discussion out of order, since opening hours fell beyond the scope of the outlet to change. This was a constraint applied in many outlets to many suggested discussion topics. In most cases, the manager's secretary recorded the discussion and produced minutes. The managers edited these, and despatched the edited version to head office as evidence of the meetings having taken place.

While the organization persisted with these events for around twelve months, no significant or useful ideas emerged or were implemented across the organization. No major changes took place in the organization's systems and procedures which would improve service quality to either internal or external customers. The whole exercise was a waste, although it could be argued that awareness of quality of customer service was raised amongst the staff, perhaps bringing some intangible benefit.

There were perhaps four major mistakes made by the organization in pursuing this quality circles initiative. First, the absolute lack of training for the staff involved. Second, the structure of the circles with managers appointed (or appointing themselves) as quality-control leaders, thus maintaining the hierarchy of decision. Third, the attempt to achieve participation was by unilateral dictat or coercion, quite apart from the staff not being persuaded that there was a problem to solve. Fourth was the failure by the senior management to understand the structure of the enterprise which they managed, a structure which, in effect, determined where problems could be solved. Any large retail organization adopts standardized systems and procedures to ensure continuity and accuracy of service delivery across its outlets. Even in the 1970s, these were increasingly tied to the capabilities of centralized computer networks. The operation of these networks, and their interaction with other organizations in the same industry, controlled large parts of the customer-facing activity, dictating what it was, or was not, possible to deliver. Changes proposed to these systems were ruled out of order by managers, thereby closing off any possible communication to those running the organization of the customer needs as perceived by the staff who actually dealt with those customers. What was possible to change locally was the way in which individual staff members dealt with customers, a change which could not be created through the chosen mechanism but only through individually focused training efforts.

This was a classic case of the senior management of the organization appearing to 'blame' the staff for poor customer service, while blinding – or perhaps deafening – themselves to the potential for improvement which lay only within their own power.

Ishikawa suggests that quality circles should be an integral part of the quality effort, not an isolated approach. They have met with success and failure both in the West and in Japan. Bendell (1989: 19) comments that 'Even in Japan, many Quality Circles have collapsed, usually because of management's lack of interest or excessive intervention.' Both Crosby and Juran are stated to have questioned their effectiveness in the West, and the experience outlined in quality circles inaction (see Vignette 8.1) demonstrates some of the scope for failure. Crosby is reported to consider that quality circles are abused as a cure for poor employee motivation, productivity and quality, while Juran suggests that if an organization's management are not trained in quality, quality circles will have limited effectiveness.

The quantitative techniques of Ishikawa's approach are referred to by Bendell as the 'seven tools of quality control' (Figure 8.3). Taken together, they are a set of pictures of quality, representing in diagrammatic or chart form the quality status of the operation of process being reviewed.

Ishikawa considered that all staff should be trained in these techniques. They will be elaborated in Part Four, as they have a useful role to play in managing quality.

This chapter will examine only the Ishikawa or Fishbone diagram, since this is the only technique that originated with Ishikawa. He developed the approach while at the University of Tokyo, to explain relationships between factors. It subsequently became part of his quality tools portfolio, and has been widely adopted throughout industry.

Kaoru Ishikawa:

Tool 1) Pareto Charts: used to identify the principal causes of problems.

Tool 2) Ishikawa/fishbone diagrams: charts of cause and effect in processes.

Tool 3) Stratification: layer charts which place each set of data successively on top of the previous one.

Tool 4) Check Sheets: to provide a record of quality.

Tool 5) Histograms: graphs used to display frequency of various ranges of values of a quantity.

Tool 6) Scattergraphs: used to help determine whether there is a correlation between two factors.

Tool 7) Control charts: used as a device in Statistical Process Control.

Figure 8.3 Seven tools of quality control.

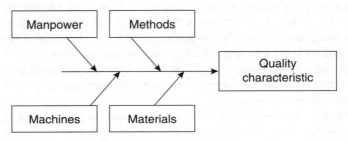

Figure 8.4 The Ishikawa or 'fishbone' diagram.

The Ishikawa diagram, Figure 8.4, is essentially an end or goal-oriented picture of a problem situation. The goal or objective is placed at the head of the fish, and contributing factors categorized. Gilbert (1992: 111) suggests that major categories, such as 'Men, Machines, Materials and Methods', may provide a useful first set of categories. Each of these categories is then subdivided again, the 'fishbones' gaining further ribs and sub-ribs as the whole issue of concern is explored. Other forms of categorization, such as processes, technology, knowledge or information systems, may also be appropriate. The approach is also useful in enabling and encouraging participants to express their views.

The approach does not carry with it any automatic means of prioritization of issues, and ideas emerging are not constrained by any limitations. The pragmatic world of management, however, does impose constraints of issues such as time, technology and capital, and these may affect the value of the approach. Issues emerging, which are not responded to adequately by those responsible, will cause discontent and, perhaps, fragmentation of the quality effort. The diagram can easily be used as a device for apportioning blame rather than enabling improvement.

Equally, the diagram assumes a linear 'cause–effect' chain of events. Such an understanding of any problem is limited, in that it does not address the potential for interrelationships between causes or for the possibility of dynamic or time-related effects. For example, the interrelationship between workers and machines, called ergonomics, can have a substantial impact on the ability to produce a quality product or service, whereas looking at either in isolation may produce no clue as to the cause. A successful 'cure' to any problem may mean making adjustments or changes in a number of places, both to fix the specific problem and ensure that the whole system remains in balance. Often, changing only one aspect can push other aspects to a point where they may fail.

Summarizing Ishikawa's approach, it can be seen to contain both quantitative and qualitative aspects, which, taken together, focus on achieving 'Company-Wide Quality'.

8.4 Successes and Failures

Ishikawa's worldwide reputation and the widespread acceptance of his ideas suggest that his approach has met with considerable success. That he is best known for the Fishbone diagram should not inhibit appreciation of the value of his other works. Similarly, that quality circles have been successful cannot be doubted, notwithstanding the level of failure that has been seen in some organizations. This idea, which has been adopted to the extent that Bendell (1989: 19) reports: 'more than 10 million circle members' in Japan alone, has undoubtedly been useful.

Summarizing from Flood (1993: 34–5) the strengths of Ishikawa's approach are:

- its emphasis on participation;
- the variety of quantitative and qualitative methods;
- its whole system view;
- that quality control circles (QCCs) are relevant to all sectors of the economy.

The main weaknesses can be seen as the following:

- Fishbone diagrams are systematic, but not systemic;
- QCCs depend upon management support;
- there is a failure to address coercive contexts.

Reviewing the strengths: participation and the development of tools usable by the stakeholders are of undeniable value. They enable people at all levels in the organization to make a meaningful contribution, in their own terms, to the process of achieving quality. Promoting creativity and increasing motivation have value, both for the organization and the individual.

The choice of a mixture of methods and tools, which are both qualitative and quantitative, is seen to encourage a broader understanding of the organization than would be achieved with a simple focus on either a single tool, or a purely qualitative, or quantitative approach. The holistic perspective proposed is again supported by the current view that a systemic approach is vital in the contemporary organizational context.

While agreeing that QCCs are relevant to all economic sectors, there remain considerable reservations as to their practical value. It is rare in the West to discover an organization where more than lip-service is paid to the QCC movement. It is very often used as a device for allowing workers to feel that they are involved, but with little real commitment from managers. That is to say that the theory in practice is rarely as successful as the theory in theory.

As for the weaknesses, it is easy to concur with Flood's view that the 'causal chain', or linear view of problems proposed by the Fishbone diagram, is useful but limited. It would perhaps be better to recognize that symptoms of problems are often interacting, and that the relationships are far more complex than the Fishbone approach will reveal.

The second weakness identified by Flood is the failure faced when management is not prepared to listen to the ideas emerging from quality circles, an aspect which has already been covered. In this case, the organization is probably facing the third weakness: that the approach struggles in a political or coercive context. The view has already been espoused that any human system is to some extent political and/or coercive, and a particular tendency currently prevalent in the West seeks someone to blame. In a culture such as this, genuine commitment to, and participation in, the quality issue is unlikely to emerge, since it implies acceptance of responsibility for both successes and failures. In a blame culture, wholehearted participation will not easily occur, since failure is met with some form of disciplinary action or punishment rather than being treated as an opportunity to learn.

8.5 Critical Review

There seem to be three founding elements to Ishikawa's work: an attempt at a holistic view, participation and communication through a common language, and simplicity of approach.

The first of these should be valued highly. As with the work of the other gurus, however, its use is limited by two failures. First, it does not take full account of interrelationships (consider the linear view of the Fishbone diagram). Second, it fails to break down and work across organizational boundaries in any systemic sense. For example, QCCs are focused on a single area, or workshop, rather than being formed along interacting processes. These represent severe limitations of the approach in the contemporary context.

Participation is again highly valued, and the idea of training everybody in the same tools, language, and techniques is a sound method to encourage this. However, it again relies rather too heavily on a willingness to participate, which is often not easily found. The third strand, simplicity, is to be criticized for ignoring the complexity and inter-relationships of organizations.

The roots of Ishikawa's approach can be found in his early training and development as a chemist. That is a science which has traditionally been associated with a reduction-ist scientific method, and is heavily reliant on analysis and fragmentation of problems. This is clearly carried across into the quality sphere, with the use of simple analytical tools and the breaking down of processes into manageable parts.

Similarly, and as with Feigenbaum, there does not emerge from Ishikawa's work an overarching methodology which binds together and integrates all the different strands of his thinking. Thus, while many of the tools and techniques are useful in isolation, there is no clear means of implementing an 'Ishikawa' programme.

This element may itself explain, to some degree, the failure of quality circles in so many organizations. They appear to stand alone as a device for quality improvement, rather than being seen as one part of a holistic process of management leading towards quality improvement. Taken in isolation, they are almost certainly doomed to failure, since changes in management attitudes, generation of a common language, and creation of a common set of problem-solving tools have not been developed to go with them.

Ishikawa appears to have taken account of developments in the human relations school of management, emerging in the West from the works of those such as Mayo, Maslow, and Herzberg. However, he does not seem to have recognized other develop-ments such as the emergence of systems approaches, for example, organizational cyber-netics, soft systems thinking, and the critical systems perspective. Recognition of these approaches would have enhanced and further enriched his already substantial contribution.

Finally, recognition must again be given to the multidimensional approach espoused by Ishikawa. Unlike Deming, his methods are not predominantly quantitative (although he uses these methods widely), but incorporate a substantial qualitative element. Aspects such as attitudinal change, participation, and communication are seen as vital elements in the management process.

Ishikawa's substantial contribution to the quality movement must be recognized, although the lack of a clear methodology is an obvious weakness.

Summary

This chapter has outlined the principal work of Kaoru Ishikawa through the five-point critical review. Interested readers should refer to Ishikawa's own works to develop further their knowledge and understanding.

KEY LEARNING POINTS

Kaoru Ishikawa's definition of quality: quality of product, service, management, the company itself and the human being

Key beliefs:
systemic approach, participation, communication.

Principal methods:
seven tools of quality control, Fishbone diagram, quality circles.

Question

Quality circles are Ishikawa's principle method for achieving participation. Critically review the idea of the quality circle.

9 Joseph M. Juran

... the vital few, the useful many ...

(Joseph M. Juran)

Introduction

Joseph Juran, a naturalized American, died in 2008. He started his initial career as an engineer in 1924, subsequently working as an executive, civil servant, professor, arbitrator, director, and management consultant. His strong professional background supported his first work in the quality field, the *Quality Control Handbook*, which is seen by some, for example, Bendell (1989: 8), as having led to his international pre-eminence in the field of quality. Along with Deming, Juran worked extensively with the Japanese in the 1950s, when the focus of his work was with middle- and high-ranking executives, since he considered that 'quality control should be conducted as an integral part of management control' (Bendell, 1989: 8).

Juran received numerous awards for his work including, again like Deming, the Second Order of the Sacred Treasure by the emperor of Japan, in recognition of his contribution to Japanese quality control and friendship with the USA.

Juran is described by Bendell (1989) as charismatic, by Bank (1992: 70) as 'perhaps the top quality guru', and by Logothetis (1992: 62) as having made 'the greatest contribution to the management literature of any quality professional'. Juran has published twelve books, which have been translated into thirteen languages. Perhaps the most relevant of these is the work entitled *Juran on Planning for Quality* (1988). This is seen as the definitive guide to his thinking on company-wide quality planning.

9.1 Philosophy

Juran's philosophy is perhaps best summed up in the saying, cited by Logothetis (1992: 62), that 'quality does not happen by accident, it has to be planned'. This is reflected in his structured approach to company-wide quality planning, an aspect already met with in the work of other gurus, for example, that of Ishikawa and Feigenbaum. He is considered by Logothetis (1992: 62) and Bendell (1989: 8) to emphasize management's responsibility for quality, with Bendell (1989: 10) quoting him as saying that 'management controllable defects account for over 80% of the total quality problems'. The emphasis of his work is on 'planning, organizational issues, management's responsibility for quality, and the need to set goals and targets for improvement' (Bendell: 1989: 8). Juran's first two beliefs can be derived from this. First, that management are largely responsible for quality. Second, that quality cannot be consistently improved unless the improvement is planned.

Logothetis (1992: 64) considers another aspect to Juran's work: the avoidance of slogans and exhortations. He cites Juran's view that 'the recipe for action should consist of 90% substance and 10% exhortation, not the reverse!' Here, Juran's third belief can be seen: that planned improvement must be specific and measurable. Logothetis sees in this aspect a 'formula for results', which consists of four elements:

- to establish specific goals to be reached, identify what needs to be done, and the specific projects that need to be tackled;
- to establish plans for reaching the goals, provide a structured process for going from here to there;
- to assign clear responsibility for meeting the goals;
- to base the rewards on results achieved, feed back the information, and utilize the lessons learned and the experience gained.

This approach indicates a clear reliance on quantitative methods, rather than on any vague or woolly-minded aspirations to higher quality, what Flood (1993: 19) refers to as Juran's concern that 'Quality has become too gimmicky, full of platitudes and supposed good intentions, but short on real substance.'

Juran's definition of quality constitutes another strand of his philosophy. He defines quality as 'fitness for use or purpose' (Bank, 1992: 71). Bank suggests that this is a more useful definition than 'conformance to specification', since a dangerous product could conform to all specifications but still be unfit for use. This may be compared with Crosby's definition of 'conformance to requirements'; it would probably be reasonable to assume that safety in use would be a requirement for Crosby, although he does not say so.

The final important strand to Juran's thinking is in his trilogy of quality planning, quality control, and quality improvement (see Figure 9.1).

This essentially simple approach encapsulates the demand for substantial action inherent in all of Juran's work. Juran's emphasis in this respect is in three areas: changing management behaviour through quality awareness, training, and then spilling down new attitudes to supporting management levels. This top-down approach reflects Juran's belief that management is largely responsible for quality problems.

Joseph Juran:

- Quality Planning: determine quality goals;
  implementation planning;
  resource planning; express goals in quality terms: create the quality plan.

- Quality Control: monitor performance;
  compare objectives with achievements; act to reduce the gap.

- Quality Improvement: reduce waste;
  enhance logistics;
  improve employee morale; improve profitability;
  satisfy customers.

Figure 9.1 Joseph M. Juran's quality trilogy.

Vignette 9.1 Fletcher Challenge Steel, China: Planning and Politics

Fletcher Challenge Steel formed a joint venture with Datong City Government in China – Fletcher Challenge Steel, China – to upgrade the Datong iron-making plant and build a new melt shop to melt and cast steel billets. The team from Fletcher Challenge had created a plan for the venture, involving increases in both volume and quality of output and reductions in manning levels. Making a significant investment in new equipment, the overall aim was to achieve levels of performance comparable to Western mills. Fletcher Challenge had previously undertaken best-practice studies, and were successfully implementing performance improvements in their domestic steel operations in New Zealand.

Following the formation of the joint-venture company, a management team was appointed, comprising some of the established local Chinese managers, the project team from New Zealand, and selected new appointees with Chinese origins but Western technical education and knowledge. It was recognized, right from the outset, that cultural barriers to success would exist, and that effective communication would be vital. In part, this communication was seen to rest on common language and shared cultural background.

Well behind the planned timescale, the plant began to approach the levels of output performance necessary to be self-supporting in the long run, and to justify the substantial investment made in it by Fletcher Challenge. The initial financial investment consisted of US$25 million, but this was supported by a substantial investment of personal credibility by Fletcher Steel chief executive, Mike Smith. Smith, an Englishman, had persuaded the group board of Fletcher Challenge to make the investment, and, despite his success in the New Zealand plants, could not afford to have this venture fail.

The delays in achieving the planned performance improvements did not result from poor technical planning, but from an inadequate appreciation of the political difficulties and resistance that would be met from the Chinese partners. The local managers were suddenly faced with both technical and managerial challenges to the ways in which they had been accustomed to run their business. Such challenges alone are often sufficient to inhibit any change programme. When those challenges are reinforced by cultural and language differences between the parties, significant problems are almost inevitable. Equally, the plans were externally derived. The local established management were not involved in the planning process; rather, the results of that process were presented to them, a factor which would further inhibit acceptance, particularly when the standards of performance proposed were considered unachievable as they were outside the scope of local experience. These factors combined to generate significant internal resistance to the implementation of the plans, and without the commitment of the local senior management, workforce acceptance was also inhibited.

This story emphasizes that quality is not just a technical issue, and that success in designing and implementing a quality programme really does depend on the wholehearted commitment and active participation of all of those involved in, or affected by, the programme. It can never be enough to cajole and persuade either managers or workers to support the programme. A mechanism must be found which enables genuine participation and commitment from all parties.

Summarizing Juran's philosophy, five key beliefs can be identified:

- management is largely responsible for quality;
- quality can only be improved through planning;
- plans and objectives must be specific and measurable;
- training is essential and starts at the top;
- there is a three-step process of planning, control and action.

9.2 Assumptions

The assumptions about the world which seem to underpin Juran's approach are discussed below.

The first point to be examined is Juran's apparent assumption, which he holds along with Deming, is that there is a quality crisis. It is certainly the case that consumers' expectations of products and services have increased, and that there is a lower tolerance of faults than was once the case. We all expect our watches to keep time, our cars to start every day, and that services will be reliably and consistently provided.

There are at least three potential views of the quality problem. First, it could be argued that the quality gurus 'created' the quality crisis by raising awareness of the quality issue, focusing attention on the negative aspects, and driving up consumer expectations, which in turn has forced producers and providers to improve. A second argument is that awareness of the costs of poor quality amongst providers and producers increased, leading managements to focus their attention on improving quality, which then became a virtue for their product (and bottom line). A third view is that consumers have driven the quality movement through increasing expectations, and that there is an unwillingness to tolerate defective or shoddy goods and services.

The truth probably lies in a combination of all of these arguments, with interrelationships between the factors being the driving force. This moves the quality argument away from a linear view of the world, seen in Crosby and Ishikawa, towards a more holistic approach.

Looking at wider issues, it can certainly be argued that in the world of relatively mature consumer market, the substantial growth in availability of goods and services must lead to a focus on performance. Poor quality represents a major threat to organizational survival. Achievement of quality becomes not an ideal to aim for but, like profit, a fundamental requirement for staying in business.

To argue that there was a quality crisis implies a decline in quality. It is more likely that there was an increase in expectations. As has often been said, 'if we can put a man on the moon, why can't we make a toaster that works?'

A second assumption is that management of both the organization and quality are processes. This idea has considerable appeal. Management is often thought of as a set of discrete, separate activities, but this view is rather narrow and simplistic. To recognize that management is a process, with all actions and decisions interacting with all others, is a much broader, and perhaps more realistic, view. There can be little argument with Juran in this respect, especially as much current thinking in management revolves around the ideas of organizing ventures on process lines, and on 're-engineering' those processes.

A third assumption is of the potential for continuous improvement. This has already been addressed in the sections on Deming and Ishikawa. To briefly reiterate, continuous improvement is a reasonable view in a continuous world. However, when change outside the organization becomes discontinuous, continuous improvement may lose its value. Discontinuity in the environment probably demands discontinuity in the organization. In a discontinuous business environment, a step change in performance – a 'discontinuous improvement' – may be what is required for survival.

The fourth and final assumption to be examined is that relating to quantification. Juran's work focuses very clearly on measurement and specific objectives. Again, as with other gurus, the validity of this approach must be questioned. Many aspects of quality, particularly in the service sector, are difficult to accurately and reliably quantify. Significantly, some aspects are outside the control of the organization providing the service. This leads to two problems. The first is the tendency to measure those aspects which are easily accessible, rather than those which are most important. The second is how to measure individual customer expectations, expectations which may vary each time the service is purchased. The normal response is to provide a standard service and educate the customer to understand what they can expect. A different, and rather more difficult, response is to adapt the service to meet individual expectations.

There is a clear bias towards the use of quantitative methods which can be considered as rooted in Juran's industrial and manufacturing-based background. This perhaps provides a certain limitation on the application of his ideas in the service sector.

9.3 Methods

While Juran's quality trilogy of planning, control, and improvement offers the guideline to his approach, his overarching methodology for achieving quality is the 'Quality Planning Road Map' (Bendell: 1989: 9). Recognizing both external and internal customers, the road map (Figure 9.2) offers a nine-step guide. These steps will be briefly reviewed in turn.

The first two steps, that is identifying and determining the needs of the customers, refer not just to external customers but also to the customers of processes within the organization. These steps are normally seen as identifying the single next step in the

Joseph Juran:

Step 1) Identify who are the customers;

Step 2) Determine the needs of those customers;

Step 3) Translate those needs into our language [the language of the organization];

Step 4) Develop a product that can respond to those needs;

Step 5) Optimize the product features so as to meet our [the Company's] needs as well as customers' needs;

Step 6) Develop a process which is able to produce the product;

Step 7) Optimize the process;

Step 8) Prove that the process can produce the product under operating conditions;

Step 9) Transfer the process to operations.

Figure 9.2 Joseph M. Juran's quality planning road map.

process, that is, translating these needs into the language of the organization, although a more useful view might be to identify the whole chain and all of the interrelationships. It could be the case that a particular feature of a product is of no significance to the immediate customer, but has enormous impact for one at a later stage of the process. It is therefore important to recognize and take account of the requirements of all possible customers in the chain.

The third step is really about effective communication. A package of requirements that is expressed in a language unknown or unfamiliar to the people in the organization will be of no help. Obvious examples of this are converting words in general or common usage, the customer's language, into the specific technical jargon of the organization. Less obvious are internal requirements. Here it is important that the requirements are expressed in terms meaningful to the working group involved. For example, a condition expressed in the language of accounting to meet a particular budget in terms of profit and loss may be meaningless to a group of engineers. It is essential that their 'budget' be expressed in relevant terms, such as required throughput, machine utilization, or levels of waste.

Developing a product that responds to customer needs takes the quality issue back to its most fundamental aspect: building quality in rather than inspecting defects out. This is one aspect where other gurus agree. It is better and cheaper to establish quality from the outset than to engage in rectification. Optimizing the product to meet the organization's or department's needs, as well as those of the customer, should ideally be seen as a constraint on the development process of the previous step, rather than as a separate issue. It is, or should be, a design constraint that the product meets these requirements simultaneously.

The development, optimization, and testing of a production process – making it operational – is an area that historically has received little attention. Consulting experience has shown that often products have been developed by the research and development staff, and then simply handed over to the production staff with the instruction to make it. More recently, many companies are taking account of manufacturing requirements in the development process. Ease of manufacture (and designing in low manufacturing or assembly costs) is becoming accepted as a design constraint.

The final step is to transfer the process to operations. Again, historically this has been done very badly, and there is no argument with Juran's proposal. A useful device to assist with this aspect, and something which is being adopted by many companies, is to create teams for product development which include operational staff and managers. If the idea of designing for manufacture is adopted, this step becomes very straightforward.

Supporting this fundamental approach to designing quality into the systems and processes is what Bank (1992: 70) refers to as Juran's ten steps to continuous quality improvement (see Figure 9.3).

Here it can be seen how Juran's philosophy is carried across into practice. The first step begins to establish a quality-oriented culture in the organization, through the process of raising awareness of the need and scope: a qualitative approach. The second is quantitative, establishing objectives, that is, goals, for improvement. The third step is an attempt to institutionalize quality, to embed the quality process in the management process, so that it becomes an ingrained part of the organization.

The fourth step takes the organization forward to train the entire staff. This is seen as helping to make quality an integral part of everyone's thinking.

Joseph Juran:

Step 1) Create awareness of the need and opportunity for quality improvement;

Step 2) Set goals for continuous improvement;

Step 3) Build an organization to achieve goals by establishing a quality council, identifying problems, selecting a project, appointing teams and choosing facilitators;

Step 4) Give everyone training;

Step 5) Carry out projects to solve problems;

Step 6) Report progress;

Step 7) Show recognition;

Step 8) Communicate results;

Step 9) Keep a record of successes;

Step 10) Incorporate annual improvements into the company's regular systems and processes and thereby maintain momentum.

Figure 9.3 Joseph M. Juran's ten steps to continuous quality improvement.

The fifth and sixth steps, 'carry out projects' and 'report progress', recognize that while continuous improvement is the objective, it must be achieved within visible and measurable elements. The reporting process is seen as enabling experience and learning to be shared, and to allow those involved to share their sense of achievement. This also allows the seventh step, 'show recognition', to be actioned. The sixth and eighth steps are linked, 'communicate results' being a call to share the successes (and failures) throughout the organization.

The ninth step, keeping a record, is again an aid to organizational learning. A record may be thought of as an organizational 'memory' to which reference can be made in the future. While Juran suggests that this record should be of successes, it is just as important to remember those strategies and schemes that do not work as those that do. This true form of knowledge management may enable the organization to avoid, or encourage, appropriate actions and behaviour in the future. Most important of all – for both success and failure – is to understand why changes have succeeded or failed. To be able to distil the general principles of success from a specific instance, or series of instances, is to create a true basis for organizational learning. After all, the specific instance will never arise again – but the principles underpinning the solved problem will almost certainly recur many times – and the practice of problem-solving is enhanced by understanding at the general, rather than at the particular, level.

The tenth step is a corporate level and public commitment to the achievement of higher quality. This should be seen as reaffirming the quality process in the minds of both employees and customers.

Juran shows awareness of the phenomenon of resistance to change, which is so common in organizations. Logothetis (1992: 75) reports Juran's belief that 'resistance to a technological change is due to social and cultural factors'. Juran proposes two principal methods for dealing with this. First, he considers that all those affected by the change should be 'allowed to participate' (1992: 75), second, that 'adequate time should be allowed for the change to be accepted'. These approaches are seen as providing an opportunity for evaluation and experimentation, promoting ownership of the changes and helping to overcome resistance.

Underpinning the two processes outlined above – 'the road map' and the 'ten steps' – Juran uses a variety of statistical methods. Like Deming, Juran studied under Shewhart, and so shares many of the same approaches, for example, control charts. Perhaps one of the best known of his approaches is using Pareto analysis to help separate the 'vital few' problems from the 'useful many'.

9.4 Successes and Failures

Like the other gurus, it must be accepted that Juran has been hugely successful in developing and promoting his ideas. That his books have been translated into thirteen languages, and his ideas accepted and exploited by so many organizations and in so many different countries, is a measure of the perceived value of his contribution. However, his work has not been applied universally, and can be seen to be less effective in the service sector than in manufacturing.

Adapting from Flood (1993: 21–2), the strengths of Juran's approach are:

- concentration on genuine issues of management practice;
- a new understanding of the (internal *and* external) customer;
- management involvement and commitment.

The main weaknesses are perceived as:

- the literature on motivation and leadership is not addressed;
- workers' contributions are underrated;
- methods are traditional, failing to address culture and politics.

Another criticism is that the body of systems knowledge, and in particular managerial and organizational cybernetics, which could have enhanced and enriched Juran's approach, has, like human relations theory, been largely ignored.

The first strength identified by Flood is one with which most people would agree, although a programme which fails to motivate and develop the majority of the workforce, is one which may well be seen as consisting of 'hype'.

The second strength, that of recognizing other parts of the organization as customers, is again welcome. Readers will recall that this can also be found in the work of Deming, and is now embedded in the ISO 9000: 2000 standard as well as in other quality management system standards.

The third strength is management commitment and involvement. This is not simply because, according to Juran's measure, 80 per cent of the total quality problem resides there, but also because the power, control, and leadership reside there. A management which is seen by the workforce to be committed to quality will breed a quality ethos for the organization. Workers wishing to progress and be content within a quality-oriented environment will probably emulate the behaviour and attitudes of their managers. If this occurs then the quality ethos will tend to spill down through the organization over time.

Turning to the weaknesses, Flood's understanding that Juran fails to incorporate adequately theories of motivation and leadership is accepted. However, Juran is a practitioner; he deals best with the practice of quality rather than the theory. It might be suggested that the second statement of weakness, that Juran undervalues the contribution of the worker, is countered to some extent by the explicit incorporation of participation.

Flood further suggests that Juran emphasizes a somewhat 'mechanistic' view of the organization, although he does take account of the organization's environment, that is, of its markets. This view is largely evident in the unstated assumption that what is good for the organization – higher quality – is also good for the individual. This, perhaps, reflects the thinking of early management theorists such as Taylor, Weber, and Fayol. In the contemporary world of 'knowledge workers', high-technology equipment, and increasing emphasis on human rights, often what is good for the organization may appear to be bad for the workers. This applies to both the short- and long-term views. A company operating in the face of maturing or mature markets, and not positioned to exploit emerging markets, with fresh, lower-cost base competitors from newly industrializing countries, may be unable to absorb spare capacity through growth. This leads to the need, to use the politically correct terminology, to 'retrench' workers.

The interests of the organization and the individual worker may come into direct conflict. The organization wishes to improve quality, to preserve and protect its customer base, to reduce its costs, and ensure its survival. The workers may recognize that these same attributes can have different consequences for them, for example, job losses, pay freezes, reductions in overtime, or loss of other benefits. Often the pursuit of quality can lead to the deskilling of jobs and the loss of craft skills, in which individuals take great, and justifiable, pride. There is little incentive for the workforce to contribute to the quality programme if a successful outcome for the company threatens their own – short-term – sense of security. They may well seek to preserve their position in the short term, while accepting the inevitable longer-term threat. Events in France and Germany during 1997 perhaps give this point extra emphasis. Compared with the UK, organizations in those nations had undertaken little in the way of radical change and restructuring. Despite the emergent threat to jobs in those economies, arising from high costs, questionable productivity, and overseas competition, the workers, as represented by the unions, were strongly resisting change. The appeal for participation must deal with issues of this type if it is to have any hope of success. Juran offers little in this regard.

9.5 Critical Review

The founding idea of Juran's work might almost be called 'Design and Build'. His approach stresses planning as the fundamental requirement for quality, followed by action. This orientation towards the setting and achievement of objectives perhaps reflects Juran's engineering and statistical background.

The 'Quality Trilogy', 'Quality Road Map', and 'Ten Steps to Quality' may all be considered as systematic, somewhat mechanistic, approaches. While Juran established a new understanding of customers (the internal and external), he does not explicitly recognize the importance of the interdependence of processes and the interactions between people within the organization. This prevents his systematic approach from becoming systemic. Juran seems to be making the assumption that improvement in the individual parts will necessarily improve the whole organization, a view which is challenged by the systems-thinking community.

With regard to management, two issues should be stressed. First, Juran views management as a process. Second, he sees management as responsible for quality, having control of 80 per cent of the problems. As regards the first of these issues, Juran's view is to be welcomed. An organization which recognizes that every action and decision is inextricably linked with every other in a continuous process of management, must be considered to be on the verge of a breakthrough in its behaviour. Even today, management in many organizations is fragmented into pseudo-independent functions: marketing is separate from finance, which in turn is separate from production, and so on. Each of these units attempts to maximize its own function independently from the others. Similarly, even within departments, tasks are often seen as independent rather than interdependent. For example, recruitment is often seen as a separate function within the personnel or human resource function, which has no relationship with training and development – and, crucially, no relationship with the units where those recruited will work. In such an organization it is not surprising that there are conflicts, disputes and difficulties in matching people to tasks. A more holistic, integrated, and interdependent process view is essential. While Juran moves towards this approach, he does not go far enough.

Turning now to the second issue, management responsibility, perhaps the question that should be asked is why 80 per cent? Deming, for example, has provided statistics suggesting that the figure is 94 per cent, while Crosby's work may be interpreted as suggesting that the bulk of the responsibility lies with the workers. An argument can be proposed whereby management take complete responsibility for quality. If, as Fayol (1916) suggests, it is the responsibility of management to 'Plan, Organise, Command, Control and Co-ordinate,' then responsibility should lie with them. The argument is this: management is expected to have control of every aspect of the organization:

- what is done
- how it is done
- when it is done
- where it is done
- who does it
- why it is done.

This suggests that there should be no matter internal to the organization which is beyond the scope of management to address. Random errors in production, for example, might be eradicable through changes in design or process, so that it becomes impossible to assemble a part incorrectly. Human error might be eradicable through training, adjustment of work rates, increases (or reductions) in relaxation time, or a range of other variables which could be altered to enable improved performance.

It is suggested that the ultimate responsibility for quality should rest with all those who are involved in the production of a good or a service, that is, every employee within every part and function of the organization. However, the power to achieve higher quality rests in the hands of those who have authority (power) to change things. If that power is in the hands of the management alone, they have full responsibility. If, on the other hand, the power is shared throughout the organization, perhaps through empowerment initiatives, quality circles, and other participative approaches, everyone who shares in that power is responsible.

The strong emphasis by Juran on management responsibility fails to address adequately the needs and aspirations of workers. He does not properly take into account the contribution that they can make to the achievement of quality, nor does he provide mechanisms through which this can be done.

Finally, the issue must again be raised of the applicability of Juran's work. It seems to be most suitable for the industrial and manufacturing sectors. It is suggested that it has limited application in service organizations, since it does not adequately deal with human issues.

Summary

This chapter has reviewed the major contribution made to the quality movement by Juran. Students should refer to Juran's (1988) own work to further inform and develop their views.

KEY LEARNING POINTS

Joseph Juran's definition of quality: fitness for use or purpose

Key beliefs:
management responsibility, planning, measurability, training, process.

Principal methods:
company-wide quality control; quality road map; ten steps to quality improvement.

Question

What can we mean by 'fitness for purpose'?

10 John S. Oakland

TQM starts at the top

(John S. Oakland, 1993)

Introduction

John Oakland is Executive Chairman of Oakland Consulting plc, and head of its research and education division – the European Centre for Business Excellence. John holds a chair in Business Excellence at Leeds University Business School. Professor Oakland is considered by many as the British guru of quality. His practice is internationally based, and he has provided substantial support to the development of quality in the UK, particularly to the quality initiatives of the government. Oakland's early industrial career focused on research and development and production management. He holds a PhD, is a chartered chemist, Fellow of the Royal Statistical Society, the Royal Society for the Arts, and the Institute of Quality Assurance. He is also a member of the Royal Society of Chemistry, the Association of Quality Management Consultants and a member of the American Society of Quality Control.

The approaches used by Oakland and his colleagues in Oakland Consulting plc are essentially pragmatic, and have been used widely in organizations throughout the UK and Europe.

10.1 Philosophy

The philosophy underpinning Oakland's view of quality is perhaps best shown in the emphasis he places on its importance when he says, 'We cannot avoid seeing how quality has developed into the most important competitive weapon, and many organizations have realized that TQM is *the* [sic] way of managing for the future' (Oakland, 1993: Preface).

In this statement, Oakland gives absolute primacy to the pursuit of quality as the cornerstone of organizational success. While organizations which do not achieve quality in their products and services will ultimately fail in the long term, it is more difficult to accept the idea of quality (in isolation) having absolute primacy over everything else. Successful and sustainable organizations are a function of their internal capabilities, and their interaction with the dynamic business environment; it is entirely possible for an organization producing 'quality' products and services to fail as a result of external factors. Purists might argue that if quality pervades the whole organization, it will recognize such threats and respond effectively to them. This is fair comment, but only applies if quality pervades the whole organization and not just its productive parts. Although quality has strategic implications (as discussed in Chapter 2) and is a strategic issue, it cannot be accepted that it is the *only* strategic issue.

On the other hand, the concept of TQM as the way of managing for the future does have considerable value. If TQM is thought of as a way of managing (as seen in Feigenbaum's work), rather than an added extra, then other management philosophies, methods and tools must be subsumed within it. This idea reinforces Oakland's view that 'quality starts at the top', with quality parameters inherent in every organizational decision. He emphasizes seven key characteristics of pursuing TQM (Figure 10.1).

First, is Oakland's definition of quality: *'quality is meeting the customers' requirements'*. This definition is simple and very hard to disagree with, as it emphasizes that quality is a characteristic or attribute defined by the customer, not the supplier. Oakland also stresses the importance of the quality chain. He emphasizes the internal supplier–customer relationships, stressing in the second characteristic that most problems are interdepartmental – that is, they occur in the interaction between process steps.

The third and fourth characteristics emphasize the purposes of quality control (QC) and quality assurance (QA). These definitions move the focus away from criticism and blame, often associated with these mechanisms, and towards the reason they are required – which is quite simply to improve quality performance. All too often, the QC and QA functions in organizations become self-serving activities, focusing on apportioning blame and identifying guilty parties rather than on improving the performance of the organization. Because of this, they frequently fall into disrepute and become disregarded by the operational personnel – who in turn focus on not getting caught rather than on not failing. A recent example of this was an organization in which every month the managers had a quality day – the day on which they ensured that all the non-conformance reports were resolved – which mainly involved lengthy explanations of why the non-conformance was not their fault. Little or no attention was paid to improvement in product or service quality.

The fifth and sixth characteristics focus on the proactive nature of the quality drive. The statement that 'quality must be managed, it does not just happen', and reflecting Juran's suggestion that 'quality must be planned', sharpens the recognition that quality is not accidental, or achieved through reactive measures. Quality for Oakland, that is,

John S. Oakland:

1) Quality is meeting the customer's requirements;

2) Most quality problems are inter-departmental.

3) Quality control is monitoring, finding and eliminating causes of quality problems;

4) Quality Assurance rests on prevention, management systems, effective audit and review;

5) Quality must be managed, it does not just happen;

6) Focus on prevention not cure;

7) Reliability is an extension of quality and enables us to 'delight the customer';

Figure 10.1 John S. Oakland's seven key characteristics of TQM.

meeting customer requirements, must be a parameter of every decision made within the organization, whether operational, administrative or strategic. Quality must then be inherent in management thinking, which in turn means that it must be part of the norms of the organization. This view is supported by the sixth characteristic: prevention not cure. Oakland suggests that one-third of all organizational efforts are wasted in error-based activity, for example, rework, rectification, inspection, and so on, with an even higher proportion in service-based organizations. Working from experience, these proportions are difficult to argue with, and in some cases represent a significant under-estimate. If quality can be achieved at the outset, rather than through detection and rectification, the total costs of the organization will always be reduced. The limitation to achieving this arises very often from the functionally-based budgeting common in organizations, where each manager seeks to reduce his or her own current period costs, with no regard to the effect on other parts of the organization.

The final characteristic deals with quality as more than a momentary attribute. Reliability has two dimensions which are related to the nature of the product itself. The first is reliability in use, and relates to durable products such as cars, domestic appliances, watches, and so on. In this case, what 'delights the customer' is enjoying the uninterrupted use of the product, other than for routine, service-based maintenance. A motor car which breaks down will not delight the customer, regardless of how it met the quality criteria upon delivery. The customer requirement is to be able to turn the key and make a journey without fear of non-completion. This means that each time the service is delivered, it must meet the customer requirements. In this context, reliability means consistency, and to achieve consistency of service means there must be a consistent and reliable delivery process.

Quality is considered by Oakland to be an organization-wide and fundamental requirement, driven by top management commitment and created through reliable, consistent organizational processes.

10.2 Assumptions

The assumptions about the world that seem to underpin Oakland's approach will now be considered.

Oakland's first assumption is that quality is the only issue for organizational survival. While this may be largely true of some organizations in fully developed, highly competitive and mature economies (those in which Oakland predominantly operates), it is certainly not true of all organizations. Some will succeed (at least in the short to medium term), because they have established such market dominance (and perhaps customer reliance) that the issue of quality simply does not arise. Customers buy the products or services because of lack of alternative rather than through choice. For example, the majority of personal computer users purchase Microsoft operating system compatible software, not necessarily because it does exactly what they require, but because it is what is readily available, and works with their Microsoft-based operating systems. Interestingly, this tendency has been challenged by the increasing compatibility of Apple products with Microsoft products, and the emergence of open-source solutions such as Linux with a new generation of users testing alternative systems.

With banking and other financial services providers, until very recently, the issue of customer choice did not arise; the products, services and costs were all substantially undifferentiated. When one supplier is as good or bad as every other, the product or service becomes a commodity and choice ceases to be a meaningful word. In other contexts, the sophistication of consumers and state of development of the market still means that providers of goods or services can predominantly focus on their own requirements, not those of the customers. Other suppliers enjoy state-sponsored or supported supply positions, and as such quality is not a concern for them – again the consumer has no choice. Oakland's first assumption can be challenged on the grounds that while perhaps correct as a matter of value, the constraint does not apply across global markets.

The second assumption, that quality must be driven from the top, carries complete support. Unless this commitment is achieved at the outset of a quality programme, and maintained at a high level of enthusiasm, the initiative will fail. The revised ISO 9000: 2000 standard focuses heavily on management commitment as a major issue, although many managements can be seen to be struggling to convert the concept into action.

The third assumption is that errors can always be prevented, through planning, design and effective processes. This is probably true, but requires a substantial shift in the traditional mindset of those in the organization, and a full appreciation of the softer, human issues, particularly in service-based organizations. As already mentioned, while a process operation can be designed to operate in an error-free way, the actual minute-by-minute delivery of service depends very largely on the personal interaction between customer and supplier. However robust the technical process may be, there is always scope for error to arise in this context. No standard form of words can cater for the vagaries of mood, sense and interpretation which influence the outcome of such transactions and determine whether customer requirements are met – Oakland's measure of quality.

The fourth assumption is that quality is an organization-wide issue. This is in common with Flood's (1993) call for quality 'across all functions and all levels', and again cannot be argued with. Quality must pervade the whole organizational atmosphere. This suggests that Oakland's approach is systemic. While he makes no direct reference in his work to the systemic approaches to management, there is a systemic, as well as a systematic, attitude reflected in his approach.

Finally, Oakland assumes the involvement of all people through communication, teamwork and participation, in other words, through redeveloping the culture of the organization. This view is again supported, and reflects a systemic mindset in his approach.

10.3 Methods

While Oakland rightly capitalizes on the many well-established methods, tools and techniques for achieving quality, he does offer his own overarching approach for TQM and some new insight. The overarching method is his 'ten points for Senior Management' (Figure 10.2).

Oakland represents the major features of this in his 'Total Quality Management model', in Figure 10.3.

Unlike some of the other gurus, Oakland focuses on the total process of achieving a TQM organization seeking to optimize the mix of qualitative and quantitative aspects. He recognizes the necessity of both, and, if anything, is slightly biased towards softer aspects as the initial drivers of quality.

The ten-point process begins with the absolute commitment of senior and middle

John S. Oakland:

Point 1) Long term commitment;

Point 2) Change the culture to 'right first time';

Point 3) Train the people to understand the Customer–Supplier relationship;

Point 4) Buy products and services on TOTAL COST (sic);

Point 5) Recognise that systems improvement must be managed;

Point 6) Adopt modern methods of supervision and training and eliminate fear;

Point 7) Eliminate barriers, manage processes, improve communications and teamwork;

Point 8) Eliminate arbitrary goals, standards based only on numbers, barriers to pride of workmanship, fiction (use the correct tools to establish facts);

Point 9) Constantly educate and retrain the in-house experts;

Point 10) Utilise a systematic approach to TQM implementation.

Figure 10.2 John S. Oakland's ten points for senior management.

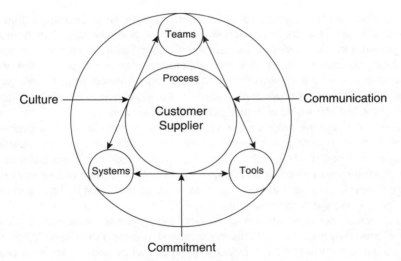

Figure 10.3 John S. Oakland's total quality management model.

management to constant improvement. Oakland suggests that the quality process must start in the boardroom. Adoption of quality at that level is fundamental to its achievement, since it is then a normative decision; a decision about the sort of behaviour that is desired. Unfortunately, this is rather more difficult to achieve in practice than is recognized. The senior management may say that they are committed to quality, but unless they change their behaviour (that is, the decisions they make, the things they say and do, the ways in which they measure and reward performance) the commitment is not genuine. This will soon be detected at other levels within the organization.

Vignette 10.1 The Hong Kong Police Force

(Formerly The Royal Hong Kong Police Force)

The commissioner of the, then, Royal Hong Kong Police Force (an organization consisting of some 40,000 personnel) publicly announced his strategy for the introduction of a service quality approach to meet the need for change in the culture and work attitudes within the Force. With no clear driver for change, the Force recognized the need for this initiative to meet the challenges ahead, and for action before it was forced to take action by external events. The programme gave equal focus to internal customers and external customer relationships.

The envisaged change was being implemented in a 'step-by-step' approach, and it was anticipated that the development and implementation of the strategy would take at least five years, probably longer. This process had been nominally structured into five phases:

- Awareness
- Understanding
- Favour
- Involvement
- Commitment

Early work focused on generating an understanding of the kinds of changes that were planned. Activities included a road-show for middle- to senior-level management, a video presentation for viewing by all personnel, publication of the strategy in various internal communications media, development of performance pledges (for the public), internal service-level agreements (for internal customer interactions), the encouragement of voluntary work improvement teams in the work environment, and the commissioning of the first of a series of regular public opinion surveys.

However, although the project team assigned to undertake all these activities was reasonably clear regarding its objectives, there was a perceived lack of expertise in knowing exactly how to achieve them. The team was also driving these changes from too far down the organizational 'food chain', and the lack of commitment from senior management was seen as a threat to success. It was at this stage that assistance was sought from a management consultancy.

After an initial scoping study, the consultants recommended refocusing the project team's efforts away from the customer interface and towards a more holistic approach. This entailed a more detailed examination of the overall purpose of the organization, how it was going to set about to fulfil it, and called for this process to start at the very top of the organization.

Until the advent of the consultancy, the project team's activities and proposals for change lacked credibility. Overnight, senior management were confronted with arguments that they could not refute. Quickly, decisions were made and commitments pledged to a broad front of Force-wide changes. The key thrust for these changes was to develop a corporate vision and mission, which was to be entitled the Force Vision and Statement of Common Purpose and Values.

From this point onwards, it was recognized that the Force would be undertaking a process of change requiring a strong sense of direction, provided by solid organization, vision, mission, and values. To this end, the commissioner and his senior management team attended a series of workshops, facilitated by the consultants, to identify the themes and elements of the Forces Vision and Statement of Common Purpose and Values.

The outcome of each workshop was further refined by a team of middle-level managers, broadly representative of the myriad of functional areas within the Force. The result was draft documents, ready for a consultation process designed to underscore the commitment of Force management to the change process in an unprecedented, heavily structured, communications approach. This was to be undertaken by way of discussion groups, rather than using the more traditional paper exercise.

Each member of the Force, from the chief superintendent downwards, attended a discussion group run by one of their managers, assisted by a consultation pack and a discussion guide. This was seen as a new approach, designed to involve and commit commanders at all levels visibly to seek genuine feedback from their staff. Over 1,400 such discussion groups were held.

The results of this consultation were made available to Force management, and the commissioner and his management team attended further workshops to consider the feedback and agree on the final version of the statement.

At these workshops, the first steps towards developing formal strategic directions for the Force were also outlined.

The finalized Statement was launched at the Force Open Day, and widespread publicity of the document followed. The process, from inception to launch, took just over one year. That signalled not the end of the exercise, but completion of the first stage. The next phase was probably the more important, which was the introduction of a strategy to give life to the vision, common purpose, and shared values that all have agreed to. This was undertaken through a programme called Living-the-Values, with the intention of preparing senior managers for the change in culture and attitudes that were needed to follow on from the launch of the statement, and the cascading of this message down through the organization to the constable on the beat.

Following on from the strategic workshops held in connection with the Vision and Statement of Common Purpose and Values, the consultants facilitated similar workshops for each of the Force departments, with a view to drawing up departmental strategic direction plans. Once all departments had been through this process, the various departmental plans were to be incorporated into the Force Strategic Directions Document.

Finally, it is worth clearly stating that it was not intended that the Force lift a TQM package from a shelf; there is no cookbook which tells them what to do or how to do it. There are plenty of success stories, and there are plenty of examples of what not to do – the Force will consider adopting only those things which should support the Force. As the commissioner has said, 'Our pursuit of excellence is providing a Service of Quality.'

This story clearly shows how, when an enlightened management begins to take the message and intent of a quality programme seriously, it can be spilled down the organization in a structured, consistent, and meaningful way that leads to substantial change.

Arising from the first process, the second requirement is to change the culture of the organization at all levels, to focus on 'right first time'. Oakland sees this as based on awareness of customer needs and teamwork, enabled by participation and use of the 'EPDCA helix'. This is a more dynamic representation of the Deming cycle already seen, with explicit recognition of the need for evaluation before planning. There is much else required in a cultural change, as is implied in the ideas of teamwork, participation, and customer needs.

The third process represents the orientation of the organization, through training, towards customer–supplier relationships, both externally and internally. Oakland suggests this must be achieved for everyone. This is an especially difficult area, which will meet with much resistance in many organizations. This is especially true where the staff of a particular process or function are traditionally poorly regarded; where there is functional organization design, or a major difference of perceived relative expertise, with the customer regarded by the supplier as being of a 'lower order'. This is a particular concern in organizations where there is a significant perceived difference between staff members and clients, for example, doctors interacting with nurses and/or patients, or chefs interacting with kitchen assistants. Arrogance based on perceived expertise can easily emerge, which inhibits effective communication and teamworking.

Process four moves away from the culturally-oriented changes to examine cost. Here, like Deming, Oakland recognizes that initial purchase price is not the sole determinant of the cost of any input. He calls for continuous improvement in everything to reduce the total cost of doing business. He recognizes that a higher initial cost of purchase may be more than outweighed by reduced lifetime cost to the organization, including running costs, depreciation, and, in response to changes in legislation, disposal or recycling costs. For example, a stainless steel machine may be initially more expensive than its mild steel equivalent, but if the maintenance and running cost is significantly lower and the longevity greater, the total cost may be less over time.

Process five examines the systems used to manage the organization, and calls for them to be actively managed to achieve improvement. While this may seem like common sense, it is often neglected. A key to success in this area is to step back and reconsider the utility and effectiveness of the systems employed. Many organizations continue to work with what the IT industry calls 'legacy systems', that is, those which have been purchased and developed over many years and which commonly require substantial investment to replace. Often such systems, like the budget, are functionally owned; that is, they reside within a single department which makes effective use of them in its own terms, but the system is not configured in such a way that it can contribute to the whole organization. The systems are often poorly understood in the wider organization, jealously guarded by their departmental 'owners' but, through lack of integration with the rest of the organization, are at best failing to add value, at worst causing damage. Often, the cost of replacing such systems is greater, within the individual function, than the business benefit to be obtained from their replacement, thus making it very difficult to obtain capital funding. Like any other capital investment, IT systems must be recognized as having a useful life, and must be replaced at the due time. In choosing the replacement, managers should have regard to the integration of information needs of the whole organization.

Process six calls for modern methods of supervision and training. This recognizes that many traditional supervision and training approaches no longer have great value in organizations. They are very often sterile, having no relationship to the particular job undertaken and are not reflected in individual performance expectations. Similarly, the 'kick butt and take names' militaristic approach to performance management is not applicable in a more enlightened environment, and is particularly foolish in an economic context of full or near full employment.

Process seven calls for organizations to be managed through processes, rather than up-and-down functional silos. While many process-based organizations have already achieved this, it is still the case that significant numbers adopt functional pillars as the basis of organization. In these cases, there remain many hand-offs (breaks within processes) which extend the range of customer–supplier relationships and create opportunities for the buck to be passed. In the process, the consumer (the ultimate customer) is often forgotten. If the organization is process-based, this tends not to happen, and communication and teamwork can be encouraged around the process flow, since all parties can visualize and share the team objective(s).

Process eight could be called the elimination round. Here, Oakland again reflects the ideas of others. He wishes to see arbitrary goals eliminated; it is useless to call for improvement without supplying the facilities necessary for those goals to be achieved, and without a formal basis for evaluation. He wants an end to standards based only on numbers, that is, on volumes. Purely volume-based output measures will always lead to quality problems. As a minimum, it is essential to measure quality performance as well – and to recognize that this may mean a lesser initial output, but that the output received should all be perfect! His third requirement is to eradicate barriers to pride of workmanship. Apart from purely measuring output volume (which is one barrier), this means the design, and redesign, of jobs, as suggested in the quality and human resources literature, to enable the particular worker to have pride in the completion of a meaningful task. Lastly, he calls for reliance on facts not fiction, proposing costs of quality and level of fire-fighting as measures of internal health. The important characteristic here is to recognize measurements that are both meaningful and factual, that is, numbers which cannot be manipulated to present a particular picture. While doctors bury their mistakes, managers frequently re-classify theirs, even to the extent in one factory of making rejects to maintain production efficiency. This particular factory supplied excess, or sub-standard, output in alternative packaging to a secondary market, and repackaged and labelled perfect goods to meet the needs of this secondary market. This was despite their inability to recover more than raw material costs from the purchaser. That secondary purchaser consequently made greater unit profit than the major and highly respected principal customer, while the factory itself lost money.

Stating quite rightly that 'the experts . . . are the people who do the job every day', at process nine Oakland calls for the experts' constant education and retraining. The dynamics of contemporary business and the rapid changes in the business environment render this absolutely essential. For maximum benefit, such training must be related back to job performance and expectations, that is, it must link to further improvement. This is a particularly strained point in many organizations, especially in times of economic downturn – the first budget items to suffer are normally the training and R&D budgets.

Finally, at process ten, Oakland calls for a planned, systematic approach to the operational implementation of TQM to realize the vision. Again, this seems like a sound platform for improvement. However, such systematization and planning must not preclude capitalizing on spontaneous and unexpected successes. The potential opportunist gain must not be lost through rigid adherence to a particular plan.

To support the implementation process, Oakland predominantly relies on what can be thought of as standard tools for achieving quality; such as statistical approaches, quality circles, process analysis and review, and so on. He does, however, enrich his approach by capitalizing on particular developments in the pursuit of quality.

The first of these is quality function deployment (QFD). This is a systematic approach to the design of a product or service around the expressed requirements of the customers. It involves members from across the organization in converting customer requirements to a technical product or service specification. The QFD process is based around seven activities (see Figure 10.4), and is intended to ensure that the product or service meets the customer requirements first time and every time. Oakland stresses the importance of recognizing the design input of those whose jobs do not include an evident design element.

John S. Oakland:

- Market Research
- Basic Research
- Invention
- Concept Design
- Prototype Testing
- Final product or service testing
- After-sales service and trouble-shooting

Figure 10.4 Quality function deployment activities.

Second, Oakland stresses the importance of teamwork in his approach, and draws extensively on the established literature in this area to explain and elaborate his approach.

This chapter is intended only to provide an introduction to Oakland's overall approach. Methods, tools and techniques will be elaborated in Part Four. This section has introduced Oakland's primary method, which relies heavily on absolute management commitment and leadership of the quality process supported by a wide selection of tools and techniques.

10.4 Successes and Failures

The use of Oakland's approach to TQM by thousands of companies speaks volumes for its utility. Quite simply, no programme could achieve such sustained success without substantial benefits being delivered to many customers.

The establishment of the European Centre for Business Excellence, and of Oakland Consulting plc, further confirms that Oakland's approach adds value to quality practice.

A number of strengths and weaknesses can be identified in Oakland's approach. The strengths are:

- a systematic, methodical approach;
- a process-based view of organizations;
- it capitalizes on developments in quality practice;

- there is a participative approach which utilizes ideas from the literature on teamwork;
- it stresses the importance of management commitment and leadership.

The weaknesses are:

- it ignores many developments in organization theory, especially the systems literature;
- it fails to offer assistance in coercive contexts;
- it justifies quality in terms of developed economies (the focus on competition);
- it ignores other aspects of strategy formulation;
- it does not explain how to obtain the commitment from senior management, on which the whole process relies.

Considering the strengths, the systematic and methodical approach provides a straight-forward, coherent platform for the quality initiative. Unfortunately, it assumes there is established agreement about the need for quality. Second, the process-based view adheres to current developments in the understanding of how organizations actually function, and how effectiveness is improved. Third, the capitalization on current developments in quality practice ensures that 'best practice' is achieved; a fundamental characteristic of quality.

Oakland's emphasis on team-working, and in particular his utilization of the literature on effective team-working, is to be admired. This shows that he has moved outside the relatively narrow discipline of pure quality to embrace other ideas which support his activities.

The final strength, emphasizing the importance of management commitment, is again fundamental to effective pursuit of quality. It is unfortunate that (as suggested by the weaknesses) he says little about how such commitment can be achieved. While the point has been made before, it is so important that it must be made again. If senior management are not passionately committed to the achievement of quality throughout every aspect of the organization, it will not happen. Unfortunately, Oakland does not advise on how to achieve this passionate commitment, or how to overcome the many functional and professional barriers which may obstruct it.

Turning to other weaknesses, the failure to incorporate other aspects of organization theory explicitly, and especially to have ignored the value to be derived from a systems-based understanding of organization (together with the associated methodologies), detracts substantially from Oakland's work.

The failure to deal with coercive contexts is common to all quality approaches, and is perhaps a little unfair as a criticism. Nonetheless, there are many organizations in the world which are characterized by potentially abusive power relations. One responsibility of the management guru or scientist must include attempting to ameliorate such conditions.

Perhaps because Oakland's practice is centred on Europe, the focus of his justification for pursuing quality is, if not entirely eurocentric, at least based on a perception of the problems and opportunities facing Western organizations in developed economies. These economies are dominated by industrial oligarchies, with a small number of major players in each industrial sector. It can be argued that effective competition on strategic issues has almost disappeared and has been replaced by a high degree of collaboration and, to some extent, a tacit acceptance of established market shares. For example, in the motor industry there are many interrelationships between manufacturers who promote distinct brands. Thus Volvo (now owned by Ford) made use of Renault (who now own Nissan) engines; Volkswagen, Seat (owned by Volkswagen) and Ford collaborate in the production of the Galaxy and Sharan, which are essentially the same vehicles but differently badged and priced. Globally, the interrelationships become even closer and more confusing.

Developing economies, on the other hand, often experience much lower levels of consumer and producer sophistication, which means that the customers are perhaps less discriminating in their purchasing choices, and place a lesser credence on Western perceptions of quality. These countries often have much more diverse industrial bases, with a greater proportion of small- to medium-sized businesses and less dominance by major players. These two factors taken together generate scope for strategic advantage to be obtained through routes other than quality.

10.5 Critical Review

Overall, the foundation to Oakland's work can be seen in his professional background and practical experience of quality. The approach is based broadly enough for it to be regarded as reflecting a systemic, as well as a systematic, view, but it fails explicitly to capitalize on developments in systemic thinking.

Oakland is clearly concerned about management commitment with his calls for passionate leadership, but the approach falls down in not making a mechanism available by which such passion can be engendered. It may be thought that the fear of competitive failure is enough to stimulate this response, but that is to rely on people running away from something – a negative reaction, rather than running to something, which is a positive reaction. In the first case, as soon as the stimulus is relaxed, that is, the current danger subsides to a comfortable level, the negative response will cease and with it the passion for quality. There is clearly a need to develop an ethos where management want quality as a means to a positive end rather than as an alternative to failure, but no tools are made available to support this.

One very positive feature is that the generality of Oakland's overarching methodology renders it potentially useful in the service, as well as the manufacturing, industry. While he says little of the public sector, it is clear that the method will also work there, although again the senior management motivation stemming from fear of competition is absent.

To summarize, support has to be given to Oakland's approach, while recognizing that it relies very heavily on well-established techniques with all the drawbacks these entail. On the other hand, he has capitalized on recent developments, and drawn on at least part of the relevant management literature to support and enhance his work. The practical success speaks for itself.

Summary

This chapter has presented the quality approach of John Oakland, through a five-point critical framework. Readers may wish to refer to Oakland's own work, *Total Quality Management* (1993, second edition), and *Total Organizational Excellence* (1999), to develop further their understanding and knowledge.

KEY LEARNING POINTS

John S. Oakland's definition of quality: quality is meeting the customer's requirements

Key beliefs:
quality is the only issue, quality from the top, errors can be prevented, quality is an organization-wide issue, quality involves everybody.

Principal methods:
ten points for senior management, EPDCA cycle, TQM model, quality function deployment.

Question

Oakland proposes that 'Quality is the only issue for organizational survival'. Discuss this proposal in the light of the contemporary challenges facing organizations.

11 Taiichi Ohno

Humpty Dumpty paid words extra and made them mean what he chose; but he could not thereby change [their] behaviour

(Stafford Beer, *Decision and Control*, 1966)

Introduction

Taiichi Ohno, who died in 1990, is less well remembered than his work. He was the creator of the 'just-in-time' Toyota Production System, which is now being emulated, at least in part, by many manufacturing and service organizations worldwide. Born in China in 1912 and a graduate of Nagoya Technical High School, he worked initially with Toyoda Spinning before joining the vehicle business in 1943, where he completed his career, eventually working primarily to develop Toyota thinking in suppliers to the business.

His most widely read work is *Toyota Production System: Beyond Large Scale Production*, originally published in Japanese in 1978, and in English by Productivity Press in 1988. In a foreword to that text, Muramatsu Rintaro describes Ohno as 'a determined man' who 'always challenged existing concepts' and was 'able to conceive of and apply improvements that are both accurate and swift'.

11.1 Philosophy

Ohno argued that, 'The world has already changed from a time when industry could sell everything it produced to an affluent society where material needs are routinely met.' He was inspired by Toyoda Sakichi and Toyoda Kiichiro, and saw the objective of the Toyota system as being the consistent and thorough elimination of waste, combining that objective with 'respect for humanity'.

Ohno (1987) states that: 'The Toyota Production System . . . will reveal its strength as a management system adapted to today's era.' His belief seems to have been that by re-engineering production processes to enable a 'small quantities in many varieties' output (contrasting with the high-volume, long-run, single-product, approach of Western organizations), Toyota could compete more effectively in challenging markets.

He demonstrates three clear beliefs. The first is in an ordered, disciplined, systematic approach to eradication of waste. The second is an acknowledgement that individual workers are capable of contributing to this improvement, given training and opportunity. Third, he uniquely emphasizes the role of the customer, suggesting that far from organizations 'pushing' their goods into the marketplace – the underpinning belief in the West – customers now 'pull the goods they need, in the amount and at the time they need them'. Taken together, these translate to a belief in the science of industrial engineering to resolve the challenges of improvement, in the value of human beings as contributors to success, and, ultimately, in the power of consumers to determine the fate of a company and its products.

Although not explicit about this, he clearly views the executive and management as having a 'top down' responsibility to drive changes in the organization. When he writes about the workers, and notwithstanding the preceding comments about humanity, he writes about initial resistance to his work, and of using 'authority to encourage them' – a clear recognition of the hierarchy in organizations. He states that this needs to be focused into the area under control, saying, 'I could yell at a foreman under my jurisdiction, but not at a foreman from the neighbouring department.' Here, we can see both the determination of Ohno to see the innovations succeed, but also a limit to personal tolerance, perhaps a measure of his personal drive and ambition which conflicts with the team-working and respect written about elsewhere.

Vignette 11.1 The Sisters of Nazareth

In 2006, the newly elected Superior General of the Congregation of the Sisters of Nazareth recognized that the Order needed to change the way it worked if it were to survive into the future and continue the mission of the foundress, Victoire Lameniere. Successful for over 150 years, the Congregational Mission was threatened by both legislative changes and the emergence of strong lay organizations offering similar services.

Particular concerns were brought into focus by the significantly increasing average age of the members of the Congregation and falling new vocations (a factor affecting every religious order). These were the challenges of progressively introducing senior lay management, and the need for the order to come to terms with the prospect of withdrawal from operational management, together raising the further challenge of the members of the Congregation needing to learn how to act in a governance capacity, more as owners than operators. This, probably the most significant change of role in their history, compelled the engagement of the whole community.

The Superior General and her council (equivalent to the board of a company) engaged with a firm of consultants to support them in renewing the spiritual life of the Congregation, enhancing their stewardship of the assets on four continents (principally care homes for the elderly but including schools, orphanages and outreach programmes), and leading their religious and lay communities to a more certain future.

Recognizing themselves as being a 'community of will', persisting only by the choice of the Sisters and the commitment of their lay staff, the General Council knew that any programme of change required the full engagement of everybody associated with the Congregation. Working with the consultants, they devised a series of engagement events. The first of these, delivered in each of the regions, brought together the Sisters Superior for each region to examine and understand the opportunities and threats facing the Congregation, and to make some decisions about the future. These included making plans to react to significant challenges to their survival: financial, organizational, and human (including falling numbers of vocations). The outputs from these events were considered by the General Council and shared, in full, with every one of their communities.

With a new shared understanding, the regional Superiors were asked to work with their houses to develop regional plans which addressed the challenges and threats for that area, aligned with the agreed plans for the global congregation. With those plans in first draft, the Superior General, working throughout with at least one member of the general council and the Regional Superior, undertook a second round of meetings, visiting each of the regions again to review the plans together, to provide the opportunity for everyone to contribute their thoughts, and to share their feelings and offer guidance based on experience and knowledge gained through the process. The outputs were again brought together, reflected upon, and shared widely through the organization.

Finally, a third global tour was undertaken presenting back to each of the regions the findings and proposals arising from the discussions, covering the global, regional and individual house plans. These workshops again provided the opportunity for all members of the community (religious and lay) to engage in the change process. Emerging from this final round was a plan to transform the congregation and its various care operations over the subsequent four years.

Although this was a hugely time-consuming process for the 'senior management', this approach enabled the general council to ensure that, when decisions were taken and implemented, the whole organization would be aligned behind them and the chances of success greatly increased. Involving over eighty meetings in a twelve-month period, every religious member of the community and probably over half the lay management, this was senior management commitment writ large.

In addition to the success in engaging the community, the Congregation has begun to be a learning organization. Each step in the process has been iterative – the questions have been posed, the answers developed, tested, and reflected on – and only then has action been taken. This learning has also occurred at the individual level. One example of this is that, of the eighty-plus meetings, the Superior General conducted forty-two of them with the representatives of individual houses. In the first of these meetings, the Superior General provided a two-minute introduction, with the assisting consultant talking for ten minutes. By the forty-second meeting, the Superior General was providing a ten-minute introduction and the assisting consultant was pretty much redundant!

To some extent, Ohno's work might be considered to align most closely with the 'machine' view of organizations, and potentially having the same limitations, particularly a reliance on the 'rightness' of the designer of the organization. While Ohno's approach increases the low level and local adaptiveness of the organization, arguably it reduces it at the corporate level.

Ohno argues that the traditional 'cost-plus' model of pricing 'selling price = profit + actual cost' is outdated and inappropriate. It is fair to say that, except in production-led industries, for example, public transportation systems and health care, organizations have moved away from this model towards value-based pricing. Increasing competition and market growth, at rates lower than growth in production capacity, have forced businesses to look in this direction. Ohno argues that 'Our products are scrutinized by cool-headed consumers . . . where the manufacturing cost of a product is of no consequence', and hence the 'question is whether or not the product is of value to the buyer'. Increasing value can, in that competitive environment, primarily be derived by driving down the cost of production – and hence the focus on elimination of waste.

Ohno might be thought of as Shaw's 'unreasonable man', adapting the world to himself rather than adapting himself to the world. Clearly a practical man of courage, determination and intelligence, Ohno's forty-year mission at Toyota is undoubtedly having a long-term impact, not only on Toyota but on management globally. As this is written, eighteen years after Ohno's death, Toyota have reduced their 2009 sales forecast by 1m vehicles and are forming a 'Profit Improvement Committee' to increase value and reduce costs across the business to protect their bottom line.

11.2 Assumptions

What assumptions about the nature of the world does Ohno seem to be making? There are several. First, and perhaps most dominant, is that the conventional model of mass-production (Ohno cites the then Ford production method) is inappropriate for contemporary businesses and markets. Ohno claims that, in 1949, Toyota produced around 25,000 vehicles, of which only about 1,000 were passenger cars. At that time, the American manufacturers were both the most advanced in production methods and the largest. In 2008, Toyota is reputed to have produced nearly ten million passenger vehicles and succeeded General Motors as the largest global producer. In early 2009, with global recession apparently looming, the three American majors, Ford, General Motors and Chrysler, approached the US government for $30bn to rescue them from failure, and Toyota is facing its first losses in forty years.

It is fair to say that there are a significant range of differences, other than the Toyota Production System, that separate Toyota from its Western competitors. In the 1940s, the Western organizations were working with a legacy of established investment in manufacturing plant, with established, powerful, functionally-oriented and disparate unions, and succeeding with their products in the market place. Where was the incentive to change? On the other hand, as the numbers above show, Toyota was building a new business and seeking to compete with the established businesses, investing in new plant and new markets, and supported particularly by American industrialists and consultants, able to study and learn from the challenges facing the Western manufacturers. Culturally, Japan was very different to the West, perhaps having a much more disciplined and homogeneous culture, whereas individuality was beginning to assert itself more strongly in the West. It is appropriate to wonder if, under alternative conditions, the Western manufacturers might have evolved differently.

The assumption that 'multi-kind, small quantity', just-in-time production is more cost-effective over time was the fundamental operating difference between Toyota and its competitors. The current situation suggests that, at least for now, Ohno was right. The ultimate expression of this approach might be reflected in B. Joseph Pines' work on *Mass Customization* (Harvard College, 1993).

Ohno's second assumption appears to be about the responsibility of management – not just for quality (which he hardly mentions) but for the whole process of managing the organization and driving continuous improvement in the eradication of waste, in achieving consistency and in minimizing costs. In this regard, although acknowledging the inspiration of the Toyoda's, it is apparent in his writing that Ohno sees himself as battling persistently against the established methods and norms, whether with the executive, from whom he undoubtedly had significant support at the highest level, or with the production workers, whose established practices he (apparently successfully) worked to change. This 'top down' approach is not unusual in organizations, and does perhaps give the lie to the reputation of Japanese organizations as being much more participative in their approach – for example, quality circles. While effective, trained workers are recognized by Ohno as fundamental to success, he clearly sees them as necessary rather than desirable – and their contribution, while perhaps wider than their Western equivalents (eventually being multi-skilled rather than mono-skilled), is constrained to their own working area. There is no scope in his system for them to query whether or not something should be done; they can only think about how the given task might be done faster, cleaner and cheaper than before. To a large extent, this is no different to many Western organizations – but it does not fully reflect a 'respect for [their] humanity'.

Ohno writes about the necessity of effective team-working, 'Teamwork is Everything', and the benefit that can bring, 'not how many parts were machined or drilled by one worker, but how many products were complete by the team as a whole'. He acknowledges that this may mean less than optimal performance from some individuals: 'distribute force equally . . . and at the same depth'. There is clearly a slight clash here with the notion of 'eliminating waste', since he seems to be accepting as part of the necessary functioning of the team that some talent or strength may not be fully utilized in the creation of the product.

The centralized 'command and control' organization implied by this approach has already been critiqued (Part One), and while encouraging low-level process improvement, it says nothing of the ability of the organization to adapt and change at a more strategic level.

A third assumption appears to be that workers will contribute 'as directed', and will, in consequence, sacrifice themselves for the good of the business. The 'as directed' again points to a requirement for individuals to follow instructions, while offering contributions to performance improvement, for example, waste reduction, which ultimately may not be in their interests – at least in the short term. It has been argued elsewhere (see Chapter One) that, in the long term, jobs cannot be protected by the perpetuation of inefficient work practices. In a competitive world, efficiency or productivity gains are essential for an organization to remain in business. As Toyota demonstrates, the relentless pursuit of process efficiency is at least one key to continued success – and provides a competitive advantage in a global economy where 'there is a surplus of everything' (Peters, 1992). However, an expectation that the average production worker will actively seek to bring about changes that lead to his or her own redundancy must be considered, at best, optimistic. While working in a predominantly growing business, Toyota employees may have considered themselves relatively immune from loss of employment. This can no longer be considered to be the case. Notwithstanding the rapid emergence of China and India as major growth economies, the mature replacement cycle markets of the West can no longer offer continued demand growth at a rate fast enough to absorb the increasing productivity of a continually improving company, and in the medium to long term this may threaten employment numbers in the East. Coupled to this is the trend by major corporations to locate their factories near to their markets (for example, Toyota, Nissan and Honda producing in Europe and the USA, Mercedes and BMW producing in the USA, South Africa and Asia) – which again may limit Toyota home country production to neighbouring Asian countries.

11.3 Methods

Unlike the other Gurus discussed, Ohno does not offer a quality programme or method for a quality project, but a business management philosophy that gives primacy to satisfying the needs of customers. This designs the production system around a 'demand-pull', rather than a 'production-push' approach. Ohno argues that this approach works to eliminate waste, as only those things which are demanded by customers are produced. Although simple to say, this philosophy requires a complete reversal of the thinking that drove the development of Western economies. It is not a philosophy that can be adopted in part, or from which the 'juicy bits' can be extracted and applied; it is very much 'all or nothing' if it is to be successful.

The key elements to Ohno's thinking, the fundamentals of the Toyota Production System, seem to be:

Learn: Citing Toyoda Kiichiro, then Toyota President, saying 'Catch up with America in three years. Otherwise the automobile industry of Japan will not survive', Ohno saw that learning from, and about, competitors was fundamental to success.

Revelation: A different understanding of the world which, in effect, denies the existence of a mass market to focus on the customer as an individual.

Flexibility: Recognition that a 'slow-growth' economy demands cost-effectiveness in small batch sizes, and frequent tool changes, in contrast to the traditional 'long-run, large batch' mentality.

Waste: Elimination of waste and reduction of cost as the basis of survival and efficiency enabled by the 'just-in-time' meeting of needs and the development of autonomic systems which generate self-control in the production flow process – which becomes the basis of organizational design. Ohno sees price as value-based rather than cost-based – and value is determined by the consumer not the producer.

Information: The idea of *kanban*, a communication device for the production process which informs the preceding step *and* controls its rate of output, is startling in its simplicity and effectiveness. *Kanban* eliminates a mass of planning, reporting, controlling activity, and information systems that impose enormous costs on traditional organizations. Information also manages the essential process flow, from customer demand backwards to supplier management, and is used to smooth or 'level' demands to minimize peaks and troughs.

Autonomation: Rooted again in the notion of self-control, 'autonomation' (Ohno, 1978) requires that machines be designed in such a way that they monitor their own performance and stop themselves if they are not performing within pre-set parameters, or are producing defective product. This cybernetic thinking eliminates waste in three ways:

- no more than one defective part is produced (eliminating scrap and rework) because the machine monitors itself;
- human talents can be put to more effective use than 'machine-minding';
- final products are not assembled using defective parts.

Coaching: With autonomation taking over much of the role of production supervision, the supervisor and manager are free to focus their attention on developing the skills and talents of the workers, and in supporting their development as multiskilled workers able to carry out a range of tasks.

Needs: In the Toyota Production System innovation and improvement are based on identified need, drawing on the information generated by the system. The need is used to drive thinking about the change – so management is not fad- or initiative-oriented but is consistently focused on understanding the ongoing need for improvement, on identifying through accurate information the opportunities for it, and to taking deliberate action to achieve it.

Ohno offers a mechanism (Figure 11.1) for the complete analysis of waste, moving beyond traditional measures of 'yield' or 'scrap', and suggesting that: present capacity = work + waste, and identifying waste in the following ways:

overproduction;
time on hand (waiting);
in transportation;
processing;
of stock on hand (inventory);
of movement;
of making defective products.

For Ohno, then, the focus on waste emphasizes that 'the ratio of value-added work is lower than most people think'. The elimination of waste might then be thought of more positively as increasing the proportion of value-adding work, which for Ohno means 'actually advancing the process towards completing the job'. While there has been much work on process improvement in many companies over recent years, there is still a surprising amount of 'waste' in many, if Ohno's definition is accepted. For example, a project undertaken to improve performance in the management of a sterile supply chain revealed that, for some products, the proportion of overhead in terms of process time was 94 per cent, that is, for 94 per cent of the time, the product was 'waiting', while in terms of the non-value adding work, this ranged from 36 per cent up

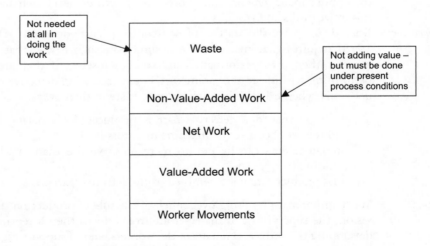

Figure 11.1 Understanding waste.

to 67 per cent, depending on the proportion of fixed to variable elements in the product. Redesigning the process to eliminate these factors both significantly reduces process cost and dramatically improves process output. The benefits are realized in financial terms and improvement in customer service.

In 1988, Ohno proposed that Toyota, having already achieved substantial performance improvement (reduction in waste), was able to focus on the 'Order to Cash' time line, reducing it by 'removing all the non-value-added wastes'. For a capital-intensive industry such as motor manufacturing, reductions in the order to cash cycle substantially reduce the working capital needs of the business. This focus is not available to organizations that have not already largely eliminated waste or slack in their production facilities.

11.4 Successes and Failures

That Ohno's work has had major impact is irrefutable. It has been adopted and adapted by many large organizations (often as 'lean manufacturing'), and his approach is now researched and taught in universities and business schools. The growth of Toyota vehicle manufacturing to become first or second in the world can, at least in part, be credited to the adoption of Ohno's work, although no doubt there have been many other factors that have affected the growth of Toyota, such as the vision of the Toyoda family, the availability of low-cost labour in a number of Asian countries, and the favourable economic conditions that prevailed for much of the period from the late 1940s through to the turn of the century.

As a manufacturing approach, Ohno's methodology works well. However, it is not without its limitations. Particularly in an established organization and supply chain, the adoption of parts of the Toyota process can be problematic and even inappropriate where the supplier technologies or worker capabilities are not aligned. While the implementation of this method on a new or growing facility is relatively straightforward, the difficulty of application and use in an established factory should not be underestimated.

The focus is on manufacturing, and although some (for example, Seddon) have revised the approach to focus on the service sector, its success is very much more limited in circumstances where the process is less influential than the human interaction. Similarly, the idea of 'autonomation' applied in a production environment works well; employed in a service environment it is inadequate – an automated (or autonomated) system cannot deal with the infinite variety of human behaviour. If you doubt this, think about your last experience of dealing with an automated telephone call handling system!

Human behaviour also exposes another significant weakness. Although Ohno expressly includes the workforce within the methodology, the workers are included as small-part players, that is, they are expected to contribute to their part of the grand central design, but not to be full participants in the decision processes. The core ownership of the ideas is clearly reserved for the directors and senior managers, with workers expected to follow that lead. That said, the emphasis placed by Ohno on the customer (as the focus of the process) places the whole organization at the mercy of customer desire. However, he says nothing of how the organization can and should seek to understand the customer, or how the customer should be influenced to want what the organization has to offer.

11.5 Critical Review

Ohno's core idea might best be characterized through the call to eliminate waste of all types. With its roots in the desperate straits of post-war Japan, and the urgent need to maximize value from every aspect of the economy, this makes much sense. It is also very supportive of the more contemporary need to minimize environmental impact caused by business operations and the use of products.

The adoption of his ideas throughout the world are testament to the value and resilience of the approach under changing circumstances, but that adoption has in many cases been somewhat partial, with organizations attempting to cherry-pick the parts that they want (usually those that appear to immediately save money). It is noticeable that investment in training for workers has, certainly in the West, been more challenging to achieve than the implementation of *kanban*-type systems.

Ohno, bizarrely, does not offer a systematic methodology for the development and adoption of the Toyota System – though this can be derived from his work (Ohno, 1978). He says little or nothing of how to start the implementation process – and in particular nothing of how to engage the hearts and minds of the company directors whose support, encouragement, and funding will be necessary for successful implementation. Inspiration for a systematic methodology can be drawn from other areas. For example, there is now a substantial literature on the subject of 'lean production', with authors such as Feld (2001), Levinson (2002), Dennis (2007), and Junewick (2002) who, each in their own way, seek to systematize, organize, synthesize and homogenize the Toyota System. Each brings a slightly different perspective. Secondly, the underpinning method that drives improvement in the Toyota method is the use of 'feedback control'. There is a whole body of knowledge (cybernetics), of which feedback control is but a small part, ranging from Wiener (1947) through Beer (1959, 1966, 1979, 1981) and, more recently, Beckford (1993, 1998, 2002) and Dudley (2000).

The focus on 'method' in Ohno's work, the science, perhaps understates the nature of power relations in Japan generally, and Toyota in particular (at least at that time). It is likely to be the case that in countries and businesses with different power structures and relationships, the same success story may be harder to achieve.

Summary

This chapter has introduced the work of Taiichi Ohno, and has considered his substantial contribution to the global quality movement. Students are encouraged to read Ohno's own work to inform and develop their views further.

KEY LEARNING POINTS

Taiichi Ohno: **father of the Toyota Production System**

Focus on:
the elimination of waste.

Scientific methodology:
very successful in manufacturing organizations.

Adopted by many businesses worldwide under the 'lean production' banner.

No clear methodology for engagement and implementation.

Question

Consider what challenges would be faced by a traditionally managed organization in adopting the Toyota Methodology. Identify tools from all the gurus that might help overcome them.

12 Shigeo Shingo

Admit your own mistakes openly, maybe even joyfully
(Robert Townsend, *Further Up the Organization*, 1985)

Introduction

Shigeo Shingo, who died in 1990, is perhaps the least well known of the Japanese quality gurus in the West. Educated as a mechanical engineer, he became a consultant in 1945, subsequently working with a wide variety of companies in many industries. These companies included Toyota, Mitsubishi, Matsushita, and Sony. During his later career, he became involved with a large number of Western organizations. Norman Bodek, president of Productivity Incorporated, in the Foreword to *The Sayings of Shigeo Shingo* (1987), cited by Bendell (1989: 12), says:

> If I could give a Nobel Prize for exceptional contributions to world economy, prosperity and productivity, I wouldn't have much difficulty selecting a winner – Shigeo Shingo's life work has contributed to the well-being of everyone in the world.

Shingo is regarded by Gilbert (1992: 24) as 'one of the 20th century's greatest engineers', and he made a number of significant contributions to engineering. He wrote fourteen major books, with several translated into English and other European languages.

12.1 Philosophy

Shingo's early philosophy embraced the 'scientific management' ideas originated by Frederick Taylor (1912). This approach was based on what is now called the 'economic man' theory of motivation, which was briefly reviewed as scientific management in Chapter 4. The approach was adopted extensively by Shingo, until in mid-career he became aware of 'statistical quality control' methods. He adopted these methods, until in the 1970s he was 'finally released from the spell of statistical quality control methods' (Bendell, 1989: 12). The breakthrough in his thinking arose when he came to believe in defect prevention. This led to his major contribution to the quality debate.

Essentially, Shingo believed that 'statistical methods detect errors too late in the manufacturing process' (Flood, 1993: 28). He suggested that instead of detecting errors it was better to engage in preventative measures, aimed at eliminating sources of error. Gilbert (1992: 166) suggests that Shingo meant that we need to change our attitude of mind and 'to organise and then behave in a way' which allows mistake proofing to happen.

Thus, over time, Shingo effectively rejected the scientific management 'economic man' theory with all its attendant difficulties; rejected control after the event; and focused on prevention. He became concerned with the total manufacturing process, and Gilbert (1992: 24) cites him as saying that:

> he would prefer to be remembered for his promotion of the understanding neces-
> sary behind the concepts of looking at the total manufacturing process and the
> elimination of transportation, storage, lot delays and inspection.

Much of this approach has become embedded in the *kanban* systems, often called 'just in time'.

Shingo continued to believe in mechanizing the monitoring of error, considering that human assessment was 'inconsistent and prone to error'. He used people to identify underlying causes and produce preventative solutions.

There is a clear belief, like Crosby, in a 'zero defects' approach. However, unlike Crosby who emphasizes worker responsibility, exhortations and slogans, Shingo's approach emphasizes zero defects through good engineering, process investigation, and rectification. Bendell (1989: 12) reports that Shingo shared the concern of Deming and Juran that 'posting defect statistics is misguided, and that instead the defective elements in operations that generate a lot of defectives should be hunted down'.

12.2 Assumptions

The assumptions about the world that seem to underpin Shingo's approach will now be reviewed.

Perhaps unsurprisingly, given his mechanical engineering background and training, Shingo can be seen to have adhered to a mechanistic approach to organization through-out his career. From engineering jobs and people in the scientific management approach of his early work, he moved to the quantitative methods of statistical quality control, and, finally, to error prevention through good engineering.

Many management theorists and practitioners have challenged the mechanistic view of organization. It is criticized for failing to take account of human needs and desires, and failing to recognize the interactions within an organization, and between the organization and its environment. Further criticisms have been aimed at the reductionist nature of the approach, which tends to fragment organizations, their systems and processes, rather than deal with them holistically. An approach which does not take account of these factors in an increasingly complex and dynamic world must be flawed.

The adoption and then abandonment of statistical methods, rests on the belief that it is possible to develop processes which are error free. While it can be seen that in an engineering context it may be possible to achieve the zero defects objective, it is considered unlikely that this is possible in other sectors. Food production, as was seen with Chesswood Produce in Chapter 5, relies on natural processes which cannot yet be engineered to achieve absolute reliability. While it is possible to improve materials and yields, the processes are still subject to forces which are outside the influence or control of the organization and its people, for example, temperature, humidity, wind, soil condition, and crop diseases. Similarly, in the service sector, as previously discussed, there are many variables which cannot be controlled to the extent that Shingo's approach requires.

It has been consistently argued in this book that an appropriate balance of both qualitative and quantitative approaches is most useful. Here, Shingo's assumptions must be challenged by suggesting that ignoring the human relations aspects of organization, and abandoning statistical methods, largely limits the potential applications of his methodology to the manufacturing sector.

12.3 Methods

Shingo can be considered as the first management thinker and practitioner to engage in what has recently come to be called 're-engineering' (Hammer and Champy, 1993), although the term was used as early as the 1940s in the discipline of operations research. His achievement in reducing hull assembly time from four months to two months at Mitsubishi, and the development of the Single Minute Exchange of Die (SMED) system at Toyota as part of the 'just-in-time' concept, were both substantial contributions in their own right.

However, Shingo's principal contribution to the quality field is the mistake-proofing concept *Poka-Yoke*: 'Defect = 0'. This approach stops the production process whenever a defect occurs, defines the cause, and generates action designed to prevent recurrence. Alternatively, on-line adjustment to the product or process may be made, enabling continuous processes to be managed. For example, in the chemical and steel industries it may be both impractical and expensive to stop a production process.

Poka-Yoke relies on a process of continuously monitoring potential sources of error. Machines used in the process are equipped with feedback instrumentation to carry out this task, as Shingo considered that human personnel are fallible (Bendell, 1989: 12). People are used to trace and resolve the error causes. Installation of the system is expected over time to lead to a position where all likely recurring errors have been eradicated.

Vignette 12.1 Cybernetic Systems

The idea of *Poka-Yoke* is similar to the concepts employed in cybernetic systems, which, in the process of going out of control, put themselves back in control again. The simplest and commonest form of cybernetic system is a domestic heating system, which, on receipt of 'feedback' information about the air temperature from the thermostat, turns the heating system on and off in the attempt to maintain a set temperature. A similar example is the cooling system on an engine, where the thermostat opens and closes to control the flow of water through the radiator, keeping the engine at its optimum operating temperature.

The 'goal' of these systems is a particular temperature. In the case of *Poka-Yoke*, the goal is zero defects. In each case, the goal is determined outside the system – by the design engineer for the car, the house occupier for the heating system, or the factory management for the production process.

The concept is now widely employed in industrial control systems for production processes. For example, the baking industry uses a system of this type to control the chamber temperatures in travelling ovens, aiming to ensure that the product is appropriately heated at each stage of the cooking process. The employment of these techniques can reduce or eliminate the need for human monitoring of processes, and, as Shingo suggests, enhance reliability.

Advances in information technology, and approaches to information management, make the application of these techniques much simpler. It is now possible to design and build control systems which operate in real-time, and are capable of both detecting errors – and, perhaps more importantly, anticipating errors (on the basis of the information being received), and stopping the line before the error occurs.

A common failure amongst managers in organizations is fully to appreciate what it is now possible to achieve in this regard, and to rely on outmoded techniques of management. In pursuit of quality it is useful to adopt proven, reliable techniques, but it is essential to embrace new approaches which have the latent capability to bring about substantial improvement.

The concept has been adopted to some extent in the food processing industry, through the system known as Hazard Analysis Critical Control Points (HACCP), which has already been outlined in Chapter 7. Clearly, it would be unacceptable for even one defective food item to move through a system which generated risk to health. However, as is regularly seen, even such rigorous systems cannot entirely remove the risks, as, for example, with the E. coli food poisoning outbreak in Scotland during 1996, which led to several deaths.

12.4 Successes and Failures

There is no doubt that Shingo's ideas have made a substantial contribution in a variety of areas. The adoption of all or some of his methods by companies throughout the world, and his extensive consulting in many countries, stand as testament to his success. There are, however, apparent limitations.

While Gilbert (1992: 166) suggests that the *Poka-Yoke* concept can be applied equally to administrative procedures and production processes, this is, at best, arguable. A production process may well be fully or extensively automated, thus minimizing the opportunity for human or machine error. Administrative and book-keeping procedures, which rely for the most part on the communication and transcription of information, cannot be automated to the same extent, thus allowing scope for error. (An error rate of 2 per cent – two keystrokes in one hundred – is regarded as normal for a competent keyboard operator.) Human interaction and intervention in the system is inevitable, and as Shingo himself said, humans are fallible. A second strand to this is the potential for misinterpretation of data. Language relies on two levels of understanding: the syntactic (signs) and semantic (meaning). While syntactic understanding can be relatively reliably conveyed, even automated, semantic understanding cannot be guaranteed. It is therefore not possible to build an administrative system which can guarantee that the message, including its meaning, transmitted by one party is received and understood in the same way by the other party.

Flood (1993: 29) provides the basis for the main strengths of Shingo's approach:

- on-line, real-time control;
- *Poka-Yoke* emphasizes effective control systems.

The main weaknesses are:

- source inspection only works effectively in manufacturing processes;
- Shingo says little about people other than that they are fallible.

Considering the first of these points, there is little doubt that in a fast-moving and rapidly changing world, on-line real-time information is not just desirable but essential. However, the feasibility of halting many production processes is questioned.

The use of automated feedback and control mechanisms is a sound starting point for the control of a process in operation, and is to be welcomed. However, little is said about the management attitudes towards accountability and responsibility that must go with it. It could be argued that a management unsupportive of this approach would not implement it. However, a technical system of this sort provides information which an autocratic management could use in a way which might be considered inappropriate – as a stick with which to beat people rather than as a tool for improvement. Nonetheless, as Wiener (1947) stated, in the early stages of the development of modern cybernetics, there are 'great possibilities for good or evil', and it is up to managers to use the knowledge wisely.

Turning to the weaknesses, the applicability of the ideas to the service sector has already been questioned. Regarding the attitude to people, it is clear that Shingo's work assumes a willing, co-operative workforce, although he says nothing about how this state can be achieved and maintained. The body of literature concerning this topic, which arose during the middle and later years of the twentieth century, has not been accounted for.

12.5 Critical Review

There appear to be some consistent themes to Shingo's views, despite the apparent developments in his thinking, from scientific management, through statistical quality control, to mistake-proofing.

In the main, Shingo seems to have adhered to an 'economic man' view of people involved in the organization. The wisdom of this view, and his failure to address the body of theoretical and practical knowledge which challenges it, has to be considered a major weakness of his work. While in some Eastern cultures there remains a strong allegiance to collective societal values, notably in Japan, other nations have moved away from this. Many Western countries have seen a significant move towards the pursuit of individual values and objectives, which often translates into the pursuit of individual, rather than corporate, benefit from work – often reinforced by the style of corporate rewards offered. In a situation where that is the case, the individual may not be willing to contribute in the way that Shingo's work suggests is necessary.

A second, clear and consistent theme has been the concentration on good engineering. This is unsurprising, given Shingo's background, and his contribution must be considered substantial in this area. However it does limit the application of his ideas to organizations and processes where the concepts are most readily applied.

The concept of mistake-proofing (inevitably sitting comfortably with the work of Taiichi Ohno), by refining and redesigning processes, is of great importance. While it will generally be most easily applicable in the manufacturing sector, there is little doubt that the concept, if not the practice, can be carried across into service organizations. The danger is that it may give rise to additional administrative, auditing, and checking procedures which, far from reducing costs and speeding up processes, may well serve to increase costs and slow down service. Associated with this is that the procedures may become 'institutionalized', thus inhibiting or preventing adaptation and learning by the organization. Manual methods, once ingrained, can become the fabric of each individual's daily task – and very difficult to change. Nonetheless, the underlying emphasis on prevention of error is to be welcomed.

Summary

This chapter has reviewed the major contribution of Shigeo Shingo to the quality movement. Students should refer to Shingo's work (1987) to enhance and develop their own understanding.

KEY LEARNING POINTS

Shigeo Shingo's definition of quality: defects in process

Key beliefs:
defect prevention through eradication of defective processes, human fallibility, 'mechanistic' view of organizations, real-time information processing.

Principal method:
Poka-Yoke (zero defects).

Question

Consider the implications of mistake-proofing for lean manufacturing (Toyota Production System).

13　Genichi Taguchi

All things are numbers

(Pythagoras)

Introduction

Genichi Taguchi trained as a textile engineer, prior to his service in the Japanese Navy. He subsequently worked in the Ministry of Public Health and Welfare, and the Institute of Statistical Mathematics. In that post he learned about experimental design techniques and orthogonal arrays. He began his consulting career while working at Nippon Telephone and Telegraph. His early work in the field of quality was mainly concerned with operational production processes – the shift to a focus on product and process design occurring during the 1980s. It was during this period that his ideas began to be adopted in the USA. Logothetis (1992: 17) describes Taguchi's contribution as an 'inspired evolution' in the quality movement, by eliminating the need for mass-inspection through his process of building quality into the product at the design stage.

Taguchi was awarded the Deming prize and the Deming award for literature on quality. His best-known works are *Systems of Experimental Design* (1987) and *Management by Total Results*, which he co-authored.

13.1　Philosophy

The two founding ideas of Taguchi's quality work are essentially quantitative. First is a belief in statistical methods to identify and eradicate quality problems. The second idea rests on designing products and processes to build quality in, right from the outset. Logothetis (1992: 13) sees Taguchi's view of quality as a negative, the cost of non-quality, meaning 'the loss imparted to society from the time the product is shipped'. Taguchi's prime concern is with customer satisfaction, and with the potential for 'loss of reputation and goodwill' associated with failure to meet customer expectations. Such a failure, he considered, would lead the customer to buy elsewhere in the future, damaging the prospects of the company, its employees, and society. He saw that such losses not only occurred when a product was outside its specification but also when it varied from its target value.

Flood (1993: 30) suggests that Taguchi's view 'steps back one further stage on the technical side', thus pulling back quality management into design. This is achieved through a three-stage prototyping method (Figure 13.1).

The first stage is concerned with system-design reasoning, involving both product

Genichi Taguchi:

- System Design;

- Parameter Design;

- Tolerance Design.

Figure 13.1 Genichi Taguchi's three-stage prototyping method.

and process. This is an attempt to develop a basic analytical, materials, process and production framework. This framework is carried forward into the second stage: parameter design. The search at this stage is for the optimal mix of product variation levels and process operating levels, aiming to reduce the sensitivity of the production system to external or internal disturbances. Tolerance design, the third stage, enables the recognition of factors that may significantly affect the variability of the product. Further investment, alternative equipment, and materials are then considered as ways further to reduce variability.

Here, a clear belief can be seen in identifying, and, as far as possible, eradicating, potential causes of 'non-quality' at the outset. This ties in with Flood's (1993: 32) view that Taguchi's work perceives quality to be a 'societal rather than organisational issue.' He further recognizes that Taguchi's method relies on a number of organizational principles (see Figure 13.2).

Clearly, Taguchi recognizes organizations as 'open systems', that is, systems which interact with their environment, influencing and being influenced. The emphasis on communication and control – the systems view – recognizes interdependence between processes, something which he has been criticized for ignoring. Logothetis (1992: 340) considers this unreasonable, and says that 'Taguchi, contrary to common opinion does recognize interactions'. He says:

> If one assumes a linear model thinking it correct, then one is a man removed from natural science or reality, and commits the mistake of standing just upon mathematics which is nothing but idealism.

Genichi Taguchi:

Principle 1) Communication;

Principle 2) Control;

Principle 3) Efficiency;

Principle 4) Effectiveness;

Principle 5) Efficacy;

Principle 6) Emphasis on location and elimination of causes of error;

Principle 7) Emphasis on design control;

Principle 8) Emphasis on environmental analysis.

Figure 13.2 Genichi Taguchi's organizational principles.

Summarizing, there appear to be several beliefs. The first is in quantitative methods, providing measurements for control. The second is in the eradication, as far as possible, of causes of failure at the outset. The third is in the societal cost of non-quality. The fourth perhaps reflects the third, and is the systems view of interdependence and interrelationship, both within the organization and with its environment.

13.2 Assumptions

Assumptions, which are considered to underpin Taguchi's approach, will now be addressed.

The first, and quite critical, feature is that he seems to assume that quality can always be controlled through improvement in design. While this may be the case for many aspects of manufacturing, its validity in the service sector must be questioned. Similarly, where products exhibit either natural properties – as in the case of food – or contain aspects of 'craft' skill – cabinet making, pottery, or precious metal work – this may be inappropriate.

A second assumption relates to his attitude to people. While it will be clearly seen in the next section that he values their creative input to the design and development process, it is perceived that they are not considered a significant factor in the production of quality goods. Little or nothing is said about either them or the management process.

It has already been mentioned that the work has a clear focus on the manufacturing sector. Nothing is said about how to manage the quality process in service industries.

The third assumption is again quite critical. Taguchi seems to assume that the organization can wait for results, that delays between product conception and production will be acceptable. While these delays are to some extent inevitable, the contemporary market demands are such that they need to be minimized. 'Time to market' has become an absolutely crucial element in success for many organizations. In pharmaceuticals, for example, the first in the market with a new treatment becomes the market leader, and thenceforward the position is often unassailable. A similar profile arises with information technology, where the most recent innovation tends to act as a key attractor for what marketing people call 'early adopters' – and the innovator attracts a significant degree of loyalty. It is essential, therefore, if Taguchi's ideas are to be fully implemented that they are not additional to, but are an integral part of, the product development process, and that the process is designed in such a way that 'time to market' is a key consideration. A conflict may arise between the business need to be fast into the market and the business need to achieve high quality. Adopting the Taguchi method after initial product design must be seen as unacceptable. It is suggested that quality parameters should be as much a part of a basic design brief as timing, markets, and prices.

It is easy to see that much of Taguchi's work has been informed by his background in engineering and quantitative methods. What is less obvious is how his systems perspective arose. The adoption of a systemic view, while not apparently extending to the management process of the organization, is certainly a step forward from the work of many of his fellow gurus.

13.3 Methods

The principal tools and techniques espoused by Taguchi centre around the concept of *kaizen* thinking, that is, continuous improvement. His backward step into the design process helps to ensure a high basic quality standard. Other than the 'quadratic loss function', the other statistical methods are common to many thinkers and will be reviewed in the appropriate chapter. This section will consider the following:

- suggested steps for experimental studies;
- prototyping;
- quadratic loss function.

The suggested steps (Figure 13.3) fall into the 'parameter design' (Logothetis, 1992: 306) stage of product development. It is within this process that Taguchi utilizes people. This scientific method is very reminiscent of Deming's 'Plan, Do, Check, Action' cycle, and is perhaps not surprising given their common background in statistics.

The first stage is concerned with developing a clear statement of precisely what problem is to be solved. Taguchi considers it very important that the experiment should be exactly targeted. The second stage links with the first. It is important to determine what output characteristics are to be studied and optimized through the experimental process, and what measurements are to be taken. It may be necessary to run control experiments in order to validate results.

The third stage is brainstorming. At this point, all the managers and operators related to the product or process are required to come together and determine the controllable and uncontrollable factors affecting the situation. Here, the aim is to define an experimental range and suitable factor levels. Logothetis (1992: 306) suggests that Taguchi prefers to consider as many factors (not interactions) as is economically feasible. Whether this represents a sufficient involvement by people in the solution development process is debatable; perhaps they should be involved at all stages. Nonetheless, their involvement in experiment design, and their contribution of knowledge to the debate, must be considered invaluable. It is normally the case that those who actually perform a task know more about it than anybody else. The opportunity for them to articulate that knowledge in an informal session such as brainstorming is to be welcomed.

The fourth stage is experiment design. At this point, the controllable and uncontrollable (noise) factors are separated for statistical monitoring purposes. This is followed by the fifth stage, the experiment itself.

Genichi Taguchi:

Stage 1) Define the problem;

Stage 2) Determine the objective;

Stage 3) Conduct a brainstorming session;

Stage 4) Design the experiment;

Stage 5) Conduct the experiment;

Stage 6) Analyse the data;

Stage 7) Interpret the results;

Stage 8) Run a confirmatory experiment.

Figure 13.3 Genichi Taguchi's eight stages of product development.

The sixth stage is to analyse the performance measures recorded, using appropriate statistical methods. This is followed by interpretation of the results at the seventh stage. This aims to identify optimal levels for the control factors, which seek to minimize variability and bring the process closest to its target value. Prediction is used at this stage to consider the performance of the process under optimal conditions.

The eighth and final stage is to validate the results so far obtained by running further experiments. Failure to confirm results by further experimentation generates a need to revisit stages three to eight.

This whole process may be regarded as similar to the 'black box' technique used in cybernetics. In that case, altering inputs and monitoring the effect on outputs is an experimental device or method for determining the function of a unit. This technique could be used from a 'macro' perspective in a production or manufacturing facility, to determine areas of maximum concern for detailed analysis through the Taguchi methods. Interested readers should refer to the work of Beer (1981) for a more detailed discussion of this approach.

Prototyping is the technique which Taguchi uses to develop what Gilbert (1992: 24) calls the 'up and limping' prototype. This has already been seen in the review of Taguchi's philosophy. The technique consists of three stages. The first, System Design, is aimed at applying scientific and engineering principles to the development of functional design. It has two elements: product design and process design. The second stage is Parameter Design, which looks at establishing process and machine settings that minimize performance variation. A distinction is made at this stage between controllable and uncontrollable factors (parameters and noise). The specification criterion is for optimization and is usually expressed as monetary loss arising from variation. The third stage is Tolerance Design. This is aimed at minimizing the total sum of product manufacturing and lifetime costs.

Vignette 13.1 Prototyping Services

SAP is believed to be the largest provider of business management software in the world. Its core product extends to include process control, procurement, people management, financial management, and recording, as well as a whole raft of specialized applications supporting specific industry sectors. In 2008, SAP acquired 'Business Objects', thereby significantly extending its range of management information solutions.

Despite this extensive range of products – and the industry solutions and business consulting offers built around them – there are always unique or special situations which the standard solutions do not quite reach. To address this, SAP has created the Centre of Excellence (CoE) for value prototyping. Based at global HQ in Walldorf, Germany, and with representation throughout the world, the CoE offers a prototyping service to SAP and its clients. Clients with unusual or extended business needs whose requirements cannot be addressed within the constraints of the established solutions are introduced to the CoE.

The CoE works in a unique way. Populated only by skilled specialists with a very deep knowledge of the capabilities of SAP solutions, they have created a rapid prototyping process which commences with what they call a 'lab' – a dedicated team and workroom focused exclusively on a particular client and problem. Together with the client, they evaluate the existing system and determine the business needs and initial ideas for a solution. Taking this information, they use their massive dedicated computer centres and software development capability to create an initial prototype. As an example of their capability, they frequently create a copy of the client's SAP landscape in their own environment, so that they can develop the solution and test its performance in as near a live situation as possible.

While the prototyping process duration runs through as many iterations as necessary to solve the problem, it is punctuated by fortnightly deliverable deadlines on which progress is reported. The CoE team pride themselves on always achieving the desired deliverables on time – frequently working late into the night to achieve their objective.

This 'lab-based' process delivers rapid, working and cost-effective solutions to some of SAPs largest clients in dramatically shorter timescales than could ever be achieved through a conventional development approach.

The quadratic loss function is Taguchi's principal contribution to the statistical aspects of achieving quality. The point of this calculation is to minimize the cost of a product or service. In this, a particular quality characteristic (x) is identified and a target value (T) set for it. Proximity to the target value is expressed as $(x - T)$. The result of exceeding or failing to achieve T is a financial loss to the organization, hence the result must always be positive. This is achieved through squaring the answer, $(x - T)^2$. This result is multiplied by a cost co-efficient (c) which puts a cost on failing to meet the target (T). A further co-efficient (k), representing the minimum loss to society with a value always greater than 0, is added. The sum represents the total loss (L) to society. Thus:

$$L = c(x - T)^2 + k$$

This may be viewed, in some respects, as a measure of efficiency and of effective utilization of resources. Of critical importance to its use are the correct selection of criteria and the accurate development of the co-efficients c and k. If any of the values selected for the calculation are incorrect, the whole process becomes useless.

13.4 Successes and Failures

As with each of the other gurus reviewed, Taguchi is accepted as having made a substantial contribution to the field. His books, and his consulting, indicate the wide acknowledgement of the utility of his approach.

Adapting from Flood (1993: 32–3), the following strengths to Taguchi's work are suggested:

- quality is a design requirement;
- the approach recognizes the systemic impact of quality;
- it is a practical method for engineers;
- it guides effective process control.

The principal weaknesses are that:

- usefulness is biased towards manufacturing;

- guidance is not given on management or organizational issues;
- it places quality in the hands of the experts;
- it says nothing about people as social animals.

Looking at the strengths, it can again be argued that Taguchi does not go far enough backwards into the design process. Quality parameters are to some extent already determined once the product has moved beyond the initial concept stage, since certain factors such as market and price range will often be decided at that point.

The recognition of the total cost to society of defective products is useful – and particularly relevant in the light of legislative and regulatory changes concerning corporate social responsibility and environmental impact. However, since, as Flood suggests, little account is taken of the people or management process in the organization, the definition of total cost has to be open to question.

That the method is developed for practising engineers, rather than theoretical statisticians, perhaps serves to make it useful. However, the validity of the quadratic loss function should be questioned if each application is not properly understood and underpinned by a validated statistical base.

Turning to the weaknesses, Flood's assessment that the model is of no use where measurement produces no meaningful hard data can be supported. This, perhaps, limits its usefulness outside the manufacturing sector. That nothing is said about managing people and the organization is also agreed, and is considered to be a major drawback to the whole approach.

Taguchi's failure to recognize organizations as social systems contrasts quite sharply with his recognition of quality as a societal issue. There is no explanation in his work for this. He appears to consider the people within the organization as 'machine parts', who will perform whatever function they are allocated to. No account is taken of human variability in the measurement of processes; perhaps he regards variability, unsympathetically, as noise!

13.5 Critical Review

There can be little doubt that Taguchi's work makes a substantial contribution to the quality movement. This contribution has, however, been focused very narrowly.

His engineering and statistical background quite clearly underpins the approaches which he espouses, and this, to some extent, has limited the value of his work. He relies absolutely on quantitative measures of quality, and this makes his approach quite unsuitable for application to the service sector – where quality is often defined by observers at a much more subjective level.

Nevertheless, his emphasis on quality of design and the process of prototyping are invaluable, even if perhaps not far-reaching enough. The impact on total (organization) cost of developing quality products and processes must not be underestimated. They will enable substantial reductions, or even complete eradication of processes of inspection, re-work, and reject. Each of these items substantially impacts on the operating costs of many organizations, and are often directly related to the inadequacy of the design and development work.

Taguchi's lack of concern with people and managing organizations must be considered the second major flaw in his approach. He says nothing about how to implement his approaches, which, from experience, would meet major resistance in many organizations.

The necessary reorganization and alteration of corporate structures, the shifts in power, and perhaps the change in budgets associated with his method would all be expected to generate substantial resistance within the organization. Handling this resistance is not addressed.

Summary

The review of the work of Genichi Taguchi is now complete. Readers should refer to his original work, *System of Experimental Design* (Taguchi: 1987), in order to develop their own appreciation of his contribution.

KEY LEARNING POINTS

Genichi Taguchi's definition of quality: the loss imparted to society from the time the product is shipped

Key beliefs:
statistical methods, quality as inherent in design, quality as a societal issue.

Principal methods:
prototyping method, eight steps of parameter design, quadratic loss function.

Question

Taguchi believes that quality is a societal, rather than an organizational, issue. Consider whether this is a reasonable belief.

Part Three

Contemporary Thinking

User Guide

Part One showed how quality has become a major organizational issue, and placed it in the broader context of early management thinking. In Part Two, the work of the quality gurus and its relationship to that thinking was considered. In Part Three, the aim is to bring quality thinking up to date by placing it in the context of contemporary assessments of management.

Management thinking has developed substantially over the last thirty years, although the dominant literature about quality has not, for the most part, explicitly embraced the potential benefits emerging from that development. It was shown in Part Two that the work of the quality gurus relies principally on the 'machine' view of organization, with some writers moving towards human relations theory, but failing to take full advantage of the substantial body of work in that area. For example, Ishikawa emphasizes participation, and provides a potentially useful tool for achieving it, but says nothing about the aspects of human behaviour which enable or inhibit meaningful participation. Similarly, the value of holistic or systemic thinking about organizational issues is achieving increasing prominence in other areas of problem-solving (for example, Peter Senge's *Fifth Discipline*), but is largely ignored in the quality literature.

This part of the book explores and explains these holistic approaches to understanding organization. Holistic thinking seeks to move away from treating quality as a technical exercise in improving production performance and product quality, to embrace less mechanistic, softer issues of culture, stakeholder relations, and organizational politics, as well as offering assistance on the technical aspects. From a holistic perspective, it is believed that the pursuit of the traditional, narrow interpretation of quality is just one of many strands in the achievement of organizational effectiveness, although quality purists might argue with this. Systemic thinking is as much concerned with the interaction between elements of production, as with the performance of the elements themselves, since it is the interaction which is considered to create 'the system'.

Selecting contemporary themes to include in this section was challenging. There are so many books and ideas published each year in the field of management. The works and authors selected have met five criteria. They are, or purport to be:

- systemic;
- contemporary (either recently produced or currently popular);
- practical (they have a well-worked-out and tested methodology);
- original;
- directly relevant to the pursuit of organizational effectiveness through quality.

These criteria led to the exclusion of specific or extended study of many other significant management thinkers and writers, for example, Drucker, Peters, Kanter, and Mintzberg. It is not the intention to detract from, or deny, their substantial contributions to management thinking — indeed readers are encouraged to study their work. Their exclusion simply means that they did not meet the criteria established for this book.

The chapters in this part are organized along two broad lines. First, they are in approximate 'date order', that is, the earliest ideas are in the earliest chapters. Second, they broadly follow a continuum from 'hard' thinking — how to solve a defined problem, to 'soft' thinking — defining the problem itself. Readers may again work through the chapters in the order presented, or dip into the ideas they find most interesting or relevant to their particular interest. The aim of this section is to help the reader identify and understand the various strands of management thought which are currently emerging, and to enable informed selection from amongst those approaches. Finally, in Chapter 21, the notion of systemic quality management is introduced, developed from the idea of 'skills-based quality management' (Beckford, 2002). That chapter attempts to integrate the 'traditional' and 'systemic' methods for achieving quality into a coherent whole.

14 Contingency Theory

The behaviour of the elements and their effects on the whole are interdependent

(Ackoff, 1981)

Introduction

Contingency theory initially arose from the body of work concerning leadership and motivation. The principal proponent of this psychology-based approach is F. E. Fiedler (1967), whose work suggested that the best leadership style depended upon the particular set of circumstances of organization. He identified two styles of leadership: 'relationship-motivated' and 'task-motivated', which were equally valid under different conditions. 'Relationship-motivated' leadership he sees as appropriate when the technical task is relatively easy, but the relationships are difficult to manage; 'task-motivated' leadership as appropriate when the technical task is difficult but the relationships are easy to manage. There is a sliding-scale or continuum of variations between these two extreme positions. Overall, Fiedler's work, unlike that of earlier writers, suggests that there is no 'one best way' of leading or managing.

14.1 Contingency Theory and Organization Design

During the 1970s, contingency theory developed from its roots in leadership and motivation theory to become a common approach to organization design and management. It reflects some of the developments of systems thinking, to be discussed in the following chapter, but is based on observation and practice rather than theory, and pre-dates much subsequent work which has popularized the systems field.

Contingency theory considers the organization systemically, as an interacting network of functional elements bound together in pursuit of a common purpose. Each element is essential to the success (that is, the survival, efficiency and effectiveness) of the organization. Within this paradigm, the needs of each element must be met within the context of the organization. In other words, an appropriate balance must be struck between them. This balance is dynamic, since the environment and the needs or demands of the elements are continually changing. As with riding a bicycle, stability relies on continued dynamism. Like systems thinking, but unlike the Classical and human resources theories, contingency theory recognizes that the organization is contained within an environment with which it interacts, both influencing and being influenced.

Burns and Stalker (1961) proposed that 'organic' organization structures and systems were most relevant to organizations in a dynamic state, where conditions and requirements were continually changing. They identified the key variables influencing the structure as being the product market and the manufacturing technology. Joan Woodward (1965) and her colleagues studied the relationship between technology and organization design through a survey of manufacturing organizations in south-east Essex (UK). Woodward found that there were substantial variations between the organizational characteristics of different firms, with notable differences in the spread and number of subordinates to any given position, the number of levels of management, and the formality of communication. Further research showed that a key factor in these differences was not the size of the organization, as was originally assumed, but the technology employed and the production method. This led to the suggestion (Pugh and Hickson, 1989: 16–21, 4th ed.) that the 'objectives of a firm . . . determine the kind of technology it uses'. This in turn may be seen as driving the organizational structure, that is, that the design of the organization is to some extent 'contingent'. It could be argued today that for information-based businesses such as Google and Microsoft, the technology *is* the organization.

Jackson (1990) considers that there are five strategic contingencies, called subsystems, which affect each other and influence the choice of organization structure. They are:

- goals
- people
- technical
- managerial
- size.

The goal sub-system is concerned with the survival of the organization in both the long and the short terms, with normative, strategic, and operational objectives. These goals need to meet the aspirations of the stakeholders, to match the dynamism of the environment of the organization, which in turn needs to be reflected in the decision-making structure. Contemporary mantras such as 'think global, act local' reflect this demand for appropriate autonomy in goal-setting. For example, HSBC refers to itself as 'The world's local bank' reflecting an organization which is global in reach but highly localized in operation.

Goals are determined within and by the organization, although the normative goals (decisions about the nature of the organization) are strongly influenced by the socio-economic context in which the organization exists. All goals need to be thought of as dynamic and evolutionary, sometimes revolutionary, to avoid the danger of complacency. It can be argued that the economic crisis of 2008 was, to some considerable degree, driven by a complacent attitude to espoused goals and their interrelationship with the business environment.

The goals are driven by a number of aspects. The influence of the environment (socio-economic context) has already been mentioned. The expectations of the managers or controllers of the organization are significant, as are the expectations and needs of the workforce and, increasingly, of the community of shareholders and other stakeholders surrounding the organization, thus recalling again the idea of corporate social responsibility (CSR). It may be argued that CSR has really arisen amongst those thinking differently about organizational goals and objectives – and that these are necessarily systemic thinkers.

The people or 'human' sub-system is concerned primarily with the evolving needs of the employees of the organization. These needs must be met if people are to be content within the organization, to be attracted to it, and to be fulfilled by their work. It is reasonable to suggest that these needs will vary with the context in which the individuals are employed, that is, the demands of London-based employees may be very different to those in New York, Melbourne, or Hong Kong. Essentially, the design of the organization must take account of the needs and capabilities of the staff.

While Jackson draws a boundary, which emphasizes differing perspectives for people within the total system to those outside in the 'environment', it must not be forgotten that the boundary is itself arbitrary. It traditionally reflects legally established relationships, it will be for the most part porous, and it will allow transduction to take place. Reflecting briefly on the work of the gurus and others, the notions of 'supplier development', the 'value chain', the 'internal supplier-customer chain' and 'customer feedback', all imply a much closer relationship between the system and its environment, almost to the point that the boundary ceases to exist. Perhaps as Beer (1979: 94–5) suggests, this creates a 'diffusion' of information within the larger system. The relationships may be seen as symbiotic: interaction for mutual benefit. Thus, while a distinction may be drawn between suppliers, staff and customers, it may be more appropriate to see staff as both *in* and *of* the system, that is, they work within it and are largely loyal to it. Customers and suppliers are *in* but not *of* it. They work *with* or *buy from* the system, but not for it; their primary loyalty lies elsewhere. They do not necessarily directly share in, or benefit from, the system's objectives.

Increasingly today, the boundaries of organizations are blurred and amorphous. Growth in the number of small businesses, often working in partnership with other small businesses, means that many 'virtual' organizations now trade. They do not conform to the norms of traditional organizations. Perhaps like pilot fish, they are organized on collaborative lines, and their mechanisms of structure and control are rooted in contracts rather than in conventional bureaucratic and hierarchical forms.

The technical sub-system refers to the technology employed by the organization in carrying out its work. As already stated, it was found by Woodward (1965) that organizations employed different forms of organization according to their size and production technology. She discovered that 'typical' organizational forms had developed within particular industries, and that the most successful firms employed these structures. To some extent, this may be regarded as a predictable result – the practice now called benchmarking is not new. Although the more formal exchanges which take place today may be more rigorous in their use, there is little doubt that there has always been a fluid movement of ideas between participants in the same industry, particularly when there has been high mobility of labour and low job security. Equally, if a particular technology is appropriate to production of a product or product group, it should be no surprise that the organizational form which succeeds with manufacturing and servicing the product for one business will also work for others. Interestingly, breakthroughs in organizational form and in process, utilizing new or emergent technology, often provide the catalyst for change in a mature industry. The emergence of 'low-cost airlines' since the mid-nineties has been enabled by process-change and information technology. These budget airlines have, like the supermarkets before them, used process change to outsource some of their costs to their customers. Today you will perhaps carry your own bags, have no seat allocation, and market price differences are exploited (arbitrage) to secure lower landing fees (essentially by using less popular airports and outsourcing the additional travel costs to passengers). Advances in information technology are exploited to eradicate other costs (for example, ticketless travel eradicates paperwork and the distribution costs of tickets).

The role of the managerial sub-system is to co-ordinate and enable the activities of the others. Current thinking recognizes that the management of an organization can enable it to respond to developments in the environment through the implementation of strategic choices. Thus, rather than being at the mercy of the environment, the organization can, through its management decisions, be active in dealing with it. Since the scope for the organization to influence the environment is recognized, the management sub-system as observer can, to some extent, create the environment through its observations and its interference with it (Dudley, 1998).

Jackson (1990) suggests that what he calls the deterministic origins of contingency theory are flawed, and that the managerial sub-system is an important determinant of organizational success. This criticism pushes the argument away from the mechanistic view of Woodward – 'technology determines structure' – towards a more organic, interactive view.

Pugh recognized the importance of size as a factor in organizational structure, as did the Aston group in studies (Pugh and Hickson, 1976; Pugh and Hinings, 1976), which considered larger organizations than those studied by Woodward. Their work showed that increasing size reinforces the need for delegation and decentralization of decision making, while simultaneously increasing the need for structured, formal activities. This perhaps can be linked to Fayol's call for an appropriate balance between centralization and decentralization.

While not listed as one of Jackson's key factors, the environment is important to the effectiveness of the organization. It is considered that differing environmental demands and constraints require different organizational formats to be employed. Overall, there appears to be a correlation between the level of environmental complexity and turbulence, and the requisite level of adaptability or flexibility of an organization. To ensure the survival of the organization, it must be capable of responding at an appropriate rate to changes in its environment, and, perhaps through marketing and other activities, of influencing the environment in favour of itself.

14.2 Reiteration

To summarize, contingency theory views the particular organizational form existing as the product of interactions between goals, people, technology, management, and size. These factors, in conjunction with the environmental influences, feed managers' decisions about the shape of the organization, leading to a particular structure, which in turn pre-controls organizational performance. These ideas are represented in Figure 14.1.

14.3 Is Quality Contingent?

This question has two distinct dimensions. The first is concerned with quality as an output measure of the organization's performance. The second is concerned with defining quality itself.

Dealing with the first dimension, the answer must be yes. The quality of any product or service is a function of the interaction of all of the elements of the system and its environment. If any of the inputs, procedures or processes of the organization are

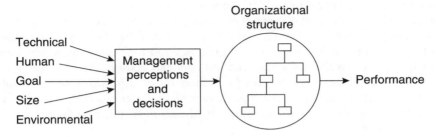

Figure 14.1 The contingency perspective.

flawed – that is, if the demands or influences of the environment are not appropriately responded to, or if the expectations of the customers in the environment are not understood – the product or service may be considered by those customers not to be 'quality'. Therefore, achievement of quality must be contingent upon the effectiveness of every part of the system. This perception demands a holistic approach to creating and managing the organization to achieve quality.

Dealing with the second dimension is much harder, since this is concerned with the definition of quality. The gurus reviewed in part two of this book each offered definitions of quality that rested on well-defined, measurable characteristics of a product or service. These are expressed in the form of 'the one best way'. In one form or another they state that *this is quality* (their various definitions) and *this is how it is achieved* (their different methodologies). It is clear that there are substantial differences between the gurus' definition of quality and how quality should be achieved, for example, Deming's statistically-based approach is very different to Ishikawa's participative approach, as is the internal evangelical focus of Crosby's work compared with the societal concerns expressed by Taguchi.

Are they *all* right, or are *none* of them right? *What is quality?* For Crosby it is 'conformance to requirements', for Deming and Shingo it is eradication of error, for Feigenbaum 'best for customer use and selling price', for Ishikawa it is the product, service, management, the company and the people – very near to the contingency view of organization. Juran sees quality as a function of planning, while Taguchi focuses on the cost imparted to society.

It is suggested here that, in the contemporary dynamic and turbulent organizational environment, quality cannot be adequately defined in these absolute terms as something fixed and necessarily quantifiable. Perhaps as Hume (*Of Tragedy, Essays*) suggests, quality is like beauty, 'Beauty [quality] in things exists in the mind which contemplates them.' Perhaps customers experience, rather than receive, quality of service or product. As each customer has different expectations, they – the customers – continually and individually redefine quality in terms of their past experience and changing expectations. This means, of course, that the pursuit of quality, like the hunt for the Loch Ness monster, the American Bigfoot, or the Yeti, is doomed to failure because, like the monster, quality is mysterious and ethereal rather than substantial and absolute. Quality, then, *is* contingent, but upon the customer *not* the organization, its products, or services.

This perspective on quality poses a problem for organizations pursuing quality programmes. If quality is not an absolute, then what are they aiming for and how do they know when they have achieved it? The answer seems to be that the quality target is continually shifting, and that organizations must pursue 'rightness' or 'appropriateness' in their products or services. Products and services must fulfil the varying purposes for which they are purchased. They, and the processes and procedures by which they are produced, must be error free – within the limits of expectations already created in the customer's mind. Those processes and procedures must minimize cost (land, labour, capital and entrepreneurship – the four factors of production), and, crucially, every aspect and activity of the organization and its management must be focused on doing the right job right.

The key to success in such a scenario rests on communication, both within the organization and between the organization, and its environment. If internal communication is defective, staff may do the right job wrong, or the wrong job right. Communication with the environment rests in understanding the expectations of customers (communication into the organization), and creating or modifying the expectations of customers (communication out to the market). If this communication is not effective, there will be flawed understanding on either (or both) sides, and hence there will not be quality – because however technically good the product or service may be, the expectations of one party from the other will not be met.

Vignette 14.1 'That's Quality!'

During a seminar on quality in Hong Kong, a student and I went for lunch together, taking an opportunity to discuss his forthcoming project work. The purpose of the lunch was the discussion, eating was incidental – a necessary activity. We found a run-of-the-mill Italian fast-food restaurant. The menu was predictable: pasta, pizzas and pollo. The decor was unassuming; the food served quickly, and, as ordered, was fully acceptable. The service was surprising: just the right blend of courtesy and friendliness to meet our, admittedly not very high, expectations. We thoroughly enjoyed both our meal and our discussion, paid, walked out into the street, turned to each other and said in unison: 'That's quality!' We had experienced it, but could not adequately describe it; the best that could be achieved was to say that it was *all* right on *all* counts.

If asked to nominate a 'quality' restaurant in advance, neither of us would have chosen the chain to which that restaurant belonged. The experience, though, has changed our expectations. If we went there again, would we be disappointed with exactly the same experience?

This story underlines the importance of the customer in defining quality. The food and service no doubt varied to some extent from day to day. Our expectations were low – and the organization as a whole exceeded them. We were then pleased and surprised.

Summary

This chapter has briefly introduced the concept of the contingency view of the world. The emergence and background of contingency theory was explored, and its roots in the empirical study of organizations explained. Readers wishing to extend their knowledge should refer directly to the work of the various authors to whom reference has been made.

KEY LEARNING POINTS

Contingency Theory

Definition:
organizational effectiveness is the product of the adequacy of managerial response to five key effectors on the organization: technology, human, goal, size and environment.

Key belief:
there is not one best way of structuring an organization.

Contingency and quality:
quality is contingent upon the expectations of the customer, not on the products or services offered.

Question

Consider how the application of contingency theory to the work of Deming or Crosby might enhance the contribution of their approaches to the pursuit of quality.

15 Organizations as Systems

'Contrariwise.' continued Tweedledee,
'if it was so, it might be; and if it were so,
it would be; but as it isn't, it ain't. That's logic'

(Lewis Carroll, *Through the Looking Glass*)

Introduction

Contingency theory is seen as systemic. From an organizational, opposed to psychological, perspective, its roots reside in the application, rather than development, of theory, its main tenets being drawn from observation. Thinking about organizations as systems must have strong theoretical foundations, if this strand of organization theory is to be more than simply 'best observed practice' of others, which may provide good, but not best, practice. Theory enables the development of general principles upon which rigorous and coherent best practice can be built and tested. This chapter briefly focuses on the theoretical development of systems thinking, and provides the platform for the various approaches outlined in subsequent chapters.

15.1 Systems Thinking

Systems thinking emerged after the traditional and human relations (HR) models, and falls within the organic view of organizations. The systems approach is fundamentally different to the reductionist view on which much of modern science rests. The shift in thinking is 'not a gradual evolution, but a discontinuity' (Singleton, 1974: 10–11). A discontinuity in this context means a total change of paradigm, that is, a complete break from traditional, reductionist approaches. Reductionism implies fragmentation: the breaking down and analysis of organizations on a piecemeal basis; while systemic thinking implies stepping back from the individual parts and understanding the organization, its behaviours, and the interaction of its parts as a whole.

Systemic thinking attempts to deal with organizations as 'wholes' rather than parts: hence the expression 'holistic'. As with contingency theory, it considers the organization as a complex network of elements and relationships, and recognizes the interaction with the environment in which the organization is contained. Thinking about organizations as 'systems' builds upon the early work of Barnard, Selznick, and von Bertalanffy, and has become a major, if not yet dominant, approach for management thinkers and practitioners. The 'language' of systemic thinking is being increasingly used, but the practical application still tends to be reductionist. In practical terms, thinking systemically has profound implications for organizations, but is not easy to adopt for those educated in a reductionist approach to the world. An explanation of systemic thinking is attempted below.

If we remove the engines from a jet aircraft, neither they nor the aircraft will fly. Flight is a product of their interaction and interconnectedness; it is a synergistic outcome. It is a property which belongs only to the complete aircraft and not to any of its parts. Properties such as this are called 'emergent'; they 'emerge' from the interaction of the various system elements. This means that, when examining the properties and performance of an aircraft, we must look at the aircraft in its totality, not just at its components, since the whole has properties (exhibits performance characteristics) not found in any of the components. Equally, the parts may have properties not found in the whole. For example, the turbine of a jet engine rotates at high speed, while the engine as a whole does not. Similarly, where is the voice in a radio, or the picture in a television? These things are observable outputs of the interactions within such systems, and with their environment (the reception of radio or television signals), but cannot be found by reductionist examination or analysis of them.

Russell Ackoff (1981: 18) perhaps offers the most lucid explanation of thinking systemically:

> suppose we bring one of each of these . . . [types of automobile] into a large garage and then employ a number of outstanding automotive engineers to determine which one has the best carburettor. When they have done so, we record the result and ask them to do the same for engines. We continue this process until we have covered all the parts required for an automobile. Then we ask the engineers to remove and reassemble these parts. Would we obtain the best possible automobile? Of course not. We would not even obtain an automobile because *the parts would not fit together*, even if they did, *they would not work well together. The performance of a system depends more on how its parts interact than* [on] *how they act independently of each other.*

15.2 Systems Thinking and Organizations

Parsons and Smelser (1956) attempted to 'elaborate four functional imperatives to be fulfilled for a system, by its sub-systems, if that system is to continue to exist' (Figure 15.1). The imperatives they identified are adaptation, goal-attainment, integration, and latency (pattern maintenance), which make up the AGIL mnemonic.

Jackson (1990) interprets this somewhat differently, seeing four primary sub-systems of an organization as essential prerequisites: goal, human, technical, and managerial. These reflect his contingency theory perspective. He considers that effectiveness and efficiency are attained through the interaction of the sub-systems in pursuit of the purpose of the system in its environment.

The goal sub-system is concerned with the purpose of the system and the means of achieving that purpose. The human sub-system deals with the people and their management and motivation. The technical sub-system handles the operations (that is, input – transformation – output), and the managerial sub-system co-ordinates and manages each of the others, thereby balancing the relationships and attending to the environmental interaction.

Parsons & Smelser:

Imperative 1) A = Adaptation; the system has to establish relationships between itself and its external environment.

Imperative 2) G = Goal-attainment; goals have to be defined and resources mobilized and managed in pursuit of those goals.

Imperative 3) I = Integration; the system has to have a means of co-ordinating its efforts.

Imperative 4) L = Latency (or pattern maintenance); the first three requisites for organizational survival have to be solved with the minimum of strain and tension by ensuring that organizational 'actors' are motivated to act in the appropriate manner.

Figure 15.1 Functional imperatives of a system.

Figure 15.2 The organization as a system.

The systems model adds value to the practice and theory of management, in that it demands explicit recognition of the environment and of internal organizational interactions. The generic system model is of great utility in a descriptive mode, enabling the elaboration of the elements and interactions of the system. However, while this description frequently enables diagnosis of faults and failures in the connectivity of the system, it does not offer a prescriptive model for improvement or change based on a projection of an organizational ideal. In terms of weaknesses, the systems model perhaps underplays the essential, purposeful role of individuals within organizations, and the extent to which human interactions can affect outputs, unless the context of the discussion fully embraces systemic thinking.

The systems model takes account of the environment and focuses on the generality of survival rather than specific organizational objectives. It does not attempt to quantify the success of an organization, and says little about 'how' organizations adapt. The potential for relative autonomy is not explored and little advice is offered in terms of specific, general remedies for ineffective organizations.

The emphasis in this view is on harmonious internal interaction, whereas conflict and coercion are often present amongst the human actors. Change is perceived as being environmentally driven, rather than initiated by the organization.

15.3 Systems Thinking and Quality

The shift from the classical management school of thought to the human relations school represented a change of emphasis within the reductionist paradigm, from a focus on the needs of the organization to that of the individuals and groups within it. This shift in thinking has not been strongly reflected in quality literature, although quality gurus do generally recognize in their work the importance of the commitment of all staff to quality initiatives, and some acknowledge the importance of dealing with the totality of the organization. The shift from reductionist to systemic thinking about quality is much more fundamental, involving the acceptance of a new paradigm, a reframing of the entire way in which we think about the world. The impact on thinking about quality is substantial.

When thinking systemically about quality, the focus on improving the performance of individual parts of an organization becomes less important, with emphasis shifting to their total interacting performance. This means examining not just the performance of functional units, such as production, sales, finance and personnel, as would be the case in a reductionist approach, but, crucially, assessing how the performance of those parts is enabled or inhibited by other parts, that is, how they interact to produce goods or services, and the impact of change in one part on each of the others.

Conventionally, most quality initiatives focus on the technical performance of production systems, whether products or services. They examine in detail the characteristics of machines (Shingo); they study the accuracy and reliability of the human and technical inputs to the production system (Deming's special causes of error); and they sometimes look at the internal supplier–customer relationships. Few quality programmes go beyond these technical aspects in any substantial manner.

In a systemic world, the examiner needs to step back and consider how each of the parts of the organization interact with every other. So, for example, financial objectives, recruitment and training policies, and inbound logistics, all impact on production capability and the ability to meet quality targets. Similarly, the sales function and the commitments given to customers by sales personnel are strong determinants of the level of after-sales service, which must be provided to meet customer expectations, and the cost of providing it. These sales commitments also interact with the production elements of the organization, creating demands which need to be met. Overlaying all of these aspects are the internal politics of the organization, that is, the ways in which people interact, the coherence or otherwise of their behaviour, the degree of mutuality in their objectives, given that individuals tend to compete for preferment within the organization – and sometimes at its expense.

Vignette 15.1 A Systems Problem

The following story, received from a reliable source in the IT industry, is reported as true; it is also an illustration of the need to think systemically about problems.

Dialogue between a customer and customer support help desk:

CS: 'I'm a computer assistant; may I help you?'
Customer: 'Yes, well, I'm having trouble with WordPerfect.'

CS:	'What sort of trouble?'
Customer:	'Well, I was just typing along, and all of a sudden the words went away.'
CS:	'Went away?'
Customer:	'They disappeared.'
CS:	'Hmm . . . So what does your screen look like now?'
Customer:	'Nothing.'
CS:	'Nothing?'
Customer:	'It's blank; it won't accept anything when I type.'
CS:	'Are you still in WordPerfect, or did you get out?'
Customer:	'How do I tell?'
CS:	'Can you see the "C" prompt on the screen?'
Customer:	'What's a sea-prompt?'
CS:	'Never mind. Can you move the cursor around the screen?'
Customer:	'There isn't any cursor: I told you, it won't accept anything I type.'
CS:	'Does your monitor have a power indicator?'
Customer:	'What's a monitor?'
CS:	'It's the thing with a screen on it that looks like a TV. Does it have a little light that tells you when it's on?'
Customer:	'I don't know.'
CS:	'Well, then, look on the back of the monitor and find where the power cord goes into it. Can you see that?'
Customer:	'. . . Yes, I think so.'
CS:	'Great. Follow the cord to the plug and tell me if it's plugged in to the wall.'
Customer:	'Yes. It is.'
CS:	'When you were behind the monitor, did you notice that there were two cables plugged into the back of it, not just one?'
Customer:	'No.'
CS:	'Well, there are. I need you to look back there again and find the other cable.'
Customer:	'. . . Okay, here it is.'
CS:	'Follow it for me, and tell me if it's plugged securely into the back of your computer.'
Customer:	'I can't reach.'
CS:	Uh huh. Well, can you see if it is?'
Customer:	'No.'
CS:	'Even if you maybe put your knee on something and lean way over?'
Customer:	'Oh, it's not because I don't have the right angle; it's because it's dark.'
CS:	'Dark?'
Customer:	Yes, the office light is off, and the only light I have is coming in from the window.'
CS:	'Well, turn the office light on, then.'
Customer:	'I can't.'
CS:	'Why not?'
Customer:	'Because there's a power outage.'
CS:	'A power . . . a power outage? Aha! Okay, we've got it licked now. Do you still have the boxes, and manuals, and packing stuff your computer came in?'
Customer:	'Well, yes, I keep them in the closet.'

CS:	'Good! Go get them, unplug your system, and pack it up just like it was when you got it. Then take it back to the store you bought it from.'
Customer:	'Really? Is it that bad?'
CS:	'Yes, I'm afraid it is.'
Customer:	'Well, all right then, I suppose. What do I tell them?'
CS:	'Tell them you're too stupid to own a computer.'

The point is not that we are too stupid for the organizations in which we work and the technology we use, but that the conventional reductionist mindset leads us to explore only the issue of immediate concern. We ignore the wider issues, which a systemic mindset suggests may have implications for the resolution of our particular problem.

Complicating the situation further is the issue of measurement, and the associated rewards and punishments related to performance. It has already been suggested in Chapter 3 that, in general, 'we get what we measure', and for many organizations, and the individuals within them, the measurements are narrow, simple and taken in isolation at a single level. Such systems tend to lead to a focus on one aspect of performance at the expense of others. So, for example, if the measurement system (or the boss) emphasizes production efficiency, that is what the management will aim for. In a systemic world, production efficiency cannot be measured in isolation, but must be related to the demands of the marketplace, the availability of inputs to the system (land, labour, raw materials), and to the capacity of the organization to provide financial support. We cannot simply measure one dimension of the organization, but must measure many simultaneously, and build the reported characteristics into a systemic picture of the performance of the whole system. We must learn to measure organizational effectiveness, not just productivity or efficiency.

Systemically, quality is not something that can be achieved through enhancing only independent functional units, however effective they may become individually. Equally, quality cannot be measured in purely technical terms by some inherent and visible characteristics of the product or service, such as size, shape, colour or conformance to requirements. Systemically, quality must be recognized as a more or less measurable property of the total organization. It must be inherent in each process and each interaction within the system, and must persist in the organization's dealings with its environment. For example, the products or services of a company may be admired for their apparent quality. However, if the process by which they are made is unnecessarily environmentally damaging, or the management system abuses the employees within the organization, then it cannot be considered a quality organization – except by that single output measure of operational performance. In the event that the processes are environmentally damaging or abusive of people, then quality is achieved at some other cost which may not be acceptable at a societal level. The growth in the measurement of environmental impact, and the demands for demonstrably greater commitment to corporate social responsibility, reflect the increasing importance of these aspects – and they are not 'instead of' other measurements, but additional to them. The complexity this generates demands a whole new approach to measurement and reporting.

Summary

This chapter has briefly introduced the idea of thinking about organizations as systems, and has attempted to explain systemic thinking. The implications of systems thinking for quality have been addressed. In subsequent chapters, three different strands of the development of systemic thinking will be explored. Organizational cybernetics stems from the relatively hard, solution-oriented approaches, while soft systems thinking reflects a more means-oriented approach. Critical systems thinking embraces both of these strands in a systemic enquiry process.

KEY LEARNING POINTS

Organizations as systems

Key definition:
the study of organizations and their interactions as wholes, not as an assembly of individual parts.

Key beliefs:
the 'system' exhibits behaviour which is not exhibited by any of the parts, and has 'emergent' properties which belong to none of those parts individually.

Implications for quality:
there is a shift of focus from just the individual parts to embrace the interactions between those parts; a recognition that the internal customer chain creates the organization; therefore quality must be recognized as an emergent property of the system rather than just a technical measure of output.

Question

What do you think might be the 'emergent' properties of a university? Why?

16 Organizational Cybernetics

... I'm not complaining, but There It Is

(Eeyore, in *Winnie the Pooh*, A. A. Milne)

Introduction

Cybernetics emerged as a branch of management science during the 1940s. Norbert Wiener was the founding driver of twentieth-century cybernetics, working primarily on machine systems. His work has subsequently been developed extensively by others in the modern field of robotics. Weiner's group was interdisciplinary, bringing together mathematicians, biologists, operational researchers, and physicists in a groundbreaking approach to developing a unified science for solving complex problems.

For nearly forty years, Stafford Beer, who died in 2002, led the application of cybernetic principles to the study of organizations, developing what we now call 'management' or 'organizational' cybernetics. His work extends from the 1950s, and has undergone continued development by Beer and others, including this author and colleagues. Beer defines cybernetics as the 'science of effective organization', something from which quality may be considered to result.

This chapter is concerned with the theory and principles of cybernetics, and the contribution this branch of science can make to the achievement of quality in organizations. In this context, organizations are conceived as social systems composed of people, and existing, as proposed in the previous chapter, as the product of their actions, interactions, and of the technical artefacts which link and support them. Early work, from which the cybernetic principles were developed, addressed such diverse fields as automation, computing, and radar, and built upon earlier discoveries, such as Watt's steam engine governor, which are used to illustrate what Jackson (1991) has called 'management cybernetics'.

Organizational cybernetics builds upon, and draws ideas from, that fundamental work, but 'breaks somewhat with the mechanistic and organismic thinking that typifies management cybernetics' (Jackson, 1991: 103). The distinction is drawn by Jackson on the basis of two differences between the work of Stafford Beer and that of others in this field. First, in *The Heart of Enterprise*, Beer (1979) builds a model of 'any organization' from the first principles of cybernetics. Second, he pays significant attention to the role of the observer, whose presence influences the situation observed. Accepting the intellectual insights of Stafford Beer, it is possible to make use of the principles of cybernetics without relying on analogies between the organization observed and other natural phenomena. Analogies are useful as ways of helping us to order our thoughts about a situation, and to assist us in explaining our observations to others. It can be recognized that the existence and behaviour of the organization studied is, to some degree, a function of the perceptions of the observer.

The role of cybernetics is to help the manager (defined as any person legitimately attempting to command and control an organization) to understand:

- how an organization works (or doesn't work);
- why it works in a particular way;
- what to do to improve it.

This is because 'Cybernetics . . . treats not things but *ways of behaving*' (Ashby, 1956).

16.1 Cybernetic Systems

'The truths of cybernetics are not conditional on their being derived from some other branch of science' (Ashby, 1956: 1).

This section deals with the major characteristics of systems susceptible to cybernetic diagnosis and improvement. Notwithstanding the above quote from Ross Ashby, a number of the principles have been derived from, or inspired by, 'some other branch of science'. It is in taking account of the role of the observer that they reflect the essentially cybernetic operation of those natural systems which have been studied. The principles of cybernetics can be observed operating in nature (see, for example, Gell-Mann, Gleick, Lovelock, Hawking, and Penrose) and are concerned with 'general laws that govern control processes, whatever the nature of the system under governance' (Jackson, 1991: 92), and that includes quality systems.

Beer (1959) considers that, in order to be a worthwhile subject for the application of the cybernetic approach, the organization will be likely to demonstrate three characteristics (see Figure 16.1).

Beer (1959: 12) designates as 'exceedingly complex' any organization which is so complicated that it cannot be described in a precise and detailed fashion. To explain this point, the wiring loom of a car is, in Beer's terms, 'complex but describable'; its design and connectivity can be completely documented. An example of an exceedingly complex organization would perhaps be an interaction between two people in a meeting. This transaction, while apparently simple to observe and record, would not be describable. The individual interpretation of words, inflections of speech, degree of eye contact, and bodily postures adopted, all form a part of the interaction. The recognition of this complexity helps us to understand why managing service quality, which is about human interaction, is so different from managing product quality.

Stafford Beer:

Characteristic 1) extreme complexity;

Characteristic 2) a degree of self-regulation;

Characteristic 3) probabilistic behaviour.

Figure 16.1 Characteristics of cybernetic systems.

Self-regulation describes the ability of an organization to 'manage' itself towards its purposes or goals while interacting with environmental disturbance; for example, maintenance of body temperature in humans and animals. The temperature control system behaves in an autonomous manner, needing no active direction or management from the brain – although the brain is where the *'rules'* of temperature control are generated.

Probabilism exists where there are elements of the organization whose behaviour is at least partly random. Returning to the example of the car-wiring loom, it is not only 'complex but describable' but also 'deterministic'; its behaviour can be known in advance as any given input to the system. For example, operating a switch will (in the absence of a fault) generate a precisely predictable outcome. The outcome of the meeting between two people, however, would be 'probabilistic'. This is because, while the agenda for discussion may be known in advance and a 'most likely' outcome predicted, the variables in the meeting, such as mood, posture, and experience of the parties, separately and together make the outcome uncertain.

16.2 Tools of Cybernetics

There are three principal cybernetic tools for dealing with these exceedingly complex, self-regulating, probabilistic organizations (see Figure 16.2).

Complexity is dealt with by the black box technique. Schoderbek *et al.* (1990: 94) consider that complexity is a property of an organization, which, when examined from a non-quantitative viewpoint, is the product of the interaction of four main aspects: the number of elements, their interactions, their attributes, and their degree of organization. It is a factorial problem.

The interaction of those four determinants, because they are factorial rather than linear, can generate what may be seen as an exceedingly complex organization. As such, it does not lend itself to the reductionist analysis of a classical or human relations view; such an approach would break down the organization and cause the emergent properties to disappear. The organization then examined would be different from that which was initially identified.

The need to study the organization, while interfering minimally with its internal operation, leads to the use of the black box technique. This is a way of gaining knowledge about the operations carried out by an organization, without the need to reduce it to its component parts. The black box technique involves manipulating the inputs to an organization, and recording the effect on its outputs, in order to establish patterns or regularities in its behaviour. As knowledge or understanding of the organization's behaviour is acquired, the manipulations can become more structured. The black box technique is shown diagrammatically in Figure 16.3.

All of us are familiar and deal with complex black box organizations in our daily lives, without ever needing to know or understand how they work. Indeed, the black box technique will never reveal how the transformation process works or how efficient it is.

Tool 1) the black box technique – to address extreme complexity;

Tool 2) feedback – to manage self regulation;

Tool 3) variety engineering – to handle probabilism.

Figure 16.2 Tools of cybernetics.

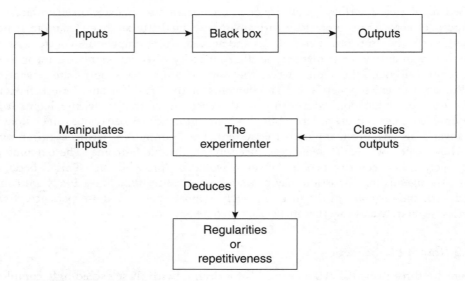

Figure 16.3 The black box technique.

Vignette 16.1 Everyday Black Boxes

1. Drivers need not know how an engine works in order to drive a vehicle.
2. No understanding of electronics is needed in order to use the computer on which this book is being written.
3. Children need know nothing of the internal workings of a video recorder in order to record and view their favourite programmes, something that so many adults cannot manage.
4. Regarding a facsimile machine and photocopier, the operator need have no knowledge of how the machine converts an image on paper into a stream of binary digits, sends those digits down a telephone line and converts them back into the image – only how to dial a number and insert paper.
5. Finally, parents learn to manage their children – and children their parents – long before they have a common spoken language with which to communicate and explain their actions. Nobody would propose a reductionist analysis of a baby to 'find out how it works' in order to control it; it is simply managed as a black box.

Managers in organizations, usually unknowingly, perform many tasks using the black box technique. It is not possible to grasp the full complexity of the organizations which are managed. Management is achieved by manipulating the inputs to the organization, recording the outputs, and deducing patterns of response. These patterns can then be used to inform future actions. In order to use the black box technique effectively, it is vital to measure the effect on output of changes in input. Unfortunately, most managers, and most of the performance management systems on which they rely, are not integrated in this way. They deny the black box its effectiveness by not recognizing the connectedness of input and output in an appropriate way.

Feedback is the process which makes self-regulation possible and describes 'circular causal processes' (Clemson, 1984: 22). Self-regulation occurs in both an organization and its environment, and is consequently of major importance. If it is not understood that an exceedingly complex, probabilistic organization to some extent regulates itself, or how this occurs, the predictability of the outcomes of managerial actions in relation to that organization is reduced. Self-regulation generates a degree of stability, but if an intervention is undertaken, either in an organization or by an organization in its environment, this stability may be disturbed. If the 'circular causal chains' have not been adequately understood, the intervention may produce unmanageable instability. The linking of input change and output effect, as described in the previous paragraph, is what makes feedback systems effective.

The simplest form of feedback occurs when two parts of an organization continuously interact with each other, such that the output of one determines the next action of the other. There are two types of this 'first order' feedback behaviour. In the first, negative feedback or goal-seeking behaviour, the organization will resist disturbances that take it away from its goal. That is to say that the reaction of one element is to inhibit change in the other, and vice versa. A common example of first order feedback behaviour is the thermostatic control of a heating or air-conditioning system; the thermostat switches the system on and off in order to maintain a given temperature.

The opposite of negative feedback is positive feedback. In this case, deviation by one element will be amplified rather than reduced by the action of another. These systems, while potentially highly unstable, are also useful. A good example of this is the level of interest acting on a bank account. Positive feedback results in the interest compounding, in effect, running away out of control.

A second order feedback system is capable of choosing between a variety of responses to environmental changes to achieve its goal. For example, the 'climate control system' in a motor car can choose between activating the heater or the air-conditioner to achieve its goal of a particular temperature. A third order system is even more sophisticated. It is capable of changing the goal state itself in response to feedback processes, determining the goal internally as opposed to externally, as in the first and second order systems. Figure 16.4 shows an example of a closed-loop feedback system.

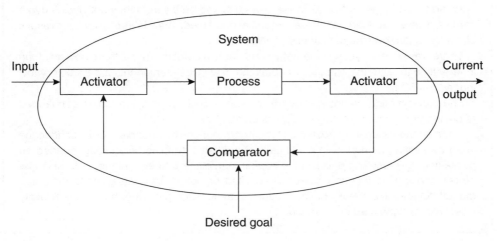

Figure 16.4 A closed-loop first-order feedback system.

The description of feedback has so far dealt with simple situations. In organizations, the feedback systems may be highly complex, containing large numbers of elements connected in a number of ways, and consisting of both positive and negative loops. It may also be the case that at any time the 'sum' of the loops may operate in a positive or negative manner, and in human systems (such as organizations) they need not be physical.

Vignette 16.2 Psychological Feedback

'Given two teams that are roughly evenly matched, if one team plays very well and begins to pull slightly ahead, the other team is stimulated to greater effort and tends to catch up, i.e. the two function as a negative loop in minimising the score difference between them. However, suppose one team is having a horrible night and gets completely demoralised in the first ten minutes. As the game goes on and they get more and more hopelessly behind they will tend to play less and less well and the better team will relax and everything will go right for them. In this case, the two teams are functioning so that the overall feedback loop is positive in maximising the score difference' (Clemson, 1984: 23).

Observation of football matches can help us to understand the notion of feedback. Much more explicit (although perhaps equally well hidden) feedback systems are observed in many other fields. The financial markets rise and fall to some, often significant, degree on 'confidence' – the way that traders and investors 'feel' about the prospects of companies rather more than the underlying profit generating performance of those companies.

The years 1998–2000 saw a massive investment in 'dotcom' enterprises – those established to capitalize on the supposed new world of electronically-based organizations, and trading in a world without boundaries with none of the usual fixed costs of traditional enterprises. Money from investors was very easy to acquire, and all the usual measurements of organizational performance were ignored. The whole market was propelled by confidence.

In 2001, the continued failure of many of the dotcom companies to stop the 'cash burn' and start to generate substantial revenues and profits from their activities led to a complete reversal. Many of these organizations failed, their failure to deliver results ultimately shattering the confidence of investors.

There was never anything inherently good about a dotcom – nor is there now anything inherently bad – but the chances of obtaining new investment in this area are very low indeed.

The over-optimism originally shown turned into an over-pessimism. Little has changed about the performance of the companies themselves.

In the economic crisis of 2008 the same behaviour can be observed. Over-confidence in an ever rising market, with continually rising sales enabled by liquidity founded on packaging and reselling debts in the capital markets, led to ever higher risk taking by certain banking institutions. Once one had failed, or looked like it was going to, the entire market deflated like a leaky balloon, banks ceased lending to other banks, the liquidity dissolved, and the markets crashed.

Clemson draws from this that: 'there is nothing structural or in the "essence" of the system, about whether the loop is positive or negative.'

Ultimately, systems that include feedback loops are capable of demonstrating exceedingly complex behaviour, and large changes in that behaviour may be brought about by small changes in the direction or extent of internal relationships. Chaos and complexity theories both rely on this notion of feedback.

There are several key criteria for the design of effective feedback mechanisms (see Figure 16.5) which will be further elaborated in Part Four.

Criterion 1) All the elements of the system must be working properly and the communication channels between them must be adequate.

Criterion 2) In an organization, responsibility for action, which carries with it accountability, must be clearly allocated.

Criterion 3) Controls must be selective.

Criterion 4) The control must highlight the necessary action.

Figure 16.5 Design criteria for feedback systems.

Variety is the measure of complexity in an organization, that is, the number of possible states it can exhibit; probabilistic behaviour exists when the behaviour of some of the elements of the organization is considered to be at least partly random. A principal argument of cybernetics is that the mechanisms that are used to manage this complexity must answer to Ashby's 'Law of Requisite Variety', which states that 'only variety can destroy variety'. This means that, in order to manage a situation effectively, the management must generate as much variety as the operation(s) it seeks to control.

Variety engineering consists of the two prime methods of achieving this control, either reducing the variety of the organization to be controlled (variety reduction), or increasing the variety of the management (variety amplification). In fact, variety can neither be absolutely reduced nor absolutely increased, only managed through appropriate techniques (see Figure 16.6). This process must be undertaken in a manner that is suitable for the particular organization being managed, and should contribute to the achievement of its goals. There are a number of management techniques which are in common use and may be seen as the tools of variety engineering if employed appropriately. These techniques need to be used thoughtfully, and with full awareness of their possible consequences, rather than randomly, or politically, as often seems to

Variety Management:
Reduction:
Structural: delegation (autonomy or decentralization), functionalization or divisionalization
Planning: establishing objectives and priorities;
Operational: budgeting, management by exception;
Rules/policies: instructions and 'norms' of behaviour.

Amplification:
Structural: team work and groups
Augmentation: recruit/train experts, employ independent experts.
Information: management or executive information systems (which may also act as attenuators).

Figure 16.6 Variety reduction and amplification techniques.

happen in organizations. Actions or processes that work to reduce the variety faced by managers are known as 'filters' or 'attenuators', while those that act to increase the variety of the manager are amplifiers.

Recursion is the final topic for this section. In this context, recursion refers to the 'organizational and interactional invariance' (Beer, 1981: 72) between levels of an organization. In essence, each level of an organization contains all the levels below it, and is contained in all the levels above it. The organization then exists within a chain of embedded systems – a sample chain is provided in Figure 16.7. In the cybernetic context, the principal elements of structure necessary for decision, information flows, and interactions within the organization are perceived as identical at every level. This invariance provides for great ease of understanding of the structure at every level, and enables the determination of the relevant autonomy of the system studied. Each level of organization then manages surplus variety from its contained levels, and enjoys a degree

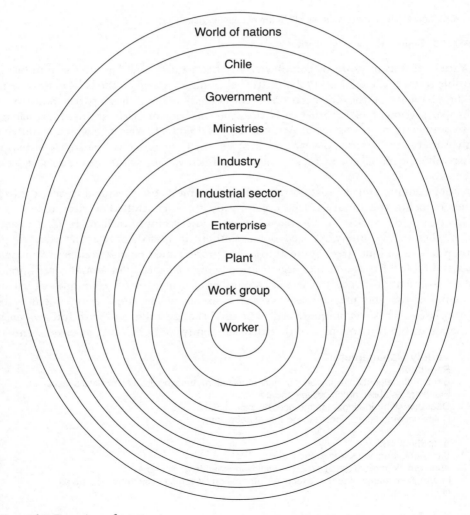

Figure 16.7 Recursions of a system.

of freedom in managing variety at its own level, constrained by its membership of the next higher level.

16.3 Cybernetics and Quality

While the systems and contingency approaches to management progress well beyond the clear limitations of the classical and human relations schools of thought, they each only offer a way of describing organizations. They are descriptive models. However, the ability to describe a situation or problem does little to improve or solve it. The cybernetic model, like these other models, can be used to provide a description of how the organization works, but the work of Beer adds to this the capability to diagnose organizational faults and thence to provide a prescription of changes to enhance the situation. The cybernetic approach, then, through Beer's Viable System Model, can be used to provide a description, diagnosis, and prescription for any organization. The application of that model will be revealed in Part Four.

The adoption of cybernetic principles generates several challenges to the established ways of thinking about organizations and achieving quality. First, the cybernetic model of organization relies on appropriate distribution of information. In other words, information is held at the lowest level in the organization where it is relevant. The design of the information system ensures this, and provides the opportunity for local decision making − metaphorically, the equivalent of reflex reactions in the human body. Information received locally may be reacted to locally, provided that reaction is consistent with the needs of the whole organization. Every feedback loop contains a comparator, which implies the capacity for making decisions. The organization provides as much autonomy as is consistent with organizational cohesion. Therefore, the local operation may not undertake activities, or engage in reactions which are different from its agreed role, or which challenge or threaten the organization, but it does have the freedom to react to those matters which are only of concern to itself.

This raises the second issue. If information is distributed, then power is distributed. A common basis of operation in organizations is for power (the right to make decisions) to be relatively highly centralized. Beer, using the expression 'dysfunctional overcentrality', contends that in many organizations decisions are taken at higher levels than is necessary or desirable for their effective functioning, and raises two points relating to this. First, it is highly inefficient and wasteful of resources. Second, it reduces the adaptability and flexibility of the organization inhibiting the ability to react to threats and opportunities. In some cases, the result of this will be the demise of the organization, since failure to respond appropriately and rapidly to a threat may cause 'organizational death', that is, liquidation, receivership, or bankruptcy.

A third issue directly challenges a key assumption which underpins much of early management thinking concerning the abilities of workers. Taylor (1911) provided a prime example of this thinking when he suggested that 'no man suited to the task of handling pig iron is capable of understanding the science that applies to it'. This negative view of the capabilities of workers suggests, of course, the opposite view of management: omniscient, god-like creatures of a higher order of intelligence than workers. Whether this view had validity in Taylor's time may be considered open to debate. Certainly its relevance to the contemporary world is highly questionable. The generally higher levels of education now in evidence, coupled with the technology-driven move towards knowledge industries, have created a situation where Taylor's view is clearly unacceptable.

This generates a significant difficulty. The adoption of cybernetic principles in the design of organizations demands that those who currently hold power in organizations must release it. Thus the solution to many problems rests in the hands of those least likely to use it. This is a major criticism of cybernetic thinking. In a highly political or coercive situation the solutions which cybernetics proposes would not be applied. The approach is also criticized for being open to abuse by those with autocratic intentions. It is certainly the case that the concepts and principles underpinning cybernetics may be used in this way. Such applications, though, would be to corrupt the intent of the work of cyberneticians, and in the medium to long term would be likely to fail. They would in any event be highly inefficient, demanding a high level of inspection or 'policing' to maintain themselves.

Comparing the cybernetic approach with the various approaches to quality, a number of parallels are revealed – most clearly and transparently with Ohno's (1978) Toyota Production System, and the principles explored in this chapter. Ohno's use of information and feedback to control production and prevent error directly reflects the necessary cybernetics.

The cybernetic demand for distributed information, coupled with the devolution of decision making in the organization, reflects the demand in the quality literature for participation and improvement centred on the particular process or workshop. The idea of 'knowledge workers' supports the concept of quality circles – the assumption that the workforce do have the capacity to bring about sustainable, substantial, and constructive improvement in quality performance. Cybernetics demands that power be distributed throughout the organization, and utilized by those who have the information to make a decision, rather than by those whose position on the organization chart suggests that they have power. This in turn reflects the quality call for management commitment. A management that is serious about the pursuit of quality will facilitate and encourage this distribution of power, recognizing that it is both necessary and desirable. If their managerial actions and behaviour do not support their open calls for improvement, the psychological feedback loops inherent in any organization will act to inhibit quality performance improvement.

The achievement of quality itself may also be seen as a cybernetic function. Any production process, whether for goods or services, will include a feedback system of the type shown in Figure 16.4. This was a model of any feedback system. In Figure 16.8 the same model is used, but this time modified to be explicitly about quality improvement. In this more specific model it can be seen that the input to a process is modified to reflect some desired quality improvement. The output of the process is measured in some way and the results fed back to a comparator. This compares the actual output with the desired output. The desired output is itself being continually modified by the *kaizen* process. Results are used to modify the input further to bring the actual output closer to that which is desired. The *kaizen* process itself consists of a further, similar set of feedback systems, dealing with people, technology, processes, materials, and so on. Each time a quality improvement is made in one of those aspects, there is a consequent change in the desired output.

The cybernetic view considers organizations as made up of closely interacting feedback systems. The action of each system is continually modified by the actions, changes and outputs of each of the others. This conception of organization serves to bring

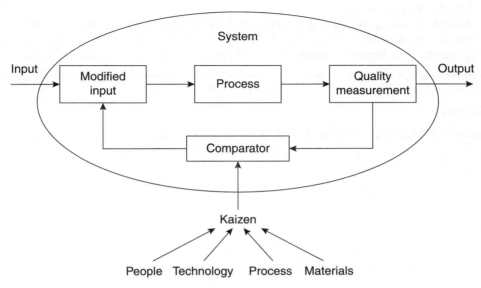

Figure 16.8 A closed-loop quality feedback system.

the organization 'alive'. It can be imagined as constantly active – engaged in a continual process of self-maintenance and self-improvement, steering itself towards a better future rather than as a static, management-driven, controlled machine of earlier views.

Summary

This chapter has provided a brief overview of the field of organizational cybernetics and its relationship with quality. Many writers, for example, Beckford, 1993, 1995; Beckford and Dudley, 1998a, 1998b, 1999; Beer, 1959, 1979, 1981, 1985; Dudley, 2000; and Espejo and Schwaninger, 1993, have worked with and sought to develop cybernetic ideas on effective organization.

KEY LEARNING POINTS

Organizational Cybernetics

Key definition:
the science of effective organization.

Key beliefs:
quality is a product of effectiveness; organizations are extremely complex, exhibit self-regulation, are probabilistic.

Tools of cybernetics:
the black-box technique, feedback, variety engineering, recursion.

Cybernetics and quality:
descriptive, a diagnostic and prescriptive model, offers parallels to mainstream quality thinking, knowledge workers support quality circles approach, distributed power demands management commitment, the cybernetic view supports and enables *kaizen*.

Question

Compare Ohno's Toyota Production System with the principles of cybernetic systems.

17 Soft Systems Thinking

It Ain't Necessarily So

(Ira Gershwin and Dubose Heyward, *Porgy and Bess*)

Introduction

Every venture has a fundamental reliance on human input for control and development, no matter to what extent it is automated and its products or services are believed guaranteed by the excellence of its technical artefacts. If there is an aim to create a quality organization, it is vital that the people, whether relatively unskilled workers or highly qualified experts, in a consultancy or research organization, are committed to that aim. This cannot be achieved if they are excluded from the development and decision making processes of the organization or its quality programme. They may tolerate the programme, or accept it at a superficial level, but they will not take ownership of it, regard it as their own, and drive it forward. A programme for quality that is not actively supported at every level in the organization will fail.

17.1 Soft Systems Explained

Organizational cybernetics is often considered by those not fully familiar with its breadth and depth as applicable to 'hard' problems, that is, problems where the end – the objective – is known, and any debate is about means. Soft systems thinking, largely represented in the work of Peter Checkland (1981), proposes the study of human activity systems, those 'soft ill-structured problems of the real world'. Checkland suggests that in 'soft' problems, the identification of the objectives themselves is problematic, and his work focuses on defining a systemic methodology which helps participants to understand social systems.

The study of 'soft systems' is considered as ends-orientated. It is concerned with discovering the purpose of the system. It presumes that the problem of what to do must be solved before the problem of how to do it can be addressed.

Hard systems thinking assumes that the problem to be tackled 'is to select an efficient means of achieving a known and defined end' (Checkland, 1978), a criticism often levelled at the cybernetic understanding discussed in the previous chapter. Soft systems thinking supposes multiple perceptions of reality. This simply means that reality is not assumed to be the same for every observer. The existence and purpose of the organization are considered to be functions of the observer, rather than objective statements of fact. Contrasting with the hard approach, the desired end needs to be defined because only limited agreement about it is believed to exist.

For example, a rainbow exists as a result of the action of light through water droplets suspended in the air, but it can only be observed from the outside and from particular angles. When approached, it disappears; it is a mirage. While we cannot grasp or physically handle a rainbow, we can describe it and understand how it is structured, even though from a different perspective – literally, a different angle in this case – the rainbow simply isn't there! Another example is to consider an entity such as the City of Kowloon in Hong Kong. There is only one Kowloon, and all parties can agree about its objective existence. However, consideration of Kowloon from vantage points on the eight hills surrounding it would generate different descriptions of that objective existence. Each of the descriptions would be 'right' for the particular observer and viewpoint, but each would describe a different reality.

Similarly, each observer's perception is informed by past experiences, personal desires, and expectations; each observation is unique. This means that even if the same organization is studied from precisely the same physical viewpoint by a variety of people, differing aspects of the organization will be highlighted. Examining Kowloon through a fixed set of binoculars from a hilltop will reveal different sights to different people: an architect may see the buildings, a town planner the roads, an anthropologist the people, and an entrepreneur the profit opportunities.

Accepting this very different, 'interpretive' (Burrell and Morgan, 1978) perspective on organizations demands a completely different approach to problem-solving and organizational management. The nature, existence, and purposes of an organization can no longer be taken as facts within an established framework; they must be negotiated through a participatory discussion between those observing it. The first step in any problem-solving or improvement process then becomes to develop consensus about the existence and nature of the organization, and the problems or issues to be addressed.

The adjective 'soft' does not refer to a characteristic of the system itself, but is a function of the perspective taken of the system by those who set themselves up as its problem-solvers. It reflects their particular interpretation of how organizational problems should be solved. Thus soft systems thinkers propose that the dominant element in a problem-solving situation is generating agreement amongst the participants, with the agreement itself leading to improvement in the situation. The generation of agreement will highlight aspects of the organization which do not meet the terms of that agreement, and must therefore be modified to fit.

17.2 Tools for Soft Systems

At a fundamental level, the tools of soft systems may be seen to be cybernetic. Effective communication between members of a group may be interpreted as operating through positive and negative feedback loops, using comparators of achievement against expectations, and adaptation or modification of attitudes in order to work towards defining goals. The processes by which this takes place, though, make more explicit use of interpersonal action and debate. For example, in Strategic Assumption Surfacing and Testing (SAST) (Mason and Mitroff, 1981) there are four phases (see Figure 17.1).

Each of these phases relies heavily on open, effective communication (speaking *and* listening) between the participants. Phase one is concerned with structuring groups on the basis of some common ground. Phase two involves the individual groups

Mason & Mitroff:

Phase1) Group Formation;

Phase 2) Assumption Surfacing;

Phase 3) Dialectical Debate;

Phase 4) Synthesis.

Figure 17.1 Four phases of SAST.

developing an agreed perspective on the problem. Phase three is based on advocacy, with each group presenting its approach and explaining the assumptions which underpin it. Dialectical debate, that is, debate based on logical argument oriented around the underpinning assumptions of the respective arguments, follows between the groups. At phase four the attempt is made to converge the two different views into a consensus view shared by all the participants. Reiteration of the process with additional information is encouraged where consensus cannot be achieved.

It can be seen that this process relies on a number of key characteristics:

* agreement by the participants to open debate;
* a common language – both syntactic and semantic;
* freedom of expression;
* advocacy skills;
* the capacity of the individuals to express themselves, hence freedom from fear;
* sufficient commonality of opinion at the outset for agreement to be a feasible potential outcome.

The tools are the tools of human communication, perhaps best understood and expressed through the science of human psychology. While admirable in theory, some of the characteristics of debate outlined above can be difficult to achieve in practice.

Vignette 17.1 Cathay Pacific: Service Straight from the Heart

Cathay Pacific Airline launched the programme called 'Service Straight from the Heart' (SSFTH), as a means of developing cultural change within the airline focused on improving customer service. As airline users will know, service is the principal means of differentiating between airlines, and is highly influential in customer choice.

Cathay Pacific recognized in early 1995 that the organization and management style of the company needed to create the conditions which would make it possible for SSFTH to be delivered to the customers. A leadership training programme was developed with the purpose of enabling managers to:

* focus on developing a culture supportive for SSFTH;
* understand the company's expectations of its managers;
* understand the impact of personal and organizational styles;
* understand how personal leadership affects service quality;

- experience leadership of high performance teams;
- identify and plan for the challenges to be faced in delivering enhanced service.

The programme addresses a number of leadership behaviours:

- sharing the strategy and vision;
- supporting others;
- enabling others;
- encouraging others;
- modelling – leading the way.

Crucial in this process of development is the emphasis on enabling the effective participation of staff in decision making. For example, in the section on 'enabling others', managers are required to involve others in planning, to develop co-operative relationships, to treat others with dignity and respect. Under 'encouraging others', the programme suggests celebrating achievements, recognizing contributions, and sharing successes. All these aspects are expected to have the effect of encouraging and enabling a sense of community and shared purpose within the organization.

Within this programme, Cathay Pacific has expressed its understanding of the importance of the people within the organization, and its recognition of the contribution of those people to its success. By putting people at the heart of its own efforts, they can expect those people to put the customers at the heart of their efforts.

The company has enjoyed considerable success with its SSFTH programme, and these results are fast becoming measurable where it matters, that is, where the airline serves its customers.

17.3 Soft Systems and Quality

Traditional approaches to quality predominantly focus on its technical aspects, paying relatively little attention to the human side. They are 'hard' approaches, which assume that the pursuit of quality necessarily leads to improvement. However, such an approach examines quality only from the perspective of the owners, or managers, of the organization. If quality means less cost and higher profits, then, in a profit-oriented world, quality is good for managers and owners. The assumption which underpins such an approach is that 'economic man' will fall in line with the corporate expectations.

However, as has been discussed by numerous writers over the last thirty years, the theory of man as being purely economically motivated does not stand up to practical examination. People work for many different reasons, and while, for some, money is a strong, extrinsic motivator, others derive the greater part of their value from the intrinsic value of the work itself. From yet another perspective, it is argued that people work simply because man is a social animal and needs both company and work for social and psychological reasons.

If the motivation underpinning an organization's drive for quality is simply economic, as it so often is, the probable outcomes include reduced numbers in the workforce (assuming a stable output), and changes to working practices and the established social mores of the organization. If management does not appreciate the differing perspectives of the other members of the organization, and accommodate them within their mental models of what is to be achieved, they will meet varying degrees of resistance to those changes. This resistance will arise from the different interpretations which the individuals put on the organization and its actions.

When resistance to the quality programme is met, the programme will almost certainly fail to fulfil all its stated objectives. Blame will be placed on the 'workers': 'they failed to make it happen'. The soft systems thinker, however, will immediately recognize that the failure belongs to management because it failed to create the conditions which would have made it possible for the programme to succeed. The management have failed to discover and accommodate the different viewpoints within the organization.

This thinking re-emphasizes the points made in earlier chapters about the need for effective communication, and is a reminder of the comments made by various gurus that most of the responsibility for quality lies with the management.

Summary

This chapter has introduced the concept of 'soft' systems. In this view, organizations are not products of objective reality but products of the interpretations put on them by their members. The different approach to solving organizational problems necessitated by this view was introduced, and the implications for the pursuit of quality discussed. Readers wishing to expand their knowledge of 'soft' systems should consider the work of Checkland (1981), Mason and Mitroff (1981), and Checkland and Scholes (1991).

KEY LEARNING POINTS
Soft Systems

Key definition:
the study of problems in human activity systems.

Key beliefs:
objectives must be agreed through participation before the study of methods becomes meaningful.

Tools of soft systems:
participation, debate, consensus building.

Soft systems and quality:
participative approaches can reduce conflict; quality programmes must address hearts as well as minds.

Question

When do *you* use 'soft' approaches to problem-solving in your day-to-day life? Why do you use them?

18 Critical Systems Thinking

... to transcend their alterable, historical and essentially ideological limitations ...

(John C. Oliga, 1988)

Introduction

Critical systems thinking, which began to emerge in the late 1970s and early 1980s, is founded on the pursuit of three goals: 'complementarism', 'sociological awareness', and 'emancipation'.

Complementarism recognizes that different situations lend themselves to different problem-solving approaches. Critical systems thinking proposes that the most appropriate methodology should be applied to a problem, and that this *must* be done with full understanding and respect for the theoretical underpinnings of the approach.

Sociological awareness is simply a commitment to the understanding that the nature and culture of societies is different between varying organizations and nations, and alters over time. It is suggested that choice of methodology must be guided by the acceptability of a particular approach in a given context. Without such contextual awareness, any approach is likely to fail. It is essential that the conditions demanded by a methodology, or way of working, are met. Thus it might be of limited value to apply a very 'hard' methodology in a very liberal environment, for example, in a creative organization. Similarly, it might be inappropriate to apply a very 'soft' approach in a prison camp or a dictatorship, since the approach would be doomed to failure by the power relations within the system.

Emancipation and human well-being are cornerstones of the critical systems approach, and act to support the development of human potential and freedom from externally imposed constraints. Theoretical support for this aspect is drawn from the work of Habermas (cited by Flood and Jackson, 1991) who suggested that the two fundamental conditions underpinning the 'socio-cultural' form of life are 'work' and 'interaction'. Work is goal-oriented and enables improvement in material things, generating a 'technical interest' in control. Interaction is a 'practical interest', concerned with the development of understanding between people. A further and major concern is with the way in which power is, and has been, exercised in forming social arrangements. Awareness of the power of individuals or groups in a given organizational context frequently disrupts the free flow of discussion, inhibiting the potential for genuine debate.

It should be clear that taking these three strands of thought together creates the potential for management problem-solving through all available and theoretically substantiated routes, thus enabling technical, practical and emancipatory interests to be fully served.

18.1 Total Systems Intervention

Flood and Jackson (1991) suggest that the world of management problem-solving and systems thinking has divided itself along three principal routes: pragmatism, isolationism and imperialism.

The first of these concentrates on practical solutions – what works for the manager or consultant – and it might be argued that the varying approaches of the quality gurus fall into this category. Concern is expressed that solutions developed without the appropriate theoretical underpinnings are somewhat sterile, as we cannot learn from them (since they only apply in the given situation), and that such solutions lead to distortion or abuse, in that they are 'simply serving the powerful'. It is also observed that without the ability to move from the particular to the general, there is no management science which can usefully be passed on to future generations of managers.

Isolationism, on the other hand, suggests that only one method, based on only a single rationality, is appropriate in *all* circumstances – in other words, it fits the problem to the solution, rather than the solution to the problem.

The dangers of 'imperialism' are also highlighted. Imperialism occurs when alternative methodologies are subsumed into the preferred theoretical position of the user. This must cause concern when, as was seen in Part Two of this book, each approach is based on a particular set of assumptions about the world. The results postulated by the approach can only be achieved if that set of assumptions is recognized, respected and adhered to by the user, and the prevailing organizational conditions allow the approach to flourish.

For example, in Chapter 16 it was shown how the application of organizational cybernetics required substantial devolution of power to make decisions within an organization to achieve maximum benefit. Such devolution forms part of the philosophy of the approach. It is undeniable that the understanding of organizational interactions derived from the cybernetic approach can be used, at the 'tool' or 'method' level, to achieve greater centralization of power. There is nothing inherently devolutionary about cybernetic interactions. However, to use the tools in a centralizing manner is a denial of the founding philosophy, and negates the power of the approach – thus making sterile its objective of improving the total efficiency and effectiveness of the subject organization.

Taking action on this theoretical work and connecting it with the work of Jackson and Keys (1984) on the development of a 'system of systems methodologies', Flood and Jackson have developed a meta-method for problem-solving, which enables the informed use of each systems methodology in its most appropriate context. This approach is called Total Systems Intervention (TSI).

18.2 Principles of TSI

The practice of TSI in the quality context will be considered in Part Four. In this chapter we are concerned with its principles and philosophy. There are seven underpinning principles to TSI (Figure 18.1), which will be considered briefly in turn and their relevance reflected upon.

Flood & Jackson:

Principle 1) organizations are too complicated to understand using one management 'model' and their problems too complex too tackle with the 'quick fix';

Principle 2) organizations, their strategies and the difficulties they face should be investigated using a range of systems metaphors;

Principle 3) systems metaphors, which seem appropriate for highlighting organizational strategies and problems, can be linked to appropriate systems methodologies to guide intervention;

Principle 4) different systems metaphors and methodologies can be used in a complementary way to address different aspects of organizations and the difficulties they confront;

Principle 5) it is possible to appreciate the strengths and weaknesses of different systems methodologies and to relate each to organizational and business concerns;

Principle 6) TSI sets out a systemic circle of enquiry with iteration back and forth between the three phases;

Principle 7) facilitators, clients and others are engaged at all stages of the TSI process.

Figure 18.1 Seven principles of TSI.

Taking the first principle, 'organizations are too complicated to understand using only one management model', it is certainly the case that the many extremely large organizations of today are very complicated and that the complexity of their problems is beyond what could have been envisaged by the management writers of the earlier parts of the twentieth century.

But what of small organizations – those which make up the bulk of the world economy? A significant proportion of the world's businesses are classified as 'small to medium' (as defined by the Companies Act, 1985, criteria of turnover below £5.75m, and less than 250 employees). These are generally owner-managed, independent organizations, with minimal influence on pricing within their industry or sector. In these cases, it might be thought that lesser tools would be adequate. However, it seems to be the case that the problems of these organizations are in many ways more complex than their larger brethren. On the economic side, the smaller business is seeking to maintain viability in a market place dominated by large organizations that have significant advantages in cost and in economic information, thus increasing the challenge to the small player. In human terms, the intimacy of small organizations may be considered to lead to an increase in the relevance of people management and relationship issues, where people are often personal friends, not simply reference numbers on a payroll. In management terms the small business is again at a disadvantage. They are relatively unattractive to many managers because they often cannot, or do not, offer the same level of either monetary or non-monetary reward (extrinsic rewards) as the larger organizations – although the intrinsic rewards arising from the work itself are often greater. They are not well placed to attract the highest calibre staff, and frequently lack the resources to properly educate and train those which they do attract.

Turning to complexity, it must be suggested that this is not necessarily a function of the size of the organization. Complexity may be seen as a product of dynamism (the frequency of interaction), the number of elements (the number of relevant sub-systems within the organization studied), and the necessary rate of change of the organization and its environment. These are factors which may be considered to be more predominant in small organizations than in large ones.

Vignette 18.1 Business Banking: Size doesn't Matter

In the late 1980s, a major high street bank reviewed the way in which it managed its relationships with business customers – those whose accounts were not held purely for personal purposes. This review led to the development of a wholly new operating struc- ture, based on the separation of customers according to their industry, rather than the traditional alphabetic division. It was felt that in this way the bankers could develop higher levels of industry-focused expertise and understanding, in turn generating higher levels of customer service and lower levels of risk.

This new form of division created difficulties. It was no longer considered adequate to simply 'lump' customers together and shuffle their problems up and down the hierarchy as had hitherto been done. If relationships were to be the basis of satisfying customers, it was essential that the customer-facing staff must be able to deal with the majority of the particular customer's problems and needs.

Traditionally, the organization had assumed that size (particularly borrowing require- ments), complexity and risk were positively correlated – the bigger the amount borrowed, the greater the complexity and risk associated with the account. The staff suggested, however, that this assumption might be flawed, and that an alternative division based on complexity of requirements and difficulty of control should be considered.

The staff involved undertook the task of dividing the relationships into industry sectors, at the same time allocating a complexity code (which would determine the seniority of the member of staff who subsequently managed the relationship) according to their knowledge and experience of the customer. It emerged that many of the largest accounts (either by turnover or borrowing requirements) were the simplest to manage, and were categorized as 'simple' by the staff. Their requirements were easy to under- stand, relatively unchanging, and the sophistication of the customer matched the needs of the organization. In contrast, many much smaller accounts were designated 'very complex'. These smaller businesses often had rapidly changing requirements (because of rapid growth, or the unexpected demands and opportunities facing small businesses) and had less financially sophisticated staff requiring a greater degree of more sophisticated support from the bank.

The second principle, the use of systems metaphors, is useful because it enables individuals to generate high-level descriptions of their circumstances without the need for great elaboration or reductionist analysis. The 'meaning' conveyed by descriptions such as 'prison', 'brain', 'culture' is usually relatively clear to the listener, since there exists a common understanding of the word. The use of metaphor provides a systemic language which can be easily shared. A good source for further exploration of the use of metaphors in this context is Morgan (1986).

The third principle follows from the second. The image generated by a particular metaphor is linked to a group of methodologies. The methodologies so identified are considered applicable to organizations which display the 'metaphorical' characteristics.

The assumptions about the world which underpin the methodology match the behaviour of the actors within the organization. Thus a 'prison' is suggestive of a coercive environment, with a relatively low level of interaction between the stakeholders: one group is dominated by the other. The methodology proposed for this situation is Ulrich's *Critical Systems Heuristics* (Flood and Jackson, 1991).

The fourth principle addresses the issue of 'complementarity' which has already been adequately elaborated at the outset of this chapter.

The fifth principle is of particular importance. It acknowledges that any given methodology has both strengths and weaknesses; there are situations for which it is useful and situations for which it is not. This specifically addresses the issues of isolationism and imperialism raised in the previous section. No craftsman uses only a single tool for the completion of all his tasks. He or she selects from the range of tools available one that is appropriate for the task in hand. Management scientists should adopt the same methodology.

The sixth principle reflects the dynamic nature of contemporary organizations. Total systems intervention is proposed as setting out a 'systemic circle of enquiry', with iteration back and forth. This issue is perhaps understated in much of the literature. A key assumption which underpins much of management thinking is that problems can be solved. Beer (1981) prefers to think that, through the application of organizational cybernetics, rather than being solved problems can be dissolved. While there is truth in both of these positions, the author tends to the view that rather than problems being solved, situations can be managed. While any particular and discrete management problem may have a definable solution, the overall problem of managing can never be complete. The continual changes, both within the system of interest and in its environment, ensure that effective management is a non-stop activity.

Thus it may be more helpful to think of TSI as a systemic meta-model for managing, rather than as a meta-methodology for problem-solving. Taking this view, it is easier to understand that the process may be simultaneously at different stages for different problems, and that more than one metaphor may be employed simultaneously with another to describe a given organizational situation.

The final principle addresses the issue of emancipation, again raised in the previous section. TSI requires that all relevant parties should be involved throughout the process. There is much scope for debate and consideration about how to make such participation meaningful under certain circumstances – particularly where coercion exists.

18.3 Three Phases of TSI

TSI consists of three phases of work: creativity, choice, and implementation.

The first phase, 'creativity', asks questions in two modes: which metaphor best describes the current situation (the 'is' mode) and which best describes the desired situation (the 'ought' mode). A third approach to the enquiry is to consider which metaphors help to explain the difficulties and areas of concern. Metaphors suggested by Flood and Jackson indicate the organization as a 'machine', 'organism', 'brain', 'culture', 'team', 'coalition', and 'prison'. This list is by no means exhaustive, and the participants may use any other metaphor. What is essential, however, is that the description can be linked to one of the systems approaches.

Encouraging participants to go beyond the metaphors suggested by Flood and Jackson may encourage more creative thinking about the situation. In one case, a large

Hong Kong-based corporation, the metaphor used was 'elephant': slow-moving, lacking in colour (no flair), deliberate but instinctive rather than reflective. This perhaps suggests a mechanistic view with organismic overtones, a rather more complex description which captured the essence of the situation for the participants. The result of this phase is a choice of a dominant metaphor, which is used to guide the selection of methodologies in the next phase. It is appropriate to use 'dependent' or subordinate metaphors to capture areas of secondary concern.

The choice phase utilizes Jackson and Keys' (1984) 'system of systems methodologies' (SOSM) (Figure 18.2) to provide a framework for choosing between approaches. The SOSM offers 'guidelines' to assist the participants in making their choices. The SOSM typology sorts methodologies according to two dimensions: the relative complexity of the system studied, and the relative plurality of views of the participants.

A 'simple' system will have few elements, a low level of interaction, a high degree of determinacy, and will be highly organized and highly regulated. It will be relatively static and closed to environmental influence. A 'complex' system will have a large number of elements in highly dynamic interaction. It will exhibit probabilistic behaviour, a lower level of apparent organization, and will be evolutionary.

'Unitary', 'pluralist', and 'coercive' refer to the relationships between the participants in the system. A unitary view suggests common interests, values and beliefs between the participants, with general agreement about ends and means and actions matching objectives. In a pluralist situation, the participants have a basic common interest, but divergent values and beliefs. They can compromise on ends and means, and will also act in line with agreed objectives. In a coercive situation, there is no common interest; values and beliefs are in conflict; compromise is not possible; and some parties may be coerced by others.

TSI interventionists must select a methodology or methodologies (albeit one of their own choice or design not included in the SOSM) in order to move to the next phase: implementation. The framework of the SOSM should enable the users to select a methodology which reflects the characteristics of the situation studied.

	Unitary	Pluralist	Coercive
Simple	Operations Research Systems Analysis Systems Engineering Systems Dynamics	Social Systems Design Strategic Assumption Surfacing and Testing	Critical Systems Heuristics
Complex	Viable System Diagnosis General Systems Theory Socio-technical Systems Thinking Contingency Theory	Interactive Planning Soft Systems Methodology	?

Figure 18.2 The system of systems methodologies (adapted from Flood and Jackson, 1991).

Implementation rests in the coherent application of the chosen methodology to the situation, in accordance with its own theoretical assumptions but constrained by the recognition of those secondary characteristics highlighted during the choice phase. Thus the approach to the methodology must be modified or 'tempered', to ensure that the use is suitable. Flood and Jackson (1991: 15–22) provide an example of the use of TSI in the quality context.

18.4 Critical Review

TSI, while appearing complex, serves to simplify and perhaps demystify choice amongst systems methodologies, while also enabling coherent understanding and debate in a common language about the characteristics of a situation. It provides a framework for the exploration of issues of concern to an organization, and for the 'dominant' issues to be highlighted.

While the SOSM framework may appear to be almost reductionist in its approach, this is too literal a view. Flood and Jackson acknowledge this in their own critique, and refer to the framework as offering 'ideal type' proposals. In any given situation, the practitioner must exercise professional judgement in choice of methodology, and recognize that most situations have a significant degree of 'grey' in their make up, compared to the simple 'black and white' so often sought by clients and apparently suggested by the SOSM. This area is one which demands sophisticated knowledge and understanding by the user (and may account for some of the inadequate uses of the TSI process).

In terms of use, TSI adds much of value to its users, provided that they are prepared to deal with the uncertainty and complexity which rigorous application of the technique may provide. For those who perceive all of an organization's problems as simple and trivial, the method is of little value, since the users have decided before the start of the exploration what the problem is and how it may be solved.

While the theoretical foundations of TSI appear essentially sound, there are two principal limitations. The approach is so complex in use that it may be difficult for managers to use without the appropriate background knowledge. Maximum benefit requires expert facilitation. The first of these limitations may lead managers to avoid the approach, preferring something simpler and more straightforward. The second limitation opens the whole model to the potential for abuse of power, for which other models have already been criticized. In this context, the facilitators are the powerful, who may divert the model to their own ends.

18.5 Critical Systems Thinking and Quality

Critical systems thinking has great relevance to the quality movement (and to the content of this book which reflects that thinking). Simply, critical systems thinking rejects the idea of 'one best way' of solving any problem (whether or not a problem of quality). Instead, it proposes that each method has potential utility in those organizational contexts, which reflect the theoretical assumptions that underpin the approach being applied, and that human freedom and well being is respected.

In the quality context, this suggests that, far from any one quality guru being absolutely right and the others absolutely wrong, they are all right *and* all wrong. Similarly, the various strands of thinking that are being introduced in this part of the book are equally right and wrong, depending upon the circumstances in which their use is attempted.

For example, in a certain situation the statistically-based approach espoused by Deming may be most appropriate, while in another the participative approach preferred by Ishikawa may have greater utility. Equally, at a higher level of intervention, both those approaches may be rejected in favour of a systems-based approach, which embraces the whole system of interest in the pursuit of quality.

A word of caution is appropriate at this juncture, at the risk of offending some readers. It is not only quality methodologies and ways of thinking about the world that have different value in different contexts. These differences also apply to the words we choose to use, and the concepts which we attempt to apply. Thus, such concepts as freedom of choice, participation, and emancipation, have different meanings and value in different contexts. These ideas are essentially products of Western thinking, reflecting primarily what philosophers consider important in societies which are relatively complex in both the economic and the social senses. They are aimed at furthering the interests of those parts of societies already supposed capable of exercising substantial political and economic choices, and accustomed, even if for relatively short periods of history, to making those choices. Such parts of societies may be thought of as enjoying significant psychological maturity.

However, other societies operate under different sets of opportunities, demands and constraints; they may be considered less psychologically mature. Thus, while in a mature society the idea of participation in process design and improvement may be wholly applicable, in some contexts, some members of the society may not be wholly familiar with the concept of a job. Consequently they may require a totally different (although not dictatorial) management approach, perhaps placing greater emphasis on the parental role of the manager. This difference in approach does not apply solely to emerging or developing economies but also to those parts of Western economies which have suffered high levels of unemployment over many years; for example, the steel, coal-mining and ship-building regions of most Western economies. In these regions, there are significant numbers of people for whom the concept of a job is wholly unfamiliar, since work has been unavailable to them, in some cases for two or more generations. This might be thought of, in part, as a product of the failure of employers and employees to embrace changes in management thinking and practice which might have enabled organizational survival. Critical systems thinking enables the thoughtful manager to recognize and reflect upon these aspects of the circumstances in which he or she works, and to choose quality implementation methods accordingly.

18.6 TQM through TSI

In 1993, Robert Flood undertook the task of exploring Total Quality Management (TQM) through the ideas of critical systems thinking, seeking to establish a sound platform for the theory and practice of TQM. His findings are encapsulated in his book *Beyond TQM* (1993). He defines quality as: 'meeting customers' (agreed) requirements, formal and informal, at lowest cost, first time every time'.

Flood sees ten principles (Figure 18.3) emerging from this definition. These are, to some extent, a distillation and synthesis of the work of the gurus already explored in Part Two of this book.

The first principle, the call for agreed requirements, implies a need for a high degree

Robert Flood:

Principle 1) There must be agreed requirements, for both internal and external customers;

Principle 2) Customers' requirements must be met first time and every time;

Principle 3) Quality improvement will reduce waste and total costs;

Principle 4) There must be a focus on the prevention of problems, rather than an acceptance to cope in a fire-fighting manner;

Principle 5) Quality improvement can only result from planned management action;

Principle 6) Every job must add value;

Principle 7) Everybody must be involved, from all levels and across all functions;

Principle 8) There must be an emphasis on measurement to help to assess and to meet requirements and objectives;

Principle 9) A culture of continuous improvement must be established (continuous includes the desirability of dramatic leaps forward as well as steady improvement);

Principle 10) An emphasis should be placed on promoting creativity.

Figure 18.3 Robert Flood's ten principles of TQM.

of communication, both within the organization and with the customers in its environment. The demand for agreement implies that the communication must be focused on discourse not dictat; it must be a two-way process of finding out and informing rather than a matter of giving orders. To be effective, there must be under-standing and voluntary consensus.

The second principle of 'first time, every time' reflects Crosby's call for zero defects. The clear implication is that there is no benefit to be gained from failing to meet customer requirements, and that achieving quality is a matter of consistency. The third principle is the belief that 'quality improvement will reduce waste and total costs'. The important issue here is the positive nature of the statement. Note that Flood uses the unconditional word 'will' – not 'may', 'could', or 'should'. This is of great importance as a belief, since many quality improvement programmes, initially at least, produce solutions which seem to have the opposite effect; increasing costs and waste in the short term while new techniques or processes are learned and embedded. Often managements not fully committed draw back from the changes in response to this negative short-term effect, and hence fail to achieve any of the expected benefits.

The fourth principle, 'focus on prevention', again reflects ideas of the mainstream gurus, and is fundamental to the achievement of quality. If the previous principle is to hold good, then clearly the process of achieving quality has to start with error preven-tion, since, as soon as an error occurs, extra cost is incurred in either rectification, rework, or after-sales support. As Crosby suggests 'It is always cheaper to do it right first time'. This links neatly to the fifth principle, 'planned management action'.

Planning is at the root of success in all manner of activities in life. Planning implies intent, which in turn implies commitment to a particular course of events. All too often, managements attempt to deal with some form of operational organizational crisis (usually a cost-based crisis) by trying to achieve 'quick hits' through an instant TQM programme. This is sure to fail, since the focus is wrong. The banner headline may read 'quality', but the sub-text reads 'save money' and, since the latter is much easier to understand and measure, that will become the focus of the exercise. Some money may be saved in the short term; what is almost certain, however, is that greater quality will not be achieved. A commitment to quality improvement is long term, and planning is the key to success.

Vignette 18.2 Ensuring Failure in Quality Implementation

In late 1996, a food manufacturer decided, within the context of its overall quality improvement programme, to investigate the poor performance of an established food factory. The plant had been built some ten years previously, but had never achieved the levels of productivity and profitability expected.

The investigation was undertaken by a team despatched from the head office, who proceeded to undertake a thorough review of all activities at the plant. Their findings were extensive, showing poor utilization of equipment and labour, inadequate mainten-ance, poor record-keeping (of production, quality, waste and yield), and abuse of the shift system by some employees. Findings were presented to the local manager, together with a well-worked out performance improvement plan.

The manager demanded 'instant' improvements – a focus on the simple operational matters requiring attention – in order to reduce current year budget deficits. The team from head office argued for a systematic, fundamental overhaul of processes and procedures, designed to achieve sustainable improvement over time.

No agreement was reached, and eventually the manager banned the team from head office from the premises. The dispute was referred to the lowest level manager, with reporting lines to both parties. To date, the problem has not been solved.

There are several mistakes evident in this process:

- the problem-solving team was imposed on the factory, rather than being invited in (while the problem belonged to the factory, the solution belonged to head office);
- a 'them and us' situation was guaranteed by the exclusion from the process of any members of the factory staff;
- no 'agreed requirements' were developed between the 'customer' (factory manager) and the 'supplier' (head office team);
- no educational process was undertaken, that is, no sharing of knowledge by either party;
- not everybody was involved;
- the protagonists allowed themselves to be distracted into a 'tribal war' rather than focusing on the particular problem faced.

The sixth principle, 'every job must add value' is perhaps recognition of the extent to which organizational processes are characterized by jobs and tasks which do not add value, being either unnecessary or obstructive to the process. It is interesting to note that 'every' does not just apply to production-focused jobs, but to *every* job in the organization – from the board downwards! This again links to the seventh principle –

'the involvement of everybody' – at all levels and all functions. This takes the responsibility for quality away from the quality assurance or inspection department, and places it firmly in the hands of those responsible for actually doing the job.

The eighth principle – 'emphasis on measurement' – is not taken as a call for reliance on purely statistical methods, but as recognition that without some form of measurement there is no effective basis for evaluation of performance. The importance of effective, integrated measurement systems was explored in Chapter 15 on organizational cybernetics.

The ninth and tenth principles can be taken together – 'calls for continuous improvement and the promotion of creativity'. The first of these relies on the second. In the ninth principle, Flood specifically recognizes that continuous improvement should include 'dramatic leaps as well as steady improvement'. In this case we can argue with word choice, and suggest that 'continual' improvement implies a more dynamic frame of reference for these 'dramatic leaps' than 'continuous', with its implications of incremental behaviour. Figure 18.4 attempts to highlight the difference perceived between continual and continuous improvement.

Quality is then considered by Flood as a function of effective communication between the organization and its customers. This communication clarifies expectations, and is supported by consistent effort from all those within the organization to meet those expectations. This necessitates meaningful measurement, and a creative approach to continual improvement.

18.7 Assumptions

Flood's assumptions about the world in the quality context will now be explored. First, it can be seen that Flood assumes willingness on the part of organizations to communicate and negotiate with their customers. This suggests recognition of equality of power between the supplier and customer. In practice, such equality of power is rare, with one party or the other usually assuming a dominant role in the relationship. When

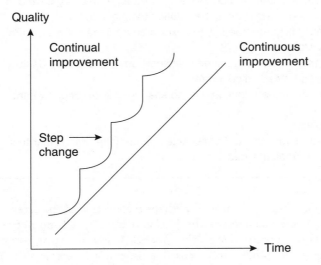

Figure 18.4 Continual and continuous change.

power is unequal – that is, one party is reliant on the other for its continued existence or financial well being – it is unlikely that equality will be maintained in negotiations about quality. For example, it is often the case in the motor industry that component or sub-assembly manufacturers rely on orders from a single manufacturer for the majority of their business. This means that the buyer can dictate quality standards and prices. Similar behaviour is seen in the food industry, where the major supermarket groups exercise enormous power over their suppliers. The banking and telecommunications industries often demonstrate similar characteristics in relation to their customers.

Secondly, Flood's approach assumes willingness within an organization to distribute power amongst the members, since this is the clear implication of his seventh principle of involving 'everybody, at all levels and across all functions'. However, the relatively low power held by many employees, and their vulnerability to loss of employment in many contexts, makes it more likely that managers will behave autocratically, dictating how things will be. This will not lead to full commitment and co-operation – which Flood requires – but does more accurately reflect the power relations in many contemporary organizations. This assumption is also implicit in the ninth principle – the culture of continuous improvement. Again, it suggests effective sharing of power within the organization.

Flood's second assumption is that it is possible to be 'right first time, every time'. While in the manufacturing context this is not at all an unreasonable expectation, in the service and public sectors it is arguably extremely difficult. The technical aspects of any transaction are, of course, no more difficult to get right than the technical aspects of a physical product. Where the service and public sectors will always have difficulty is where the organization meets the customer. While the technical aspects of any particular transaction are constant, each transaction is unique since it depends upon the mood and expectations of the particular customer and of the member of staff at the particular point in time. There are then three variables within any given transaction which are largely beyond the scope of the organization to control. It is inevitable, therefore, that there will be an occasional mismatch between expectations and delivery.

The final assumption, which distinguishes Flood's work from that of others, is the wholehearted embrace of the systemic approach. This comes through in his recognition of both external and internal customers, and in the use of the word 'every' in relation to meeting expectations, to jobs adding value, and to the involvement of all levels and all functions. He does not preclude the involvement of customers in this, although he does not specifically require it.

Overall, Flood's principles rely on a systemic world in which people behave as if they are in partnership. Power is distributed, with those having the information making the decisions, and collaboration rather than competition as the keynote of success. This is a rather different world to the one which many people experience each day.

Other aspects of Flood's approach will be examined in later chapters. The practice of TQM through TSI will be considered in Chapter 22. This section has simply outlined the overall process he proposes.

18.8 Successes and Failures

It is too early to make properly informed judgements about the success or failure of this approach as, unlike the approaches reviewed in Part Two, it has not had the benefit of extended development and empirical study. It is, however, reasonable to attempt some preliminary evaluation of this work. The probable strengths are:

- it attempts to be truly holistic;
- it is systematic, methodical and iterative;
- it embraces much of value from the established approaches, overcoming some weaknesses previously recognized;
- it is rooted in a substantial appreciation of management and organization theory.

Perceived weaknesses include the following:

- the theory and practice of TSI is not yet accepted as part of mainstream management theory;
- TSI is regarded by many practitioners as too complex in itself;
- there is a lack of widely reported case studies in the literature;
- substantial empirical development has been principally undertaken by Flood himself;
- as with the other approaches already considered, the approach is of limited value in a truly coercive context.

Reviewing the strengths, the truly holistic view stems from the meta-methodological, complementarist, framework of TSI, which underpins the approach and tries to avoid the isolationist, pragmatist and imperialist criticisms made of other methods. The systematic, methodical and iterative process provides a heuristic aspect, which reflects the Deming or Shewhart cycle of learning. The embrace of established approaches recognizes that there are strengths in them, and supports them with a broader conceptual framework, thereby increasing their potential utility. Finally, the appreciation of management and organization theory recognizes that quality is only one aspect of organizational effectiveness, and opens the pursuit of quality to the importation of ideas from other frames of reference within the total knowledge set.

With regard to the weaknesses, the lack of acceptance of TSI amongst mainstream theorists is not necessarily a fault of the approach itself, but a function of the different paradigms within which people are educated and work, and the complexity of the world itself. Unfortunately, contemporary problems can not always be addressed through simple techniques. In fact it could be argued that many of the failures of problem-solving approaches rest on their simplicity, rendering them inadequate for the problems which they attempt to address.

The lack of available case studies and empirical experience are functions of the time which has been available for development. While the work of many others has been under development for forty years or more, Flood's work has only been in the public domain for fifteen years, and TQM has never been the primary focus of his work.

The final weakness – limited value in truly coercive contexts – is common to all the quality methodologies reviewed (and indeed to other problem-solving approaches). No adequate methodology exists to address this weakness. For many practical purposes, this may be regarded as relatively unimportant. Power relations in most organizations are distorted to some degree, but in most contexts there are practical limits. If the organization becomes too oppressive, people will leave; thus the power of those in charge is finite. In many contexts, employees do have choices.

In fully developed, as well as in developing countries, there are situations where a considerable degree of practical oppression does exist, where the employees do not have effective choices. This might be the case in communities which have experienced high unemployment, or where there is a single, dominant employer. In these situations, it must be hoped that the effective pursuit of organizational survival and quality will ultimately force those in power to adopt a less dominant position, and engage the willing co-operation of the workforce by recognizing that quality cannot be achieved without it.

18.9 Critical Review

Flood's adherence to the concept of a complementarist approach to organizations, and to problem-solving, opens up a new holistic avenue for the pursuit of the quality ideal. He precludes no ideas which are theoretically substantiated, requiring only that they be used in full understanding of the principles and world-views which underpin them.

The principal tenets of various strands of quality management are subsumed into his approach, thus ensuring the use of participation; the value of appropriate measurement; the informed use of a wide range of tools; and the coherence generated by a deeper level of understanding. Overall, therefore, the approach offers a considerably enhanced perception of the 'quality problem'.

The generality of the approach would appear to render it directly relevant to both manufacturing and service industries, although it will suffer many of the same shortcomings as the dominant approaches when dealing with the very soft aspects of organizational behaviour. For example, it may be possible to specify what words should be used in any given transaction – and this is often done. What cannot be specified is the sincerity with which the words are spoken, and most certainly not the response of the particular customer to each utterance. The sincerity conveyed is probably more important to the customer than the exact form of words. Sincerity can only be attained when the staff member truly believes in what he or she is saying. No methodology exists which can guarantee such belief, although approaches do exist which make it possible.

Pending further reported and substantial empirical work, with the use of Flood's approach by a broader range of practitioners, the conclusion must be that it appears to have potential to enhance the implementation of quality programmes. This, however, has yet to be proven.

Summary

This chapter has introduced critical systems thinking, and the use of the TSI methodology in a quality context. Readers wishing to extend their knowledge should consider the various works by Jackson (1991), Flood and Jackson (1991) and Flood (1993) to develop and enhance their understanding.

KEY LEARNING POINTS

Critical Systems Thinking

Critical systems thinking has three goals:
complementarism, sociological awareness, emancipation.

Key belief:
management problem-solving has become divided amongst pragmatists, isolationists, imperialists.

Total Systems Intervention (TSI) (the meta-methodology of CST) has six principles:
complexity demands sophisticated approaches;
metaphors add value by aiding thinking;
metaphors link to problem-solving approaches;
each method has strengths and weaknesses;
problem-solving must be systemic and iterative;
participation and engagement of actors is essential.

CST and quality:
rejects the idea of 'one best way';
all approaches and gurus are both right and wrong;
beware of imposing an alternative value set;
encourages reflection and choice.

Question

What difficulties might be encountered in attempting to adopt a TSI-based approach to quality management?

19 Business Process Re-Engineering

> . . . ideas are good for a limited time – not forever
>
> (Robert Townsend, *Further up the Organization*, 1985)

Introduction

Business Process Re-Engineering (BPR) emerged as a formal business practice in America during the 1980s and early 1990s, although the term was used in the discipline of operations research (Weiner, 1947) as early as the 1940s. In its current incarnation, it is an essentially pragmatic approach that resulted from observation and evaluation of the efforts of several companies to reinvent themselves. It can perhaps be most usefully thought of as a form of business strategy, focused on gaining competitive advantage through efficiency improvement and exploitation of information technology, rather than as a theoretically rooted approach to management problem-solving. Michael Hammer and James Champy (1993) formalized and crystallized the approach, which is characterized as systemic, and capitalizes on many established problem-solving methodologies and techniques.

19.1 What is BPR?

Business Process Re-Engineering challenges many assumptions underpinning the way organizations have been run for the last two centuries. First, it rejects the idea of reductionism – the fragmentation and breaking down of organizations into simple tasks – preferring the systemic recognition of flows of interconnected activities with a common purpose. Second, it encourages organizations to capitalize on substantial developments made in technology, particularly those of the last decade. The role of information technology (IT) as an enabler of the radical redesign of organizations is emphasized – although it is stressed that using IT is not the point of BPR. Third, BPR enables organizations to take advantage of the more highly developed education, skills and capabilities of the staff they employ. People are treated within BPR as McGregor's (1960) capable 'theory Y' individuals, rather than as lazy, incompetent 'theory X' machine parts.

BPR embraces many of the developments in management thinking arising in the recent past, particularly those concerned with the management of human resources. Ideas such as empowerment are fundamental to the BPR-oriented company.

19.2 Discontinuity, Chaos and Complexity

Central to the BPR process is one key idea – that of 'discontinuous thinking', a notion raised by Hammer and Champy (1993), but earlier given prominence by Handy (1990a) in *The Age of Unreason*. Discontinuous thinking and the idea of 'discontinuity' demand some explanation.

The Western world relies on continuous thinking, largely derived from scientific thinking. Continuous thinking is incremental; that is, an apparently seamless, flowing approach based on small, incremental changes. This has served the West extremely well, and retains immense value in certain areas. It is reflected in the continuous improvement (*kaizen*) approach to quality, which has been adopted successfully by many companies throughout the world. However, this approach is inadequate for solving problems currently besetting organizations, or for realizing the true potential of the dramatic advances in the ways that organizations can capture data about performance, manipulate it, and generate information for decisions. Readers will recall Handy's view cited in Chapter 3.

The call for discontinuous change may be seen as 'special pleading' by management gurus and consultants seeking a 'new' product to sell. It is, perhaps, just another form of organizational snake-oil; a solution in search of a problem – after all it does represent the opportunity for major projects and large fees! This, however, is an extremely cynical view and ignores the substantial theoretical support which can now be drawn upon in this area from the 'hard' sciences, particularly biology and quantum physics. That Hammer, Champy, and other writers in this area have not drawn on these sources does not negate the value of their work; it merely reflects different backgrounds and knowledge bases. It is fair to say, though, that the explicit recognition and use of the insights contained in these sciences would substantially enhance their work. As suggested by Flood and Jackson (1991), if there is no underpinning science to the work of management gurus, they have nothing to rely on but experience, and nothing to pass on to subsequent generations but stories.

The mathematically substantiated science of organizational cybernetics (discussed in Chapter 16) is concerned with the control of dynamical systems: those that are changing or evolving. This science has, in its contemporary interpretation, been evolving since the 1940s. It embraces potential discontinuity as part of its structure, and enables organizations to become discontinuous in the way they operate; embracing a whole new philosophy of management and decision making, and distributing power in ways previously unheard of. Early development of this work involved mathematicians, biologists, physicists and engineers. As has already been shown, this work has reached its most developed and useful form through the writings of Stafford Beer.

More recently, other developments of this work in the hands of physicists, biologists and others have proved (according to scientific methods) that discontinuities may be considered as natural phenomena. Catastrophe theory (a branch of mathematics) is cited as the original identifier of the 'butterfly effect' – in which a butterfly beating its wings in one part of the world may generate a thunderstorm in another – the potentially massive consequences of a relatively minor disturbance or perturbation in a dynamic system.

Complexity theory (Waldrop, 1992) has shown how, in dynamical systems, equilibrium (a stable state) emerges from apparently random or chaotic behaviour, and how indescribably complex systems can be studied and their behaviour understood (see

Black Boxes, Chapter 16). These systems again can be disturbed from their stable states by minor perturbations, and then, changing discontinuously for a period, settle into a new point of stability. Studies of complexity in systems show that patterns are often present in what at first sight appear to be random oscillations.

Chaos theory (Gleick, 1987) – which some might argue is not significantly different to complexity theory – has shown how systems apparently evolve chaotically while, under further examination, pattern and order can be discerned in movements relating to a representative point in phase space. Often, system behaviour is almost repeated in a kind of spiral dynamics forming orbits around a fixed point. The orbit may never be quite the same twice, but the fulcrum (or turning point) of the orbit remains the same. Again, minor disturbances can cause major effects.

These developments reflect much of the earlier thinking in the systems and cybernetics paradigms, and are given great credence by the contemporary facility to model such systems on computers. This allows us to observe the consequences graphically for the first time. Early studies, which did not have this advantage, relied upon the mathematical knowledge of the reader for their proof.

Grasping the concept that discontinuity is as natural, if not more so, as continuity, while discomfiting to many, must ultimately be seen as reassuring, since many discontinuities are met in life. The task of management is to drive and exploit the discontinuity, steering the organization in a way that leads to its survival. The ultimate alternative is the discontinuity that is death, or, in the case of organizations, liquidation and bankruptcy. Discontinuity is sure to arise within organizational systems, but its consequences are a function of management decisions and actions.

19.3 What Drives BPR?

Hammer and Champy (1993: 1) suggest that the alternative to BPR is for 'corporate America to close its doors and go out of business'. The comment describes the behaviour of organizations for many years. When faced with increasing costs at home and competition from abroad, many have chosen, in effect, to export jobs rather than products. It is an argument already adequately explored in Chapter 1 of this book, and given new life in the economic crisis of 2008. The same imperatives which drive the quality movement should drive BPR.

Thus, a key impetus for BPR is the imperative of economic survival for mature organizations and nations. While the focus for Hammer and Champy is the US economy, the arguments apply equally well to the UK, Europe, and to certain Asian economies. The message is to stop exporting jobs and start reinventing the way we perform work, in order to match the lower costs of manufacturing elsewhere.

It must be recognized at this stage that the imperative does not simply apply to the manufacturing sector but also to service industries and the public sector. The export of information processing-based tasks, supported by the explosive developments in the capabilities and use of information technology, is already exporting jobs.

Resistance to BPR and reluctance to use its application in both the public and commercial sectors of the economy arise from the same sources. The focus of both tends to be short term – a product of government financial systems and commercial employment contracts. So long as there are profits (or an adequate budget) today, there is no need for action to be taken. Even where the need can be identified by those with the power of decision, they often lack the will or commitment to take action, since the consequences of failure, or benefits of success, will not be felt during their own incumbency.

19.4 What Does BPR Mean?

Hammer and Champy define BPR as: 'the fundamental rethinking and radical redesign of business processes to achieve dramatic improvements in critical, contemporary measures of performance, such as cost, quality, service and speed.'

This underlines that most established organizations have grown up with, and still adhere to, outmoded, traditional methods of work which are now relatively inefficient and often ineffective. These methods have often led to convoluted, complex ways of dealing with activities with many steps, checks and balances. These are, in many cases, rendered redundant by the development of both production and information technology, by the universal spread of education, and by our current understanding concerning the needs and capabilities of people. Added to this should be the exponential growth in our understanding of the systemic nature of the world, and the sophisticated methodologies and tools which have been developed in order for us to manage our organizations more competently. The key words (Figure 19.1) in the definition will now be examined.

Key word 1, 'fundamental' is a clear call for the organization to examine itself at the most basic level. Hammer and Champy suggest the question 'Why do we do what we do?' Perhaps this should go further and ask the question 'What do we do?' This second question demands that the participants focus on the purpose that they perceive for the organization – that is, a redefinition of the organization's goal – without which any improvement, however radical, may actually become trivial or banal. It is important that the organization focuses on doing the right thing to the best of its ability – not on doing the wrong thing better!

For Hammer and Champy, key word 2, 'radical', means 'not making superficial changes or fiddling with what is already in place, but throwing away the old'. Within the rigorous process of Interactive Planning, Ackoff (1981) offered the process stage of 'idealized redesign'. Ackoff simply asks the question: 'If you were designing the organization today what would it look like?' This implies *not* working from established processes and procedures, but designing the organization from scratch on a clean sheet of paper. In impact it is much the same as zero-based budgeting, since it forces a fundamental reappraisal of every activity within the organization.

Key word 3, 'dramatic', implies that BPR does not seek to achieve marginal or incremental improvement in performance – the normal 5 to 10 per cent. For companies

Hammer & Champy:

Key word 1) Fundamental

Key word 2) Radical

Key word 3) Dramatic

Key word 4) Processes

Key word 5) Performance

Figure 19.1 Business process re-engineering: key words.

with that scale of problem (if they are sure of it), the process of BPR may be too powerful. The focus is on companies which want, or need, to achieve much more substantial performance improvements. Personal experience shows that through effective BPR practice, improvements of 35 to 50 per cent are achievable. Within certain processes, up to 70 per cent is claimed to be possible. It is suggested that every company should undertake a study of its processes to determine what level of improvement might be achievable. Simply being at, or near, best in class, which seems to satisfy Hammer and Champy, is not enough. If you are the best, but another organization finds a way of being better, you will face the re-engineering challenge anyway. Far better to undertake this activity while ahead of the pack and profitable, than while running behind trying to catch up.

'Processes', key word 4, are best defined as the 'value-chain' or 'cost-chain' running through the organization and linking its inputs to its outputs. A process is the series of revenue-generating or cost-incurring steps involved in delivery of a product or service to a customer. Certain industries, for example, chemical and oil producers, are inherently process-focused at an operational level. Processes describe the enchained patterns of activity of the organization. Many other organizations are broken down into functional departments with 'baronial' (Jay, 1987) responsibilities for parts or sub-set activities. Those involved often have limited awareness that they form part of the overall chain, and sometimes have no idea what value or cost they generate for the organization. They are narrowly focused on a particular task, with no knowledge or interest in how this contributes to fulfilling the purpose of the organization or the needs of its customers. Readers will realize the relevance to quality when recalling Deming's contribution to the quality movement in his recognition of internal 'supplier–customer' relationships.

Key word 5, 'performance', while not highlighted by Hammer and Champy, is a very significant word. Performance does not necessarily mean profit, although this is the common interpretation. Rather, it should be taken to mean the fulfilment of the purposes of the organization, and the effective utilization of resources.

BPR, then, relies on several unconventional ideas. First, the orientation of the organization towards its processes rather than towards its functional, and often fragmented, activities (an orientation becoming more common). Second, it requires drive and ambition to make far-reaching and 'dramatic' improvements – and this must arise from senior management. Third is what Hammer and Champy call 'rule-breaking', that is, a willingness to challenge the conventions of the organization. Finally, there is the creative use of information technology. This means using it to enable genuine improvements in performance, rather than to set the established ways of working in electronic tablets of stone.

Added to these should be the concepts of bravery and determination, so often absent from corporate life; attentive readers will recall the quote from Machiavelli in this regard in Chapter 1.

Prior to concluding this section, it is worth noting what is *not* meant by BPR. For Hammer and Champy, what it does not mean is: downsizing, rightsizing, restructuring, automating, or any other management activity which may, or may not, be necessary or desirable. These things should happen anyway, and, of course, may result from re-engineering, but that is not the purpose of the BPR process. If, however, that is how the organization interprets re-engineering, two things are certain. The first is that the process will fail (as do over 50 per cent of so-called re-engineering projects), as the management commitment and understanding needed to really make it work will be absent. Second, the organization will grow back all of the parts reduced in size, since no fundamental change in its basis of operation will have occurred. The problem will simply be deferred, rather than solved, dissolved, or resolved.

Vignette 19.1 Business Process Tinkering

In 1995, the author was invited to present a seminar to senior members of a very large public sector organization in Asia. The topic was to be Business Process Re-engineering.

Established knowledge of the organization was reinforced through lengthy discussions with two managers concerning re-engineering projects then ongoing within the organization. The organization was essentially information driven, and the projects rightly had a high information technology content. Study of the projects suggested that the organization had rather missed the point of BPR. They had not identified their core business processes and could not model or critically examine them. Nonetheless the projects were going ahead with full approval and all possible speed. The projects were, in the author's view, tackling problems of mind-boggling triviality with regard to the central concerns of the organization, such that they were probably not worth the effort – hence the expression 'business process tinkering'.

Needless to say, this information and view was allowed to colour the presentation given to the senior management, and the live projects were used as examples of what not to do. The projects were set in the context of a different perception of the problems which the organization needed to address: overmanning in some areas; ineffectiveness in others; lack of resources in the 'front line'; too many senior managers in 'make-work' jobs. The audience seemed to thoroughly enjoy the somewhat challenging, combative, and participative seminar, which concluded with a very lively and forthright question and answer session.

The most senior of those present arose at the end to propose thanks, concluding his short speech with the words: 'A fascinating and provocative seminar, but it seems to me that we need not take any further action.'

19.5 The BPR Process

The process of undertaking BPR draws on a wide variety of tools, approaches and understanding. Many of these have been, or will be, elaborated within this book: for example, statistical methods, communication issues, problem-solving tools, process-mapping tools and the use of information technology.

In this brief section, the focus of attention will be on the overall process, called the 'Business System Diamond'. This is presented in Figure 19.2.

When adopting a process-based approach to an organization, it is essential to identify the key processes. These in turn control the number, nature and content of jobs, which leads us towards the definition of structure. Arising from the new expectations concerning desirable outputs (the results of processes), and the activities of employees, it is possible to define the management and measurements systems necessary for performance (and it should always be remembered that the tendency is for those characteristics which are measured to be delivered). Finally, with the other

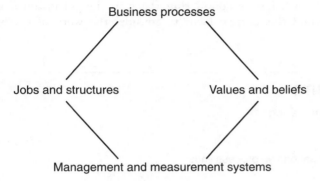

Figure 19.2 The business system diamond.

linkages in place, the values and beliefs of the members of the organization will be modified.

It can easily be seen how each stage in the diamond drives the next. The diamond also suggests an iterative process – having successfully re-engineered, the culture of the organization should be supportive of aspirations to further development. This may be interpreted as a call back towards continuous improvement.

19.6 BPR and Quality

There is some ongoing debate as to whether BPR replaces or subsumes the pursuit of quality, or quality subsumes BPR. This debate is sterile. The pursuit of quality is about 'rightness' in all the actions and interactions of an organization, both internally and externally. The greater part of the quality methods and tools are incremental in their impact, and lead the organization towards the *kaizen* philosophy of continuous improvement. This implies linear, continuous change in the organization. BPR is about embracing the hidden potential for change by recognizing that incremental change only improves what is already done, while BPR may fundamentally change what is done. If a procedure, or part of a process, is redundant, in the sense that it adds no value to a product or service, improvement in its efficiency is a false gain. While efficiency improvement reduces the amount of waste, the procedure still remains as a cost in the system. The adoption of BPR techniques in process analysis can help to overcome this problem, eradicating procedures rather than improving them. BPR and quality are complementary, not competitive.

Perhaps somewhat perversely, and as with the strategic process outlined in Chapter 2, it is vital that the BPR process itself exhibits appropriate quality characteristics. If the BPR process is flawed, the outcome will also be flawed.

Summary

This chapter has introduced the concept of Business Process Re-Engineering and placed it in the context of theoretical developments in recent years. The links to systemic approaches based on cybernetics, complexity science and chaos theory were explored. In the latter half of the chapter, BPR was defined and its key process explained. While this chapter draws heavily on the pioneers of BPR (Hammer and Champy: 1993), readers may wish to extend their knowledge by considering the work by Johansson *et al.* (1993), and by moving beyond this narrow focus to consider the work of systems thinkers in depth.

KEY LEARNING POINTS

Business Process Re-engineering

BPR definition:
radical reinvention of organizations on process lines.

Key Characteristics:
pragmatic and empirical, not theoretically-based, systemic, exploits developments in technology.

Central themes:
discontinuity, radical change, cybernetic understanding, complexity theory, chaos theory.

Key drivers:
economic, social, environmental.

Method:
The business systems diamond, process analysis, job and structure review, management and measurement systems, values and beliefs.

BPR and quality are complementary.

Question

What barriers would you expect to meet in designing and implementing a Business Process Re-engineering programme?

20 The Learning Organization

Education makes a people easy to lead, but difficult to drive; easy to govern but impossible to enslave

(Lord Brougham, 1778–1868)

Introduction

The chapters on Critical Systems Thinking and Business Process Re-Engineering have both espoused iterative processes which should lead to the continuing evolution, and perhaps revolution, of the organization. This chapter introduces early ideas about adaptation and learning, based on Ross Ashby's *Design for a Brain* (1966), before considering the specific work of Peter Senge (1990), author of the best-known current text in this area: *The Fifth Discipline*. Senge's *Fifth Discipline Fieldbook* (1994) identifies five principles for learning and seven learning disabilities which inhibit the development of truly successful organizations. Flood (1999) revisited this theme in *Rethinking the Fifth Discipline*, to bring to the field a deeper and more robust appreciation of the breadth and power of systemic thinking applied to the notion of learning. This current book cannot provide a fully comprehensive review of the literature in this field, which has grown substantially in recent years. Readers should refer to Karl Weick's *Imagining*, Gareth Morgan's *Images of Organization* and *Innovation* by Andrew Pettigrew and Evelyn Fenton to develop their understanding further.

Learning itself is a cycle of planning, experimentation, reflection and consolidation, which the PDCA cycle and EPDCA cycle from Deming and Oakland reflect. A learning organization needs to be capable of employing these cycles systemically throughout its horizontal and vertical dimensions. This means that learning must be embedded in the organization's processes, systems, and structure, and in the behaviour of its people.

20.1 Organizational Learning

Organizational learning is commonly associated with issues of data mining and knowledge management (physical retention of documented records) in an organization. The presumption is that in knowledge-based economies such information constitutes an organizational asset, and that it should be managed in the same ways as other assets. This has given rise to growth in document management systems, data mining technologies, and the creation of more substantial organizational archives. All of which rather misses the point!

Organizational learning is not about recording history, that is, the storage and retrieval of data; it is about organizational processes and behaviours which co-adapt with changes in the internal and external environments. A learning organization learns from, and about, its environment, but also 'teaches' the environment – influencing it to be more susceptible to the products and services offered. Two typical examples of this are marketing activity and political propaganda. This learning and teaching must occur at least at the same rate as the environment is changing. Changes in behaviour of the people must also happen; they must actively support and encourage adaptation rather than inhibit it.

Lessons can be drawn from the work of evolutionists, such as Darwin, which help us to understand that in a persistently evolving environment those species that survive are those which are best adapted to their environment over time. Those characteristics of a species which enable its survival in any one time period may ultimately lead to its failure when the environment changes. Thus there is a conflict. To maximize opportunities for survival in the present requires characteristics which meet the demands of the present environment. To maximize opportunities for survival in the long term necessitates characteristics which cannot even be known about, but which the species or entity must be capable of evolving into if it is to survive. This capability must, to some extent, detract from the closeness of fit to the current environment. In effect, it makes it inefficient (in terms of purely short-term measures), but effective. This conflict applies at least as much to organizations as it does to living species. It may be argued that the organizational case is stronger because, in general, the economic ecology changes faster, and sometimes more drastically, than that of the world in general.

Drawing on Ashby (1966) to resolve this conflict for organizations, it is necessary to do three things simultaneously, and at various levels of an organization. It must:

1. pursue efficiency in its current interactions with the market place; persistently pursuing faster, cleaner, and cheaper means of delivering present products and services to present markets;
2. monitor (that is, understand as well as gather data) the organizational environment searching for new opportunities; considering the closeness of fit to the market (and influencing that market) and reflecting on past performance to create future products and services for future markets;
3. conduct a meaningful dialogue internally, thus enabling the organizational objectives, stimulated by considerations for the future, to be translated into the organizational reality of the future.

In essence, the organization is attempting to move smoothly to ensure a continuous fit between its product and service offerings, and the changing demands of the customers. Such an approach means that the organization must structurally separate, either literally or in the behaviour of its employees, the roles which are necessary to enable evolutionary, adaptive behaviour to occur. Usually organizations are oriented around current products, services and markets. Often, little or no attention is paid to the future, and consequently the organization is hit with unexpected events for which it has carried out no preparation. The demands of operating today's business nearly always override the necessity of creating tomorrow's, and therefore the organization dies – usually by being absorbed by another.

Organizations do not exist (except in the sense of a legal entity) other than through the interactions of their members. They are socially constructed devices, assembled to achieve a common aim, and ultimately cannot learn except through the interactions of their human members. The collective memory of an organization is best described through its culture, that is, the ways of thinking and behaving which are common to its members. Organizational learning is therefore not about the addition of data to a corporate memory – although such memories are capable of being created – but about change in the behaviour of the organization through structural change, and adaptation of the individual and collective behaviour of its members. In Figure 20.1, the author offers a cybernetic interpretation of how such adaptation might take place.

Members of the company, through their interactions with the environment, come to question the way in which things are done ('questioning'), by comparing their real world experience with the organization's model of 'self' (their model of the organization and its environment). They conceive potential solutions to the defined problem ('conceptualization'), and design an experiment to test their hypothesis ('experimentation'). The results of the experiment are fed back to them, and the organizational model is modified according to their new experience ('consolidation'). They proceed to manage the organization in accordance with the modified model. Learning fails to take place when the last of these steps, 'consolidation', does not occur.

Alert readers will have noticed the direct comparison which can be drawn here with other learning approaches, such as the Deming Cycle (Plan, Do, Check, Action),

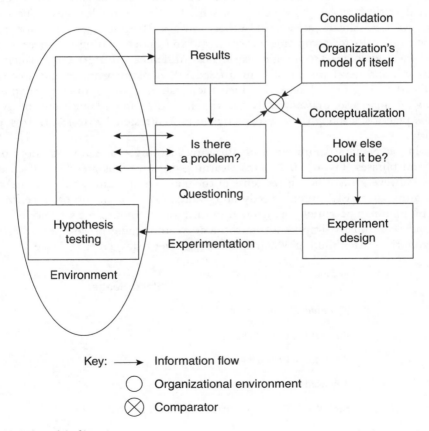

Figure 20.1 A model of learning.

Ishikawa's quality circles (which focus on problem-solving) and Taguchi's prototyping methodology. Questioning, conceptualization, experimentation, and consolidation are drawn from Handy (1985).

The structure for an adaptive organization has been considered in theory here, and extensively in Chapter 16. The practice of organizational cybernetics will be assessed in Part Four.

20.2 Senge's Learning Organization

Senge defines a 'learning organization' simply as one where:

> people continually expand their capacity to create the results they truly desire, where new and extensive patterns of thinking are nurtured, where collective aspiration is set free, and where people are continually learning how to learn together (Senge, 1990).

The idea is supported in other parts of the literature. Beer (1979, 1981, 1985) writes about adaptive, ultra stable systems – organizations which are capable of reacting to situations and conditions not envisaged when they were designed. Ackoff's (1981) work and that of Checkland (1981) both call for participation, exploration and critical reflection, which are essential activities for learning. The critical systems work of Flood, Jackson and others can also be called upon to support this view, with its calls for complementarism (requiring understanding of different theories and methodologies), sociological awareness (different cultures) and emancipation (the growth and development of human freedom). A recent work in this area comes from Flood and Romm (1996), in which they elaborate an approach to 'triple-loop learning'. Senge also draws widely on the literature in organization theory and business practice, although not systems dynamics (Forrester, 1961, 1969), to support his work.

Looking at Senge's definition of organization learning, there are a number of key words and phrases (Figure 20.2). First, learning organizations are clearly focused on people. However, this is not in the sense of the mainstream human resource literature, which aims to satisfy human needs and wants, but in an approach centred on developing human potential – which will in turn lead to those same satisfactions.

Second, 'continually' implies a commitment to an ongoing process, a further move away from the static thinking which dominated earlier management science.

Peter Senge:

Key word 1) People

Key word 2) Continually

Key word 3) Create the results

Key word 4) New patterns of thinking

Key word 5) Collective aspiration/Learning together

Figure 20.2 The learning organization: key words and phrases.

Vignette 20.1 Learning Stimulates Learning

Berkshire Young Musicians Trust is a highly successful music education organization. The public face of the Trust is its highly successful bands, which compete in music festivals at national level and regularly tour internationally, entertaining audiences in many countries. These competitive successes and international tours are seen by the head teacher as a bonus, rather than being the real work of the Trust. He sees the real work and achievement as the opportunity given to every child within the Berkshire community, regardless of ability, to take part in musical activities and succeed to their own best level.

The philosophy adopted is:

> Every child can grow through music;
> every child should be given the chance.

The successes of the Trust are attained through a number of factors such as enthusiastic staff, a large core of young musicians, and exciting, stimulating music and projects. To enable this, the Trust operates on a highly devolved structure, with day-to-day decision making delegated as far as possible. Understanding that the work of the Trust stands or falls by its teachers, the head teacher aims to recruit the best and retain them. Performance is monitored through a system of curricular heads, led by the head of education. Monitoring includes observation of lessons and assessment of problems, as well as the sharing of opportunities and experience.

The known strengths and weaknesses of the staff are seen as the basis for the development of training programmes, designed to capitalize on the strengths and overcome the weaknesses. The opportunity is taken to use outside speakers when appropriate, and bring fresh ideas and experiences into the organization.

Staff are encouraged to find new and creative ways of stimulating the learning of their pupils, rather than simply regurgitating the lessons they themselves received as young musicians. Many members of staff write and arrange music specifically for their groups. They are passionate about music, and aim to achieve the best possible results.

The only selection criterion applied to pupils wishing to study with the Trust is their desire and expressed interest in the instrument they want to learn. In discussion, the head revealed how recent research into the effects of learning music showed that this stimulated other learning by the child. Three groups of students were studied. The first group received music instruction, the second computer instruction, the third received no extra tuition. While the second and third groups demonstrated no change in their performance, the group receiving music instruction showed a 30 per cent improvement. The conclusion (however preliminary) is that learning music stimulates other learning.

Third, 'create the results' suggests that the people's abilities enable them to control and create the future of organizations. This reflects the thinking of Ackoff and others. However, it must be acknowledged that limits exist regarding the potential control exerted by organizations; these limits being enforced by the actions of others in a competitive world.

Fourth, 'new patterns of thinking' reinforces the points made earlier in the work.

While not necessarily rejecting all the old thinking, the new should be capitalized on where appropriate. Finally, there is collective aspiration and learning together. Here, Senge appears to object to much of the development of Western society in recent years. This has seen a move away from collective, shared values and hopes, towards a rather more selfish world in which the individual is considered supreme. This is perhaps reflected in life in such areas as divorce rates, executive compensation packages, the increasing trend towards litigation over relatively minor matters, and the drift away from religiously-based societies towards a more secular approach.

The issue of learning is given real prominence when the leaders of large industrial organizations take it seriously. Senge quotes from Arie De Geus, then head of planning for Royal Dutch Shell: 'The ability to learn faster than your competitors may be the only sustainable competitive advantage.' The American business guru Tom Peters makes the comment 'there is a surplus of everything'. This is taken to mean that there is more capacity in the world to create goods and services than exists to consume them. This can only generate further competitive pressure, thus driving down prices and margins, and consequently profits. It is not simply about learning to work 'smarter' to do better, but simply to survive.

20.3 The Learning Disabilities

Senge suggests that even the 'excellent' companies may only be performing at a mediocre level (again reflecting some of the thinking behind Business Process Re-Engineering). He proposes that the ways we design and manage our organizations, which reflect the narrow, convergent ways in which we are taught to think and to interact, create 'fundamental learning disabilities'.

Learning Disabilities:

Disability 1) I am my position;

Disability 2) The enemy is out there;

Disability 3) The illusion of taking charge;

Disability 4) The fixation on events;

Disability 5) The parable of the boiling frog;

Disability 6) The delusion of learning from experience;

Disability 7) The myth of the management team.

Figure 20.3 The learning disabilities.

The phrase 'I am my position' argues that we become what we do for a job. The classic example of this is when we meet someone for the first time, and are almost always asked 'What do you do?' Our response, 'I am a . . .' define us as being our work. Alternatively, we might argue that we do what we do because we are who we are.

'The enemy is out there', reflects our human tendency to place blame or guilt elsewhere, rather than to acknowledge the faults in ourselves. This tendency has been recorded in literature since at least biblical times. Commenting on the illusion of taking charge, Senge suggests that when we think we are being 'proactive', very often we are just being differently reactive. He proposes that 'true pro-activeness comes from seeing how we contribute to our own problems'.

Our reductionist views of the world, the tendency to scientifically analyse, leads us to a simple 'causal chain' view of the world; hence the fixation on events rather than processes and interactions. This has already been challenged with the recognition of the systems-based approach. Senge suggests that in this area our focus on events prevents us from seeing the patterns in continuing processes, which tell us much about what is actually happening.

The parable of the boiling frog was fully rehearsed in Chapter 3. It is the recognition of the need for discontinuous change and, perhaps, learning to be uncomfortable with continuity in a non-linear world (chaos! complexity!).

Taken at the simple, individual, level, if we reflect on our actions and their consequences, then we learn. There are many people in the world who, while claiming thirty-plus years' experience, actually have one year's experience thirty times – they do not reflect and cannot learn. We do not always learn from experience as, particularly in organizations, consequences of our actions cannot be known in this way. They may well extend across organizational boundaries and have impacts for future time, which we are not in a position to assess. Beer's Viable System Model (VSM) starts to address this point, with its emphasis on information management. The VSM calls for an internal model of the organization within the meta-management, and for abandonment of the traditional functional silos or stovepipes of management.

Suggesting that management teams are often little more than gentlemanly turf wars, Senge (following Beer and others) talks about the 'myth' of the management team. He recognizes that appearances are often more important to people within organizations than reality. This means that often the management team is not a team at all, particularly when under pressure. In reality, each member is fighting to defend his or her own credibility and position in adversity. Often, polite divisions are drawn between areas of responsibility, which simply avoid the potential for conflict, rather than resolve tensions and enable mechanisms to be developed for working together, as would be the case in a real team environment. By definition, members of a team can only win as a team, never as individuals – thus all of their efforts should be directed to that end. But we end with what Argyris (cited by Senge, 1990) calls 'skilled incompetence' – 'teams full of people who are incredibly proficient at keeping themselves from learning'.

All readers will be familiar with these issues within their organizations. Senge requires that familiarity with these issues is made within ourselves – a much more difficult task.

20.4 The Five Disciplines

Senge proposes that in order to overcome our difficulties with organizations and learning, we must adopt five disciplines (Figure 20.4), that is, become disciples of five beliefs.

Readers of this book will be familiar with the ideas of 'systems thinking'. Senge's work draws heavily on the theories and practice of systems dynamics, developed by Jay Forrester. Flood and Jackson (1991) offer a full critique of that approach. Here, it is sufficient to say that the work studies the behaviour of non-linear dynamic systems.

'Personal mastery' refers to the discipline of personal growth and personal learning. It demands an open-minded, inquiring approach of the individual, leading to the creation of his or her own future. Taking into account the critical systems commitment

Five Disciplines:

Discipline 1) Systems thinking;

Discipline 2) Personal mastery;

Discipline 3) Mental models;

Discipline 4) Shared vision;

Discipline 5) Team learning.

Figure 20.4 The five disciplines.

to 'sociological awareness', it can be suggested that the extent to which personal mastery is achievable will be a product of the capabilities, and the cultural and educational background, of the individual.

'Mental models' are formed, because it is clearly impossible to know in finite detail all there is to know; our minds carry only abstractions from reality. These are necessarily more limited than the full richness of reality, and, as Beer (1985) suggests, are 'neither true nor false but more or less useful'. Problems arise when the models are significantly flawed, which is often the case, or when it is forgotten that they are simply models and become perceived to be reality itself. In such cases, reliance on them is certain to be equally flawed. Senge suggests that it is critical to learn to unfreeze and regenerate our mental models of the world.

'Shared vision' is the call for all stakeholders in the organization to have a common (or unitary) view of what the organization is, and what is to be achieved. Senge suggests that when there is shared vision, the desire is for the same things for everyone. To achieve this, the vision cannot be 'handed down from the mountain' like the ten commandments as is so often the case, but must be built from the grassroots. This calls for the type of participative approaches espoused by Checkland (soft systems methodology, 1981), Ackoff (interactive planning, 1981), Beer (Syntegration, 1994) and Ulrich (critical systems heuristics, 1983).

'Team learning' does not easily occur, but is driven by a number of key characteristics. Senge suggests that the team members must have first embraced the other four disciplines already described. The first key characteristic is alignment (the shared vision); the team can accomplish little unless there is a commitment to the same outcomes. Second is the need to think and consider 'insightfully' [sic] about complex issues. Third is the need for co-ordinated action. Here Senge refers to championship sports teams and jazz ensembles enjoined in 'operational trust'. Finally, there is recognition of the need for the teams' effectiveness to be spilled over into other connected (and usually) subordinate teams. This final point reflects the concept of recursion from the systems literature.

Holding all of these insights together is one, so far unstated, requirement. That is the need for effective communication, both vertically and horizontally, throughout the organization. Effective communication requires a subtlety of approach often absent from daily dialogues. It means effective listening, as well as effective speaking. It sometimes requires discussion and at other times direction. It does not mean the generation of conflict or, as is so often the case, adopting rooted, entrenched positions, or reliance on dogma or ideology. These ways of 'communicating' more often lead to breakdown and obfuscation or unsatisfactory compromise, which conflict with the other disciplines.

20.5 Quality and Learning

This brief section seems now almost redundant. The whole basis of the pursuit of quality rests in the idea of learning, in finding ways of carrying out activities so that the outputs of an organization more nearly match the requirements of its customers. If the same mistakes are repeated, then clearly no learning is occurring and no quality improvement is being attained. The *kaizen* philosophy demands improvement in all processes, all of the time. Learning is implicit in this. It can then be argued that any organization successfully pursuing quality is also learning, and any organization pursuing learning is also improving quality. The two words imply each other in the organizational context; the organization needs to be structured in a way which makes this possible.

Summary

This chapter has given a brief introduction to the idea of organizational learning and the 'Learning Organization' according to Senge. Readers should refer to the works suggested in this chapter to develop their understanding and knowledge further.

KEY LEARNING POINTS

Organizational learning

The organization must be structured to:
  interact with the present more efficiently;
  monitor and anticipate the future;
  manage the interaction of the two.

Organizational learning is *not* about data mining and knowledge management, but about structural and behavioural adaptation.

Senge's learning organization

Key definition:
a learning organization is one engaged in an iterative, circular process of evolution.

The seven disabilities:
  I am my position;
  the enemy is out there;
  the illusion of taking charge;
  the fixation on events;
  the parable of the boiling frog;
  the delusion of learning from experience;
  the myth of the management team.

> The five disciplines:
> systems thinking, personal mastery, mental models, shared vision, team learning.
>
> Organizational learning means adaptation of individual and collective behaviour.
>
> Learning implies quality, quality implies learning.

Question

Compare and contrast the learning models of the quality gurus with the learning model outlined in this chapter.

21 Systemic Quality Management

A Knowledge-Based Approach

> No matter how long the procedure it never quite reaches the customer
> (Beckford and Dudley, March 1999)

Introduction

In the previous edition of this book, this chapter's ideas were in Part Four under the title of 'Skills-Based Quality Management'. In this edition, however, the ideas have been substantially revised to deal more widely with the issue of quality management as a whole. The original chapter drew on an international series of seminars, aimed at introducing a fundamentally different approach to quality management for the service and professional sectors. The ideas were subsequently developed into a paperless quality management system, compliant with ISO 9000: 2000. This chapter considers the notion of quality as an emergent property of the 'system' or organization in three dimensions of knowledge, and offers an approach to management of the whole, which will enable the delivery of quality products and services – however they may be defined. The three dimensions of knowledge considered are:

    know why: purpose, outcomes, vision, values;
    know how: behaviours, attitudes, skills and competences;
    know what: systems and processes.

In considering these dimensions, the chapter will seek to reflect the idea that no problem of quality can be solved through a single approach or paradigm, but only through an integrated systemic approach that 'solves' the problem in multiple dimensions simultaneously. This is because, in altering any one of the three dimensions, we necessarily impart tension to the others, meaning that they, too, must change – otherwise the tension will, as is so often the case, cause the organization to revert to an approximation of its previous state.

This is seen in organizations when 'the quality project' becomes tired, superseded or subsumed into another, at which time the quality issues, which have been suppressed, remerge. Similarly, the dominant approaches explored in the second part of this book, perhaps despite the intent of their originators, largely address the issue of quality at the level of 'symptom' rather than 'disease' – with the possible exception of Ohno's Toyota Production Method. Like painting rotten wood, these solutions 'solve' the problem of presentation, but do not address the underlying problem.

The critiques of the quality gurus identified that none really addressed the question of how to engage senior management fully with the idea of pursuing a quality strategy.

While each talks about this as necessary, they say little or nothing about how to achieve it. 'Know why' lies at the heart of this. Many organizations pursue quality (and other) strategies as a response to environmental change – either in the regulatory regime ('you must have ISO 9000 in order to tender for this business') or the market ('everyone else in our market is pursuing quality, we had better do it too'). In neither case is quality being pursued as a good thing in its own right. Knowing why is really asking about the purpose of the organization, the reason it exists, and designing a strategy which ensures that the purpose is fulfilled in the most effective manner. Knowing why provides a focus on the organizational purpose, in the context of which, quality methods, tools and techniques are useful. Without a sense of purpose they are relatively sterile or limited in benefit.

Various methods already outlined in the preceding chapters can be useful for this determination of purpose. Soft systems methodology (Chapter 17) is a seven-step methodology designed to uncover the objectives and desires of human actors in any situation and, through semi-structured discussion, allow the generation and alignment of individual and organizational purposes. The process of this methodology is laid out in Figure 21.1. Further discussion on practice will be found in Part Four.

Similarly, organizational cybernetics (Chapter 16) enables the diagnosis of the current purposes of the organization. It achieves this through a structured analysis that uses the 'Viable System Model' (Beer, 1979, 1981, 1985) as an idealized solution, with which the reality of the situation can be compared (see Figure 21.2). This allows identification of the purposes the organization is currently capable of fulfilling, comparing the purposes with the desires and objectives of the senior management, and defining a decision space within which management can make choices about the present and future of the organization.

For any strategy to succeed, it is vital that the actors in the organization have defined their purposes, explored their values and beliefs (the things that bind them together) and, in the context of those definitions, have decided what success means.

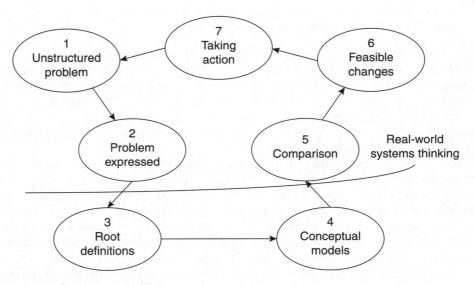

Figure 21.1 Soft systems methodology.

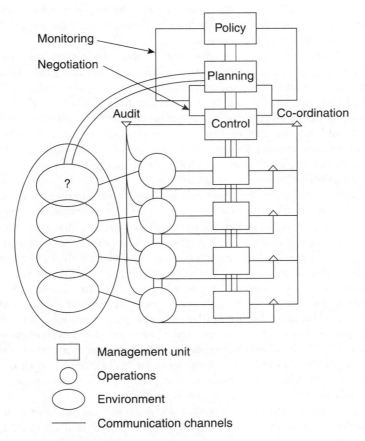

Figure 21.2 The Viable System Model.

It is vital that success is defined in a way that has shared meaning for all members of the organization, providing direction and purpose to all the decisions that they make. Here, I am reminded of the tale of three bricklayers. On being questioned, the first said, 'I lay bricks', the second, with a broader view, said, 'I build walls', the third, understanding the purpose and vision of the organization, said, 'I build cathedrals'. Once the purpose has been determined, senior managers must always act and speak consistently with what has been decided, as this demonstrates their commitment to the purpose. The purpose having been determined has the beneficial side-effect of simplifying many management decisions, since all that has to be asked is: 'Does this decision or action contribute to or detract from the fulfilment of our purpose?'

The second dimension of knowledge is 'know how', that is, the skills, competences, behaviours, and attitudes that will enable the formation of effective working groups or teams, and the application of those skills and competences to the delivery of services and products. Again, 'know why' creates the context in which the right tools and methods – the 'know how' – can be chosen to support any particular strategy. These tools are widely written about in the quality and human resources literature, and need not be explored here. It is vital that all the actors in the organization have, or will acquire, the blend of skills and talents necessary to achieve the purpose. Where they do not exist, the primary task of management is to facilitate their learning. This learning must be set in the context of the strategy.

'Know what' (systems and processes), that is, what people do with the skills and competences they have, can, in the context of the purpose and skills, be designed to support the achievement of the purpose. Again, there are many tools and methods for system and process design. With a clear understanding of purpose, there can be clear criteria for determining whether or not a system or process is effective. If it is a 'core' activity, it should act directly to fulfil the purpose of the organization. If it is an 'enabling' activity, it should support the core activities. If it is neither 'core' nor 'enabling', it is discretionary – and in this case it is legitimate to ask whether the process or system should continue in operation.

Each of these three dimensions of knowledge, which are largely about understanding the 'self' of the organization and its capacity to be sustainable, is now objectively measurable. Through this, we can evaluate the effectiveness of the organization, and the extent to which it incurs *muda* (waste) in its operation. Quality is an emergent property of the interactions of the three dimensions of knowledge; it is not isolated from them, or a function of only or any one dimension. For example, if there is no clear definition of purpose or rationale for the organization, it is impossible to know whether quality is being achieved in its pursuit – because it is measured against the purpose. Similarly, having the most highly skilled and competent workforce is only relevant where the requirements of the task (the 'know what') make effective and efficient use of those skills. Any skills across the organization that are not required for the fulfilment of the task are 'waste'. Systems and processes must also be designed in the context of the purpose to be fulfilled. Any non-utilized process, or system not focused on the achievement of the organizational purpose, is wasted.

The task of management is to recognize and embrace the tensions that necessarily exist between these three dimensions, and manage them in such a way that, over time, the purpose is fulfilled and waste in each dimension is minimized.

21.1 The Service Quality Problem

In a manner which parallels past experience in manufacturing, recent years have brought about an increasing pressure on the service sector to address the quality issue. However, the drive to improve quality, which has not been overwhelmingly successful in the manufacturing sector, seems to have been even less so in the provision of services. There are two basic reasons for this. First, quality has been described in this book, and widely in the literature, as conformance to specification, or fitness for purpose or use. Quality is then often equated with standardization. Hence, the level of quality is perceived as the inverse measure of deviation from a specification, rather than the warm rosy glow of the experience of a good thing. Second, in service quality, there is often no tangible product resulting. Service, and therefore service quality, is an emergent property of the process of its provision.

The interaction of these points has perhaps driven the proliferation of paper-based 'quality systems' for the control of service quality – which are unusable. The attempt to capture the richness of service provision in flow-chart format makes the systems so large and complex as to be unintelligible. The fact is that no system, which is internally consistent, can completely capture the complexity of the organization. Hence, it is

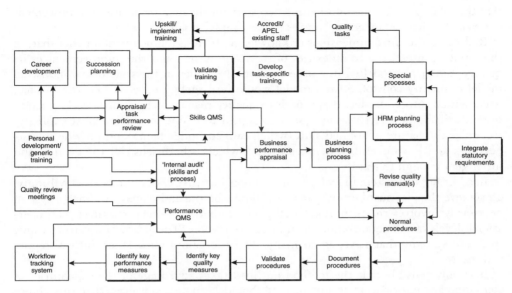

Figure 21.3 The skills-based quality management system.

incapable of achieving the purpose for which it was designed. Such quality management systems are, by their own definition, poor quality. What is needed is a re-thinking of quality, and quality management, appropriate to the service sector. This rethinking is laid out in Figure 21.3.

Figure 21.3, with business performance appraisal and planning at its heart, shows the chain of relationships throughout the business that enables performance. This almost circular, causal chain represents a form of organizational homeostat, showing how each area impacts on each other, and how ultimately all loops back to impact performance. The requirements of the lower half of the figure are well resolved in much of the quality literature; they are requirements concerned with tasks and procedures. The upper half of the figure is concerned with skills, that is, the knowledge, talents and capabilities that individuals bring to bear on the fulfilment of their duties. Historically this has been neglected.

21.2 A Systemic Quality Management System

The essence of a systemic quality management system (SQMS) is simple. The professions in particular, and the service sector in general, rely for service quality on the professionalism and judgement of the individual employee or partner. Not everything can be proceduralized and, in the service sector, the customer often falls through the gap between alternative procedural outcomes. The only way to solve the problem of quality in the service sector is to employ appropriately trained, educated staff, and grant them the necessary freedom to do the job.

A systemic quality management system is an approach to quality, and to the construction of an effective and manageable quality management system (QMS), based on the development and recording of the skill base of a service organization, and its systems and processes in the context of its purposes. 'Effective' in this context means that the QMS provides the information necessary for the maintenance and improvement of service quality. 'Manageable' means, quite simply, small.

Reflecting the three dimensions of knowledge, there is a fundamental belief that, in the service context, the complexities of service provision and the improvement of its quality cannot be modelled in a once and for all manner in the style of the industrial model of quality control. Such a model would be largely ineffective. The traditional, documented, procedure-based approach to quality management is ultimately guaranteed to fail. To be effective, any system designed to maintain quality must explicitly recognize the nature of applied skill (which calls for judgement), and provide robustness in practice – and embed it in a structure which is both sensitive to new data and intelligent enough to learn.

In addition, the system must be small and non-intrusive enough to be used willingly. To achieve this, it must be transparent to those who use and manage it. Such a system necessarily involves the planning, intelligence gathering, human resources, and operational levels of the organization in an integrated whole. The alternative is to continue to create systems that have, in so many service organizations, fallen into disrepute and disuse.

It is only sensible that the method outlined takes advantage of the capabilities of contemporary information technology. It should be noted, however, that this choice of technological platform for the approach is a convenience rather than a necessity. The concepts are independent of the choice of information media.

21.3 The Overall Structure

A systemic quality management system is based on a model of organization rooted in the viable systems approach outlined in Chapter 16, and elaborated in the three dimensions of knowledge mentioned above. Figure 21.3 illustrated those parts of the organization that relate directly to quality. The process of delivering quality is the result of the interactions of highly interconnected sub-processes, and it is important to note that many of these continue to be susceptible to traditional performance monitoring and control methods. The model is made more robust by this and by their utilization in an intelligent manner. This element of the model is represented by the flows in the lower half of the diagram.

When the links to the environment available through the business planning process are activated ('Why are we here?' – 'What are we going to do?'), the whole model represented by the diagram provides the ability for the organization to learn from its experience. Thus, it can change its behaviours and even its values over time, in relation to environmental (market) and internal changes. The diagram is a simplification of a highly complex process, which contains many circular and self-referential sub-processes. Unfortunately, managers all too often argue for the simple: 'Give me simple propositions, simple charts and simple answers.' Unfortunately again, these do not work.

The idea of using skills (know how) to ensure quality is not new (consider the medieval craft guilds), even amongst the quality community. Section 6 of the ISO 9001: 2000 standard explicitly deals with the effective management of skills, and this was also possible under the 'special processes' clause of the 1994 standard, though its potential was usually ignored by quality experts and auditors. The distinguishing factor of the SQMS approach is that it explicitly uses skills as the basis of quality, with the organizational processes being captured at a higher, less detailed, level. This means that task and procedure descriptions are minimized, or even eradicated, in many situations.

The quality of the outputs in this approach is assured through the determination of the abilities and competence needed to deliver the service; a process known as 'qualification'. Once a process is 'qualified', formal quality assurance is achieved by ensuring that only those operators whose skills match those needed for the special process are permitted to work on it. This, though embryonic and static, is the beginning of a skills-based QMS.

The traditional attraction of process control is based on the premise that the better you control the process, the less error, and the less error, the higher the quality. As service is a process, the less error in the process, the higher the provision of service quality. How can this be achieved?

All services are 'special processes', in the sense of ISO 9000: 1994. Fundamental process control can be achieved by recognizing and treating them as such. A further chapter – or even a whole book – could be written about the interpretation of 'control', but it is not the purpose of this text to explore it. Readers should be aware that, in this context, 'control' refers to a situation being created where the individual can be self-controlled. This is because he or she shares the objectives of the organization, has the skills necessary to complete the task, and the autonomy required to adapt service delivery to the needs of the individual customer.

Services are delivered by people. Therefore, process control, in the context of service provision, is the control of the behaviour of the people providing the service. Appropriate behaviour, assuming the absence of malice, is behaviour which is likely to achieve the purpose of the service being provided. This is assured by ensuring that the provider of the service has the skills, knowledge and competence deemed to be necessary for the provision of the service.

Services are also delivered to people. People (especially clients, patients, passengers, customers) vary, therefore no two service-provision events are ever the same. Even assuming an impossible situation, such that the education of the service provider ensures that the service-provision events are consistent in approach, there will be as many variations on a single service as there are recipients. This is why the complexities of service provision arise, and judgement is required. It is the potential variety of the situations that arise in service provision which, of necessity, defeat the traditional process-engineering approach to quality management. It is not possible to model all possible situations in advance; therefore it is not possible to specify all activities and solutions in advance. It is therefore not possible to chart the process fully in advance – not even with charts a mile long – and it is the very attempt that creates the bureaucracy.

In contrast to machines, people are extremely good at dealing with complexity. And this ability to deal with complex situations and make sensible decisions in the absence of complete data (to exercise judgement) only becomes prominent when the people involved have become skilled, educated, or trained for the task at hand, and have a clear understanding of the purposes to be fulfilled.

Utilizing this human ability to deal with complexity has two distinct advantages over the traditional 'chart, measure and count' approach to ensure quality in service provision. The first is that it significantly reduces the amount of paper necessary for the operation of the system. Quality-relevant procedures can be stated in a descriptive form.

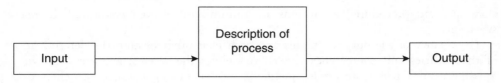

Figure 21.4 A process.

The ideal situation in this model is:

- **Input:**   client with a problem;
- **Process:**   negotiate a solution to the problem;
- **Output:**   client without a problem.

While it must be accepted that this ideal will be difficult to achieve in some cases, complicating the documentation of the process to be undertaken will not make it any less difficult. Indeed, the production of rigid procedural charts (which, as has been argued, cannot entirely capture any situation) may give a false impression of the operation of the process. A procedural chart may very well remove the things that would allow a solution to be reached – negotiation, informed choice and compromise – thus creating a 'jobsworth' mentality.

The second advantage to be gained runs in parallel with the first. By ensuring that individual service providers have the skills necessary to carry out the tasks they have been set, it is possible to devolve responsibility.

Because professionals draw on a shared body of core knowledge (see Figure 21.5) in their decision making processes, it is possible to predict the range of solutions professionally available to the front-line providers with a degree of accuracy. This standardizes the outcomes at the level of 'client perceived quality', without the necessity for standardizing the potential solutions available to non-standard clients.

The professionalism implicit in this model allows the quality of the outputs of the organization to be 'process-controlled' rather than 'post-delivery inspected' (see Figure 21.6) – which is meaningless in the service context as it can only ever be

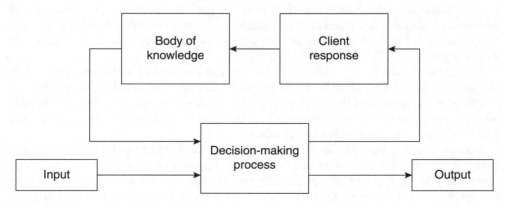

Figure 21.5 Applying skills.

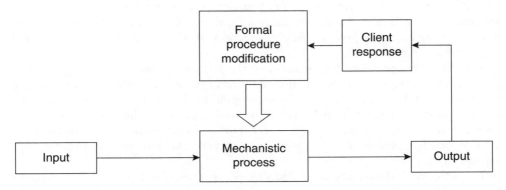

Figure 21.6 Applying procedures.

complaint management. This is because the evaluation of the service provided using a mechanistic process is possible only after the event, rather than being an integral part of it. By defining the skills necessary to the fulfilment of the task:

- the complexity of the procedural system necessary for its control is reduced; process definition is transformed into a statement of professional competence (less paper);
- the level of managerial and supervisory intervention is reduced; tasks become owned by the front-line provider (less overhead cost);
- the level of perceived autonomy at the individual level is increased, and greater personal responsibility is taken for the delivery of quality (lower alienation from the task);
- the process becomes more flexible; the potential for client perception of quality is increased (fewer complaints).

21.4 The Model for a Systemic QMS

In its purest form the creation of a Systemic QMS is very simple:

- identify the tasks to be undertaken;
- identify the skills necessary to undertake the tasks;
- ensure that only those people that have these skills undertake the task.

In practice, however, each of the three stages will contain sub-tasks and require ongoing operational validation. Identification of the tasks to be undertaken is, effectively, a mapping of those processes that are vital to service provision. Outcomes of the first stage of the approach should be:

- key tasks identified;
- relevant flow diagrams produced;
- statement of those tasks that cannot be reduced to flow diagrams;
- identification of tasks which are routine or frequently repeated, and thus susceptible to standard performance measures.

The selection of key tasks tends to be a negotiation process between the QMS designers and the users. It is advantageous to keep an open mind regarding the perception of what is and is not a key process; decisions made at this stage can return to haunt the intervention later on.

Selection of the processes for inclusion on the skills-based side of the design process is based on a heuristic relating to the complexity of the charting necessary to map the process. If it is possible to achieve significant complexity reduction through the acceptance of some minimal level of skill on the part of the operator, it can be assumed that there are also significant operational efficiency gains to be made by using a skills-based approach to the quality assurance of the process (see Figures 21.4 and 21.5).

The demands of the quality management model presented in Figure 21.3 are satisfied by the outcomes of this stage of the approach through the production of:

- documentation of those processes that can be represented as linear flows, including control points and performance measures (Figure 21.5);
- generic description of those processes that cannot be represented as linear flows but are 'routine', including control points and performance measures (see Figure 21.7);
- a statement of those processes that cannot be represented as linear flows and are 'non-routine'.

With the operational elements of the model defined (in the case of the linear processes), or described (in the case of non-linear processes), and performance measures stated, it is possible to move on to skills definition. It should be noted that there are two assumptions in Figures 21.7 and 21.8, that is, that the processes themselves are fixed. For the most part linear processes are input-controlled, and routine skills-based processes are activity controlled.

The skills used in an organization are categorized into three types:

- generic
- role specific
- professional

Each of the skill types, and their level of development and importance to the operation of the organization, have an impact on the type of QMS appropriate and the potential success of the skills-based approach. This categorization, shown in Figure 21.9, indicates a model of the interrelationships between the varying skills

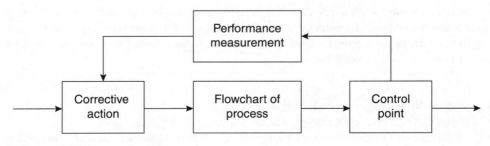

Figure 21.7 Performance management.

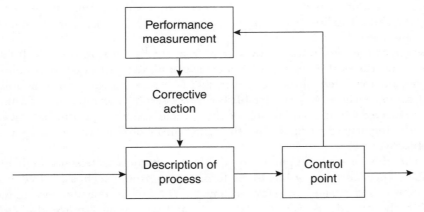

Figure 21.8 Performance improvement.

Generic	Role	Professional
MBA	Specific masters and research programmes	Memberships and professional recognition
NVQ level 5	Knowledge-based quality management	
4	Skills-based quality management system	Product assurance and development
3	Procedure-based quality management	

← Records →

Feeds ———————————→   ←——————————— Feeds

Figure 21.9 The hierarchy of skills.

available in a service organization. It also provides a basis for deciding the extent to which a planned education and development programme can be used to enhance performance and, therefore, the type of QMS appropriate to support it.

In practice, the effective professional service organization will rely on a balanced utilization of the three skill types. Each share the common characteristic that, as the operations of the organization move toward a dependence on skills typical of the upper half of the diagram, it will become increasingly difficult to control quality using the more traditional charting approach. A quality management system that aims to support the improvement of the performance of the organization will focus on role performance. Hence, the skills baseline in any organization is the ability necessary to follow the process flow charts.

However, as the organization moves away from the baseline, to the 'non-linear but routine' tasks, the skill necessary to absorb the complexity generated moves on to the lower end, and to the left, of the scale. Such skill levels are consistent with the ability to operate competently within the established processes. This competence within processes is reflected throughout the left of the diagram. As the operator becomes more skilled, the imperative changes from the achievement of objectives to the setting of these objectives.

Tasks in this category might be typified by such roles as telesales or help-desk operation. They are susceptible to performance measures such as, 'How many?', 'How often?', 'How long?' or 'How accurate?'. The human operators are trained to deal with the procedural aspects of the task, and have some limited discretion to deal with 'non-standard' occurrences. As the individual moves up this scale, he or she contributes to the organization through his or her management or administrative skills.

To the right of the scale, the emphasis is very different; it relates to the consideration of what the processes can or should be. Professional knowledge brings with it the capacity for critical reasoning around the structures through which the service is provided, and forms the basis of the non-linear, non-routine skill set. At this end of the scale, the imperative is not 'What are the objectives?', but 'What are suitable indicators to measure the objectives by?'

It is not possible to set commercial performance indicators for professional skills, as the focus of these skills is based on the integrity of the professional discipline. The professional contributes to performance through the appropriate application, and, in some cases, extension, of the body of professional knowledge to the furtherance of organizational objectives. To a large extent, the only performance indicator applicable to the professional is the performance of the core product in the market.

Choice of skill type (that is, generic, role-specific, professional) should be based on the contribution to the process, and will provide (in conjunction with the appraisal process and personal career ambitions) indicators as to the appropriate development strategy for individual role incumbents.

At this point, it should be possible to assign qualifications or skills lists to the roles identified. The lists should also identify those qualifications where possession is a legal requirement. Ensuring the skills-to-task link has two main elements:

- skills assessment
- records management.

The skills possessed assessment section of the link comprises the appraisal process of the organization. Operational service quality can then be assured through the creation of an auditable documentation system, which demonstrates that the skill sets of operators at least meets the skill set necessary to carry out the specified task.

The idea is that organizations possess a body of skills held by their personnel, and a set of skills needed that have been identified through role analysis. It is relatively simple to construct a relational database to carry out this task, and to extend its utility to the creation of personal development plans, pre-selection for internal promotions, and the generation of job specifications for recruitment purposes. At its most simple, the database need comprise no more than two tables, each containing a set of triples.

The adoption of this approach to quality management has a clear impact on the role of the human resources department in a large organization. It becomes very clearly the focus of a strategic operation, whose role is to ensure that the individual and aggregate skill set of the employees is at least equivalent to the needs of the organization all of the time. This approach has implications for training, recruitment, promotion and retention policies, and is the key to consistent service quality. Strategic human resource development, as a sub-set of the wider strategic function, forms the link between current and future performance by managing the skills base of the organization.

21.5 SQM Review

For an organization to maximize its gain from investment in ISO 9000 certification, the QMS must have the lightest possible negative impact on the organization, while generating the maximum business value. That is, it should not be cumbersome or bureaucratic, and must generate more benefit than it generates cost. In particular, it must directly act to enhance, rather than inhibit, the performance of the organization in every respect. Experience shows that most organizations fail to achieve this.

The SQM approach differs from traditional systems in a number of ways. First, it is rooted in the purposes of the organization, and based on a dynamic, learning model of the organization, driven by events within the process, and linking directly to business planning, staff performance, and staff development processes. It learns at two levels. First, it promotes learning by individuals – the improvement in skills and competences – which closes the 'know how' gap. Second, it stimulates learning at the organizational level, adapting itself on the basis of recorded experience, and enabling informed, structured adaptation of the organization. The third key difference is that the approach directly supports the business or organizational needs. It is driven by business performance appraisal and planning, operational processes and active skills management, and feeds the outputs directly back into them. It thus links directly to the achievement of purpose.

The systemic QMS represents a major challenge to the dominant methods of addressing the problem of quality. It has significant benefit in a service environment, and also provides new insights into manufacturing management quality programmes. While the approach has been developed, certified to ISO 9000: 2000, and applied in a number of sectors – chemicals manufacturing, healthcare, chemicals research, and property management – it undoubtedly requires further development and refinement.

Summary

This chapter has considered a wholly new approach to systemic quality management, focused especially on the service sector. Readers should refer to the work of Dudley and Beckford (1998a, 1998b, 1999 and 2000), and Dudley (2000), to extend and develop their knowledge.

KEY LEARNING POINTS

Services are different to manufacturing

Skills-based quality management recognizes:
management and development of professional skills is the key to service quality; procedures can never substitute for human interaction and judgement.

Skills are acceptable as the foundation of an ISO 9000: 2000 quality management system.

SQM has been tested in a variety of sectors; it is in need of further development.

Question

Outline the benefits and drawbacks of adopting a skills-based approach to quality.

Part Four

Quality in Practice: A Case Study

User Guide

In the first three parts of this book, a substantial platform has been developed for thinking about quality theory and the dominant methods. Those parts have been built on a theoretical platform, with practical insights provided through the vignettes, which have presented theory in practice.

In the two prior editions, Part Four continued that structure, and built upon the knowledge platform by examining methods for implementing quality. It explored general methods, such as process analysis, and those specifically focused on quality, such as ISO 9000 and quality circles. In this edition, Part Four reverses the approach and, through an extended case study, presents practice in theory – embedding descriptions and critique of methods, tools, and techniques as they are called for in the telling of the story. The story is 'real', in as much as all of the issues described actually occurred; fortunately, they did not all happen to only one business!

It is hoped that this approach will be both more helpful and more interesting. The methods, tools and techniques will be introduced in context, and their strengths, weaknesses and utility considered – but they will not be fully described or evaluated.

Each has a supporting reference base through which it can be fully explored; the reader is encouraged to examine the original sources for a detailed understanding of their application.

As with Parts One, Two, and Three, Part 4 can be used in two ways. It can provide a straightforward critical introduction to those tools for achieving quality, which are derived from the various theories already explained. For those with a practical focus, this section provides a comprehensive tool kit, enabling the pursuit of a quality initiative in a way that is both practically informed and theoretically sound.

22 SB Foods: A Problem of Quality?

Now do THIS!

(Stafford Beer, 1985)

Introduction

This chapter sets out the background to SB Foods, which will be the subject of the extended case study, and begins the process of discovery, which is the first stage in the consulting process. To avoid doubt, SB Foods does exist, but not by that name, and it does not have all the problems and issues that are ascribed to it here. The actual situation has been extended, with additions taken from other case studies to ensure the presence of those characteristics necessary for completeness in the study. Names and places have been changed throughout, and any remaining similarity to real people or places is entirely coincidental.

22.1 Background

The following information was discovered during an initial telephone conversation with the directors of SB Foods.

SB Foods is a company within the Sundries division of Victuals, a major supplier of manufactured and processed food to multiple retailers. SB Foods has two factories, A and B, as well as a head office which deals with sales, central buying, finance and distribution. It is these head office functions that primarily deal with the Sundries division management of Victuals.

A major extension and refurbishment of factory A has been completed. It was expected to enable factory A to absorb the production currently obtained from factory B. This plan has proved to be impossible, as output volume has increased at factory A, absorbing the capacity as it has become available. For two years, while the factory A extension was being built, factory B, which has a poor industrial relations record, operated under the threat of closure, a threat which was well known to management, staff, and customers. The inability of factory A to absorb production from B has led to a reversal of the closure decision, and the senior management of SB Foods now wish both to retain factory B and develop its volume to ensure long-term viability.

SB Foods has recently appointed general managers, with profit responsibility, to both factories. The general manager of factory B recognizes that change is needed, but needs help to determine the current state of the operation, what changes should be made, and how the organization will benefit.

The outcome of the telephone call was an invitation to propose a scheme of work, initially to investigate the situation, diagnose the problems, and resolve the issues.

22.2 Initial Reflections

This is clearly a dynamic and complex problem situation. It exhibits a number of characteristics reflective of complex systems: enormous variety, questions of purpose and intent, human issues, and ongoing change. Working from the information gathered so far, it is clear that a 'scheme of work' that properly addresses the range of issues identified will be quite extensive. Thinking about what is now known highlights that there are:

— *cultural and relationship issues with the workforce* — these are partly historical and embedded, and partly arising from the recent threat of closure and past management behaviour;
— *structural concerns* — SB Foods is an organization embedded as a subsidiary of Victuals, so it is inevitable that any work will need to consider the relationship between the two and respond to Victuals's demands, and will need to take account of the SB Foods' head office functions. The internal organization structure of factory B is unclear at present, but it is likely that this too will need to be considered in resolving any performance and management problems;
— *management concerns* — both general managers are newly appointed, and will have inherited issues from their predecessors; they will also be facing the need to secure their new positions.
— *productivity concerns* — factory A is unable to absorb production from factory B, and this will need to be investigated; the directors have already stated that they need help to understand and resolve the problems;
— *viability issues* — if the directors are concerned to secure 'long-term viability', they clearly recognize that they are, to some degree, under threat. It is also apparent from the information provided that the business critical problems to be addressed reside in factory B, and that needs to be the initial focus of attention. Resolving the viability of factory B will ensure its survival, and allow the necessary interventions at factory A and SB head office to be addressed later.

This is not, then, a simple problem of quality; indeed, quality has not been mentioned so far. There are undoubtedly aspects of the problem situation that lend themselves to a traditional quality-type approach, but, given the range of issues, which one could be sensibly chosen?

The methods of Crosby, Deming, Feigenbaum, and Oakland would all lend themselves to key aspects of the production issues and the workforce engagement process. Ishikawa, Ohno, Shingo, and Taguchi would all have much to say about the purely operational aspects. However, none of these approaches could support an initial intervention.

The methodology of Total Systems Intervention (TSI) (Figure 22.1) might be adopted. However, to be consistent with the TSI methodology, the project would

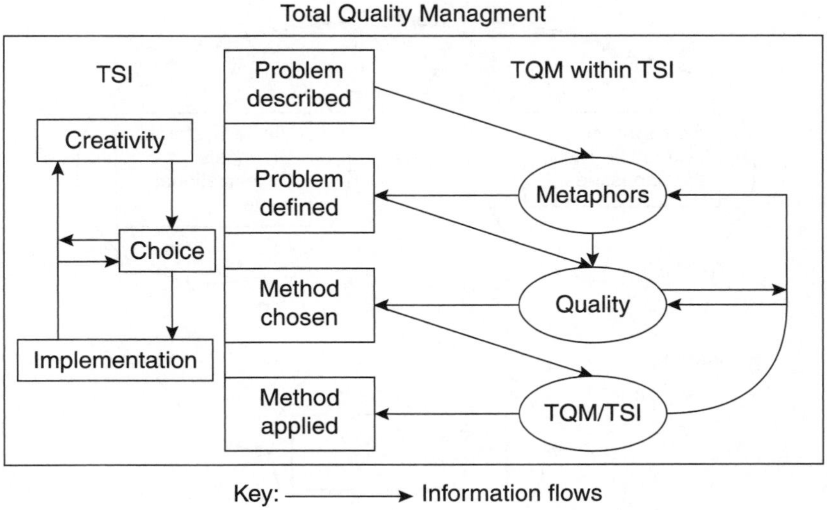

Total Quality Managment

Key: ———————▶ Information flows

Figure 22.1 TQM within TSI within TQM.

have to give primacy to one dimension of the problem situation, thus necessitating solving the identified problems in series. The situation, however, demands a parallel approach – one in which several aspects of the problem situation can be resolved simultaneously.

The requested intervention (or scheme of work) will need to be designed around a whole systems, synthesized, approach. At this stage of the process, the prime candidates for this are soft systems thinking (Chapter 17), using soft systems methodology (Checkland, 1981), briefly introduced in Chapter 21, which will cater for, at least, the initial stage of engagement with the directors. This can be deployed in parallel with organizational cybernetics (Chapter 16), using Beer's Viable Systems Diagnosis (Beer 1985, Beckford 1993) (briefly introduced in Chapter 20), which can focus on the organizational and informational issues, and provide a base for exploring the process issues – for which another tool, process analysis, will be required.

To obtain the information necessary to understand the problem situation, and to address all of the interconnected problems, initially at least, it will be necessary to use the first stage of soft systems methodology, organizational cybernetics and process analysis concurrently (Figure 22.2). The process of enquiry for each will inform the others.

These different approaches, based on different views and assumptions about the nature of the world, will provide at least three perspectives on the nature of the problems to be solved. These views and assumptions can then be synthesized, through dialogue and discussion, into a single, very rich, understanding of the situation (Figure 22.3).

Soft systems thinking and organizational cybernetics have already been introduced; brief methodologies for their use are included in Chapter 23. Readers seeking a deeper understanding of Viable Systems Diagnosis should refer to the work of Beckford (1993, 1995) and Beer (1985), and for soft systems methodology, Checkland (1981). Process analysis and a method for its application are outlined in Chapters 23 and 24. For a fuller

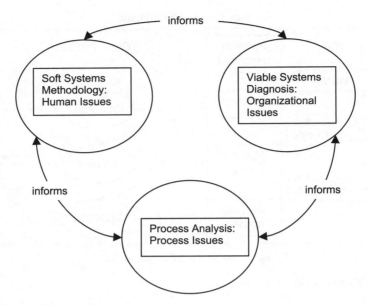

Figure 22.2 Tools for the first intervention.

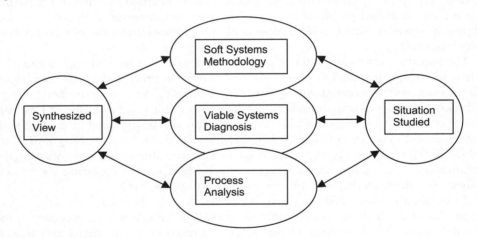

Figure 22.3 Synthesizing the diagnosis.

source, readers should consider Kanji and Asher, 1996. This chapter will concentrate on the integrating framework.

22.3 Iterative Methodology

It must be clear that the problems of SB Foods will not be solved with a single programme, solution, action, or intervention. It seems rather more as if the organization needs to go through a series of interventions, each of which moves it one stage closer to 'solving the problem'. These will need to be designed to diagnose and validate the interrelated problems, develop a framework for their resolution and an implementation pathway.

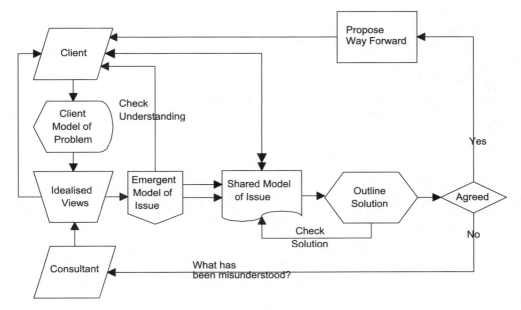

Figure 22.4 Developing a shared model.

VS method, Figure 22.4, provides a process map for the conversation between SB Foods and the consultant. The purpose of the method is to develop, at the centre of the process, a shared model of the problem to be addressed; that is, a single picture of the situation which expresses the viewpoints of all the relevant participants and the findings of the different methodologies. Achievement of this unified view enables the development of possible solutions and agreement about the next steps to be taken.

The method is based on enabling the participants to articulate their views and compare them with what is understood about idealized organizations (theoretical models of how organizations 'ought' to be if they are to be successful). These theoretical models can and should embrace all possible valid perspectives on the situation – a perspective is valid if it expresses the views of one or more participants – and appropriate levels of detail.

The initial outcome, the shared model of the problem, is the basis for action in the next stage – which might include further investigation and analysis, some direct improvement action, testing of possible solutions, and so on. Figure 22.5 shows how the method cycles through a process of enquiry, testing/evaluating, reflecting (and reaffirming or modifying the chosen direction), and then taking further action. The figure shows four iterations (this is entirely arbitrary; the number of iterations is a function of the size and complexity of the problem situations being addressed).

Alert readers will have noticed that this method is in many ways a variation on the Shewart or Deming PDCA cycle (Chapter 6) or Oakland's EPDCA cycle (Chapter 10). However, there is a major difference. This method, unlike the others, explicitly includes a requirement on each cycle to re-engage with the relevant client and revalidate the shared model of the situation. This is vital; needs change and emerge, the organization evolves, individuals change roles and perspectives, and the external environment in which all of the activity is ultimately carried out is also dynamic. A reflective cycle that

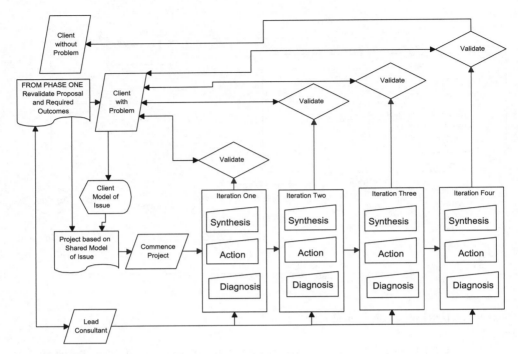

Figure 22.5 An iterative framework for action.

does not include refreshing the shared understanding will inevitably generate divergence between the optimum solution and that which, in the end, will be imposed rather than jointly developed.

The subsequent chapters of Part Four will follow the method outlined.

Summary

This chapter has introduced the problem situation at SB Foods, and argued for an overarching, iterative, methodology for addressing the issues raised. The next chapter will pursue the first iteration of the formal project.

KEY LEARNING POINTS

Client problems and issues do not come as neatly packaged as academic and consultants' methodologies.

Selection of any one methodology, to the exclusion of all others, necessarily means that some aspects of the situation will not be considered, or that others will obtain undue prominence.

A selection of methodologies, simultaneously applied, with their findings integrated through a rich dialogue, will produce the broadest understanding.

An iterative methodology must include refreshing and reaffirming the shared model of the world developed in the initial investigation.

Question

Consider the SB Foods information from the perspective of either Crosby or Deming. What issues would their approach have highlighted, and which might have been played down or ignored?

23 First Intervention

Be not curious in unnecessary matters

(Ecclesiasticus 3:23)

Introduction

This chapter considers the process and findings of the first intervention, while introducing and reviewing the core methodologies. While the three chosen methodologies were applied concurrently and the findings synthesized into a whole systems view of the problem situation (see Figure 22.3), the findings of each part of the intervention are described here sequentially. The synthesized view is elaborated in the next section. The use of the selected methodologies will reveal those aspects of SB Foods which appear to be important, based on the initial conversation. They will not reveal some other aspects, and one challenge for the consultant conducting the study is to separate those things which are important and must be acted upon from those which are, perhaps, interesting but unimportant.

23.1 Soft Systems Perspective

This element of the intervention was primarily focused on engaging the senior management. It involved developing an understanding of the purpose, vision and values of the management, that is, their objectives for the organization, the constraints under which they perceive themselves to be working, and, importantly, the rationale for their choices. Soft systems methodology is outlined below.

23.1.1 Soft Systems Methodology

PRINCIPLES AND CONCEPTION

Soft systems methodology (SSM) (Checkland, 1981) rests on the assumption that the resolution of complex problems, of which achieving quality may be considered one, relies on the innate subjective views of the participants in the situation. SSM has been developed for use in ill-structured situations, where there is an absence of clarity in the definition of the problem and no agreement as to what action is required to solve it. The system enables a variety of viewpoints to be elaborated and evaluated by a group of problem-solvers, allowing them to make informed choices about the future. It is considered that by exploring the various viewpoints in an open forum, and evaluating their strengths and limitations, an approach can be generated to which all participants will commit themselves. Solutions generated through the seven-stage process of enquiry, which is the methodology of SSM, will normally lead to changes in three dimensions: attitudes, structure and procedures. It is considered that as many people as possible should be involved in the SSM process; it does not have to be driven by 'experts'. It can be used by managers as part of their everyday working practice.

SSM – METHODOLOGY

SSM consists of a seven-stage process and should be used in an iterative manner. Although this description starts at Stage 1, any other starting point would generate an equally valid result. Members of the organization pursue the methodology, although it may be facilitated by a 'problem-solver', often a consultant.

Peter Checkland:

Stage 1) Finding out;

Stage 2) Rich picture;

Stage 3) Root definitions;

Stage 4) Redesign;

Stage 5) Real world comparison;

Stage 6) Debate and decision;

Stage 7) Taking action.

Figure 23.1 Seven stages of soft systems methodology.

The first two stages take place in what is called the 'real world'; that is, they are based on the experience and knowledge of the participants, and how things are perceived by them.

Stage 1 consists of exploring the problem situation and gathering information about it through observation, evaluating formal data (such as company records), and interviews.

Stage 2 is often an entertaining stage and is usually expressed in the form of a cartoon, called a 'rich picture'. This consists of creating a representation of the problem situation as experienced by the participants. Stages 1 and 2, taken together, lead the participants to define a number of themes or systems that they need to examine. These can usefully be thought of as processes within the overall organization studied.

Stages 3 and 4 are abstract processes, designed to explore how things could, and arguably should, be, rather than how they are – as perceived by the actors. They are concerned with what Ackoff (1981) calls 'idealized design'. Stage 3 develops concise statements about the purpose of the various systems or processes, called 'root definitions'. The root definition presents an ideal view of what the relevant system 'ought' to achieve, and is refined through the use of six principal elements (Figure 23.2) and six key questions (Figure 23.3).

6 Elements of a Soft System

Customers: those who gain by or suffer from the activity;
Actors: those who perform the activity;
Transformation: the action itself;
Weltanschauung: the world-view of the situation which validates the action;
Owners: those who can stop the activity (often the management);
Environment: external constraints upon the system behaviour.

Figure 23.2 Six principal elements of a system.

'Root Definitions'

Question 1) What is required?
Question 2) Why is it required?
Question 3) Who will do it?
Question 4) Who will benefit?
Question 5) Who will be hurt or damaged?
Question 6) What external factors constrain the activity?

Figure 23.3 Six questions for defining root definitions.

Stage 4 uses the validated root definitions to redesign the activities (the transformation process), which aims to overcome the limitations of current transformations. The conceptual model developed identifies the minimum set of activities necessary to ensure that the transformation achieves its purpose. The set of activities is ordered into a process based on how the activities would occur in the real world; this ensures that carts are not put before horses! It may be necessary to define sub-sets of activities which naturally group together, perhaps under the headings of operations, control, co-ordination and so on, (rather like the viable systems methodology model seen in the next section).

The aim of *stage 5* is to compare the models constructed with the real-world understanding of the group members. This enables them to highlight possible changes in the actual situation to bring it closer to the systemic ideal now developed. Devices for this might include highlighting areas of difference, generating and ranking – for evaluation – options, and generating projections of possible futures (in the style of the scenario planning technique used by Royal Dutch Shell (Johnson and Scholes, 1993)).

At *stage 6*, the comparisons drawn in the previous stage provide the basis for discussion and debate amongst the participants. This should lead to the selection of culturally feasible changes in the actual situation, that is, changes which are systemically desirable and are considered achievable within the culture of the particular organization.

There are few, if any, absolute rights or wrongs at this stage. The point of the exercise is more the process itself (for generating mutual understanding and appreciation) than for the outcomes – although unless these lead to practical and beneficial changes in the organization, it may be seen as somewhat sterile. The final outcome should be a set of changes to which all parties are willing to commit themselves.

The final stage of the process, *stage 7*, is taking action, that is, implementing within the real-world situation the changes that have been proposed. These may affect any part of the totality of the organization studied, that is, its structure (organization design, job design), attitudes (the culture and values), and procedures (the actual operations of the organization). The total process is shown diagrammatically in Figure 21.1.

CRITICAL REVIEW

While SSM does not preclude the inclusion of large numbers of people in the process, the approach is often recognized as working best with relatively small numbers. The SSM methodology offers no specific help in a situation where there are large numbers, where some degree of 'order' needs to be brought into the enquiry process (for example, in a factory employing 2,000 workers, or in a total organization which might employ hundreds of thousands of staff in a distributed network of offices and factories). An apparently more useful approach for such organizations is Ackoff's Interactive Planning (IP) (Ackoff, 1981), which will be discussed in the next section. This approach adheres to the participative and subjective views recognized in SSM, but provides a structured method for involving all of the people in the organization in the process of creating its future.

SSM has great strength in its capacity to bring together groups with diverse opinions, and offer them a structured process through which those opinions can be debated. However, it does not offer any form of desired, or ideal-type, outcome. It does not suggest any principles to which an ideal solution should adhere, other than the forming of a consensus view. The solutions proposed, therefore, will ameliorate the concerns of those participating in the process but not necessarily others who, either willingly or not, are excluded from the process. Neither will it necessarily adhere to any specific organizational, cultural, or procedural principles which might be thought desirable. Unless these things are already present within the *weltanschauung* ('worldview') of the participants, or introduced at the problem definition stage, there is no scope for them to be considered.

The key findings arising from the application of the first stage of soft systems methodology are now discussed.

It is quite clear, both from the initial telephone call and from the subsequent structured discussion using the first stage of SSM, that the purpose imputed to the situation by the senior management is the sustainable viability of both factories, profit being recognized as a constraint upon their continued existence. In order to achieve sustainable viability, they recognize the need to establish a co-operative working environment and to realize the potential of the factories. A number of issues were discovered during this stage that will need further inquiry and possible action.

While the general manager at factory B has a very open style and wishes to have managers working for him who will manage, there are no routine, planned management meetings. The 'grapevine' is, after the union, seen as the most reliable information source, and communication is such that one senior manager only found out about a major factory visit by the most important customer through a member of the cleaning staff. Management appears thoughtless; that is to say, the prevailing method of decision making is to do that which has always been done.

While a number of basic management courses have been run in the short period since the appointment of the general manager, a large number of candidates have not attended, as either they consider it a waste of time, or their managers have refused to make them available. One manager, who has completed the course, was unable to implement changes on his return due to lack of support from the senior management.

Morale is poor in the factory, and this has not been helped by the recent replacement of the manufacturing manager and the junior manager in the mixing bay by two staff from factory A, where the general manager was also previously based. Foremen throughout the factory consider that their future careers are threatened by these moves, as vacancies at this level have, for thirty years, been filled internally. There are no job descriptions in force for the managers and supervisory grades. Replacement staff are not available to cover absences through sickness and annual leave. The personnel officer will not obtain relief for these absences, instructing managers to 'cope'. This is normally achieved by substantial overtime working often until 9 p.m., at which time a shift premium of 17.5 per cent is payable for the whole shift.

Communication is poor throughout the organization. At a personal level, some of the foremen do not have the ability to speak, write or understand the English language – and SB Foods is in an English-speaking country.

Health and safety requirements are frequently not achieved, machines often being in a hazardous condition. The engineering manager has advised production managers that 'no funds are available for that repair'.

The personnel officer carries out the entire personnel function. The line managers direct all problems, complaints and grievances to her. She has no executive authority in any of these matters.

The health, safety and hygiene co-ordinator takes responsibility for the running of the canteen, which has two foremen and four staff, and the staff shop, which has one foreman and one member of staff. Also reporting to him is the assistant hygiene manager who, through his two supervisors, is responsible for the cleanliness and hygiene of the factory and equipment.

23.2 Viable Systems Perspective

This element of the intervention was primarily focused on understanding how the organization functioned and was controlled, why it worked in the way it did, and the issues that this gave rise to. The work involved developing an understanding of the structure, measurement and information systems, and how these aligned with the desires and expectations determined in the soft systems intervention, embedded in work processes, are dealt with in the next section. Viable Systems Diagnosis is outlined below.

23.2.1 Viable Systems Methodology

THE VIABLE SYSTEM MODEL IN THEORY

The Viable System Model (VSM) was developed by Stafford Beer from the principles of organizational cybernetics, the science of effective organization (Chapter 16).

Beer considered an organization viable when it is capable of survival in a given environment, and capable of learning and adapting to changes in that environment. To achieve this ultra stable state, the process of its management must have five functions:

implementation, co-ordination, control, planning and policy, which, taken together, constitute the viable system.

The model enables multiple interpretations of any organizational situation to be developed, all according to the same principles, but focused on the different purposes imputed to the organization by its various observers. Through this modelling process, dialogue and debate is generated, from which an agreed organizational purpose can be derived, and a most useful approach developed.

The approach to cybernetics espoused by Beer rests on five principles:

- observer dependency
- systemic thinking
- black box method
- self-regulation
- Ashby's Law of Requisite Variety

(see Beckford 1993).

VSM: CONCEPTION AND CONSTRUCTION

The VSM is a general model of any organization. It is concerned with mechanisms of adaptation, communication and control. It consists of the stated five sub-systems, each of which is of equal importance to the viability or effectiveness of the organization. A network of information loops in continuous operation richly interconnects these sub-systems. The whole system is capable of learning, which in this context means co-adaptation between the system and its environment – perhaps a form of Lamarckian evolution.

Implementation creates the products or services. Co-ordination and control mechanisms ensure cohesion of the organization, and allow for the maximum appropriate autonomy to implementation. This maximizes the self-regulating tendencies, and enables the resolution of problems as near to source as possible. This in turn generates two outcomes, each of which has clear relevance to the pursuit of quality, while autonomy enables greater motivation at more junior levels in the organization. Higher management is freed to concentrate on the issues of greatest relevance to them.

Planning enables the organization to interact with its environment: influencing and being influenced. This function helps to ensure that changing customer requirements are known to the organization – a vital part of the quality process.

Policy is responsible for the whole organization, creating and sustaining its identity and arbitrating between demands for change and stability. It is the policy function that determines whether or not the venture will be organized for quality.

The organization is considered as embedded in an environment and consists of two parts: operations and management (see Figure 23.4). The boundaries between these three elements are thought of as permeable. This permits the continuous communication that is necessary between the elements. The diagrammatic conventions demand that these normally be shown as discrete information channels, and this will be the case in subsequent diagrams.

Figure 23.5 demonstrates the next step in building the VSM, by separating the three elements and showing the communication channels, which are used to either amplify or attenuate variety. The organization and its management absorb the variety of the environment, and operational and managerial variety are amplified into the environment. The standard strategies by which this is achieved were reviewed in Chapter 16.

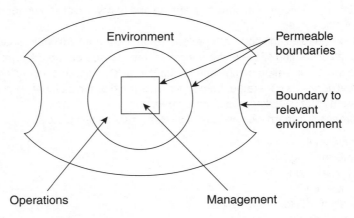

Figure 23.4 The organization in its environment.

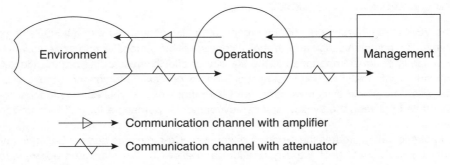

Figure 23.5 The environment, operations and management separated.

Figure 23.5 provides an overview of an entire organization interacting with its environment. Most organizations will consist of a set of implementation units embedded in a total organization, for example, the divisions of a multinational company, the branches of a bank, or the production lines within a factory. Each must have the capability to be viable, within the constraints imposed on it by its membership of the containing organization. Equally, within each unit further lower level units will be found, each of which must again be viable. The lowest level unit for practical purposes is the individual worker. This 'nesting' effect is called recursion, and constitutes a special form of hierarchy built on organizational logic rather than on power.

A chain of recursively embedded viable systems is presented in Figure 23.6. Each oblong box encapsulates a complete recursion.

Figure 23.7 shows all of the operational elements of a company at the same level of recursion, for example, the divisions of the company. As stated, this set constitutes the implementation function of the organization, the parts which carry out the purpose(s) of the organization. The communication channels are simplified in this presentation.

This shows that for each division there is some degree of overlap between the environments. This could represent shared customers, physical overlap between geographical marketing areas, or competition for customers whose requirements could be satisfied by either of two or more product ranges from the same company. For example, for a computer manufacturer, the overlap might represent customers whose requirements could be satisfied by either a large PC network, or a mid-range system.

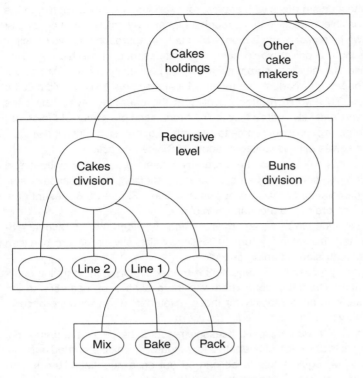

Figure 23.6 A chain of recursively embedded viable systems.

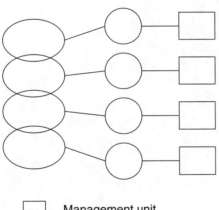

☐   Management unit

○   Operations

⬭   Environment

———   Communication channels

Figure 23.7 A set of implementation elements.

A co-ordinating mechanism deals with sources of oscillation or conflict between the parts. It would be possible to achieve this through a higher level edict – a set of rules or policies handed down by senior management – but such an approach has two principal effects. Every exception to policy would need to be sanctioned at the highest level, which would increase the volume of communication and potentially overload the senior management. The degree of freedom that the individual elements enjoy would also be severely constrained. This would reduce flexibility at the operating level, inhibit the development of *kaizen*, and fail to utilize fully the self-regulating properties of the organization. Finally, the organization would come to be seen as oppressive, since individuals would perceive themselves to have limited freedom of choice and action.

Prime examples of this co-ordination are progress chasers/production controllers in factories, the creation of a timetable in an educational institution, the allocation of service bays in a car dealership, or telling windows in a bank. Figure 23.8 presents the organization with the co-ordinating mechanism in place.

A second feature included in this diagram is the links between the operational elements. These represent the informal communication, which always occurs between stages in a process, or divisions of an organization.

The next stage in the process of management is the regulation of the ongoing activities of the organization. Control is concerned with the allocation of resources to the operational elements, with accountability for those resources, and with adherence to corporate and statutory regulations.

This is achieved through two principal processes: resource bargaining and auditing. Resource bargaining is the process of budgeting for resources, which is carried out in all organizations. The VSM requires this to be carried out on a negotiated basis. The control functions and the operational elements should engage in meaningful discussions

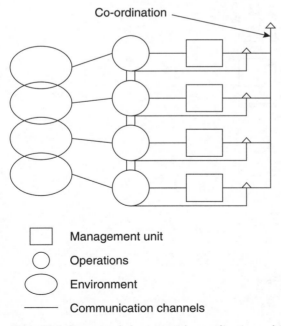

Co-ordination

□ Management unit

○ Operations

⬭ Environment

─── Communication channels

Figure 23.8 Operational elements with co-ordination and interaction.

about what resources are required and what objectives are to be achieved with them. The resource bargaining process should encompass all the resources utilized and objectives set: money, staff, equipment, profitability, quality standards, and so on.

The control function is made up of the various departments involved in regulatory activity. This would include units such as administration, personnel, production management, perhaps the general or divisional manager's office, and quality assurance.

Audit is a sporadic intervention by each of the control departments in the operational elements. This serves to increase their knowledge and understanding of how those functions are performing. It is essential that these audits are sporadic; if they are not they will lose their effect.

The control function being in place, the organization may now be considered to be self-regulating. It will be able to function effectively, carrying out its allotted tasks. Parallels may be drawn between this and devices such as heating/air conditioning systems, which are self-regulating against a target temperature in the same way. Figure 23.9 presents the model at this stage.

An organization that is simply self-regulating will not be viable in the longer term, since it cannot respond to environmental changes. Neither will it be capable of generating continuous improvement, since it has no facility for development. This brings us to planning.

Planning covers all of the research and development activity of the organization. It may be concerned with market research and marketing activity, product development, financial planning, staff training and development, and most certainly is the root of quality planning. The planning functions interact with the emergent environment,

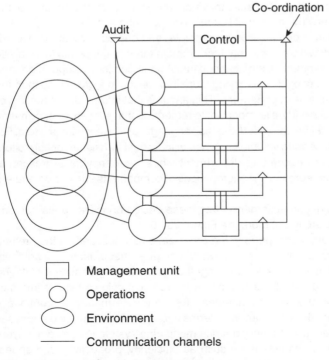

Figure 23.9 The self-regulating organization.

considering possible courses of action for either adapting the organization to the environment, or, where appropriate, influencing the environment towards the organization. The planning and control functions also interact with each other, continuously renegotiating the resource allocations and objectives of the organization.

This process of negotiation will almost inevitably lead at times to conflict and dispute, because the control functions wish to maintain the status quo, while the development functions wish to promote change. The conversation between them will be monitored by the last management function, policy, which arbitrates between them according to the ethos of the organization.

The ethos is the set of values and beliefs that underpin the philosophy of the venture. Policy may be considered to be fulfilling an equivalent function to that of co-ordination at the implementation level. There is, however, one significant difference. The policy function represents the entire organization to the outside world, and is the formal link to the next higher level of organization. The complete Viable System Model is represented in Figure 21.2.

At this stage, the model can be linked back to the prior writings on quality, with the consistent demands from all writers for top management commitment. It is clear that without this commitment the quality initiative will fail, and such commitment demands changes in both the words and actions of the senior management. If organizations are as closely linked as is suggested by the Viable System Model (and from experience they seem to be so), the actions and behaviour of the policy-making group may affect the behaviour of those in the rest of the organization. If they are serious about quality, this message will filter through very rapidly; if they are not, the message will be received just as fast. Through the cybernetic model, the justification for senior management commitment to quality is realized, because they transmit vital messages throughout the organization and to the environment, that is, the customers and suppliers.

The model of an effective organization is complete, and one constructed in accordance with this framework will be viable, but there remain three major points to be made at this stage. First, the communication channels must be in continuous operation, and second, that they must be capable of carrying more information in a given time than the transmitting system is capable of generating. This ensures that information is not lost or distorted in the system. Similarly, it is important to remember that every time information crosses a boundary it must be converted into the 'language' of the receiving system. For example, a message concerning volumes or types of individual transistors or capacitors may have no meaning for a receiving department whose 'currency' is expressed in financial terms, or in units representing aggregations of components such as computers or keyboards.

An organization designed in accordance with these design principles does not look like the conventional hierarchy, but more like Figure 23.10.

In this diagram, the operational parts of the organization are focused on the present market. The management is considering the wider market – other present and potential future opportunities. Strategy joins the two together, representing continual dialogue between the corporate and operational managers. In order to provide adequate information to all managers for effective management, the corporate managers continually review the interaction with the environment in terms of business performance appraisal. The operational managers use the performance monitoring system to consider current performance in relation to characteristics such as efficiency, productivity and speed. Information arising from that system is also provided to the corporate managers for

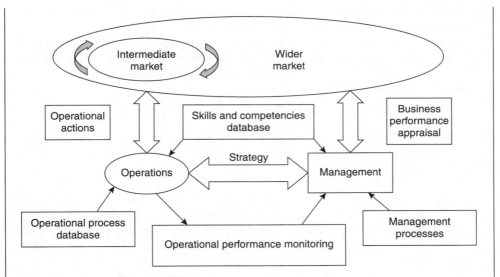

Figure 23.10 The ultrastable organization.

inclusion in the business performance appraisal. The operational processes, management processes, skills and competencies record provide the standing information necessary to support management decision making. An organization designed along these lines will be viable.

It is perfectly legitimate to use this approach specifically to examine only a single aspect of the organization. It is possible, and often useful, to model only the quality management function. Such an approach ensures that the effectiveness of the quality programme is understood at all levels in the organization. It may be found that while the senior management have implemented a quality programme, this has been done only at the operations level, and no changes have been made in other parts of the organization to support it. For example, control may be focusing purely on volume as an output measure and ignoring the quality issue. Development may be focused on the demand for new products, while ignoring customer calls for better quality of existing products.

CRITICAL REVIEW

The VSM can be, and has been, applied to organizations of all sizes and types, from one-man businesses to entire nation states. It has a general applicability and utility, which exceeds that of other organizational models. The model fully embraces the interaction between the organization and the environment in which it is embedded, and caters for the definition of the organization and its purposes by its stakeholders.

The model is criticized for being difficult to use in practice, but although the methodology appears lengthy and complex, it can be very rapid in use. The standard modelling format generates great economy.

The model is also criticized for focusing on static rather than dynamic goals, although this criticism rather misses the point of the model. Similarly, it is argued that the model can lead to, and support, autocratic management behaviour. While this argument is easier to sustain, it must be noted that the principles of the model call for appropriate levels of autonomy; if this is not granted the organization will not be viable. The major barrier to its use is the necessity of devolving power within the organization, and this requirement frequently generates resistance from those already in power.

In the field of quality systems, the model has been used by Flood (1993) to deal with structural elements of the organization, while Beckford and Dudley (1998a, 1998b, 1999) and Dudley (2000) have used it as the basis of a complete approach to skills-based quality management.

When SB Foods factory B is diagnosed using the Viable System Model, what is actually happening is compared with the ideal as represented by the model. The following is discovered.

Factory B production is arranged on three floors. The top floor is a preparation and mixing area, while staff on the middle floor cook and pack three product ranges, Unit, Corn and Bar, representing 40 per cent of total output (split 30/5/5). During the second six months of the calendar year, an additional product range, Christmas cake, is also produced on a second line on the middle floor. The ground floor staff cooks and packs a single range of products, Slab, representing the balance of output. The ground floor also houses the stores and despatch departments.

During the period of threatened closure, the caretaker manager, whose brief was to maintain production at all costs, made a number of short-term operational decisions. These included staff being granted higher status positions, for example, foreman, leading hand, supervisor, in order to 'buy off' problems with the union. This was done, regardless of the need for a higher grade in the functions to be fulfilled: there were several supposed supervisors with no subordinates. Similarly, procedures and working practices were allowed to deteriorate. Morning and after-noon tea breaks were stretched from fifteen minutes to thirty minutes; the lunch break stretched from thirty to forty-five minutes; an end-of-shift shower break was taken by staff in the mixing department; toilet breaks were treated as routine rather than exceptional and minimal interruptions to work. Absenteeism ran at around 15 per cent, and staff commonly took 'sick leave' up to the limit beyond which sick pay ceased. Across the factory, standards of hygiene had become inadequate and maintenance of plant and equipment was only undertaken in the event of a breakdown.

Both managers and staff systematically abused overtime and shift payment sys-tems, intended to reward staff adequately for long or unsocial working patterns. This was tolerated as a way of 'keeping the peace'. The level of basic pay at all grades was such that the factory had one of the lowest paid workforces in the local community.

Line managers had no responsibility for setting or managing the budgets of their departments, and there appeared to be no meaningful mechanisms for monitoring departmental, process or personal performance. The only performance measure-ment was of labour utilization for the production managers, on the first and ground floors. This operated in such a way that the managers were working to maintain production, regardless of the level of customer orders. This approach was funda-mentally flawed, in that while managers were maximizing labour utilization, they were ignoring the other costs of overproduction: the costs of transport, freezing, and stocking of excess output. Similarly, there was no workload or staff monitoring system in use; managers operated according to the numbers they had always used. There was no explicit requirement for them to attempt to reduce numbers through revised working practices or applied automation.

There was no flexibility of labour between the processes or the product lines, although the workload in one area would frequently peak while there was a trough elsewhere in the process.

Provisional customer orders were received on a weekly basis, with daily confirmation of final out-loading requirements. The production managers ignored these provisional orders which were notoriously inaccurate. They preferred to produce according to the previous week's final orders, with an adjustment for 'instinct and experience'. Daily production was always within 10 per cent of final orders, usually by way of an excess. The factory had never cut a customer delivery for lack of output. Final orders were used only by the despatch foreman for loading vehicles.

The stores foreman ignored both provisional and final orders, and ordered stores to maintain a stable supply of all items. The factory rarely ran out of any item, but frequently had cause to throw away perishable items (such as raw liquid egg) that had been overstocked.

There appeared to be no process control system in place, so that batches could not be tracked in their progress through the factory, although 'tracking and tracing' were on the verge of becoming mandatory requirements to comply with food safety legislation.

While managers considered that foremen needed constant guidance and instruction throughout a shift, including control and setting of equipment (for example re-lighting burners on ovens), both the workforce and management considered that they were producing a consistently high quality output, notwithstanding an ongoing reject rate of around 10 per cent. Quality inspectors in the line were expected to undertake 100 per cent inspection of output. When running, each production line had an output rate of around ninety units per minute; inspectors were required to check presentation, size, appearance and labelling for each item. There were six quality inspectors to deal with the two production lines, as well as all other quality control aspects of the factory.

At the management level, communication between production staff and product development staff was minimal. Product development staff reported to the commercial director, not to the general manager of the factory. Product development staff were not involved in pre-production trials of new products on the plant, nor did they advise production staff of forthcoming changes until the last moment. This was largely a function of the relationship between SB Foods and its customers. Once a product specification had been agreed with a customer, it would normally be launched within a few days.

SB Foods head office consisted of a managing director who reported to Sundries division management. He was supported by a commercial director, who also acted as salesman to the principal customers. There was also a general trades salesman and two product development teams, one at each factory.

The finance director reported to the managing director, and was supported by a plant accountant at each factory and a team of accounts staff at head office.

The operations controller, reporting again to the managing director and through his head office-based team, acted as buyer of raw materials and packaging. He also handled product distribution.

A personnel controller reported to the managing director, and took direct responsibility for the entire personnel function, with particular responsibility for management development. He was supported by a personnel officer at each factory.

A general manager reported to the managing director, and was fully responsible for the operation of factory B with the support of the manufacturing manager, who was responsible for all aspects of production from goods in to despatch.

The engineering manager, supported by an assistant manager and a foreman fitter, reported to the general manager, and was responsible for all aspects of site, plant and equipment maintenance. The engineering workforce consisted of a team of fitters and a team of electricians, together with a painter and storeman.

A technical manager, responsible to the general manager, looked after all technical aspects of the factory, including adherence to food safety standards, customer product specifications, health, safety and hygiene. He was supported by a co-ordinator (who also had responsibilities at factory A).

Three quality assurance staff in the laboratory, and six line inspectors and the specification manager, who, together with the food chemist, prepared and maintained product specifications for both factories, supported a quality control manager.

Finally, the factory had a canteen and staff shop (which sold reject output), both of which report to the health, safety and hygiene manager.

23.3 Process Analysis

This element of the intervention was focused on understanding and recording the production processes of SB Foods, and the enabling processes through which they function, including information and behaviour. The work involved, in this case literally, walking through the factory – from stores to dispatch – capturing the flow of activities and understanding how the process worked, any changes of responsibility, and how process performance was measured.

23.3.1 Process Mapping

A core process is a sequence of activities linked across an organization to deliver a product or service of value to an end-user customer. Enabling processes are internal sequences of activities, which facilitate or support the operation of a core process.

Defining processes in an established manufacturing environment is a straightforward activity, as the process is largely defined by a construction or assembly flow (see Ohno, 1978, pp. 48–50). In a service environment, however, it is often more difficult, since processes are often not recognized as such, their elements being linked across separate functional areas. For example, in a bank, processing a customer's cheque may involve the signature of an official for authorization of payment, a cashier, a computer input operator, and a filing clerk. Each of these individuals may work in a different department (functional silo) within the bank, and the process may be subject to a number of variations and sub-routines, dependent upon circumstances. For this reason, fragmentation of processes is common. For an organization serious about achieving quality, it is vital to move beyond this fragmented approach to something more coherent. Process definition is vital in this regard.

A process chart provides an overall picture of a connected set of value-adding activities by recording, in sequence, each of the operations. These operations are recorded regardless of who does them, or where they are performed. Functional boundaries within the organization are ignored for mapping purposes.

Process charting can be carried out at a number of nested levels or recursions. At the first level, the 'total process' records the process from start to finish, with a minimum of detail, and identifies where exceptions and sub-routines occur. The second level, 'process operation' or 'task', details the specific actions taken at each stage (including the exceptions and sub-routines), while a third level, 'process detail' or 'procedure', studies detail, potentially down to the level of individual hand movements (a work study level of analysis). For many purposes, especially where a skills-based approach is used, capturing information at the total and operational levels is sufficient. Figure 23.11 shows how the three levels are linked.

The process charts are developed by identifying particular operations and linking them together, along with any inspections, audits, or delays. The process may be defined in either a vertical or horizontal flow, whichever is more convenient, and, for clarity and economy of effort, ASME symbols are typically used to indicate each stage. The ASME symbols, with some additions, are provided in Figure 23.12.

It is common practice to give each process a unique name or identifier, and to number the sequence of actions. The completed process charts provide a record of the operation, and provide the basis for process analysis and critical examination. They also provide a basis for evaluation and measurement at process handover points (the connections between steps), and allow the identification of problem areas. Such charts may also usefully be overlaid on a plan or topographical diagram of the building layout, indicating paths of movement. This can prove helpful in eradicating delays and

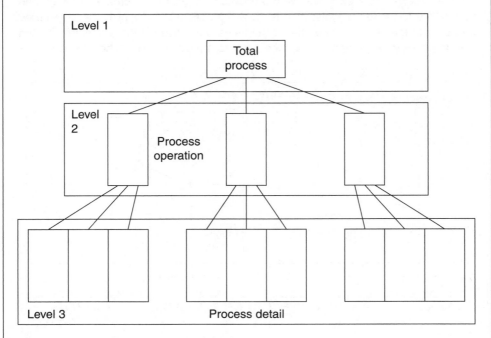

Figure 23.11 Nested or recursive process levels.

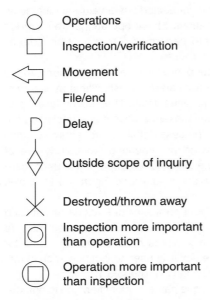

○   Operations

▢   Inspection/verification

◁   Movement

▽   File/end

D   Delay

⬦   Outside scope of inquiry

⤬   Destroyed/thrown away

▣   Inspection more important than operation

◉   Operation more important than inspection

Figure 23.12 ASME symbols.

identifying why and where quality problems occur, for example, in the storage of temperature-sensitive materials in an unprotected area. An example of a completed 'total process' chart overlaid on a building plan is provided in Figure 23.13.

This chart represents the receipt, preparation and despatch of a purchase order. The order is received by a storeman, who prepares a request form, creates a folder, and passes the folder to the typist (that is, three operations). The typist types the order, passes it to the checker, who checks the typed order against the request form, and (assuming all to be correct) passes the order to a progress clerk. The progress clerk

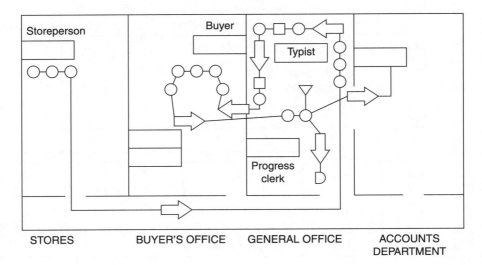

Figure 23.13 A total process chart.

passes the forms to the relevant buyer for signature and return. The progress clerk then passes the order to the supplier, passes one copy of the order to the accounts department, and holds the other in the buyer's file.

This process, which undoubtedly seems cumbersome to the reader, is a real example found in a UK factory, and while obviously inefficient is not unusually bad compared with many other contemporary situations.

Most long-established organizations have not yet properly exploited the potential for process re-engineering, enabled by innovative approaches to process management and contemporary information technology. One intervention provided an example of data being captured electronically in the first instance from a system outside the organization, and being retyped at least five times within the organization – a hugely inefficient process. Similar findings have been made as late as early 2009 in one global business, and the staff could see nothing wrong with it.

When SB Foods is examined using process mapping, the following matters are revealed, some directly concerned with the processes themselves, some relevant to the control of those processes, and some simply discovered by being on the manufacturing floors.

The core manufacturing process for all output is the same:

Mix: Raw materials brought together
Deposit: Cake mix dropped into baking tins
Bake: Tins passed through 'travelling' oven
De-tin: Cooled cake removed from tins
Cut: Cake sliced according to packing requirements
Process: Cake surface decorated
Pack: Cake sleeved in plastic and boxed
Despatch: Boxes assembled to palletized orders for loading

This process is presented in Figure 23.14.

When the process is examined at the next level of detail, several new aspects are revealed. First, the process flow is split, all mixing takes place on the second floor, while all other stages to the end of packing take place on the ground and first floors, with all products coming back together at despatch for compilation of final orders. Therefore, another view of the processes is presented in Figure 23.15.

From this view, it can be seen that the production process, which on the face of it is quite simple, has been broken up into five separately managed areas, with each process flow going across two functional boundaries just at this level of analysis. Discussion with the line managers then revealed that while there appeared to be numerous managers and foremen, there was a lack of clear delegation of

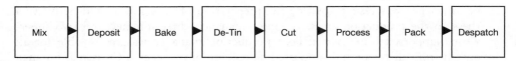

Figure 23.14 Manufacturing process.

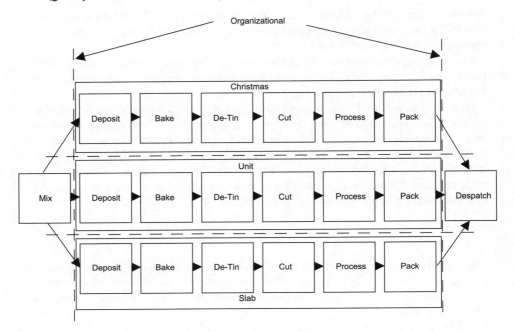

Figure 23.15 All core processes.

authority. Managers and foremen are apparently unaware of the level of decisions they can take. This has meant that they have taken decisions in the past – which subsequently have been overridden by senior management. Equally, it seems that managers and others in supervisory positions have limited understanding of their roles, and no adequate articulation of the performance expectations of the senior management. Managers recognize that they are only responsible for part of the process and, in the event of a failure, blame is passed up and down the lines of command.

The capability and professionalism of many of the managers and foremen is doubted by their peers, superiors and subordinates. The majority of them have risen to their posts from the shop floor with little or no training; it has simply been 'their turn'.

It seemed from observation that management at all levels was failing to support and implement established rules and procedures, and that the union was relied upon as an information source to a far greater degree than the management.

All of the foregoing having been said, the team reporting to the manufacturing manager included the following. A stores manager (outside the process flow) was responsible for the ordering, receipt, and storage of raw materials and packaging. A foreman, a leading hand, one operator, and a clerk supported him. The mixing bay manager was responsible for the preparation of cake mixes, and delivery of these to the production areas. A junior manager, three foremen and two supervisors supported him. A first-floor production manager was responsible for all output from this floor and supported by one junior manager, a Christmas foreman (working as an ordinary hand for six months of the year), a bar foreman (responsible for 'minding' a fully automated machine), a processing foreman, a bar packing foreman, and a corn foreman – each responsible for a particular element of the process.

The ground-floor production manager was responsible for slab output, and supported by two junior managers, a depositing foreman supported by a leading hand, two shift oven foremen, each supported by a leading hand, a cream room foreman, supported by one operator and servicing both production floors, and a packing foreman.

Finally, the despatch manager was responsible for the safe custody and outloading of completed product to customer vehicles. One leading hand, one clerk, and two operators supported him.

It had already been established during the Viable Systems Diagnosis that there was no effective process control mechanism in place, no meaningful measurement of the performance of the various processes, and only weak understanding of the role and expectations of managers.

23.4 Reflections and Next Steps

It is apparent that SB Foods factory is not as effective or as efficient as is possible. The three methodologies, used in parallel, have each worked to reveal particular issues on which they are focused, and at the same time, each has provided confirmation of findings in other areas.

Overall, the studies show that the factory needs to address numerous cultural, organizational, and process issues if the aspiration to viability is to be fulfilled. From a 'soft systems' perspective, it is evident that there is not an agreed view of the purposes of the organization, or the ways in which it should seek to fulfil them. Note, for example, the differing aspirations of the senior management (viability), from the middle management (production at all costs), and the staff ('if we have to work late we get a 17.5 per cent premium for the whole shift'). From the viable systems perspective, there are evident weaknesses in communication and in clarity of responsibility for different areas. From a resource and performance management perspective, SB Foods is 'out of control': it is over-producing and under-performing. When the examination comes from the process perspective, it is easy to see why the other characteristics might apply. The processes have numerous handover points, are probably over-managed from a 'numerical' and involvement perspective sense, but under-managed from a competence perspective, including the involvement of senior and middle managers in routine decision making. The lack of a meaningful measurement system means that managers and staff are working hard to do the wrong thing in relation to the overall objectives. Resolving the issues raised will address the three characteristics raised in Chapter 21: 'know why', 'know how' and 'know what'.

Summary

This chapter has taken the first steps in simultaneously applying three methodologies to reveal different aspects of the situation under consideration. Through this, it has provided three perspectives on SB Foods which have briefly been reported. In the next chapter, the study will progress to determine a way forward and to select tools and methodologies to help achieve success.

KEY LEARNING POINTS

No one methodology can address all aspects of a problem situation

Consider the use of multiple methodologies in parallel to reveal different perspectives and integrate them to a synthesized view.

The findings from one methodology will act to confirm or challenge the findings of the others.

Viable systems diagnosis

Key definitions:
a system is viable when it is capable of survival in a given environment, and capable of learning and adapting to changes in that environment.

Principles:
observer-defined systems, systems thinking, black boxes, self-regulation, requisite variety.

Three modes:
descriptive, diagnostic, prescriptive.

Critique:
general applicability, environmental interaction, observer definition, difficult to use, threatens established power bases, static not dynamic goals.

Soft systems methodology

Key definitions:
solving complex problems, relies on the innate subjective views of the participants in a situation.

Principle:
engage participants in the organization in changing its operation, improve commitment to outcomes, purposes must be defined before means can be decided.

Method:
seven-stage process of enquiry – finding out, rich picture, root definitions, redesign, real-world comparison, debate and decision, taking action.

Critique:
best with small numbers, brings 'order' to a debate, caters for diverse opinions, no desired or ideal-type outcome other than consensus.

Question

Use the methods and diagrammatic conventions of soft systems methodology, viable systems diagnosis and process analysis to create your own interpretation of SB Foods.

24 Second Intervention

Insanity: doing the same thing over and over and expecting different results
(Albert Einstein – attributed)

Introduction

This chapter develops the SB Foods enquiry to the next stage, both acquiring further detail as necessary and commencing action where appropriate. It continues with the process analysis, and introduces the ideas of interactive planning, process measurement, statistical process control, quality circles, and job design.

24.1 Recap

The basic situation at SB Foods having been diagnosed using the methods introduced in the previous chapter, it is now possible to use other problem-solving methods, again in parallel, and in the context of the initial findings, to address the issues raised and establish a way forward. Summarizing, it has been determined that there was:

- a lack of alignment, or shared purpose, between the objectives and intent of the senior management, the middle management, and the workforce;
- poor engagement of the staff generally;
- a weak management structure, and ineffective process control;
- poor processes, with numerous changes of poorly articulated responsibilities;
- a lack of meaningful measurement, and lack of evaluation of process and people performance;
- poor information and communication.

If the problems of SB Foods were to be properly addressed, it was necessary to achieve several outcomes. The first was to generate alignment between the objectives of the various internal stakeholders. The second was to analyse process performance, bring processes under proper control, and design a management structure and measurement system which would enable effective performance. Third was to engage the production staff in designing and delivering further improvement.

Interactive planning enables the engagement of the whole workforce in the development of the future of SB Foods, and re-establishes regular communication up and down the hierarchy. Process measurement and statistical process control provide an understanding of how well (or not) the processes are performing, and a rational basis for evaluating improvement. Quality circles, applied as complementary to interactive planning, engage the production staff in delivering locally developed process improvement. Kobayashi's twenty keys methodology (Chapter 7) might also have been used. Job design provides some useful insights into how roles can be revised to align skills and responsibilities more closely with the needs of the organization.

The mapping of methodologies originated in Figure 22.2 can now be extended to incorporate the additional approaches employed. This is represented in Figure 24.1.

24.2 Engaging the Internal Stakeholders

The soft, ends-oriented, issues at SB Foods were at this stage not resolved. Although Checkland's soft systems methodology worked well for the relatively small numbers of senior managers, the methodology is not designed, or intended, to work with larger groups. To generate the potential for alignment of the entire workforce, a different approach was required. Consideration was given to using Stafford Beer's Syntegration Methodology (Beer, 1994), however, its structure effectively limits it to groups of about thirty people, and it is, like soft systems methodology, a 'single-use' approach. In this situation, what was needed was to generate an approach to alignment and communication in the business, both horizontally and vertically, which would be of continuing use. The issues of communication and alignment would not be resolved through a single event. It was therefore necessary to adopt an approach which SB Foods could continue to use long after completion of this particular project. This led to the adoption of Ackoff's Interactive Planning.

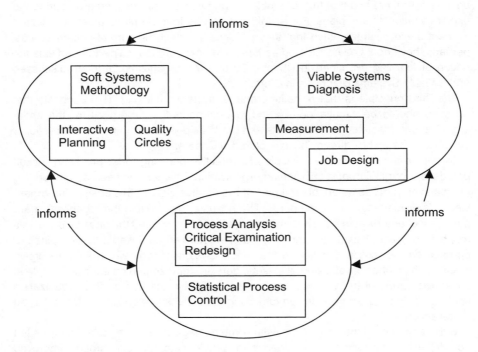

Figure 24.1 Tools for the second intervention.

24.2.1 Interactive Planning (IP)

PRINCIPLES AND CONCEPTION

Ackoff holds the view that a planning methodology is required which enables people to plan for themselves, rather than be planned for by other people. He sees this as enabling the participants to make their own values and ideals paramount in the planning process. This lets participants express their own perceptions of 'reality', rather than having the reality of others forced upon them, and it necessitates wide participation in the creation of the future of organizations. Reflecting ideas already met in other approaches, IP recognizes three sets of interests in the organization: those of the organization itself as a purposeful, viable entity, the interests of the wider community (environment) in which it exists, and the interests of the individuals who work within it.

Interactivist planners take into account the past, present and predictions about the future as inputs to a planning process aimed at creating the organization's future, and the mechanisms by which it can be achieved. The planners work with their conception of the ideal future for the organization.

Interactive planning rests on the three principles of participation, continuity and holism. The participative principle is that all stakeholders should participate in the stages of the planning process. Ackoff, like Checkland, suggests that the process of planning is more important than the plan which is produced, since it is the process which enables individual contributions to be made, and which enhances understanding of the whole organization by those involved with it.

The principle of continuity recognizes that values and ideals of the stakeholders change over time, and that further problems, and new possibilities, emerge during the implementation of any plans. For Ackoff, this means that the plans must be adapted to meet these changes, such that they continually reflect the current circumstances; perhaps they should be considered as forever in final draft form! This idea reflects the notion of learning examined in Chapter 20 and the organizational ideas discussed under Viable Systems Diagnosis in Chapter 23.

The third principle is that of holism, that is, systemic thinking. This suggests that planning should be simultaneously and interdependently carried out for the entire organization, or at least as many parts and levels as possible. The notion of holistic, or systemic, thinking has already been explored in Chapter 15.

To enable the participative principle of interactive planning to be practised, Ackoff proposes a particular form of planning organization. This form is seen as embedding the planning process as an integral part of the organization. In this design, the organization is divided into planning boards. The heads of units within the organization are members of boards at three levels: their own, the one above, and the ones below. In this respect, they act similarly to, and may be characterized as, Likert's 'linking pins', or perhaps as the 'policy' function in the Viable System Model, which links recursive levels. At the highest level, external stakeholders are represented on the board, while at the lowest level, all the workers are members of their unit board. This organization could usefully be used as a design for linking the activities of quality circles within an organization.

While apparently time-consuming, with some managers belonging to as many as ten boards, the organization is considered to derive major benefit through improved

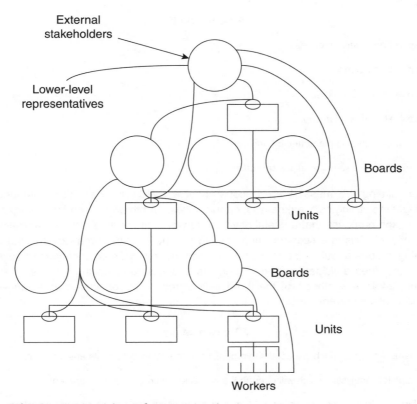

Figure 24.2 Organizational design for interactive planning.

communication, co-ordination, and integration of ideas. Morale is also improved. The organization of interactive planning is represented diagrammatically in Figure 24.2.

It can clearly be seen that this structure does not replace the existing hierarchy, but interleaves with it. It is a hierarchy of planning rather than control. This generates possibilities of communication and debate which the hierarchy of power and position tends to inhibit. It is particularly noteworthy that the approach explicitly incorporates the views of external stakeholders, who might, for example, include local government representatives, community leaders, suppliers and, perhaps, customers or consumers of the product or service – or in this case could accommodate SB Foods head office and Victuals representatives. This has evident implications for organizations pursuing quality programmes. For example, where a supplier development strategy is being pursued, suppliers can be linked into the planning process of the organization. Similarly, customer feedback becomes truly meaningful when the customers form a part of the organization.

METHODOLOGY

The methodology for IP includes five steps (Figure 24.3). Holding to the systemic requirements of the approach, the process may be run in any order, and the whole should be regarded as an iterative process with plans, as already suggested, always being in the latest 'draft' form.

Russell Ackoff:

Step 1) Formulating the mess;

Step 2) Ends planning;

Step 3) Means planning;

Step 4) Resource planning;

Step 5) Design of implementation and control.

Figure 24.3 Five stages of interactive planning.

Formulating the mess (Step 1) consists of a SWOT type analysis, intended to highlight the strengths, weaknesses, opportunities, and threats faced by the organization. Ackoff proposes that a useful device is to work out the 'future the organization is currently in'. This is a scenario representing the future of the organization, that is, if nothing is done about its internal situation, and the environment continues to develop along the lines anticipated. Ackoff suggests that this requires three types of study (Figure 24.4). A synthesis of the three sets of results is considered as a reference scenario of the current 'mess'.

3 Types of Study

Systems Analysis: which will detail the organization, how it works and its environment;

Obstruction Analysis: which will unearth the obstacles to corporate development;

Reference Projections: which predict future performance by extrapolating current performance in the given environment.

Figure 24.4 Three methods for formulating the mess.

Ends planning (Step 2) seeks to specify the future the organization wants. It begins with an idealized redesign – a vision of the sort of organization the stakeholders would create if they were free to do so. This involves selecting a mission, specifying the attributes of the design, and designing the organization. Normally, two versions of the ends planning are created, one constrained by the existing wider system, and one unconstrained. The difference between these two idealized organizations indicates to what extent the organization must address its efforts towards modifying its environment during the planning process.

Idealized redesign is a creative process, and as such permits only two constraints. First, the design must be technologically feasible – that is, it must not rely on a potential future invention or breakthrough. Second, it must be operationally viable – that is, it must be capable of functioning if created.

Flood and Jackson (1991: 151) suggest that the design should answer to the criteria of the best 'ideal seeking system' that the stakeholders could imagine. From this point, it is clear that the organization designed must be capable of learning and adaptation. Ackoff's outline design for such a system requires it to be capable of:

- *observation* – to recognize opportunities and threats;
- *decision making* – enabling a response to those opportunities and threats;

- *implementation* – actually doing something;
- *control* – performance monitoring and self-correction;
- *communication* – the acquisition, generation and dissemination of information.

The alert reader will by now have identified some similarities in ideas between IP and other approaches already discussed, such as the VSM with its requirement for implementation, co-ordination, control, development, and policy: the five functions of management. It must be stated, though, that there are some fundamental differences in the theories underpinning the approaches.

Means planning (Step 3) is the term used for the process of generating the 'hows' to support the 'whats' of the first two steps. It is concerned with making operational the changes considered necessary by those involved. Alternative 'hows' should be generated, perhaps using some of the techniques outlined in earlier chapters of this book, and comparisons made to find the most effective.

Resource planning (Step 4) looks at the requirements for materials, supplies, energy, and services – all of the inputs to the organization – as well as at facilities and equipment, personnel, and money. For every aspect, it is necessary to determine what changes need to be made to support the idealized redesign. This stage is very similar to the 'internal business audit' in a strategic review process, as it attempts to assess the capabilities of the organization and its personnel.

Implementation and control (Step 5) is concerned with ensuring that the decisions made are carried out. This involves the allocation of tasks, and the monitoring of their completion. The outcomes of implementation should be fed back into the planning process, such that necessary modifications and further changes can be made.

CRITICAL REVIEW

IP shares with SSM the criticism that its outcomes are bound by the knowledge and expectations of the participants in the process. For quality to be addressed as an issue, it must be highlighted at the outset as part of the formulation of the mess. Similarly, at the implementation phase, the need for knowledge of quality theory and practice must be recognized.

While IP and quality circles appear to have much in common, they are differentiated in two ways. First, quality circles operate only at a single level within the organization, whereas IP links all levels. Second, quality circles are focused on purely localized operational problems, whereas IP, used properly, has the scope to capture strategic perspectives from the lowest levels of the organization. Quality circles may be thought of as a problem-solving technique, whereas IP may be thought of as a way of managing the organization.

Like SSM, IP is oriented towards defining the problem. It is focused on providing a methodology for generating solutions. It does not offer any guidance as to what those solutions should be demanding, only that they are derived in an emancipatory manner.

The key outcomes of the use of IP can now be discussed. Purists might argue that the benefits of this approach were unduly limited by the prior use of other methodologies which constrained what it was possible to do, and that the approach is thereby rendered sterile. However, if it is accepted that SB Foods is not free to be whatever it wants to be, but has a degree of autonomy which is determined by its membership of the higher-order organization, Victuals, that argument is neutralized. Whatever the philosophical ambitions, SB Foods had limited freedom, and any methodology applied to resolving its problems is subject to the same limits.

The previous chapter reported a number of tensions that existed in SB Foods caused by poor communication, changes in promotion strategy, strength of the union and grapevine, and a level distrust between the managers, foremen, and workforce. It was inevitable that the first events would require the senior management to begin building trust between themselves and the workforce. An example of the distance between them was that, at the initial event, with the chairs positioned in a horseshoe with the facilitators at the open end, the general manager and manufacturing manager were positioned on one end of the horseshoe, with most of the team sitting directly opposite them. Never was positioning so expressive of tension and distrust. The process developed for each of the inaugural events was designed to build some shared ground between the apparently 'opposing sides', to expose concerns and worries, and to develop the basis of trust. To this end, participants at each event:

- proposed and adopted some 'rules of engagement';
- clarified the purpose of the events;
- ran an open discussion in which concerns could be discussed;
- exposed the limitations under which they could be run.

SB Foods belongs to Victuals, and its freedom is thereby constrained – it cannot make choices which take it outside the boundaries imposed by that ownership. Similarly, factory A and factory B are constrained in their freedom by belonging to SB Foods. There were therefore legitimate and necessary constraints laid upon the discussions. Those things that were not for debate were exposed as limitations. These were:

- if the factories are to survive and thrive, they must improve production performance;
- they must be profitable – losses were not acceptable;
- the technologies in place – and the capital cost thereof – meant that survival was as a cake factory, and not anything else.

Those limitations understood, all other aspects were for free discussion within the methodology. The principal agreement to emerge from these first meetings was the joint desire to see the business thrive and to work towards that end. It was also recognized that, with the accepted limitations, the IP boards would not be able to address the operational issues rapidly or frequently enough to deliver some of the benefits. They would, however, provide a useful integration device and enable the newly opened dialogue to be continued. They proposed, therefore, to introduce the idea of quality circles at the operational level to drive short-term, and more focused, productivity improvement and error reduction.

Interactive Planning therefore became accepted as a device for communicating vertically and horizontally throughout the business, rather than as just a planning and reinvention tool.

This breakthrough being achieved, which included greater integration of people, the second series of events focused on Obstruction Analysis (see Figure 24.4), which identified the following as barriers to development:

- lack of clarity of responsibilities;
- lack of managerial skills – at all levels;
- poor job design;
- lack of meaningful measurement;
- poor co-ordination of processes;
- no performance management or reporting.

While IP works well at the 'total system' level, it is not so useful at the level of individual work processes and tasks. These require a different mindset, and a real depth of understanding of the production processes. It was with this in mind that a quality circles approach was taken for addressing operational challenges.

24.2.2 Quality Circles

Quality circles are usually considered to be the brainchild of Dr. Kaoru Ishikawa (Chapter 8), but many companies throughout the world have adopted them in a variety of forms. The circles exist (Figure 24.5) to identify and solve quality problems associated with a particular activity or interest group within the organization.

The aims of using quality circles are to improve and develop the organization, show respect for people, enhance their satisfaction in the job, and stretch them to their potential. Each circle is made up of between four and twelve workers, led by a supervisor or manager. The focus of attention is on problems within their own area, although problems imported from a prior process should also be recognized. These become the responsibility of the supervisor or manager to address.

The effectiveness of quality circles depends upon a number of key factors. Prime amongst these is support from senior and operational management. If these levels obstruct, or inhibit, the effort – even passively – the initiative will fail. Similarly, participation by the workers must be voluntary, and both they and the leaders must be trained in appropriate techniques.

It is usually suggested that circle members have a common work background. This may be seen as perhaps inhibiting the development of solutions to problems that cross process or functional boundaries. It is certainly the case that a problem within a particular area may be solved by a circle drawing its membership from within that area. This approach, though, will not necessarily help with problems which cross internal boundaries and which denies the use of interdisciplinary teams. Inter-disciplinary working has been found to be extremely helpful in the discipline of operational research, and is continuing to gain popularity in many other fields. The principal benefit of a 'common background' circle is that the membership will not feel that a solution has been imposed by an outside, disinterested body. A sense of 'ownership' in solutions is generally recognized as a powerful means of overcoming resistance to change.

The orientation of the quality circle is towards solutions. It is very easy for them to become enmeshed in complaints about the organization and its management. This may

Quality Circle Purposes

· improve and develop the enterprise;
· respect human relations and build job satisfaction;
· stretch human potential and capabilities.

Figure 24.5 Aims of quality circles.

be made manifest in moaning about other parts of the process, or fruitless comparisons of working conditions, pay rates, and other issues which are not central to the purpose of the circle.

Organization of the circle should be a matter of normal good practice for meetings; that is, a specific (but limited) time set aside, circulation of an agenda, and invitations to attend to all members, together with managers/supervisors – at least as a matter of courtesy. It is recommended that the leadership of the circle be rotated on a regular basis, and that hierarchy in the circle be avoided. Apart from its benefit to active participation in the circle, this provides the opportunity for every member to try the role of manager, even if in a very limited sense. It may also be regarded as good training practice, and an opportunity for a manager to see how individual workers might cope with more responsible and supervisory positions.

It is generally considered important that the efforts of the participants should be recognized, although debate continues about this aspect. One school of thought suggests that a participant in a quality circle is only fulfilling his or her responsibility to an employer by showing how improvement can be achieved. If satisfaction and increased job security are achieved through this, the effort brings its own reward. The other school of thought believes that an employee is paid to carry out a specific task, and that extra responsibility should carry extra reward.

Any recognition or reward aspect needs to be related to the culture of the organization and its geographical location. Decisions need to be made on the basis of the socio-cultural context of the particular organization. This means that what may be appropriate in Hong Kong or Singapore may be wholly inappropriate in Tokyo or London.

Quality circles do not stand on their own as an approach to TQM; they must be supported by other initiatives. One important weakness in this respect is the lack of a quality circle hierarchy for working across organizational boundaries, and at higher levels in the organization. This means that interactions cannot be recognized and appropriately addressed within this conventional approach.

As far as SB Foods was concerned, having introduced the concept of quality circles and facilitated the training and initial events, it became clear that there was much scope for improvement. Some of this fell within the remit of the local circles, and they followed a systematic approach (based on that offered by Kobayashi – see Chapter 7) to deliver those improvements. However, many of the issues fell across organizational boundaries, and had an impact on the way that SB Foods was structured. For example, the circles determined that:

> Poor process control and multiple handovers of responsibility was exemplified by the fact that cake mix being 'deposited' was frequently part cooked 'in the pipe', because the 'mix' process was deemed completed when the mixture was tipped from the mixing machines. This event took place to suit the needs of the mixers and not the depositors – and their managements were separate.
>
> The approach of 'production at all costs', driven by the absence of meaningful measurement, meant that 'production push' rather than 'demand pull' drove volumes. So, while production expectations were met, there was clearly waste in the system – and output that exceeded customer demand. As the business was operated, excess production was repackaged and sold, at materials cost only, to a

secondary customer for retailing through local farmers' markets – in effect SB Foods was deliberately manufacturing for that market.

The inability of certain individuals to fulfil the role of supervisor or manager competently, on either competence or language grounds, was a major barrier to improvement.

The 'quality inspection' element of the process was simply a farce. The standards set could not be measured, the inspection regime could not be achieved, and the whole process element was adding no value.

Three of these issues demanded further analysis of the production process, while the fourth, the competence issue, drove a desire to examine job designs within the business, to determine whether better options might be available.

24.3 Improving Processes

The core processes of SB Foods having been captured, and a number of issues raised to do with control, changes of responsibility, performance measurement, and so on, it is appropriate to continue this part of the project by analysing and critically reviewing them.

24.3.1 Process Analysis

PROCESS ANALYSIS AND CRITICAL EXAMINATION

Once a process has been defined, it can be analysed. Of particular concern in the quality management context, is the recognition of where error or failure does, or may, occur in the process. This enables focus to be maintained on those aspects most in need of improvement or redevelopment. It also provides cues for key measurement points, at which statistical process control techniques may be most usefully employed.

The purpose of analysing the process at the outset is to eliminate unnecessary activities, and to identify 'triggers' which start other processes and sub-routines. The critical examination should reveal the reasons for each activity, and enable the compilation of a systematic and prioritized list of potential enhancements.

The benefit gained from critical examination is influenced by the attitude of mind of the analyst. The final result will depend upon the skill with which the process is recorded. Attention must be paid to the following points:

- actions should be recorded factually and verified;
- preconceived ideas must be abandoned;
- all aspects should be challenged and verified;
- hasty judgements must be avoided;
- small details must be recorded at the appropriate level
  (these may be more important than the major items);
- hunches and 'bright ideas' should be set aside;
- problematic attributes of the existing process must be exposed;
- new methods must wait for analysis to be completed.

There is debate as to whether the productive or non-productive parts of the process should be examined first – the former tending to lead to more rapid productivity improvements. In the quality context, and following the work of Ohno, the concern is with identifying where error and failure occur, as these are the causes of reducible waste. It is best if a systematic approach is taken: following the process from the start, and following through to the end. This is because errors made in early parts of the process may be driving failure at later stages, and it is important to eliminate these prior causes. The author recently studied a production process in which the only way the manager of the second stage of the process could succeed was by ensuring that the first stage was seen to fail. Measurement of performance and error at key points of the process may be desirable as a means of identifying where failure occurs, and in what proportions. The information derived can be used to help to prioritize work.

The examination of the identified process can be carried out through a two-stage sequence of questions, which adopt the pattern shown in Figure 24.6.

In contemporary organizations, it is useful to ask similar 'means' questions about the machines and technology used to support the process. That is: what machines are used; whether they are they suitable for the task; whether they are reliable; whether their outputs match or exceed the task requirements; and so on. These questions enable the analyst to determine precisely what the existing process is, to question it, and to identify its flaws. The movement towards quality is begun by proposing

Critical Examination Procedure:

	Primary Questions	Secondary Questions
PURPOSE:	What is done?	What else might be done?
	Why is it done?	What should be done?
PLACE:	Where is it done?	Where else might it be done?
	Why is it done there?	Where should it be done?
SEQUENCE:	When is it done?	When might it be done?
	Why is it done then?	When should it be done?
PERSON:	Who does it?	Who else might do it?
	Why do they do it?	Who should do it?
MEANS:	How is it done?	How else might it be done?
	Why is it done like that?	How should it be done?

Figure 24.6 Critical examination procedure.

alternatives and highlighting failures. Properly supported by valid statistical techniques, this 'is–ought' approach is useful.

A final issue to address in this context is process naming. What the process is called may have a significant influence on how it is treated by both management and staff.

For example, while building an ISO 9001: 2000 quality management system for a Hong Kong organization, a process called 'customer complaints' was identified. The volume of complaints was very high, relative to the total number of customers, and each was responded to effectively. However, they were regarded as an interruption or intrusion in the 'real work' of the business. The volume being high, it was anticipated that some difficulties might arise with the quality certification process. It was therefore decided to examine this area in greater detail. The examination revealed that what the organization called 'customer complaints' were actually requests for maintenance and repair work on the various premises managed by the organization. They were really 'requests for service', that is, they were, for the most part, reports of minor building defects in need of attention: blown light bulbs, dripping taps, failed door locks. These were all matters which the organization could not know about without advice from the customer.

It was therefore decided to rename the 'customer complaints' process as the 'requests for service' process. A complaint was deemed to arise where the same fault was reported more than once – that is, that the organization had failed to respond. The impact was to change the attitude of the tenants – because they perceived that the organization had created a better communication facility for them – and also to change the attitude of the staff when dealing with 'requests for service'. The number of genuine complaints fell substantially.

METHOD DEVELOPMENT

Method development covers a range of techniques which can be used to identify alternatives to the established process, and ways of overcoming quality problems. It relies on creative thinking about the situation, which in turn requires an open and inquiring mind. A lateral approach is useful, as it attempts to find fresh angles from which to view the process. Determination to succeed is important, as is an acceptance that all ideas can be treated as equally valid at the outset, even though they may appear remote from the problem. Creative thinking is supported by a variety of techniques. Readers might wish to refer to the works of Edward De Bono for further inspiration.

Brainstorming is a method of enabling groups of individuals, usually between four and twelve in number (the same as for quality circles), to generate ideas for problem-solving. The process is relatively simple. The group leader outlines the problem, and answers any questions submitted by the members. Thereafter, the group generates ideas which are recorded without comment or judgement on flip charts, white boards, or sometimes on 'post-it' stickers. After about half an hour (or when the ideas dry up) the ideas are evaluated by the group. Those that offer the most apparent value are subject to further evaluation and, where appropriate, experimentation and development.

It is vital that the leader of a brainstorming session is experienced in problem-solving, and is able to create and maintain enthusiasm amongst the group members.

Analogies are also useful. An analogy is an agreement or commonality in certain characteristics between things which are otherwise different. To use analogies is to apply alternative knowledge and experience to a problem. The problem-solvers consider items which are different but which possess similar attributes to the problem under consideration. This approach encourages cross-fertilization of ideas from different professional backgrounds and disciplines. There are three types of analogy which are particularly useful.

Functional: What else does what this process does?
Simple: What does this process look like?
Natural: How is this done in nature?

This last is a particularly helpful approach, since natural systems tend towards self-organization (see Chapter 14), effectiveness (if not always apparent short-term efficiency), and evolution.

Morphological analysis is a systematic method of creating possible lists of logical combinations of variables already known to solve a problem. It enables the range of possible solution spaces to be matched, and a 'most reliable' method to be chosen. One example of this could be solving a delivery problem as follows:

Method: post; courier; in-house delivery system
Speed: JIT (just in time); same day; overnight; non-critical
Packaging: crushproof; airtight; palletized; unimportant

The possible number of logical combinations of variables is 3*4*4 – there are forty-eight possible solutions to the delivery problem (given that each combination of variables is possible; some, such as post and same day, are 'illegal' solutions, that is to say they will not work). Once the range of possible solutions has been defined, quality and other criteria can be applied to identify those which meet expectations and requirements.

Listing and combining attributes is another way of highlighting potential for improvement in a process. This technique requires the creation of a list of the attributes that the process must possess in order to fulfil the requirements, such as zero defects. Changes to the process are then proposed which enable these attributes to be attained.

Heuristic analysis fits within the context of *kaizen* quality thinking. The heuristic method is to generate changes to the process, apply them, and review the results. The results are then used as the platform for testing further changes, and so on in an iterative cycle. This is similar to the PDCA cycle proposed by Deming (Chapter 6) and to the ideas of organizational learning outlined in Chapter 20. Heuristic improvement should never stop but, to be effective, must be used in a systematic rather than random manner. The principal disadvantage of the heuristic method lies in its inherently incremental nature. A heuristic approach may never generate the sort of radical, discontinuous, or step change in a process that may be provoked by the use of other methods.

Convergent and divergent thinking are also useful approaches. Convergent thinking occurs when the analyst(s) attempts to separate the essential items of the process from the incidental. In this way, the aim is to focus on the most important issues, reminiscent of Juran's 'vital few and useful many'. Divergent thinking is the opposite, and occurs when the analyst(s) expands the problem to take account of other information that is not central to the defined process.

The process analysis and examination showed that the core process was essentially fixed – it seems there really is only one way to make a cake. However, the way in which the process was managed, and the lack of information throughout the process, were significant problems. It was also clear that the quality control process prior to packing was ineffective.

Dealing with these matters one at a time, it seemed that the first issue to resolve was that of the management of the processes. Figure 23.15 showed how organizational boundaries broke what were, in essence, two process flows into five process areas, each with its own manager. The physical layout of the factory (mixing on the top floor, production and packing on first and ground floors, despatch on the ground floor) was such that a different approach could be taken. Fortunately, the top floor (mixing bay) was designed in such a way that discrete areas fed mixed product through to the ground and first floors. That meant that it was possible to extend the responsibility of the two production managers backwards into the mixing area, at which time they became responsible for the whole production process through to final packing. Now that the production flow problem could be addressed, it was possible to link the packing element of the process directly to the mixing process, so that the availability of stock to pass to despatch could stimulate the production of mixes and consequently drive the volumes of cake produced. A half-way house to Ohno's 'demand pull' methodology, this step at least eradicated over-production immediately, since mixing were now only creating product to satisfy the demand. At the same time, a more detailed intervention in the mixing process itself ensured that mixes were only deposited to meet demand; this stopped mixes being part cooked in the depositing tubes.

Turning to the 'quality inspection' issue, the process in place involved some six members of staff sitting beside a production line with over a hundred cakes a minute moving past them, giving them – assuming an even flow – six seconds to examine each cake and ensure perfection. This was challenging enough. However, what made the task more challenging was that the cake (the subject of the examination) had already been enclosed in a cellophane wrapper (for hygiene purposes) and inserted into a windowless, pre-printed cardboard box. All it was possible for the inspection team to assess was whether the box looked right – they had, and could have had, no knowledge of the content at all. (The quality of the boxes and printing had already been inspected at stores on receipt from the suppliers.)

While it was essential that some level of verification should be carried out at this final stage of the process, it was much more likely that a verification check during packing would reveal any quality issues with the packaging itself. Any quality assessment of the cake (the actual product) needed to be built in to the process much earlier.

It was concluded that the quality inspection should take place at the 'process to pack' stage of the production system, when every cake was being handled by a member of staff. The staff were allowed discretion to determine what did and did not constitute conformance. This was a level of trust that had not previously been seen in this business.

Although the process had now been redesigned and was being managed differently, there was as yet no real understanding of performance or measurement. While the production process could be deemed as 'under control' – to the extent that no customer order had ever been cut – there was no real understanding of what was going on, how efficient or effective it was, or how improvement might be achieved.

24.3.2 Statistical Methods

This is not a textbook on statistics; that is something best left to a true expert in the field. Here, Logothetis (1992) has already been suggested as providing a useful text.

However, it is usually necessary within any consulting intervention to undertake some level of quantitative analysis, which usually involves statistical calculations of some sort. You are necessarily working with a sample of activities, and it is important to understand how well that sample represents the whole situation being considered. This section therefore provides an introduction to some of the limitations of statistics, and how they are often (mis-)used.

Statistical methods offer techniques for measuring and evaluating performance and performance improvement on a sampling basis. However, they also offer the greatest scope for fooling both others and yourself. They must be used properly, intelligently, and with full understanding of their accuracy and implications.

Statistics are frequently used to support decision making – and support is their proper role. They should not become the only factor used to help to make a decision, for a number of reasons. First, they may not be accurate. Even when machine counted, measures of volume, throughput, and so on can often generate misleading numbers. When people are involved in the counting process, a degree of error is almost inevitable – try counting sheep in a field or fish in a pond – the difficulty of counting is similar to counting finished products on a production line or service events in a retail outlet. Similarly, however accurate the actual numbers, if some critical process event has been overlooked (for example the 'within process' recycling in the bakery example in Chapter 20), the measurements, and the statistics derived from them, will be wrong.

Second, statistics usually represent probabilities, not actualities – remember the number of 'averages' used in the calculation of standard deviation – particularly where batch or sample sizes vary. The answers given for these calculations are 'more or less' accurate, never precise. Third, since the calculations are, to some degree, 'wrong', pure reliance on them is bound to generate some degree of mismatch to the actual situation, often leading to complaints and witch hunts.

Fourth, understanding how the numbers are driven is much more important than the numbers themselves. Pure reliance on the statistics leads to a focus on improving the statistics, rather than improving the process which supports them. It is frequently observed that in a failing or struggling company, the focus is on reducing costs. Company-wide cuts are imposed: for example, 10 per cent of head count, or 10 per cent of wage costs. While in the short term this might address the specific problem of immediate cash flow, it usually does nothing for the medium- to long-term future of the company.

As it is with money, so it is with quality. A short-term, hard-nosed push for quality is a recurring feature of organizations. However, unless changes are developed for the production processes, the common causes of failure are simply overridden. As soon as the pressure is released, the system will revert to its previous behaviour. A further phenomenon is called 'squeezing the snake'. In this case, a quality problem is identified at a particular stage of a process through a statistical process control mechanism. Managerial pressure is applied to that point, and performance improvement is generated, with the quality problem reducing. What is not realized until much later is that the problem has not disappeared; it has simply been moved – either back up the process by constricting the inputs to the problem area, or further down the process by widening the exit point (usually by varying the criteria for quality).

COMMON STATISTICAL ERRORS

A headline in the UK press proclaimed that 'Women are safer drivers than men!' This headline generated much debate in the press, on radio and TV, with many men incensed by the claim (their manliness insulted), and many women and men responding to the headline by citing examples of poor driving by the other sex.

The debate was highly entertaining, but built on an entirely false premise. The headline created for the original newspaper article had one intention: to sell more newspapers. In the newspaper tradition of 'never let the truth get in the way of a good story', the journalist involved had distilled a useful headline, with strong emotional impact, from what was probably a rather dull report. The research had been undertaken by the insurance industry in relation to claims experience amongst British insurers. What the research actually established was quite simple: women, on average, make less frequent insurance claims than men, and, again on average, the size of their claims is smaller.

The research findings themselves can be accepted: they are probably matters of fact. They do not, however, establish the superiority of either female or male drivers. So what is established?

a.   The average claim by women drivers, on policies held in their own names, is smaller than the average claim by male drivers.
b.   The average frequency of claims in respect of those policies is lower for women drivers than for men.

These statements have everything to do with the claims experience of the companies participating in the research relative to female and male policyholders. However, they say nothing of substance concerning the *safety* or otherwise of either sex behind the wheel of a car and, because claims are made by the policyholder, they cannot differentiate between a wide number of aspects of the claims experience. For example:

1.   The number of claims made by female policyholders whose cars were, at the time of the damage, being driven by men.
2.   The number of claims made by male policyholders whose cars, at the time of the damage, were being driven by women.
3.   The number of vehicle repairs carried out for which no claim is made.
4.   The number of accidents for which no repair is carried out.
5.   The difference in claims between high-mileage drivers and low mileage drivers, that is, the average miles driven per claim made – a measure, perhaps, of relative safety.
6.   The relative value and cost of the repair of vehicles driven by either sex.
7.   The context in which accidents take place, that is, urban, rural, motorway.
8.   The speed of vehicles when accidents occur.
9.   The meaning, in context, of *average*.

One other key factor underpins this headline: what did the journalist mean by 'better'? It can be seen that the headline had been used for the purposes of the journalist, while the research on which it was based was almost certainly for an entirely different purpose. The headline, though probably not the research itself, was meaningless in statistical terms.

It is vital when developing and applying statistical techniques that the claims made as a result of quantitative analysis are not subverted to other ends. Some common errors are:

DATA-COLLECTION

A common error is to rely on statistics for which the raw data has been collected in an unreliable manner. A good example of this is the measurement of footfall on the pathway outside a shop or fast-food outlet. Footfall (the number of people passing by) is generally regarded as a good guide to the likely number of customers for an outlet in the location. But even with the best of intentions and concerted effort, the count of passers by will have some degree of inaccuracy, simply because the method of measurement is unreliable. Often such numbers are compiled from the 'best estimates of those who know' – in other words, the measurement is entirely subjective. When these subjective measurements are summed, aggregated, averaged, and otherwise manipulated, they give results with a degree of accuracy which is entirely spurious. If the base data is no better than subjective estimate, then neither is the end result – however well it has been manipulated!

SAMPLING ERROR

On every occasion where a sample (rather than an entire population) is used, the opportunity exists for either accidental or deliberate bias to be introduced into the survey. The sample must be sufficiently large and properly selected for any meaningful data to be derived from it.

MISSING NUMBERS

Tying in with sampling error, is failure to provide (either deliberately or accidentally) the key figures which validate (or otherwise) the statistic. If the population is one million and the sample size is ten, then a statistic which claims '100 per cent of respondents agreed with our findings' is meaningless, unless the sample size and confidence factor are also quoted. In this case, the confidence in the accuracy of the answer would be low!

THE WRONG AVERAGE

There are three different types of average: the mean, the median, and the mode. These are in turn the arithmetic average (total divided by number), the middle one, and the most frequently occurring! It is important to know which average is being used in each context, and what it really tells you. That is, for what purpose the statistic is being quoted.

SPURIOUS CORRELATIONS

It is often found that there is some apparent correlation between the incidence of two events or happenings, and that somebody, somewhere states that because they appear to correlate, one must be the cause of the other. This causal chain view of the world has already been challenged in Part Three of this book. When a correlation is proposed, it is vital to understand why the proposer suggests it, and also to examine the evidence for and against the proposal – particularly to consider what other factors might explain the coincidence of the events. For example, creative people such as musicians, artists and writers are also often seen to be heavy drinkers or users of narcotic drugs. There is a positive correlation between artistry and substance abuse. Does one cause the other? Could I be a great artist if I were to drink more? Could I drink more if I were a great artist? However, a third factor must be allowed to intrude: personality. Perhaps an individual who challenges convention in one area of his or her life will also challenge convention in others; here, the causal link is not artistry or substance abuse but arises through personality. It is necessary to challenge the assumptions which underpin the causal link view of events.

MISLEADING PRESENTATION

Many statistics are reported graphically. Pictures of a situation are often easier for people to understand than the raw numbers derived from surveys and samples, and they also make it easier to misrepresent, either deliberately or inadvertently, the real situation. For example, 'an increase in the rate of decline' can be represented as an upward path – if it is the rate of decline which is being reported! The words tell the truth – things are getting worse – but the picture with its upward sloping line suggests the opposite! Similarly, a slow rate of growth in something can be presented as fast by the simple device of shortening the horizontal axis relative to the vertical axis on a graph.

It is always important to know:

a.   Where did the statistics come from?
b.   How big was the sample size?
c.   How representative of the total population was the sample?
d.   What average(s) have been used, and for what purpose?
e.   What point was the presenter of the statistics trying to prove?
f.   What counter-evidence was found, and perhaps not presented?
g.   What assumptions underpin the points being made?

SUMMARY

Good, accurate statistics are vital for performance measurement, but they cannot replace competent, informed management. Good, that is, accurate, well-founded and reliable statistics can tell the manager much about what is happening within the processes of a organization. That is the limit of their usefulness. The statistics say nothing about why the reported events occur – which is much more important. Statistics are simply a statement of the characteristics and events the managers have chosen to record. Demanding an improvement in the statistics – as managers often do – will ensure they get just that! But the processes, products or services of the organization will not change at all. Managers need to look behind the reported numbers, and consider the deeper aspects of the organization. Aspects to consider might include the quality and amount of supervision, the reliability and accuracy of equipment, the feelings and attitudes of the staff, and the expectations of the customers. (Many complaints are, after all, the result of a mismatch of the customers' expectations, created through marketing, and the reality of the product or service, as produced by the organization.)

Readers are reminded to develop their understanding further through the use of a good text on statistical quality methods, such as Logothetis (1992), or operations management such as Slack *et al.* (1995).

The statistics for SB Foods were, in the end, quite simple. Each line produced around thirty-six cakes per minute, and the rate-determining process for each line was the 'travelling oven'. (This is a metal conveyor belt that carries cake tins full of mix through a series of heated chambers, after the last of which the cake is deemed cooked.) Increasing the rate of travel meant increasing the temperature in each chamber to cook the cakes more rapidly, and decreasing the rate of travel meant decreasing the temperature in each chamber. Given that an 'optimum cooking cycle' had been developed for each recipe and throughput was a factor, in that it became obvious that the throughput rate was fixed.

This meant that every other variable in the factory could be determined by its ability to support the oven throughput rate, **and** that the factory capacity could now simply be determined – thirty-six cakes per minute * three travelling ovens * the number of minutes available for production – 108 cakes per minute or 6,480 per hour of production. To determine whether or not the process was under control was then straightforward. It was known that the output rate should be thirty-six cakes per minute per line if all was working optimally. The reality was, of course, different. It had already been established that the quality inspectors (QI) were seeing around a hundred packed cakes per minute, whereas the capacity determined was 108 cakes per minute. A sample over two hours on each of five successive days was taken, which showed that the average rate of throughput at the QI stage was ninety-six cakes. This varied over time from as few as 68 to as many as 125, which was beyond the notional maximum rate, and suggesting some ebb and flow in the process with both common and special causes of error present.

A measurement system was devised which captured the performance of the process at each of the key handover points, to determine the reasons for the variability in production. There turned out to be two prime causes. The first was disrupted flow from the mixing to depositing elements. Any disruption to that link caused a later interruption in the process flow, which caused lost production. The second was the processing element, where the cakes were being manually split, filled, cut, and reassembled. This process involved no machines at all, relying totally on the skill and expertise of the production workers. The performance of this area was significantly affected by the particular composition of the team on any given day. When all the 'right' people were on duty the area could be highly productive, but with other people present production volumes could fall off substantially.

While the first of the production problems was addressed by the use of more effective information, the second required the business to look at both job design and the skills mix necessary to perform the required tasks, which required considerable dexterity.

24.3.3 Job Design

Job design covers a range of issues associated with obtaining improvement in quality through enhanced job performance. It involves recognizing that, to a large extent, historically jobs have not been designed but more often have been initially described and subsequently allowed to evolve. Redesign may have been undertaken in the pursuit of greater efficiency and error reduction, including the application of work-study and organization and methods techniques, but this will have often served to fragment tasks into smaller parts. Frequently, managers do not actually know how any given employee actually uses the working day. Decisions about particular tasks have often been made without understanding of the whole process, or the purpose to be served.

This section proposes a variety of approaches which help to address the problems so caused, including dissatisfaction, fragmentation, and ineffectiveness.

Often, organizations are not systematically developed and work is allocated on the basis of current workload and/or past experience. In this way, work appears to move randomly around the organization. Consequently, little sense of ownership or responsibility for particular aspects of the work is engendered amongst the workforce. On that basis of allocation, the work has little or no meaning or value to them.

Creating natural work units (Figure 24.7) means adopting a different approach, whereby logical (or natural) groupings of work are created and allocated to individuals or teams, each accepting total responsibility for the work allocated. If the employees can identify with the work, there is a greater opportunity for them to take ownership and pride in accomplishment. A sense of ownership of the task and pride in its completion will often lead to improved quality through the individual feeling a sense of responsibility for the work.

Natural or logical groupings of tasks may be developed along a number of dimensions, dependent on what is to be achieved.

It is, of course, necessary to maintain an equal work-loading in the creation of these work units. This may mean either allocating more staff to a particularly heavy workload area, or creating vertical or horizontal sub-divisions of the work. This can be achieved by cross-matching categories, for example, matching a geographical area with an industrial sector, or by delimiting authority for taking action. An example of this is the use of lending authorities in banks, which are often split both horizontally and vertically.

Natural Work Units:

Geographical: each worker is assigned work arising from a particular location, for example a Country, County or District;

Organizational: each worker may be allocated work according to its divisional or departmental source;

Alphabetical: customer processing work may be divided according to alphabetical groupings, for example A-D, E-K, L-R, S-Z;

Numerical: Work in a supply depot may be allocated to clerks according to bin locations or part numbers;

Customer: Work may be allocated according to customer size or type. For example some Banks have divided customers into four principal sectors - large corporate, small business, high net-worth individuals, mass-market – and these divisions are reflected in their allocation of work;

Industry Sector: each employee specializes in servicing customers, or making products in particular market segments; for example engineering, property, education, medical and so on.

Figure 24.7 Natural work units.

For example, a lending officer may be able to authorize loans up to £240,000 in a particular market segment, while another lending officer is able to authorize loans from £240,001 – £1,000,000 in the same sector.

Jobs have often been broken down into tasks (and even sub-tasks), so that in order to create a complete product or service a team of five or six people is needed. In the service industries in particular, these people may be in separate areas or departments.

This is apparently highly efficient (in the sense of Adam Smith's pin factory) since the individuals become highly adept at the particular task. However, simple, repetitive tasks often provide little or no challenge, and hence provoke little interest from the employee. This lack of interest leads to dissatisfaction, falling productivity, increased error-rates and absenteeism, and often increased labour turnover. This last item leads to increased recruitment and training costs. This approach rests heavily on the work of Frederick Taylor (1911), and may be considered at least partly responsible for some of the problems of industrial relations seen in Western countries throughout the twentieth century.

Recombining tasks into complete jobs can help to counter this source of dissatisfaction, allowing the employee a sense of pride and achievement in what is created. Using task combination, the employee is given the chance to manage his or her work, rather than being simply required to repeat the same simple task over and over again.

To implement this approach, it is necessary to have a comprehensive understanding of the work process. This can be obtained through the use of the process-charting techniques discussed in Chapter 23 of this book. Analysis will need to be undertaken at the process operation or process detail level. An alternative is to involve the affected staff in the redesign. They already know the process, and from experience usually have a good understanding of how changes and improvements can be achieved.

Perhaps the most famous, and certainly extreme, example of this is Volvo in Sweden. Volvo redesigned a whole car factory, abandoned the production-line approach, and created a factory where teams built complete cars. Within this set up, each team member employed a range of expertise to complete the task. This may be contrasted with a conventional, production-line approach, where each worker carries out only a single task on each vehicle.

In most organizations, the worker works, while the supervisor or manager, at least notionally, carries out the tasks of planning, organizing, controlling and co-ordinating. Conventionally, the management sets tasks, performance standards, time frames and objectives for their subordinates, with little or no consultation. This may mean that workers feel no obligation to achieve those targets which they consider as belonging to the management rather than themselves.

Vertical loading (Figure 24.8) consists of allowing responsibility to descend through the organization, so that workers are allowed a degree of freedom in setting their own standards, thereby accepting a degree of responsibility for their achievements. Equally, degrees of latitude in decision making can be increased, empowering the employee to solve problems and take appropriate action.

A willingness to accept responsibility;

Ability which matches the increased requirements;

A level of training commensurate with the new responsibilities.

Figure 24.8 Key requirements for vertical loading.

Using the vertical loading approach can enable the reduction or removal of some control and checking activity, the assignment of more demanding tasks, and increased levels of authority amongst the workforce. This, if properly handled, should lead to a virtuous circle of improvement at the lower levels, and should enable managers to concentrate more effectively on the issues which really matter regarding their own work. Successful use of vertical loading depends upon three key characteristics amongst the workforce. Workers must be willing to accept the additional responsibility, they must have the appropriate ability and the level of training, and competence must be commensurate with the need of the task.

It is the responsibility of management to ensure that these conditions are met, and to provide appropriate training where necessary. Management must also ensure that scope is provided for the empowered staff to become accustomed to their freedoms, and to learn to use them wisely. At the outset, it is almost inevitable that mistakes and errors will occur while staff learn to apply skills of decision and judgement, which were previously the exclusive preserve of the management. Mistakes must be accepted at the initial stage as part of the learning process, and management must avoid the temptation to withdraw the freedoms and retake direct control while the employees learn to work with their new-found freedoms.

Decision making is based on information. Very often, employees exist in what might be considered an information vacuum. They are unaware of performance standards (or even if they exist), receive a performance appraisal once a year (or once every two years in many public sector organizations), and gain no specific current information on how well, or badly, they are performing their particular task. Where appraisal systems do exist, they are frequently used as instruments of blame and punishment, rather than as enablers of improvement.

Under these circumstances, the employees will set their own standards, either explicitly in conjunction with each other, or, more usually, on an individual basis – doing what they think is best for them. Nature abhors a vacuum, and in the absence of information from management, the workforce will create their own. This may, or may not, be in line with management expectations. To correct this, task feedback information (Figure 24.9) must be provided, and to be effective must be driven by the process itself. It must be as near 'real-time' as possible, must be continuously provided, and must be meaningful to the recipient. Failure to meet any of these conditions will render the information useless.

The word 'feedback' is one of the most commonly abused in the English language. In this book it means information drawn from the output side of a process, which is compared with a target, with the comparison being used as the basis for adjusting the input to the process.

Using the insights provided by Ohno and the power of contemporary information technology, none of these requirements is difficult to achieve. However, the most frequent difficulties arise with the last requirement. What constitutes meaningful

Driven by the process itself;
Real time (or as near as possible);
Continuous;
Meaningful (it must be in the recipient's language).

Figure 24.9 Task feedback information.

information for a manager may be very different to that for the worker affected. For instance, a manager may wish to work with reports expressed in terms of profit and loss, that is, with monetary measurements of performance. For workers in the service department of a car dealership, monetary measures may be meaningless. They may measure performance in terms of the number of vehicles serviced, or the level of utilization of servicing bays. It is therefore useless to provide information to these individuals on profit or loss, since they cannot use that data for control and self-management purposes. It is more useful, and more effective, to use information technology to provide information to each recipient which is meaningful in their own terms.

The idea of the self-managed work team is essentially an extension of vertical loading. While an overall task is set, the team are free to organize themselves towards its achievement, having either no supervisor, or appointing their own from within the team, often on a rotational basis. In extreme cases, the self-managed work team will take responsibility for organizing holiday schedules and other activities, which have traditionally been regarded as the exclusive province of management. The team will have the freedom and responsibility to devise improvements and changes within a process, and will often have ways of communicating successes and failures to other teams.

THE QUALITY FUNCTION

The role and position of the quality function are of great importance in relation to both the job design and the position within the organization.

A normal position for the quality inspectors, quality control or assurance manager in many organizations is as a direct reportee of the production manager. This serves to institutionalize the potential conflict between them, and allows the production manager the final decision.

Such an approach enables the production manager to override quality decisions in the pursuit of some other interest, for example, shipping a full order, regardless of quality, to satisfy the customer in the short term. It also enables the manipulation of other data such as productivity, labour utilization, and even reject/rework levels.

It is vital that the quality assurance function enjoys complete independence from the production function, in order that effective inspection and audit become possible. In a company that has fully adopted the quality ethic, this becomes a much less significant issue since quality ideas will be embedded in the workforce and quality standards will be clearly defined and recognized. In these circumstances the quality decisions, to a large extent, may make themselves. There will be limited scope for arbitrary decisions.

A key factor in creating an organization for quality is the recognition of processes, and the consequent realization that each part of a process has customers, either internal or external. A company which uses these processes as the cornerstone of the way in which it is organized, and sets its quality criteria in recognition of the needs of customers, will become an organization for quality.

The change mechanisms established at SB Foods encouraged and supported the engagement of all the staff in contributing to the changes necessary. Through the mechanisms of IP and quality circles in particular, they were able substantially to participate in the redesign of their jobs (notwithstanding certain language difficulties). The redesign extended the reach and scope of many positions, reducing the number of 'handovers' in the production process, while giving purpose and focus to the role of the production managers who, for the first time, had complete control of their processes. In concert with the redesigned jobs, staff were able to determine the information they needed to allow them to carry out their tasks effectively and efficiently.

The recognition of the farcical nature of the existing quality inspection process was a major breakthrough. Historically, positions in the QI team had been allocated either to those unable to undertake the hard, physical work of cake production or to those whose seniority had 'earned them the right to an easy time'. The changes in the manufacturing process, and the devolution of effective control to the production staff, mean that the QI function was abolished. The former QI staff were redeployed as far as possible within the 'processing' element of the manufacturing process, which it had been established was the primary source of quality problems.

24.4 Reflections and Next Steps

This second intervention in SB Foods has demonstrated significant progress. Starting from the diagnosis provided in the previous chapter, the project has been able to focus at a lower level of recursion, and begin to develop new approaches to staff engagement, interaction and communication. A shared, aligned view of the future has been generated, together with an understanding of what is required to achieve it, and processes have been properly understood and control made more effective. The beginnings of effective measurement have been put in place and performance improvements have been delivered. Jobs have been redesigned with the active involvement of the affected staff, who feel a greater sense of ownership and responsibility.

Summary

This chapter has extended the case study, and has introduced a number of additional tools and techniques to help to address the situation. The intention has been to show what can be done, and to set out the logical flow of choices. The assumptions and world views underpinning the multiple methodologies in use have been respected, but given new meaning by being applied in the context of a systemic intervention. Limitations to autonomy have been understood and accommodated. A potentially sustainable improvement has been generated.

In the final chapter, tools will be introduced to help to ensure that potential is realized.

KEY LEARNING POINTS

A variety of tools and methods can be used in context, and in conjunction, with each other, to address complex problems;

Any one tool will necessarily focus on part of the problem to be addressed;

Statistical techniques are essential to aid real understanding, but must be used with intelligence and knowledge;

Interactive planning and quality circles can be used together to engage the whole workforce;

Process examination and review can highlight the potential for real improvement;

Job design can be used as a device for both engaging staff and solving the problems;

Meaningful measurement is essential to success.

Question

Consider SB Foods' production process through the 'Toyota Production System' approach, and develop an information solution to support it.

25 Final Intervention

And now, the end is near

(Paul Anka, 1967)

Introduction

This chapter completes the SB Foods case study by considering external factors. It introduces the ideas of Supplier Development, embraced very strongly by Japanese businesses, benchmarking – which is now widely used both internally and externally – and, of course, the design and development of quality management systems (QMS). Chapter 21 has already introduced contemporary approaches to the QMS; this chapter will reflect a more conventional approach.

25.1 Recap

SB Foods has progressed from its initial disordered state to one where it is internally consistent, has sound processes with well-designed jobs, and has clear internal performance criteria and achievement. This is all good progress, but it is not enough. To do the best possible job internally is one thing, but sustainability demands that the organization fully engages with the world outside itself. That means comparing its performance with that of its neighbours and competitors, working with its suppliers to bring their performance up to what is required, and, critically, exposing its performance to some form of audit through pursuit of recognition of its quality performance.

Figure 25.1 shows how benchmarking, supplier development, and QMS inform the information flows between the core elements of the process.

25.2 Benchmarking

It is inadequate to define improvement relative to internal measurements only. Organizations must define quality and improvement in terms of customers' requirements, and relative to the 'best' of the competition. The foundation for quality improvement is to know how good or bad a set of products and services are when compared to others in the same market place, particularly as regards the way they are perceived by customers. The 'fact' that one product or service is technically better than another (as might be argued for the Macintosh and Sun computer operating systems when compared with that from Microsoft) is not enough. Microsoft, through more effective interaction with its customers, has achieved and sustained a dominant market

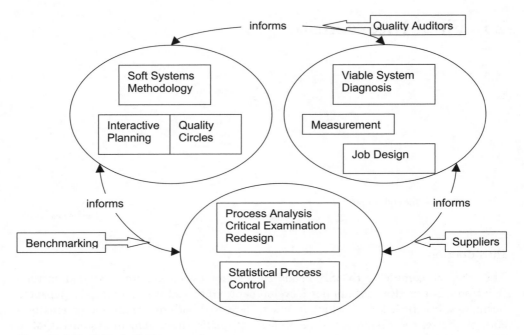

Figure 25.1 Tools for the final intervention.

position. It is creating the foundation for quality improvement – across all aspects of the product or service – which benchmarking helps to establish. One particular benchmark now being used by many organizations is the ISO 9000 series, which provides the standard for quality management systems and is thought by some to create competitive advantage.

25.2.1 What is Benchmarking?

Benchmarking, also now often called 'best practice' – and reinterpreted and broadened for the UK public sector as 'best value' – is used by large and small organizations through-out the world to help them understand their own performance against the best that they can measure. This enables them to develop and grow their businesses more profitably.

Benchmarking is a process of comparison between the performance characteristics of separate, often competing, organizations, intended to enable each participant to improve its own performance in the market place.

Benchmarking allows us to obtain a clearer understanding of competitors' success factors, and of customers' requirements. This understanding will lead to reduced complaints, a sharper focus on customer needs, and higher levels of customer satisfaction. Discovering process improvements will help to reduce the costs associated with rework, rectification, waste, and other quality problems.

Benchmarking will also enable innovations (either of process or product) to spread more rapidly through an industry, and across industries where appropriate – for example, in supply or distribution logistics, where many problems are similar regardless of the industry.

Benchmarking involves a number of simple steps. The first establishes what, from the customer's perspective, makes the difference between one supplier of a product or service, and another. It is important to remember that the customer's *perception* – not the actual, technical quality of the product or service is what matters. The second step is setting standards according to the best practice found, that is, regarding best practice as the 'benchmark' for the organization's performance. The third step is to determine by what means the benchmark organization achieves those standards. The final step is utilizing the capabilities of the staff to meet, and if possible exceed, the standards observed.

It is important to understand that what is important in benchmarking is not the industry but the core characteristics of the product, service, or activity. While it may be ideal to benchmark one airline against another, this may be difficult for reasons of competition, politics, or law (for example, where such behaviour may be regarded as anti-competitive or likely to lead to cartel pricing). On the other hand, it is perfectly reasonable to compare an airline's marketing or logistics function with those of a newspaper or a bread bakery. This is because the products share a significant characteristic: nobody buys yesterday's bread or newspaper, and no one can occupy an airline seat once the flight has left! A similarly useful comparison can be drawn between customer and enquiry handling in a bank, and that at an airline counter, or in a department store. The core process may be the same, even though the particular questions may be very different.

Benchmarking provides a rigorous framework through which the benefits outlined above can be obtained. It enables a disciplined, demanding assessment of performance in areas which are crucial to the particular organization. It also enables errors and mistakes already made by others to be avoided, thus preventing further reinvention of the wheel.

Two major limitations on performance improvement can be usefully addressed through benchmarking. First is knowledge limitation, which so often affects organizational performance. Experience and knowledge are often bound by the particular environment in which they are gained. Unless individuals have the opportunity of wider exposure, they are largely closed off from developments which could improve their process. Thus they become content with the way things are, because they know of nothing different or better.

Second, the syndrome known as NIH (Not Invented Here) can be overcome through benchmarking. NIH is a typical response by many organizations and employees to proposed changes to improve performance. It is often accompanied by remarks such as 'that might work alright in xxxx, but it just wouldn't apply here', frequently supported by 'because we're unique', 'our circumstances are different', or 'our customers don't expect', or some similar excuse. The truth is that NIH is a defensive ploy, intended to inhibit the disruption to established patterns and habits of work, and the effort that is often associated with a change programme. If, however, the employees who will be affected by a change are involved in its design through the benchmarking programme, they will be much less likely to resist change and more likely to develop unique aspects which will 'make it work here'.

Overall, benchmarking requires senior management commitment, particularly to supporting actions arising from the exploration. It also requires staff to be trained and guided in the process, to ensure that maximum benefit is obtained. Finally, it requires allocation of part of the relevant employee's time to enable it to be carried out.

25.2.2 How is Benchmarking Done?

There are only five steps (Figure 25.2) to a benchmarking process, regardless of the size of the company involved. However, larger companies may indulge in greater amounts of data-gathering than smaller ones, and may have to be conscious of issues surrounding anti-competitive or monopolistic behaviour.

The first step, appraising and identifying which characteristics to benchmark, can be achieved through Pareto analysis. While it is possible to benchmark every characteristic of a process, the return to the company from doing so will vary substantially. Remembering Juran's comment on 'the vital few, the useful many', it is worth trying to determine at the outset which activities the company needs to excel in to succeed in its particular business. A substantial improvement in a process which delivers no benefit to customers will not necessarily and directly improve the competitive position, although it may generate improvement in profit performance – which may be of great importance. Quality benchmarks might include aspects such as reliability, longevity, consistency, accuracy, levels of in-process rework or rectification, service intervals, after-sales response, and so on. Factors that affect profitability – and which may enable more effective competition through reduction in prices – include reduction in rework, working stocks, and inventory levels. Profitability is also affected by relationships between factors such as sales dollars (or other currency) per employee, enquiry to sale conversion rates, space utilization and, increasingly, the effectiveness in use of management information systems.

The selection criteria for projects should be based on delivery of maximum benefit to the customer, rather than on matters which might be considered as exciting or interesting to a particular professional group. Approaches based on the latter view often lead to major disappointment. Characteristics to be benchmarked should be:

> those which are of genuine concern to the customer;
> those which are of material importance to the organization;
> those where a problem is recognized.

The second step is deciding which other organizations to benchmark with. In the case of a very large, perhaps divisionalized, operation, it may be perfectly reasonable to start by internal benchmarking, for example, comparing the distribution logistics processes of two factories. If this is not possible, then it is necessary to look outside the organization for benchmarking partners. A starting point is to ask the customers who they regard as the best in your particular business, after all it is the customers that you are trying to satisfy. This will also help to identify those characteristics of performance which the customers regard as important.

Step 1) Identifying what characteristics to benchmark;

Step 2) Identifying benchmarking partners;

Step 3) Designing the data gathering methodology;

Step 4) Selecting analytical tools;

Step 5) Implementing changes.

Figure 25.2 Five steps in benchmarking.

Other sources include the press, trade and industry associations, industry expert consultants, or academics. Looking overseas, the various trade commissions, embassies, and state departments should be able to provide useful leads. For example, in Hong Kong the Productivity Council might be able to help, while in the UK there are a number of organizations focused on benchmarking practice and co-operation.

There are four key issues to address in selecting benchmarking partners:

a. Do the companies have some knowledge of each other?
b. Is there a customer–supplier relationship already?
c. Is the partners' experience directly relevant to our needs?
d. Are they as good as their reputation suggests?

It is quite normal for a company's reputation to outlast the quality of its goods or services; equally, some companies with established 'bad' reputations may have made substantial performance improvements. For example, in the 1970s the FIAT Company developed a reputation for building cars which rusted very quickly and very badly. This has not been the case for many years, yet the bad reputation still surrounds their products despite the evidence on the roads that the reputation is unfair.

Finally, and as mentioned before, is the exchange of information with this partner permissible? Apart from any legislative issues, organizations need to be aware of limitations on the transfer of technology to and from certain countries, and for certain purposes. These general cautions need to be supported by appropriate legal advice and, of course, with the application of common sense.

The third step, designing the data-gathering methodology, moves beyond the basics of ensuring that any statistical methods are rigorously applied and the results meaningful, to the real issue of how physically to obtain the information. The first and most readily available sources are in the public domain, for example, company annual reports, press articles, trade association journals and libraries, academic studies (where these have been undertaken and published), and from the various bodies and consultancies which specialize in enabling benchmarking. While normally direct competitors will only exchange data through a third party, such as a trade association, some may be amenable to a direct contact – particularly if the company approaching them is able to offer comparable assistance to them on another issue. For example, you may swap information on staff retention and development programmes for information on distribution logistics. As long as each party perceives there to be a fair exchange (in terms of problems solved) the volume of data will probably not be an obstruction. What is vital at this stage is that the data necessary to enable the benchmarking to be carried out is identified right at the outset. Nothing is worse than having to return to the partner for more information; nothing is more unhelpful than designing improvements based on incomplete or inaccurate information.

The fourth step reflects the similar stage in process review. The key difference is that rather than seeking general improvement, the search in the benchmarking exercise is for specific differences between processes which give one a significant performance margin over the other. This recognition of the performance gap is the basis for improvement; always recognizing that what works for one company in one set of circumstances will not necessarily work for another in a different set.

The fifth and final step is implementing changes. Technically, this is quite straightforward. New performance standards need to be set, based on the improvement scope identified. The lowest level of management with an overview of the whole process affected, appropriately supported, needs to take direct responsibility for implementing the changes. Additional resources must be provided to support the changes if required. For example, overtime working may be necessary to create a window, enabling the absorption of disruption associated with a particular change. This might occur in a despatch unit, where a redesign of the storage layout could demand that a significant amount of space be created in the short term. Finally, a performance monitoring programme must be implemented to make progress visible.

Benchmarking, like quality improvement, is never complete. It is a continuing process, and although the incremental gains from the first exercise are likely to be the largest, the process should be continued to ensure that the organization always reflects best practice in the particular area.

25.2.3 Critical Review

Benchmarking is essentially an exercise in organizational humility. It demands that rather than being complacent about how good an organization is, it is necessary to respect the idea that there may be others in the industry who carry out a particular process more effectively. Effective means cheaper, quicker and more closely meeting customer expectations. The organization then has to set out to learn from these higher performers.

Technically, as has been shown, benchmarking is not a difficult process. Each of the five steps is relatively straightforward and, overall, it amounts to emulating the best and trying to improve on their performance. As any author will tell you, it is far harder to write an original book than to prepare a review or critique of another's.

The risk with benchmarking is that the organization only aspires to be as good as the rest – and sets its sights accordingly. This means it simply copies others' practices, without adapting them to the particular and unique set of circumstances in which it operates. Relying on such a model (a model is simply a representation of reality), the organization will never achieve the levels of performance of the organization copied. This is because the model does not reveal everything about the organization or its circumstances, only those characteristics which the modeller thought important.

The second problem with straight copying is, of course, that no competitive advantage is gained. The process simply levels the playing field further, reducing diversity in the market and thereby reducing effective consumer choice. If there is no measurable difference between products or services, then purchasers will make their choices on other criteria such as convenience, accessibility, or taste (fashion), the last of which is extremely fickle.

Benchmarking is a potentially valuable technique for quickly lifting the performance of an organization. However, establishing benchmarks must be used as the platform for significant improvement over the best, if it is genuinely to improve the competitive position of the organization rather than simply keep it in the game.

The UK food production industry is characterized by strong competition between a relatively small number of major suppliers to a very small number of major customers: the supermarket chains. Benchmarking externally was too difficult for SB Foods – the only real benchmark target within the industry was a direct competitor. In this instance, SB Foods initially chose to benchmark factories A and B against each other – their processes and products were sufficiently similar for this to be meaningful. The principal benefits derived from the approach were:

– comparisons of processes which demonstrated the progress made;
– transfer of knowledge between the two sites so that the performance of both improved;
– engagement of the staff and management with each other, and the creation of friendly competition between the staff to demonstrably be the best;
– combined working on new product development by bringing together the development team with the production staff to create a more effective product launch process, because the benchmarking highlighted that as a major stumbling block.

Within the time limitations of the project, benchmarking did not extend to other businesses – although there was an approach to a nearby pie factory.

25.3 Supplier Development

Suppliers of both materials and services are critical to the achievement of quality. The quality of material inputs to a manufacturing process are strong determinants of the quality of output. The quality of bought-in services, such as distribution and logistics, accounting, information technology support, and building or machine maintenance, affects either the production process or the interface with the customer, for example through deliveries or invoicing. Clearly, a part of being a quality organization is ensuring that the external factors affecting the input and output ends of the internal processes meet the requisite quality standard.

25.3.1 What is Supplier Development?

Supplier development is best thought of as a business policy espoused by a company which is serious about achieving quality. It involves a commitment by that company to set and attain internal quality standards which meet the requirements of its customers, and to support its suppliers in enabling them to meet those same requirements.

Traditionally, companies wishing to exercise a degree of control of the upstream or downstream elements of the value chain have followed the route of vertical integration, either through development of their own services, or through acquisition. However, these traditional routes have usually proved to be less than fully successful. The company loses the focus on its core business, often operating the other parts of the business less successfully, and at greater cost than specialists, so that instead of excelling at one task it becomes mediocre at many. Equally, it is frequently the case that overall profitability is adversely affected. Supplier development moves away from this strategy, recognizing its inherent difficulties and limitations, and respecting the expertise and knowledge specific to the fulfilment of a particular need.

Supplier development requires that the company changes its posture in relation to its suppliers. Traditionally, the buyer–supplier relationship is adversarial, each party seeking to maximize its own benefit from the relationship. Supplier development requires that this relationship become co-operative or collaborative, such that buyer and supplier work together to maximize mutual interests. This demands a change in buying processes. The placing of orders based on lowest price and sealed tenders has to cease, with a change to open exchange of information and negotiations based on a willingness to achieve an equitable outcome for both parties. For example, the need for each party to generate an adequate return on its efforts must be respected.

A move towards using a single supplier is also advocated by some writers, (for example, Deming, 1986: 35–40). This policy has both advantages and drawbacks. Positively, utilizing a single source of supply should ensure greater reliability of inputs in terms of consistency, lack of variability (that is, closer adherence to standards), and the potential for continually improving standards and reduced paperwork. From the supplier's perspective, the company is perhaps assured of a particular level of order, potentially higher order values, greater certainty in its business planning and longer production runs with bigger batch sizes (reducing down-time and set-up time, which both in turn may increase productivity), more reliable payment, and availability of additional expertise (from their customer).

Looking at the drawbacks, the buying organization may close itself off to other options, reducing the opportunity for speculative or spot purchases of materials (which meet requirements), and may reduce its leverage in price negotiations with the supplier, particularly when supplier power is high (Porter, 1980). The organization becomes vulnerable to changes in strategy, tactics, or performance by its supplier. This is particularly important when the product or service purchased is critical to the process. An example of this would be when distribution is contracted out to a dedicated haulage firm which then, for reasons unrelated to the particular contract, experiences financial or other difficulties, such as a strike, or limitation on the availability of vehicles. From the supplier's perspective, becoming the sole source of supply to a particular organization may involve the dedication of a significant proportion of its resources to fulfilling that order. In this case, it in turn may become vulnerable to any difficulties experienced by its customer, or any change of product or strategy on its part. For example, if the buyer ceases to produce a particular product, or suffers from extensive competition leading to falling volumes, the fortunes of the supplier are similarly affected. This is a particular issue for small businesses acting as specialist suppliers to large organizations. The maintenance of the relationship, and the volume of resources required to maintain the supply, can swamp the small company.

The foregoing comments are general considerations which must be addressed before any sole supplier relationship is agreed. It may be that both parties feel that the advantages outweigh the disadvantages and associated risks in the particular case, and choose to proceed. On the other hand, one or the other may find that the relationship would make them especially vulnerable, in which case they should instead seek alternative arrangements.

Clearly, there is a significant degree of risk to a supplier if the agreement with a buyer constitutes a significant proportion of the total business, and for whatever reason limits the ability of the supplier to undertake business with other parties. That being said, there is also significant potential advantage to the buying organization in successfully pursuing the strategy of supplier development, particularly in the creation of a long-term and stable relationship.

25.3.2 How is Supplier Development Undertaken?

The decision to pursue a policy of supplier development can only reasonably be undertaken by an organization already fully committed to quality, and which recognizes that improved input quality is necessary to support its implementation programme. To pursue this policy when the organization is not already achieving high standards may well be seen by the supplier as an attempt to shift the blame for quality failure. Such an approach is unlikely to be well received.

Supplier development takes place in seven stages (Figure 25.3). The first stage is crucial. If the senior management are not committed to the process and its outcomes (including the need to provide short-term financial support and to commit workforce resources to the strategy), it will fail.

The second stage is to audit and evaluate the processes in which the suppliers' inputs are used, to ensure that these meet the current internal expectations. Similarly, the inputs themselves must be formally evaluated. If a process is failing because of internal factors, no amount of supplier development will cure it. Similarly, if suppliers are to be approached to improve their performance, it is vital that the buyer can precisely demonstrate the need by showing the impact on its own output.

The third stage is for the buying organization to determine what standards it expects its suppliers to achieve and, consequently, what changes are necessary and which are desirable. It is important to discriminate between those aspects which are essential to acceptable performance (that is, meeting requirements) and those which would be beneficial in the longer term, but are not currently essential. This stage, taken together with the second stage, defines the gap between the current performance of the supplier and the necessary performance. This defines the initial scope for the supplier development strategy and provides a basis for measuring subsequent performance improvement.

The first three stages simply prepare the ground for approaching suppliers. The buying organization is now equipped with the information necessary to engage in meaningful discussions. The fourth stage is the development of agreement with the identified suppliers. Clearly, if the suppliers are not willing to join in with the programme, then nothing is lost, since the organization is fully prepared to approach alternative sources with a clear idea of its expectations. The supplying organization must be prepared to make the same commitment to improving performance as the buying organization. The basis of moving forward should be a written agreement, setting out the aims and objectives of the programme and the benefits to be delivered.

Stage 1) Senior Management commitment to Supplier Development;

Stage 2) Audit & evaluation of internal standards;

Stage 3) Define and quantify the desirable or necessary changes;

Stage 4) Develop agreement with identified suppliers;

Stage 5) Form joint teams and develop training programme (if necessary);

Stage 6) Teams define precise objectives, deliverables and timescale;

Stage 7) Implement changes and monitor impacts.

Figure 25.3 Seven stages of supplier development.

Stage five is the formation of joint problem-solving teams, tasked with pursuing the various benefits. These should take the form of quality circles, and may require training or development input in order to function effectively. Ideally, these teams should include representatives of all relevant functions in the two organizations. For example, a team made up exclusively of product buyers and sales staff would not be effective, since they are likely to have only limited knowledge of the problems in use of the particular product or service. Operational staff must be regarded as fundamental to such a team, which should have the authority to draw on other resources when appropriate, for example, accounting staff (for costings), statisticians (for the development of process control measurement), and so on.

The sixth stage is the implementation phase, when the designated teams should initially define precise objectives, tasks, and timescales in the light of the current performance gap. Implementation itself should more or less follow the pattern of quality circle operation, using the same quality tools and techniques.

Finally, stage seven is concerned with implementing any changes arising, and monitoring the impacts against the expected benefits. It may be that for very large organizations a supervisory or steering board is required to oversee the implementation programme (particularly if a part of the strategy is to transfer the learning which takes place to other parts of the respective operations). For smaller organizations this should not be necessary.

Like most other aspects of a quality programme, supplier development can never be considered as complete. It is an ongoing, iterative process, which aims to improve performance continually for the benefit of both parties.

25.3.3 Critique of Supplier Development

There is clearly significant benefit to be gained by buyer and supplier organizations working together to improve performance. They can streamline processes, reduce costs, enhance productivity, and more adequately satisfy their customers' expectations. The drawbacks to this strategy principally surround the issue of vulnerability of either the supplier or buyer through dependence on a single source. This vulnerability relates to financial leverage, and to the risks of failure to supply.

To be successful, a supplier development strategy relies upon absolute commitment by both parties to making the arrangement work, and willingness and intent to act in the utmost good faith at all times.

The principal suppliers to SB Foods were the major producers of raw materials: flour, eggs, cream, butter, margarine, sugar, and so on. These suppliers were enormous compared to SB Foods – the flour supplier, for example, being one of only two significant, mass-market providers in its industry. The ability of SB Foods to work with such suppliers to deliver improvement was very limited. Their leverage was very low, and they could provide no meaningful incentive to the supplier (a Victuals Group company) to improve the product or service – although they did achieve a renewed engagement of the supplier's technical team with their own development staff. This simplified and enhanced the process of product development, which ultimately fed through to production changes.

SB Foods themselves were, of course, suppliers to the retail food industry – again dominated by a small number of very large companies. The reality for SB Foods is that they remain exposed – unable to manage their suppliers meaningfully, and with insufficient importance to their major customers to really influence them. Their core product, cake, is essentially undifferentiated and, as such, they can have only limited bargaining power.

25.4 Quality Management Systems

Without adherence to a QMS, it is impossible for the organization to know and record how well (or badly) it is performing. There are many quality management systems in existence which do not conform to the ISO 9000 standard.

This chapter will not provide a full guide to the development and implementation of a QMS. That task is beyond the intended scope of the book, and better left to a dedicated work of which there are several (for example, Hoyle, 2006). What this chapter does seek to achieve is a broad understanding of the nature and purpose of a QMS, its utility and limitations. A specific interpretation of the ISO 9000: 2000 series is provided.

25.4.1 What is ISO 9000?

ISO 9000 is one of a series of quality management systems standards developed over a long period of time, beginning with quality standards in the defence industry. For example, NATO began developing quality standards in the late 1940s, to enable a degree of harmonization between co-operating military forces. These standards were consolidated and revised in DefStans (Defence Standards) 05-08, 05-25, 05-25 and 05-28 between 1951 and 1973. Dominant systems in the civil world include BS5750 (the British standard) and EN29000 (the European standard), as well as unique local systems which have been developed in several countries and industries such as QS9000 in the motor industry. However, ISO 9000 is generally accepted as the standard for quality systems practice in most countries.

A QMS constitutes a formal record of an organization's method of managing the quality of its products or services. It enables the organization to demonstrate to itself, its customers, and, importantly, to an independent certification body, that it has established an effective system for managing the quality of its products or services. Meeting the accreditation standards permits the organization to claim quality certification for its products and services, and to advertise the fact. This is seen as an important factor by many organizations, and there is a trend in certain areas, notably in the public sector and parts of the construction industry, particularly in South East Asia, to only deal with quality accredited organizations. A QMS will also assist the organization in attempting to formalize its operations and attain consistency of outputs.

The ISO 9000: 2000 Series:

BS EN ISO 9000: 2000: Fundamentals and vocabulary;
BS EN ISO 9001: 2000: Quality management system requirements;
BS EN ISO 9004: 2000: Guidelines for Performance Improvements;

Figure 25.4 The ISO 9000: 2000 series.

As already stated, this chapter is not seen as the place for a full description of the standards. However, it is clear that they are comprehensive in their coverage, ranging from product or service development to after-sales service. There is within this series of documents a clear bias towards the manufacturing sector. After all, this is where the process started and where greatest use continues to be made of the standards. The ISO 9000: 2000 family of standards, launched at the end of 2000, attempts to harmonize all the standards and remove the manufacturing bias.

25.4.2 ISO 9000: 2000 Interpreted

The revision to the ISO 9000 family of standards was adopted in late 2000. This was a much more substantial revision than that of 1994.

Overall, the 1994 family of standards (ISO 9001, 9002, 9003, 9004) was consolidated into a single standard ISO 9001: 2000, with a new ISO 9004: 2000 providing a set of guidelines for continuous improvement. The standard has a substantially increased customer focus, while an attempt has been made to reduce the manufacturing bias. The scope has been widened to include more management elements, and all of the core requirements of the 1994 version of ISO 9001 continue to be present, but the new standard restructures these (and other elements) under four headings:

> Management Responsibility
> Resource Management
> Process Management
> Measurement and Analysis, Improvement

The aim of these changes is to encourage organizations to think about their management processes, and react to the changing demands placed upon them.

Management responsibility is extended to include a specific responsibility for ensuring continuous improvement and benchmarking (relying on ISO 9004: 2000 for guidance), and for management review. There is a much greater emphasis on supplier relationships, customer satisfaction, market and competitor analysis, and on the development of improvement opportunities.

Resource management is extended to focus very clearly on human resource management – especially the match of the skills of the individual to the requirements of the task. A major shift in emphasis here enables the organization to rely extensively on the skills-based approach and, consequently, to minimize the extent of procedural documentation required to support the system. Issues such as Health and Safety, and Environment and Financial Management, as part of the overall 'well being' of the enterprise are also given prominence.

Particular issues in this respect will be to consider the means by which the quality policy message is conveyed to employees and sub-contractors, and to ensure that all employees understand their contribution to quality. The standard expects the organization to be able to demonstrate that every employee will be provided with the opportunity to realize her or his full potential and contribution to the organization.

The shift towards process management reflects the shift in managerial thinking in recent years. Within this area there is a requirement for appropriate risk analysis, recognition of the interactions between departments and functions (the internal customer chain), capability to respond to changing customer expectations, formal and documented review of capabilities, and a focus on the delivery and post-delivery activity. It is no longer adequate for an organization to be able to demonstrate that 'we made it right' – it also has to be able to demonstrate that it was delivered 'right' and serviced 'right'. Rather than a focus on the physical aspects of product quality, the shift is towards the customers' total experience of dealing with the organization – perhaps reflecting the thinking of Taguchi and Feigenbaum.

Measurement and analysis simply requires that an appropriate performance measurement system is in place. This captures the adherence (or otherwise) of the product or service to the standards specified. This in turn enables audit of the product or service delivered and monitoring of customer satisfaction, of competitor and market performance, and demonstrates continuous improvement. For certification under ISO 9000: 2000, it's what you do with it that counts!

25.4.3 ISO 9000: 2000 – The Limitations

It is undeniable that the revised standard is a major step forward from the 1994 revision. It explicitly recognizes the process-oriented nature of many organizations, attempts to address the manufacturing bias, and pays particular attention to the 'people' issues within organizations – perhaps recognizing that this is an area in which many quality initiatives fail.

There are, however, a number of limitations:

1. Notwithstanding the process orientation, it continues to reflect a 'static' interpretation of organization. It deals with *what*, not *how*.
2. It does not explicitly address the issue of business or organizational benefit.
3. The process orientation is to be welcomed, but not enough emphasis has been placed on developing the 'special processes'.
4. The focus on people (especially in the service sector) as the heart of quality is still significantly underplayed.
5. It retains the potential limitations of bureaucracy, disuse and disrepute associated with the current standard.

As organizations have made the transition from the old to the new standard, it becomes more and more apparent that there are limitations of real understanding of organization and skills management (on both their part and that of their external auditors). This inhibits the achievement of the full potential benefits of the changed standard. The potential advantages offered could be eradicated if the designers of quality management systems continue to work with the same procedure-focused, mechanistic, and bureaucratic mindset that has so often been employed in the past.

A compliant QMS based on the traditional 'paper record' and 'checklist' approach will clearly, and very rapidly, become a bureaucratic nightmare, with ever more people required simply to maintain the system – let alone collate, analyse, interpret, and synthesize data in such a way that it can be used as a springboard for performance improvement. In the service sector in particular, the variability of requirements of individual customers would be impossible to track properly.

25.4.4 How is a QMS Constructed?

Construction of a QMS relies upon the use of the ISO 9000 series to provide guidelines and instructions, adherence to which ensures that the system will meet certification standards. As with every aspect of quality, the development of an effective QMS relies on a systematic approach.

Kanji and Asher (1996) propose a thirteen-step programme (Figure 25.5) of actions. Step 1, commitment to the quality management approach, has already been met on several occasions. This commitment is fundamental to any aspect of achieving quality. Unfortunately, managers find it far easier to commit themselves to a QMS than they do to commit themselves to quality. If you have the latter, that implies commitment to the QMS. If you only have commitment to the QMS, you have a system which will not only fail to assist the drive for quality but will enable the manager to decide precisely who to blame (other than her- or himself) for that failure. It will become an instrument of the penal system rather than a guide for the successful pursuit of quality. An effective QMS can only be created within the context of a fully supported quality programme.

Step 2, defining the scope of activities to be included, seems to be a little short-sighted. If an organization is to be effective in its quality drive, then *every* part of it must fall within the QMS. There will certainly be a need to assess priorities for inclusion in the QMS – production before personnel and the canteen, perhaps – but the ultimate

Kanji & Asher:

Step 1) Obtain management understanding of, and commitment to, the quality management approach;

Step 2) Define the scope of the activities to be included in the QMS;

Step 3) Define the organizational structure and responsibilities of those within the scope of the QMS;

Step 4) Audit the existing systems and procedures against the requirements of the standard;

Step 5) Develop a plan to write the necessary procedures;

Step 6) Train sufficient personnel to write their own procedures;

Step 7) Draft and edit the procedures and gain agreement to them;

Step 8) Compile a draft quality manual;

Step 9) Implement the system on a trial basis;

Step 10) Train internal auditors to carry out audits of the system and its operation;

Step 11) Revise the operation of the system in light of the results of audits and other information;

Step 12) Apply for registration (sometimes called third party approval) from an accredited body;

Step 13) Maintain the system by internal audit, using it as an opportunity to improve.

Figure 25.5 Thirteen steps to a quality management system.

aim should be an all-inclusive system. This system may even extend to link with those of suppliers where appropriate.

Step 3, defining the organizational structure and responsibilities, while necessary, carries the danger of inhibiting necessary organizational change. While it is vital that the appropriate organizational structure is in use, and that responsibilities are clearly defined, it is essential to realize that the correct organizational form is, or may be, a rapidly changing element. The dynamism and fluidity of the organizational environment demand this. Therefore, it must be the case that the organizational structure and responsibilities define the organization of the QMS – not the other way around.

The fourth, fifth, sixth, and seventh steps – audit of current systems and procedures and development of new procedures – are fundamental to the achievement of the QMS. However, it may be preferable to place the sixth element in fourth place, and extend the training element such that operational staff are trained to audit and review their own processes, as well as develop the appropriate documentation. No one else knows a job better than the people who do it. Step 8, the draft quality procedures manual, is a product of the four steps which precede it. A warning must be applied to the procedures issue now. The revised standard demands only a very limited set of compulsory procedures. To minimize the bureaucracy associated with the QMS, organizations should reflect on how many additional procedures they really need to ensure consistency of operation. Wherever possible, the reliance should be on active skills management rather than on procedural adherence.

Step 9 reflects Taguchi's 'up and limping prototype'. The proposed system must be tested in action, and validated or modified against empirical data. This links naturally to Step 10. Training of internal auditors is vital and, again, should draw on the experience and knowledge of those who actually carry out the operations of the organization. Use of the staff in this way, and proper training of them in the correct meaning of effective audit outputs – helpfulness, guidance, and assistance to improvement – rather than oppressive policing, is likely to lead to highly productive outcomes. This generates the modifications demanded by Step 11 as an output of the audit process.

Step 12, accreditation of the QMS, should happen almost naturally. Within the context of the overall quality programme, accreditation should be a by-product. The application and registration should be easy to come by, if the organization genuinely has quality and has taken the development of the QMS seriously.

The final step reflects the demand for continuous improvement, not only in the core activities of the organization but in everything that it does.

It must always be remembered that the purpose of the QMS is not accreditation to a particular standard, but improvement to the quality of output of the products and services of the organization. It has been observed that many more organizations have accredited QMS systems than generate quality products and services. It is perfectly possible to develop and implement a QMS with absolutely no improvement to quality whatsoever.

Conventionally, a QMS will require three core sets of information. The first will be a statement of the quality policy of the organization. This may form the first part of the quality manual. The second set is the procedures, which will be adopted to fulfil that policy. The third set is the task instructions, which set out how each activity should be performed. With the increasing trend towards process-oriented structures, it is useful to give serious consideration to documenting the procedures along process lines, rather than on the traditional functional basis. Similarly, task instructions can be minimized where skills are used as the basis of quality.

To support these three sets of information, the organization will also require a record system to provide evidence that the quality procedures are being adhered to. This record system should be simple and straightforward, but should also be proofed against corruption and fraudulent completion as far as possible. If the data is not accurate, it is less than helpful. Accuracy will decline with complexity, volume of data, and difficulty of collection. Wherever possible, data should be recorded automatically.

25.4.5 ISO 14000

The ISO 14000 series of standards for Environmental Management Systems was launched in 1996, in response to rising awareness of damage to the environment, and the need for a common set of standards which could be adopted by any organization. These standards are important, because SB Foods is focused on overall sustainability, and meeting environmental standards is a key part of that.

The standards provide guidelines on the elements that an environmental management system should have, and on the supporting technologies. The standards prescribe what should be done by an organization, but not how. ISO 14001 and ISO 14004 provide the specifications and general guidelines for the series, and allow it to fulfil the business needs of any organization: from general guidance to self-assessment and registration. Achievement of the standards is claimed to lead to genuine business benefit, with companies claiming process performance improvement, cost reductions, reduced pollution, legislative compliance, and enhanced public image.

ISO 14000 has much in common with ISO 9000, and can capitalize on systems and procedures already established. It extends from the ISO 9000 criteria of meeting customer requirements to capture regulatory and mandatory environmental requirements. While ISO 14000 is established on a voluntary basis, there are indications that some countries may enshrine the standards in environmental legislation.

25.4.6 The Business Excellence Model (BEM)

While the focused has been on the ISO standards, there are other approaches to the management of quality which, while perhaps not carrying the same global authority, have delivered significant value to their adopters.

The Business Excellence Model is sponsored by The European Foundation for Quality Management. This model is developed from the belief that contented customers, satisfied staff, and positive societal impact can only be achieved through effective leadership. In turn, leadership steers both organizational policy and strategy in relation to organizational processes and human resource actions. Taken together, this integrated approach (Figure 25.6) is considered to drive the organization towards excellence in business.

While the model refers to business, the BEM has been widely adopted in the public sector in the UK.

Using the BEM, the organization assesses itself against nine performance criteria, divided into two sets. These are 'Enablers', which are those aspects of the organization that provide the foundation for excellent performance, and 'Results', which are the impact of those enablers on staff, customers, society at large, and ultimately on business performance.

Business Excellence Model Criteria

Leadership

Policy & Strategy

People

Partnerships & Resources

Processes

Customer Results

People Results

Society Results

Key Performance Results

Figure 25.6 The business excellence model.

'Leadership' considers how effectively those who manage the organization act in relation to the drive for excellence. 'Policy and Strategy' examines how those aspects of the organization are oriented towards the achievement of total quality, and how it goes about delivering them. 'People Management', in concert with the revised requirements of ISO 9001: 2000, explicitly recognizes that quality is ultimately delivered by people, to people, through people. It is a major factor in achievement of the award. People management considers how the organization works to realize the capabilities of its employees in driving improvement.

'Resources' (or Resource Management in the ISO language) is focused on the effective use and maintenance of the organization's physical assets (buildings, finance, information, technology, suppliers and materials). 'Processes' is concerned with the design, development, production, delivery, and service processes which add value to the organization. The BEM examines how these processes are identified and managed to achieve improvement.

Results criteria focus on 'People', 'Customer' and 'Societal' satisfaction with the organization, and on the business results. This category attempts to compare the organization's actual achievements with its internal standards, with its competitors' performance and with those organizations considered to be the best in the market. Results are generally presented quantitatively, using time-series graphical representation – charts!

People satisfaction attempts to determine the degree of satisfaction of staff in terms of how the employees feel about the organization, in relation to issues such as morale, terms and conditions of employment, management behaviours, development, the work environment, and participation in the quality programme. Objective measures include issues such as staff turnover, development activity, absenteeism, and numbers involved in suggestion schemes and improvement programmes.

Customer satisfaction considers the response of customers to the goods and services provided. Again, the results are split between customer perceptions of performance on delivery, reliability, service levels, complaints, warranty and accessibility of staff, and objective measures based on error and rejection rates, actual delivery performance, numbers of complaints and warranty claims – and, significantly, numbers of repeat customers.

The impact on society examines many of the issues which would be considered under ISO 14000, such as environmental impact, impact on quality of life, preservation of resources, and internal measures of resource utilization efficiency. The model looks at external perceptions, that is, how well the organization represents itself to its community, and objective internal measures, such as employment, recycling, waste reduction, pollution, and complaints.

Finally, the BEM addresses the 'Business Results': the success or otherwise of the organization in meeting the expectations of its financial stakeholders and in meeting business objectives. This section is considering objective aspects of business performance focused on the range of measures traditionally associated with business success. These include statutory accounting information (profit and loss, margins, sales, net worth), cash flows, share prices and ratings, dividends, productivity, and returns on investments. Other aspects may include market share, performance of suppliers, error rates, process performance, and cycle times.

While the basic process of using the BEM is primarily an internal matter, companies can pursue The European Quality Award (EQA). The process leading to the award engages external assessors in evaluating the performance of the company against the award criteria – and in competition with other organizations also pursuing the programme.

Overall, the BEM is suitable for companies which have already made significant progress towards excellence in all aspects of their operations. Frankly, it is unattainable to those organizations which have not already been pursuing meaningful quality initiatives for some time. It is considered that the EQA is a target to work towards for organizations which have already achieved the ISO standard.

The key limitations of the BEM are that it relies rather heavily on perceptions, rather than on ongoing objective measures. It has been found by some organizations to be cumbersome and bureaucratic in use (especially in the public sector), and its reliance on self-assessment leaves creative managers free to evaluate their performance (at least initially) at a lower level than is actually being achieved. This enables them to demonstrate improvement at the next evaluation – without changing anything. While this criticism may seem unfair (and is necessarily difficult to prove), it is undoubtedly the case that the strategy is frequently employed.

The second major criticism relates to the lack of real dynamism in the model itself. Considered as a foundation for a management system, the BEM framework has the potential to represent a network of interrelated enablers and results. It could be used, with appropriately objective performance measurement, to drive a dynamic business model in which the impacts of change on other areas could be usefully assessed before being made, rather than being reflected upon after the event.

As an established food producer, SB Foods was accustomed to meeting regulatory demands. Similarly, the quality benchmarks set for it by its major customers were fairly high – and totally inflexible (although always biased in favour of the buyers!). Therefore, the prospect of yet further regulatory compliance had little appeal for SB Foods, until it was recognized that the expectations of each of the standards had about an 80 per cent fit to each other. That is, the difference between all the standards were so relatively small that in meeting one standard they would be sure to meet all the others. Effective use of information technology would allow them to demonstrate compliance to multiple standards with minimal additional work.

The most demanding standard they had to meet was that of their biggest customer, who set more and higher expectations in most dimensions of quality than any of the others. Where another standard had a more demanding element, that was taken as the expectation. By recording the relevant information in a database, against which each of the standards could be interrogated and performance reported, a single system enabled reporting against multiple standards. SB Foods went on to achieve accreditation to ISO 9000 and ISO 14000, and are using the Business Excellence Model as a framework to help deliver further improvement.

25.5 Final Reflections

As with any story, this one is necessarily incomplete. Much of the detail has been passed over, and there are undoubtedly some parts of the process that would benefit from more attention.

The intention has been to show how adopting a systemic mindset from the start of an enquiry, and designing that enquiry in an iterative manner, can enable a wide selection of quality thinking and tools to be brought into use in an appropriate context.

None is necessarily right or wrong; each is appropriate to a user, a time, and a situation – the trick is knowing which ones to pick and when.

Summary

This chapter has completed the SB Foods case study by introducing external relationships and a selection of tools for dealing with them. The tools have been applied in the context of the original 'why, what and how' questions raised in Chapter 23, ensuring their fit to the problem situation.

Much more could be said about SB Foods, the tools chosen – and those not chosen – and about the contexts for their use. The curious reader is encouraged to explore those parts of the quality literature that seem interesting; students are encouraged to read everything!

KEY LEARNING POINTS

Supplier Development

Key definition:
buyers working co-operatively with suppliers to improve quality throughout the value chain.

Key technique:
commitment, audit and evaluation, define changes, develop agreement, form teams, define precise objectives, implementation.

Critique:
benefits through streamlining, cost reductions, enhanced productivity, drawbacks from

vulnerability of suppliers, unbalanced power within the value chain, potential to reduce choice and variety.

Benchmarking

Key definition:
the practice of formal comparison of processes and systems with other organizations as the basis for improvement.

Key technique:
identify key characteristics, identify partners, design data collection methodology, select tools, and implement changes.

Critique:
demands humility, willingness to learn, risk – only match, not exceed competitor performance, hence danger of levelling not competing.

Quality Management Systems

Key definitions:
the ISO 9000 series is the internationally accepted standard for quality management systems; the ISO 14000 series is the internationally accepted standard for environmental management systems.

Quality Management System:
a formal record of an organization's method of managing the quality of its products or services; needs a systematic, ordered approach, leading to third party certification of the system, not the quality.

Purpose:
provides a basis for measuring and monitoring quality performance.

The Business Excellence Model:
framework of performance criteria for the achievement of the European Quality Award.

Question

Why does accreditation to external standards matter?

Afterword

Whatsoever is done rightly, however humble, is noble

(Henry Royce)

Management commitment is the single most critical issue in the pursuit of quality, or, indeed, in any other organizational objective. Without it, the programme will fail – as so many do.

Each of the writers on quality mentioned in this book mentions this commitment, though none is very specific about how it can be obtained. The reasons given for pursuing quality are negative: to avoid failure, to reduce costs, to avoid defeat by overseas competition. While these are all conveniently measurable, they are also all inherently short term. They cause management to focus on the financial return from pursuing quality. Equally, quality consultants often package their programmes in terms of the cost-benefit case. In terms of Maslow's hierarchy of needs (1970), quality programmes focused on avoidance are addressing basic organizational needs of physiology and safety. These objectives are all, of course, worthwhile – and making profits (or operating within a given budget) is a constraint on the continued existence of every organization; it is important to achieve all of them. However, once the set objectives are achieved, the focus of the organization usually moves on to some other short-term objective, such as increasing market share, or improving margins. The pressure for quality subsides in the face of increased emphasis on some other, apparently more desirable, objective. This is one of the reasons so many quality initiatives are seen as 'flavour of the month', and may be regarded almost with contempt; like buses, everybody knows there will be another initiative along in a little while.

Quality, in the absolute sense, can never be achieved. There will always be scope for further improvement, and once the pressure for improvement is released, the organization will tend to slide backwards towards a lower level of achievement.

In the context of a sustainable organization, quality is not an objective but a given. The essence of effectiveness and survival for the organization rests in 'rightness', that is, being perceived as providing a quality product or service. This 'rightness' arises from an attitude of mind which obtains satisfaction from doing the job correctly, for no other reason than that is the way the job should be done. This attitude is seen as caring; it is clear that it matters to the individual that the job is done correctly, not for the benefit of the measurement system or for the purposes of statistical process control, but just because it is right. This parallels Maslow's idea of self-actualization: to be all that one can be.

While this attitude is most obviously seen in those who work in the 'caring' professions – doctors and nurses, vicars, nuns, priests and rabbis – similar behaviour can be observed in the tradition of the guild craftsmen. Their only measure of quality performance is against themselves; have they done the best that they could do? It is met, though more rarely, in those pursuing other occupations. If this attitude is met in unexpected places, it is remarked upon; it delights customers and may exceed their expectations.

Caring reflects the aesthetic dimension of quality. The management wishing to be successful in pursuing quality must do so for the intrinsic value of its rightness, not for its short-term extrinsic benefit. They must truly believe in, and pursue, quality for its own sake.

Further Reading

Throughout this book, reference has been made to a wide selection of sources which have been found informative and interesting in the attempt to understand the role of quality in the wider context of management thinking, organization theory, and emergent social issues. A list of texts follows, which will help the reader to explore further the themes and issues raised in this book.

Beer, S. (1959) *Cybernetics and Management*, Wiley, New York. Beer exposes in detail how an approach to organizations rooted in cybernetics can be applied to revolutionize management thinking.

Beer, S. (1974) *Designing Freedom*, Wiley, Chichester. Beer discusses the impact of conventional management thinking on the development of society, and suggests ways in which the apparent threats to freedom can be overcome. This book is Beer's most lucid attempt to elaborate his philosophy.

Crane, A., Matten, D. and Spence, L. (2008) *Corporate Social Responsibility*, Routledge, Abingdon. A good selection of readings and cases, which act as a positive support to understanding the key issues and arguments in this field.

Crosby, P. (1979) *Quality is Free*, Mentor, New York. Crosby introduces his quality approach in a highly readable, accessible text.

Deming, W. E. (1986) *Out of the Crisis*, The Press Syndicate, Cambridge. Deming elaborates his fears for the future of American industry, and proposes solutions based on his quality thinking and practice.

Feigenbaum, A. V. (1986) *Total Quality Control*, McGraw-Hill, New York. This text provides a full explanation of Feigenbaum's approach to managing for quality.

Feld, W. M. (2001) *Lean Manufacturing*, CRC Press, The Everglades, Florida. This text provides a sound introduction to methods, tools and techniques for applying lean thinking.

Flood, R. L. (1993) *Beyond TQM*, Wiley, Chichester. Flood develops his holistic approach to TQM, drawing on his background in systems science. The book is readily accessible to non-specialists in systems and quality.

Galbraith, J. (1974) *The New Industrial State*, Penguin, London. Galbraith develops an argument about the power of big corporations in the future economy of the world.

Hannagan, T. J. (1986) *Mastering Statistics*, second edition, Macmillan Education, Basingstoke. Hannagan provides an introduction to the development and use of a wide variety of statistical techniques.

Hoff, B. (1994) *The Tao of Pooh and the Te of Piglet*, Methuen, London. Hoff provides an insight into Western systems thinking through a re-interpretation of elements of Chinese philosophy.

Hoyle, D. (1994) *ISO 9000 Quality Systems Handbook*, Butterworth-Heinemann, Oxford. Hoyle provides an easy-to-follow guide to developing and installing a quality management system.

Huczynski, A. and Buchanan, D. (1991) *Organizational Behaviour*, second edition, Prentice-Hall International (UK), Hemel Hempstead. This text provides a substantial and reader-friendly guide to the principal strands of management thinking which dominate contemporary organizations.

Huff, D. (1973) *How to Lie with Statistics*, Pelican, London. In an entertaining but ruthlessly critical manner, Huff explores the ways in which poor understanding of statistics are used to manipulate decision making.

Ishikawa, K. (1986) *Guide to Quality Control*, second edition, Asian Productivity Organization, Tokyo. This book, based upon Ishikawa's practical work, was originally developed as a guide for the work of quality circle members.

Juran, J. M. (1988) *Juran on Planning for Quality*, Free Press, New York. This substantial and detailed text provides the most useful guide to Juran's thinking and his approach to achieving quality.

Kanji, G. P. and Asher, M. (1996) *100 Methods for Total Quality Management*, Sage, London. The authors provide an easy-to-follow, simple 'how to' guide, covering the major activities in a TQM programme.

Kotler, P. and Lee, N. (2005) *Corporate Social Responsibility*, Wiley, New Jersey. An introductory text covering the breadth of thinking in this area.

Logothetis, N. (1992) *Managing for Total Quality*, Prentice Hall International, London. Logothetis provides a guide to the statistically-based methods for achieving quality.

Lovelock, J. (1979) *Gaia: A New Look at Life on Earth*, Oxford University Press, Oxford. Lovelock explains the development of his theory of the environment. Appreciation of this perspective helps in understanding the environmental imperative for the pursuit of quality.

Oakland, J. S. (1993) *Total Quality Management*, second edition, Butterworth-Heinemann, Oxford. Readable and well structured, Oakland elaborates in detail his programme for attaining quality.

Ormerod, P. (1994) *The Death of Economics*, Faber and Faber, London. Ormerod explores the assumptions which underpin much of currently dominant economic theory, highlighting the weaknesses and flaws which he perceives.

Pirsig, R. M. (1974) *Zen and the Art of Motorcycle Maintenance (An Inquiry into Values)*, Black Swan Edition, Arrow Books, London. Presented as an account of a man's journey with his son, the book reflects a process of enquiry into two strands of quality thinking: the technical and aesthetic.

Shingo, S. (1987) *The Sayings of Shigeo Shingo*, Trans. A. P. Dillon, Productivity Press, New York. Shingo's message is expressed through his many mottoes for achieving quality.

Stickland, F. (1998) *The Dynamics of Change*, Routledge, London. Based on his doctoral research, Stickland provides fascinating insights into the processes of organizational change through analogies with the natural world.

Taguchi, G. (1987) *Systems of Experimental Design*, Vols. 1 and 2, Unipub/Kraus, International Publications, New York. Taguchi's own guide to his process for developing quality within the product and the production process.

Waldrop, S. (1992) *Complexity*, Simon & Schuster, New York. Waldrop reports the development of complexity theory, providing insight into thinking about organizations as non-linear dynamical systems.

Warboys, B. C. *et al.* (1999) *Business Information Systems, A Process Approach*, McGraw Hill, New York. Very useful for understanding how to build information systems to support and reflect process-orientation in organizations.

Glossary of Terms and Abbreviations

AGIL:	Adaptation, Goal-attainment, Integration, Latency.
aphorism:	a short, clever saying expressing a general truth.
benchmarking:	a formal comparison of one organization against another, with the aim of performance improvement.
black box:	a technique for studying the behaviour of complex systems.
Business Process Re-engineering (BPR):	a process-oriented organizational performance discipline.
Business Systems Diamond:	a meta-methodology for BPR.
BS 5750:	British Standard quality management system (now subsumed in ISO 9000).
call-centre:	a centralized telephone enquiry service.
cowpaths:	naturally developed processes in organizations.
comfort zone:	an accustomed way of behaving and working.
complementarism:	an approach to problem-solving, in which choice and use of methodology is guided by the characteristics of the situation, and understanding of the theory underpinning the method.
CSH:	Critical Systems Heuristics.
CSR:	Corporate Social Responsibility.
CST:	Critical Systems Thinking.
culture:	the set of values and beliefs which guide behaviour in an organization or nation.
deterministic/ determinism:	entirely predictable system behaviour.
direct costs of quality:	the visible costs of quality failure.
emergent properties:	behaviour which is exhibited by a whole system, but by none of its parts.
empirical:	derived from practice or observation, not theory.
EN 29000:	European Standard Quality Management System (now subsumed in ISO 9000).
feedback:	self-regulation of a system by using output to manage input.
GDP per capita:	the amount of income generated by a nation divided by its population.

guru:	originally a Hindu spiritual teacher; now used to refer to leaders in a discipline.
HACCP:	Hazard Analysis Critical Control Points – a food production management system.
heuristic:	a process of trial and error.
holism/holistic:	the attempt to deal with whole organizations, rather than parts.
HR:	human resources.
invisible costs of quality:	consequential and hidden costs of quality failure.
IP:	interactive planning.
ISO 9000:	International Standards Organization guidelines for a quality management system.
ISO 14000:	International Standards Organization guidelines for an environmental management system.
just-in-time (JIT):	a system of supply, which delivers parts to a production process when they are required, obviating the need to hold stocks.
kanban:	the operating system to support JIT.
kaizen:	a Japanese belief system, oriented towards continuous improvement in *all* aspects of life.
lean manufacturing:	a manufacturing methodology developed to eliminate waste, usually thought to be based on the Toyota Production System.
mechanistic:	a view of organizations which suggests that they and their staff can be organized to behave like machines.
meta:	of a higher, logical order.
methodology:	a systematic set of methods for studying issues and problems.
muda:	waste.
NIH:	not invented here – a barrier to change.
normative:	concerned with defining ethics and social standards.
organismic/organic:	a view of organizations being like organisms.
organizational cybernetics:	the science of effective organization.
paradigm:	a personal framework of thought or system of beliefs.
PDCA cycle:	a systematic continuous improvement cycle.
Poka-Yoke:	defect = 0.
probabilism/ probabilistic:	behaviour which is partly random or unpredictable.
process:	all the operations required to complete a task.
QA:	quality assurance.
Quality Circle/ (QC/QCC):	a problem-solving team for quality issues.
QC:	quality control.
QFD:	quality function deployment.
QMS:	quality management system.

recursion:	structural invariance at different levels of an organization.
reductionist/ reductionism:	a way of studying organizations through fragmentation and analysis.
replacement cycle:	the time period between repeated purchases of a good or service.
rework:	fixing or repairing finished goods before despatch.
self-regulation:	the ability of a system to manage itself.
slipping clutch syndrome:	an effect on productivity and quality when a production system is placed under pressure.
SMED:	single minute exchange of die, a fast change process for machine tools.
soft systems:	the study of human activity systems.
SOSM:	system of systems methodologies.
SSM:	soft systems methodology.
stakeholder:	any person or organization affected by, or involved with, an organization.
Statistical Process Control (SPC):	a quantitative system for monitoring process performance.
statistical quality control (SQC):	a quantitative system for monitoring quality performance.
supplier development:	a business strategy of co-operation between buyer and supplier to jointly improve quality.
systemic:	an approach which deals with whole systems and the interactions of their elements and the environment.
total cost:	the lifetime cost of purchasing and maintaining a product.
Total Quality Control:	Feigenbaum's approach to quality and management.
TQM:	Total Quality Management.
TSI:	Total Systems Intervention.
variety engineering:	techniques for managing probabilism.
VSD:	Viable System Diagnosis.
VSM:	Viable System Model.
zero defects:	a quality target, focusing on error-free production.

References

Ackoff, R. L. (1981) *Creating the Corporate Future*, Wiley, New York.

Ashby, W. R. (1956) *An Introduction to Cybernetics*, Chapman and Hall, London.

Bank, J. (1992) *The Essence of Total Quality Management*, Prentice Hall International, London.

Beckford, J. (1993) 'The viable system model, a more adequate tool for practising management?', Ph.D. thesis, University of Hull, UK.

Beckford, J. (1995) 'Towards a participative methodology for the viable systems model', in *Systemist*, UK Systems Society, Portsmouth.

Beckford, J. and Dudley, P. (1998a) 'That's not very big, is it?' *Management Issues in Social Care*, 5, (4).

Beckford, J. and Dudley, P. (1998b) 'Size isn't everything', *Management Issues in Social Care*, 6, (1).

Beckford, J. and Dudley, P. (1999) 'It's what you do with it that counts', *Management Issues in Social Care*, 6, (3).

Beer, S. (1959) *Cybernetics and Management*, Wiley, New York.

Beer, S. (1979) *The Heart of Enterprise*, Wiley, Chichester, UK.

Beer, S. (1981) *Brain of the Firm*, 2nd edition, Wiley, Chichester, UK.

Beer, S. (1985) *Diagnosing the System for Organisations*, Wiley, Chichester, UK.

Beer, S. (1994) *Beyond Dispute: The Invention of Team Syntegrity*, Wiley, Chichester, UK.

Bendell, T. (1989) *The Quality Gurus: What Can They do for Your Company?*, Department of Trade and Industry, London, and Services Ltd., Nottingham.

Burns, T. and Stalker G. M. (1961) *The Management of Innovation*, Tavistock, London.

Burrell, G. and Morgan, G. (1979) *Sociological Paradigms and Organisational Analysis*, Heinemann, London.

Carroll, L. (1866) *Alice's Adventures in Wonderland*, Macmillan, London.

Checkland, P. B. (1978) 'The origins and nature of "hard" systems thinking', *Journal of Applied Systems Analysis*, 5 (2): 99.

Checkland, P. B. (1981) *Systems Thinking, Systems Practice*, Wiley, Chichester, UK.

Checkland, P. and Scholes J. (1990) *Soft Systems Methodology in Action*, Wiley, Chichester, UK.

Clemson, B. (1984) *Cybernetics: A New Management Tool*, Abacus, Tunbridge Wells, UK.

Clutterbuck, D. and Crainer, S. (1990) *Makers of Management*, Macmillan, London.

Crane, A., Matten, D., and Spence, L. (2008) *Corporate Social Responsibility*, Routledge, Abingdon, UK.

Crosby, P. (1979) *Quality is Free*, Mentor, New York.

De Bono, E. (1970) *Lateral Thinking: A Text-book of Creativity*, Spain Press, London.

Deming, W. E. (1982) *Quality, Productivity and Competitive Position*, Massachusetts Institute of Technology, MA.

Deming, W. E. (1986) *Out of the Crisis*, The Press Syndicate, Cambridge, UK.

Dennis, P. (2007) *Lean Production Simplified*, Productivity Press, New York.

Dudley, P. (2000) ' "Quality management or management quality?": an adaptive model of organisation as the basis of organisational learning and quality provision', Ph.D. thesis, University of Hull, UK.

Espejo, R. and Schwaninger, M. (1993) *Organizational Fitness, Corporate Effectiveness through Management Cybernetics*, Campus Verlag, Frankfurt and New York.

Fayol, H. (1916) *General and Industrial Management*, SRL Dunod, Paris (trans. Constance Storrs, Pitman, London, 1949).

Feigenbaum, A. V. (1986) *Total Quality Control*, McGraw-Hill, New York.

Feld, W. (2001) *Lean Manufacturing*, CRC Press, Florida.

Fiedler, F. E. (1967) *A Theory of Leadership Effectiveness*, McGraw-Hill, New York.

Flood, R. L. (1993) *Beyond TQM*, Wiley, Chichester, UK.

Flood, R. L. (1999) *Rethinking the Fifth Discipline*, Routledge, London.

Flood, R. L. and Carson, E. R. (1988) *Dealing with Complexity*, Plenum, New York.

Flood, R. L. and Jackson, M. C. (1991) *Creative Problem Solving*, Wiley, Chichester, UK.

Flood, R. L. and Romm, N. R. A. (1996) *Diversity Management: Triple Loop Learning*, Wiley, Chichester, UK.

Galbraith, J. (1974) *The New Industrial State*, Penguin, London.

Gilbert, J. (1992) *How to Eat an Elephant: A Slice-by Slice Guide to Total Quality Management*, Tudor, Reading, UK.

Gilbert, M. (1994) *Understanding Quality Management Standards*, Institute of Management, London.

Gleick, J. (1987) *Chaos*, Heinemann, London.

Hammer, M. and Champy, J. (1993) *Business Process Reengineering*, Nicholas Brealey, London.

Handy, C. (1985) *Understanding Organisations*, 3rd edition, Penguin, London.

Handy, C. (1990) *The Age of Unreason*, Arrow, London.

Heller, R. (1989) *The Making of Managers*, Penguin, London.

Herzberg, F., Mauser, B., and Synderman, B. B. (1959) *The Motivation to Work*, 2nd edition, Wiley, New York.

Hofstede, G. (1980) 'Motivation, leadership and organization: do American theories apply abroad?', *Organizational Dynamics*, summer 1980: 42–63.

Hoyle, D. (2006) *ISO 9000 Quality Systems Handbook*, 5th edition, Butterworth-Heinemann, Oxford.

Huczynski, A. and Buchanan, D. (1991) *Organizational Behaviour*, 2nd edition, Prentice Hall International (UK), Hemel Hempstead.

Ishikawa, K. (1985) *What is Total Quality Control? The Japanese Way*, Prentice Hall, London.

Ishikawa, K. (1986) *Guide to Quality Control*, 2nd edition, Asian Productivity Organisation, Tokyo.

Jackson, M. C. (1990) *Organisation Design & Behaviour, An MBA Manual*, University of Hull.

Jackson, M. C. (1991) *Systems Methodology for the Management Sciences*, Wiley, Chichester, UK.

Jackson, M. C. and Keys, P. (1984) 'Towards a system of systems methodologies', *Journal of the Operational Research Society*, 35, 473–86.

Johansson, H. J. *et al.* (1993) *Business Process Reengineering*, Wiley, Chichester, UK.

Johnson, G. and Scholes, K. (1993) *Exploring Corporate Strategy*, 3rd edition, Prentice Hall, Hemel Hempstead.

Junewick, M. (2002) *LeanSpeak*, Productivity Press, New York.

Juran, J. (1988) *Juran on Planning for Quality*, Free Press, New York.

Kanji, G. K. and Asher, M. (1996) *100 Methods for Total Quality Management*, Sage, London.

Kobayashi, I. (1995) *20 Keys to Workplace Improvement*, Productivity Press, Portland, USA.

Levinson, W. (2002) *Henry Ford's Lean Vision*, Productivity Press, New York.

Logothetis, N. (1992) *Managing for Total Quality*, Prentice Hall International, London.

Lovelock, J. (1979) *Gaia: A New Look at Life on Earth*, Oxford University Press, Oxford.

Lovelock, J. (1988) *The Ages of Gaia*, Oxford University Press, Oxford.

Lovelock, J. (1991) *Gaia: The Practical Science of Planetary Medicine*, Gaia Books, London.

Lovelock, J. (2001) *Homage to Gaia*, Oxford University Press, Oxford.

Lynn, J. and Jay, A. (1982) *Yes Minister*, BBC Books, London.

Machiavelli, N. (1513) *The Prince* (trans. G. Bull, Penguin, London, 1961).

Maslow, A. (1970) *Motivation and Personality*, 2nd edition, Harper & Row, New York.

Mason, R. O. and Mitroff, I. I. (1981) *Challenging Strategic Planning Assumptions*, Wiley, New York.

Mayo, E. (1949) *The Social Problems of an Industrial Civilisation*, Routledge & Kegan Paul, London.

McGoldrick, G. (1994) *The Complete Quality Manual*, Longman, London.

McGregor, D. (1960) *The Human Side of Enterprise*, McGraw-Hill, New York.

Morgan, G. (1986) *Images of Organisation*, Sage, London.

Oakland, J. (1993) *Total Quality Management*, 2nd edition, Butterworth-Heinemann, Oxford.

Oakland, J. (1999) *Total Organisational Excellence*, Butterworth-Heinemann, London.

Ohno, T (1978) *Toyota Production System*, Diamond Inc, Tokyo.

Ohno, T (1987) *Foreword to Toyota Production System*, (trans.) Productivity Press, New York.

Oliga, J. (1988) 'Methodological foundations of systems methodologies', in *Critical Systems Thinking, Directed Readings*, Flood, R. L. and Jackson, M. C. (eds.), 1991, Wiley, Chichester, UK.

Parsons, T. and Smelser, N. J. (1956) *Economy and Society*, Routledge & Kegan-Paul, London.

Peters, T. J. and Waterman, R. H. (1982) *In Search of Excellence*, Harper Collins, New York.

Pine, B. J. (1993), *Mass Customization*, Harvard Press, Cambridge, MA.

Porter, L. and Tanner, S. (1996) *Assessing Business Excellence*, Butterworth-Heinemann, London.

Porter, M. (1980) *Competitive Strategy: Techniques for Analysing Industries and Competitors*, Free Press, Macmillan, New York.

Porter, M. (1996) 'What is strategy?' *Harvard Business Review*, November–December 1996: 61–78.

Pugh, D. S. (1990) *Organisation Theory*, 3rd edition, Penguin, London.

Pugh, D. S. and Hickson, D. J. (1976) *Organisation Structure in its Context: The Aston Programme I*, Saxon House, Aldershot.

Pugh, D. and Hinings, C. R. (eds.) (1976) *Organizational Structure – Extensions and Replications: The Aston Programme II*, Gower Publishing, Farnham, UK.

Schmied, H. and Brown, K. (2009) *The Five Dimensions of Project Planning*, Ermite, Strasbourg.

Schoderbek, P. P., Schoderbek, C. G., and Kefalas, A. G. (1990) *Management Systems: Conceptual Considerations*, 4th edition, Business Publications, Dallas.

Senge, P. M. (1990) *The Fifth Discipline*, Century Business, London.

Shingo, S. (1987) *The Sayings of Shigeo Shingo* (trans. A. P. Dillon, Productivity Press, New York, 1987).

Singleton, W. T. (1974) *Man-Machine Systems*, Penguin, London.

Slack, N., *et al.* (1995) *Operations Management*, Pitman, London.

Taguchi, G. (1987) *Systems of Experimental Design*, Vols. 1 and 2, Unipub/Kraus International Publications, New York.

Taylor, F. (1911) *The Principles of Scientific Management*, The Plimpton Press, Norwood, MA.

Townsend, R (1970) *Further Up the Organisation*, Michael Joseph, London.

Trist, E. A. and Bamforth, K. W. (1951) 'Some social and psychological consequences of the Longwall method of coal-getting', [*sic*], in *Organisation Theory, Selected Readings*, D. S. Pugh (ed.), 3rd edition, 1990, Penguin, London.

Ulrich, W. (1983) *Critical Heuristics of Social Planning*, Haupt, Berne.

Ulrich, W. (1987) 'Critical heuristics of social systems design', *European Journal of Operational Research*, 31: 276–83.

Waldrop, S. (1992) *Complexity*, Simon & Schuster, New York.

Waller J., Allen, D., and Burns, A. (1993) *The Quality Management Manual*, Kogan Page, London.

Weber, M. (1924) 'Legitimate authority and bureaucracy,' in *Organisation Theory, Selected Readings*, D. S. Pugh (ed.), 3rd edition, 1990, Penguin, London.

Wiener, N. (1948) *Cybernetics or Control and Communication in the Animal and the Machine*, The Massachusetts Institute of Technology, MA.

Woodward, J. (1965) *Industrial Organization: Theory and Practice*, Oxford University Press, London.

Index